CLEARED
FOR THE
OPTION

CLEARED FOR THE OPTION

A Year Learning to Fly

PATRICK CHOVANEC

Causation Press
New York

Copyright © 2023 Patrick Chovanec

All rights reserved. No part of this publication may be reproduced, distributed, or transmitted in any form or by any means, including photocopying, recording, or other electronic or mechanical methods, without the prior written permission of the publisher, except in the case of brief quotations embodied in critical reviews and certain other noncommercial uses permitted by copyright law. For permission requests, write to the publisher, addressed "Attention: Permissions Coordinator," at the address below.

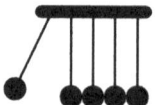

permissions@causationpress.com

ISBN: 979-8-9879481-1-8 (paperback)
ISBN: 979-8-9879481-2-5 (ebook)
ISBN: 979-8-9879481-0-1 (hardcover)

Printed in the United States of America
Illustrations by Kopp Illustration

Ordering Information:
Special discounts are available on quantity purchases by corporations, associations, and others. For details, contact orders@causationpress.com

Publisher's Cataloging-in-Publication Data

Names: Chovanec, Patrick, author.
Title: Cleared for the option : a year learning to fly / Patrick Chovanec.
Description: New York : Causation Press, [2023] | Includes bibliographical references and index.
Identifiers: ISBN: 979-8-9879481-0-1 (hardcover) | 979-8-9879481-1-8 (paperback) | 979-8-9879481-2-5 (ebook) | LCCN: 2023917565
Subjects: LCSH: Airplanes--Piloting. | Private flying. | United States. Federal Aviation Administration—Examinations. | Air pilots--Examinations. | Air pilots--Licenses. | Aeronautics. | Aviation psychology. |
BISAC: TRANSPORTATION / Aviation / Piloting & Flight Instruction. | BIOGRAPHY & AUTOBIOGRAPHY / Aviation & Nautical. | TRANSPORTATION / Aviation / General.
Classification: LCC: TL721.4 .C56 2023 | DDC: 629.132/5217--dc23

Cleared for the Option:

ATC [Air Traffic Control] authorization for an aircraft to make a touch-and-go, low approach, missed approach, stop and go, or full stop landing at the discretion of the pilot. It is normally used in training so that an instructor can evaluate a student's performance under changing situations.
—FAA Pilot/Controller Glossary

Readers should note that any word or phrase first introduced in **bold print** may be found in the Glossary at the end.

Unless otherwise noted, or unless they derive wholly from government-published sources, all photographs and illustrations are also copyrighted by the author.

This publication contains the experiences, opinions, and ideas of the author, who is an amateur, not a professional, pilot. No warranty is made with respect to the accuracy or completeness of the information contained herein. This book is sold with the understanding that the author is not engaged in rendering any professional advice or service. The author is not a Certified Flight Instructor, and this book is not intended as flight instruction. It is not a replacement for competent instruction or for the procedures defined by an aircraft's manufacturer. The author specifically disclaims all responsibility for any liability, loss, or risk, personal or otherwise, which is incurred as a consequence, directly or indirectly, of the use or misuse of any of the techniques or other content contained in this book. Pilots should consult with the Pilot Operating Handbook for the specific airplane they are flying, and the applicable FAA regulations, which frequently change.

Mention of specific companies and products in this book does not imply endorsement of such companies or products by the author, nor does it imply that such companies have endorsed the author.

The names and identifying characteristics of some individuals have been changed.

The registration numbers and call signs of aircraft in this book have been changed to ones that, according to the FAA registry, were not assigned, reserved, or in use as of the time of initial publication. The author is not aware of any prior users and assumes no liability for any such prior or future uses of these registration numbers or call signs.

The chart on p. 331 of this book is reproduced with copyright permission from McGraw Hill. McGraw Hill makes no representations or warranties as to the accuracy of any information contained in the McGraw Hill Material, including any warranties of merchantability or fitness for a particular purpose. In no event shall McGraw Hill have any liability to any party for special, incidental, tort, or consequential damages arising out of or in connection with the McGraw Hill Material, even if McGraw Hill has been advised of the possibility of such damages.

To William, who taught me to ask,
To Alice, who taught me to plan,
To Rachel, who taught me to see,
To Frances, who let me try.

Table of Contents

1	**CHAPTER 1:** Out of the Blue	193	**CHAPTER 19:** Bravo
12	**CHAPTER 2:** Discovery	204	**CHAPTER 20:** Arizona
23	**CHAPTER 3:** Medical	217	**CHAPTER 21:** Night
33	**CHAPTER 4:** Aerodynamics	225	**CHAPTER 22:** Radio
43	**CHAPTER 5:** Controls	241	**CHAPTER 23:** Independence
55	**CHAPTER 6:** Maneuvers	252	**CHAPTER 24:** Performance
65	**CHAPTER 7:** Instruments	264	**CHAPTER 25:** Emergencies
78	**CHAPTER 8:** Hood	277	**CHAPTER 26:** Stalling
86	**CHAPTER 9:** Navigation	284	**CHAPTER 27:** Helicopter
100	**CHAPTER 10:** Charts	297	**CHAPTER 28:** Ready
114	**CHAPTER 11:** Weather	308	**CHAPTER 29:** Checkride
125	**CHAPTER 12:** Luck	322	**EPILOGUE:** Killzone
134	**CHAPTER 13:** Engine	336	Glossary
145	**CHAPTER 14:** Exam	377	Acknowledgements
154	**CHAPTER 15:** Instructor	379	Notes on Sources
162	**CHAPTER 16:** Approach	381	Selected Bibliography
172	**CHAPTER 17:** Landing	397	Endnotes
184	**CHAPTER 18:** Solo	413	Index

CHAPTER 1

Out of the Blue

📡 *"Morristown Tower, Skyhawk Niner-Juliet-Papa, midfield left downwind Runway Two-Three."*

📡 *"Skyhawk Niner-Juliet-Papa, cleared for the option Runway Two-Three."*

📡 *"Runway Two-Three, cleared for the option, Skyhawk Niner-Juliet-Papa."*

I never seriously imagined I would learn to fly an airplane. In the spring of 2020, at age 50, with my entire world shutting down due to the COVID-19 pandemic, I can tell you it was the very last thing on my mind. Yet here I was, roughly a year later, flying on my own 1,000 feet over suburban New Jersey, confirming the control tower's instructions, easing the throttle back, putting in flaps, and starting my descent to land.

Over the past several months, I'd gone from being a complete newbie in the cockpit to learning the ins and outs of an airplane, cramming my head full of facts to pass a standardized written pilot's exam on a daunting range of subjects. I had recovered from dizzying spins, groped my way through the inky blackness of a night flight over the Arizona desert, and faced down my fear of the unforgiving ground rushing up at me as I attempted to land on a devilishly small runway. Soon, I'd start preparing for my final test date with the government-designated examiner, who would hand down his verdict on whether my knowledge and skills measured up to the standards required to earn a pilot's license.

But first, I had a plane to land. Completing my final turn, I lined up my aircraft with the runway ahead, making slight adjustments to the throttle and controls to stay on a steady, almost relentless path to my aiming point as it grew larger. A sudden gust of wind tossed the small plane off to one side, but I quickly corrected and put myself back on track. Taking a deep breath, I pushed the consequences of what would happen if I screwed up into a corner of my mind and reverted back to my training. It was on me now—no one else was here to put me safely on the ground. But that was okay. *I had this.*

We all fly. These days, it's the rare person who has never traveled on an airplane. But even as the experience becomes an increasingly mundane part of modern life, *how* to fly—the knowledge and skills that go into *piloting* an airplane—remains, for most of us, something wrapped in mystery. Think about the last time you were at an airport, waiting at the boarding gate. A group of pilots appears in their crisp blue uniforms and, even among the most seasoned travelers, a slight hush descends. Unlike the rest of us, these are the men and women who know what they are doing. If our trust in the technology of flight is a kind of faith, the pilots are its glamorous priests, possessors of secrets we hope will bring us safely to our destination.

That's certainly how I felt for most of my life. And I think it helps explain our fascination with news stories like the one that broke recently about an untrained passenger who had to take the controls and land a small plane in Florida, with the help of Air Traffic Control, after the pilot became incapacitated.[1] The incident went viral, in no small part because we can all imagine ourselves in that situation. If suddenly confronted with the mysteries of flight, with our lives on the line, we wonder whether the outcome would be a happy or a tragic one. What lies on the other side of that invisible barrier between cabin and cockpit, and would we be up to the challenge of meeting it, if we had to?

This book is the story of how I crossed that barrier and became a pilot. The value in telling this story lies not in its being unique, but typical. Virtually every pilot—from a hot-shot fighter ace at Top Gun to the airline captain flying your family to Florida—started by going through much the same process I did, learning the same basic skills in a similar kind of airplane. Fair warning: I purposely haven't pulled any punches or watered anything down. Learning to fly is exciting, but parts of it are tough and involve absorbing a body of knowledge that can be intellectually demanding. My goal here is to give you the real deal, so that by the end of this book, you'll have a pretty solid idea what someone learns and experiences to become a pilot.

Maybe you're a student pilot with a few lessons under your belt who is unsure of the road and challenges ahead. Perhaps you are someone who has always wondered—way in the back of your mind—whether learning to fly is worthwhile and right for you. Or maybe you're happy being a passenger, thank you very much, but still curious what exactly it is that pilots know and do. In any case, I hope this journey we're about to go on together will give you a richer understanding and new appreciation for something you already do: fly.

If you're not sure you were born to be a pilot, don't worry—neither was I. This is not a book I ever expected to write. People who know me would have expected a book about China, where I've lived and worked for much of my life, or economics, which is how I earn my living. Occupied by these ever-challenging pursuits, I always assumed that flying an airplane was something *other* people do, not me. It wasn't my lifelong dream. I never felt the "wild blue yonder" calling out to me. Unlike some people I've met, I don't have flying in my bones. What I do have, perhaps like you, is a fervent curiosity about the world and a willingness to step outside my comfort zone. And those traits have led me, on more than one occasion, to some rather unexpected adventures. This was one of the least expected.

In the spring of 2020, New York City, where I lived for the past few years, got hit early and hard by COVID-19. Schools were shut down, the streets nearly deserted, and families like ours—me, my wife, and three children—

crammed into apartments together for weeks on end. We live across from a major hospital, so ambulances were lined up and down the street. Every time I made a run to the local grocery store, I had to pass two refrigerated morgue trailers—an unsettling reminder of the specter of illness and death hanging over all of our heads. At first, I passed the time teaching my kids to play *Dungeons & Dragons*, taking a break each evening to go out on the balcony to clap and cheer the medical workers making their daily appearance on the corner. But it was a tedious existence, and we all quickly got on each other's nerves, as families cooped up together often do.

One evening I was browsing YouTube with my 10-year-old son when we came across a short promo video for *Microsoft Flight Simulator (MSFS) 2020*, the newest edition in a long-standing series of PC-based games designed to realistically simulate flying an airplane, each a technical and visual improvement over the last. I hadn't played any flight sims for a very long time, but I admired—at a remove—the steady progress they had made from the early days of squiggly, jerky lines to something that increasingly looked like the real world. But the promo blew us away. We could hardly tell the screenshots of places like London and New York, at different times of day and weather conditions, from actual photographs. Just as astonishing, *MSFS 2020* aimed to depict the entire world, virtually, using data streamed from the internet. You could fly literally anywhere, with live weather and air traffic, and see it as it really looked at that moment—or close enough.

Travel is one of my great loves in life. Before COVID-19, my work as an economist typically sent me to a half-dozen foreign countries each year. I'd dive deep into the history and culture in advance, then hop in a rental car and drive hundreds of miles to visit the locations I had read about in books. My bookshelf at home is lined with the well-creased spines of *Lonely Planet* guides. I had just returned from Algeria and was planning a trip to Tajikistan when the pandemic brought all of this to a screeching halt for the foreseeable future. *Microsoft Flight Simulator 2020* promised a virtual way out—*if* I could manage to fly an airplane.

This I found a bit daunting, even if it was only on a computer screen.

Unlike many pilots and instructors I later met, I had no family ties to aviation—no airline captains or air force fighter jocks to inspire me, no dads to introduce me to stick and rudder before I could drive a car. As a boy, I was enticed by a course catalog from a nearby military school that offered—*I could barely believe it*—a summer program that taught you how to fly a plane. But you needed to be at least 16 years old and I was too young, so it remained a vague—and unrealized—fantasy.

Ironically, it was the very first PC-based flight simulator that pushed the flying fantasy even further out of my mind. Sublogic's *FS1 Flight Simulator*, released in 1979, was an amazing and groundbreaking piece of software for its time. However, it was constrained by processing power, memory, and graphics that were but a fraction of what a pocket-size smartphone offers today.[2] Its world, on the screen of our old 64K Apple II computer, consisted of jagged geometric lines in space and a few rough-hewn dials (see Figure 1 in the color insert). I could take off—at least the grid that represented the ground got smaller—but the keyboard controls lagged so badly that I always felt about a second behind whatever the "airplane" was doing. The enemy plane that I was supposed to shoot down was a tiny dot floating around. But it was landing that did me in. I couldn't figure out how to line up with the stick-like runway, much less avoid slamming right into it. I was supposed to "flare" and "stall" to make a gentle touch down. What the heck did that mean? It all seemed very, very hard and beyond my grasp, so much so that I never went near a flight sim again.

But another experience, in an actual airplane, planted a seed—a tiny seed—of opposing hope. When I was about 12, my father took some cousins and me on a raft trip down the Colorado River and through the Grand Canyon. On the very last day, we crawled out of the Canyon on mules to a small airstrip, where a tiny Cessna waited to fly us back to our starting point at Page, Arizona. A storm was brewing on the horizon and, unlike in a large airliner, as we flew we could definitely feel the sensation of riding through the air flowing around us. What struck me, though, was that as we approached the airport at Page, the pilot turned to line up with the runway just like he was in a car turning into a driveway, and we watched the runway grow steadily larger until we touched down nice and smooth. What seemed impossible on the primitive computer simulator seemed rather natural in real life. Perhaps it could be done after all.

These two contradictory impressions coexisted in my mind for several decades but had little practical impact on my life. I didn't particularly enjoy riding in planes as an airline passenger. Whenever they banked to turn, I always felt like they must be about to crash—but that never happened, so I grew used to it. Though I knew a few private pilots—my boss at work, a journalist I had met in China—the idea of piloting a plane myself never entered my mind. That is, not until I saw the promo for *MSFS 2020*, whose vivid visuals evoked more memories of that encouraging landing at Page than of those perplexing, intimidating polygons on my old Apple II.

My existing PC, over a decade old, fell way below the minimum requirements to run *MSFS 2020*. So I took the plunge and ordered a Dell Alienware 11 with a curved, wide-screen monitor, a hefty upgrade from my old machine and pretty close to top-of-the-line. If I wanted to see the world, I rationalized, what would be the point of anything below "ultra" graphics settings? The problem was, due to COVID-19 shutdowns and the increased demand for laptops during the pandemic (for children attending school and grown-ups doing their office work remotely from home), there was a backlog on computer orders. *Microsoft Flight Simulator* would come out the next month, in August, but my new PC wouldn't arrive until mid-October.

That gave me time to rustle up some accessories, which were also in short supply due to the highly anticipated release of *MSFS 2020*. Industry observers estimated the game would generate $2.6 billion in related hardware sales, and I did my best to contribute to that sum.[3] The Logitech rudder pedals were fairly easy to order from Amazon, and some lesser-known online shop was able to ship me a throttle quadrant. But I had to call around for a Honeycomb yoke (for steering the plane), which were all sold out into November, until I found an actual pilot shop in South Carolina that had one left in stock. As the packages arrived, my bedroom desk began to look more and more like a cockpit. All dressed up and nowhere to go.

As the August release date came and went, I began watching videos on YouTube of those lucky enough to have their rigs already in place, posting their first flights on *MSFS 2020*. Several of them—Squirrel and Pilot Emilie were my go-to sources—were evidently pilots in real life, and their videos were very educational. I began having questions: How do you typically make an approach to land? When do you lower your wing flaps and why? What do the markings on the runway mean? When do you talk to **Air Traffic Control (ATC)**, and what do you say? I started watching other videos produced by various real-life flight schools like MzeroA, Fly8MA, and Boldmethod that helped answer these questions. Of course, in the process they only raised new ones, and I soon realized that the free videos online would not be enough to satisfy my curiosity.

Until recently, when people signed up to learn how to fly, they began by attending **ground school**. Alongside their first flights in an airplane, they sat in a classroom for several hours listening to lectures and taking notes on everything they would have to know to pass the FAA's required written exam for private pilots. You weren't renting a plane, so lessons on the ground didn't cost as much per hour, but they could easily add up to a few thousand dollars on top of flight lessons themselves. The Internet has upended this entire model. Today, certain flight schools—including some whose excerpts I had been watching for free on YouTube—offer video courses that you take at your own pace online. They include a standardized curriculum of explanatory videos as well as practice quizzes and tests, and cost a few hundred dollars.

After a little bit of research, in late August I bought the "Learn to Fly Course" from Sporty's, a popular pilot store outside of Cincinnati that I'd come across while hunting high and low for a Honeycomb yoke. The package cost $249 and was available instantly on purchase. I sat down in front of my laptop and began to explore the serious world of flight.

A funny thing happened as I watched the Sporty's videos. The course is designed, needless to say, for real student pilots, so they often said things like "when you are in the plane" and "when you are with your instructor" and "when you are ready for your first solo." You hear that repeated often enough and you begin to think in those terms as well. Sure, I was just waiting for my new PC to arrive so I could boot up a *game*, but what I was learning… well, couldn't I just go out and do it for real? I mean, these people obviously expected me to. For the moment I assumed that flight schools, like everything else, were probably closed due to COVID-19, but the idea had been planted.

As I learned the basics of flying from the Sporty's videos, the days of summer slowly ticked by and our initial quarantine began to ease. When I received the good news that my new PC would be arriving earlier than expected on September 17, it was all I could do not to go out and meet the FedEx delivery truck on the street corner after tracking its progress across the country.

My excitement, to be honest, was mixed with a certain trepidation. What if it actually turned out to be as hard as I remembered, so many years ago? Would smoother, more photorealistic graphics really make a difference, or did I simply lack the hand-eye coordination and depth perception required to land a plane, even on a computer? If I did, all my enthusiasm and video watching—to say nothing of shelling out money for a brand-new PC—would seem rather foolish.

PC unboxed and set up, I wasted no time downloading and installing the game. I started it up and listened for the first time to the soothing *MSFS 2020* theme song that would become the soundtrack of my life for the next few months. The flight sim has a series of tutorials, which being brand new to controlling an airplane, I knew I would need. They take place in a Cessna 152 (a smaller, two-seat version of the four-seat 172) out of the picturesque mesa-top airport at Sedona, Arizona. The first one started with the plane already flying in the air, where a virtual instructor walked you through a basic set of maneuvers (turning, climbing, descending, and maintaining **straight and level** flight).

This seemed like it couldn't be too hard, but from the very start, something was wrong. The airplane in the tutorial somehow couldn't produce enough power to stay level, even at full throttle. The gauge showing **RPM** (revolutions per minute of the propeller) wavered weakly around 1700, well below where I knew it should read. I launched the first tutorial several times, and each time the little Cessna 152 gradually, futilely nosedived into the rapidly approaching ground. What the hell? I checked and rechecked the settings and couldn't find the problem. Was there a fatal bug in my setup? Or was I just cursed to fail at flying?

Then it occurred to me. In all the videos, I learned about the little red knob next to the throttle, which regulates **fuel mixture**.[4] When a simple piston-driven plane goes up in **altitude**, the air becomes less dense, and the balance of air and fuel being introduced to the cylinders must be adjusted. You have to pull back on the red knob to "lean" the mixture, reducing the amount of fuel to match the reduced amount of air, in order for the engine to produce as much power as before. Sedona Airport sits at 4,830 feet above sea level, and the airplane started off in the tutorial about 1,000 feet above that—well above the 3,000 feet where "leaning" is normally required. So I gave it a try. And it worked. With the fuel mixture leaned, the Cessna was suddenly producing all the RPM one would expect and flew like a dream. For the very first time, something I had learned in online ground school had been applicable to a real (well, simulated) situation and had solved a problem. I actually knew something about how to fly an airplane.

The next lesson, taking off, was fairly straightforward. **Taxiing** the airplane involved (as in real life) using the rudder pedals, which in a Cessna are also linked to the nosewheel. Push on the right foot pedal to turn right, the left to go left, and press forward with the toes of either foot to apply the left or right brakes. You're not supposed to taxi very fast—no more than a "brisk walking pace" is the rule—which is good because I was pretty wobbly to start. Once you're positioned at the end of the **runway**, lined up on the **centerline** with the nose pointed toward the other end, you gradually but firmly push the throttle to maximum. As the plane builds up speed, you need to use the rudder pedals to stay on the centerline. This could be tricky until I got the right feel for it—and adjusted the sensitivity of the pedals so they didn't overreact to every slight move of my feet. In this type of airplane, once you reach 55 knots on the dial—whatever a knot is, I thought—you pull gently back on the yoke, and you're off. In the sim, at least, taking off wasn't too difficult a trick, as long as I could stay on the runway. At full power, an airplane wants to fly and eventually will.

Landing. There's the rub. I could never manage it in the crude, old-fashioned sim, and I wasn't sure if anything had changed. The *MSFS 2020* tutorial lesson starts you out all lined up with the runway and tells you to aim for the near end of it, nose slightly down, while lowering your flaps and pulling back the throttle enough to keep from gaining speed. Too high, reduce throttle; too low, add power. At the very last moment, when you're about 10 feet above the runway and over the numbers, level off and pull the throttle all the way back to **idle**—its lowest setting where the engine is still on, but the propeller produces little or no forward thrust. Then keep the nose pulled slightly up while the plane loses speed and lift and eventually settles onto the ground.

The first time I tried this, everything was looking alright until I somehow fell short of the runway. When you crash in *MSFS 2020*, the screen simply goes black and a mournful song begins to play. That was discouraging. But I went right back and tried again. The second time I made the runway, leveled off, cut the power, and plunked myself—not very gracefully, but nevertheless quite solidly—onto the runway. After a few tries, I was able to fly the whole "traffic pattern" from takeoff and back around to land. Lining up with the runway to land was, in contrast to the nightmarish geometry of my early experiences on a sim, rather intuitive. The graphics now looked amazingly like real life, and that made all the difference in terms of sensing both my alignment and altitude. Soon I was flying the final tutorial lesson cross-country to Flagstaff and beginning a "bush trip" that started along the coast of Croatia and Greece, which I would eventually continue all the way around the Mediterranean. I was airborne!

Except I really wasn't, was I? I was playing a game on a PC, a rather impressive and complicated game, but still just blips on a computer screen. The folks in the ground school videos, on the other hand, were doing the real thing—and preparing me to do the real thing. Based on what I had learned, flying didn't seem so impossible after all. Meanwhile, all around me people were bemoaning all the plans COVID-19 had sidetracked, depressed at the prospect of a whole year "wasted." But maybe this unkind year, for all its disruptions, didn't have to go to waste. Now that some things were starting to open up again, maybe—just maybe—I should explore the possibility of taking some real flying lessons.

CHAPTER 2

Discovery

Few of the pilots I talked to, at least outside of YouTube, were very keen on PC-based flight simulators as any kind of preparation for flight school. "I've never really been into flight sims," one who I deeply respected told me. "It's just not like flying a real plane. It might help you with practicing procedures, but that's about it." (I later came to conclude that this impression, while once probably accurate, is increasingly out of date.) Another warned me not to get too far ahead in my studies for the FAA written exam before starting my practical lessons in the air. "It's not for everyone," he cautioned. "See if you actually like it first."

I had no idea how to find the right flight school for me, and no one I knew had any suggestions. New York City is probably one of the worst places to decide you want to take flying lessons because of the heavily trafficked and restricted airspace for many miles around. I knew I would have to travel a decent way out into the suburbs in Long Island, Connecticut, or New Jersey—or perhaps to another part of the country altogether. Winter was soon approaching, and I wondered what issues weather might pose. So my first thought was maybe to find a school in Florida, where the skies are typically sunny and clear all year round, and hopefully persuade my wife to let me go there for two or three weeks to pack in as many lessons as possible. Was this a realistic plan? There was only one way to find out. I looked up an online list of flight schools, found one that had won numerous awards and accolades, and gave them a call to ask.

The woman I spoke to was not encouraging. "Flying is a motor skill," she explained. "You really have to develop it over time. We recommend no more than one lesson per week." Was it not possible for someone to do something more intensive? "We only did that once. A woman needed to complete her commercial license, so she did a lesson each day. It was like drinking from a fire hose. We wouldn't recommend it." *So you're saying there's a chance?* "I would suggest you find a flight school closer to your home." Do you have any recommendations? As a matter of fact, she did. She gave me the name and number of a small school out of a small airport in suburban New Jersey called Lincoln Park, which she'd worked with in the past and had given her a good impression. It looked like I was on to Plan B.

There were several flight schools with websites sprinkled across the New York City region but, not knowing one from the other, I figured there would be no harm in sticking with my one recommendation, for whatever it was worth. I called them up and, after some brief conversation, booked a "discovery flight" for the next available date: October 31, Halloween. About four months since I first heard about *MSFS 2020* and a little over a month since I started playing it at home, I would be taking flight—this time, for real.

A **discovery flight** is the typical introductory session for someone potentially interested in taking flying lessons. Sometimes people give it as a gift to a family member or friend (for a birthday, anniversary, etc.) who they hope to interest in aviation or think might just enjoy the thrill. It might lead to further lessons, or it might stop there. As the date approached, I happened to ask whether my son, who would just turn 11 a few days before, could join and fly with us. Student pilots can't fly passengers, but when an instructor (**CFI**, or Certified Flight Instructor) is in the plane, even if they're not manning the controls, they are formally the **PIC** (Pilot in Command), so passengers can come along if the CFI says it's okay. On discovery flights, it's almost encouraged because flight schools know that buy-in from family is going to be critical if the student is going to invest time and money in further lessons. My son was welcome to come along.

Someone later asked me if I ever had "the big sit-down" with my family to discuss the risks and dangers of learning to fly a real airplane. As a matter of fact, I never did, and their question made me wonder whether I should have. When I asked my wife if she'd ever felt any unvoiced concerns, however, she told me that she had not, for two reasons. First, she reasoned that the people at the flight school probably knew what they were doing. Second, my wife knows I am a pretty conservative, cautious person, not a daredevil personality by any means, so she trusted my judgment not to do anything reckless or crazy. My family was used to me traveling to far-flung countries that often were a little rough around the edges, so I guess they figured that if I had survived this long, I knew how to stay on the safe side of risky situations. But every student and every family are different, and for some, having this conversation is very important. Inviting them along on the discovery ride is one way to help reassure skeptical loved ones that you're in good hands.

The day of our discovery flight is clear and calm—something I would come to appreciate more, and take for granted less, as my lessons progressed. My son and I take an Uber over the George Washington Bridge, past the old silk mills of Patterson, to where the city's outskirts begin to give way to the first foothills of the Appalachians. The airstrip itself, down a road lined with modest homes, copses of trees, and a number of plant nurseries, is nestled below a wooded ridgeline running from west to north. I had never spent much time around small airports, so the languid, bucolic pace of the place catches me somewhat by surprise. The peaceful quiet is only occasionally, and briefly, interrupted by the buzz of a propeller as a small airplane gently bumps to a landing. Beside the parking lot, a sign declaring "Learn to Fly" fills the window of a small office between two barn-like hangars. An older woman, the owner Abbie, greets us as we step inside.

They have only one plane, she says, a Cessna 172. It's out for another discovery flight but will be returning shortly. The Cessna 172 Skyhawk is the workhorse trainer at most schools, not only in the U.S. but around the world. First flown in 1955, over 44,000 of the high-wing, all-metal 172s have been built, more than any other airplane in the world.[5] They are still being made today out of Kansas, and a brand new one costs around $400,000. I've seen used 172s listed anywhere from $70,000 to $500,000 depending on age, upkeep, and amenities. When well-maintained they last for a long time. A 50-year-old automobile is considered an antique and a rare sight on the roads, but there are plenty of 50-year-old Cessnas flying as good as new.

For a while, we pace the sunlit waiting room, gazing out the window, unsure what to expect. Shortly, though, we hear the lawnmower-like sound of the Cessna taxiing around the corner and parking on a small patch of grass outside. A woman in her 20s named Tess (who would become my instructor for the next year) climbs out and comes over to introduce herself. She is tall with brown curly hair, sunglasses, and a relaxed smile. Tess already has our weights to make sure the plane is properly balanced—a crucial requirement in any small aircraft, as I would later come to appreciate. So the first part of my lesson is to learn how to do the **pre-flight inspection**, a process I would repeat every time I returned.

There are all sorts of things that can happen to a plane when it's sitting on the ground, so you can't just hop in and take off. The manufacturer provides a **checklist** for examining each and every critical part of the airplane, inside the cockpit and out, to make sure nothing is damaged and everything is functioning. Tess walks us around the plane, pointing out its different components and ticking them off the list as we go. We wiggle the bolts on the flaps and ailerons, listen for the avionics cooling fan, look for any pink brake fluid leaking under the wheels, and make sure each antenna is in place. We drain samples of the sky-blue-colored fuel into a clear plastic bottle—a process called **sumping**—from five taps under each wing and three under the engine, looking for either water or sediment that may have gotten into the fuel tanks and could cause the engine to suddenly cut out if not discovered and removed. The checklist can eventually come to feel tedious when you're eager to get airborne, but this morning is my first time physically touching a

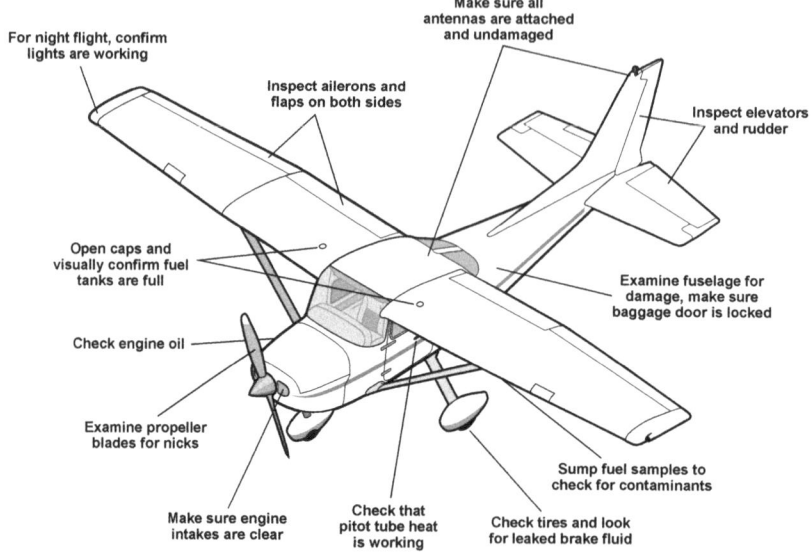

Some of the main steps in performing a pre-flight ground inspection on a Cessna 172.

plane I will fly, so each little task feels like a milestone.

This particular Cessna, I later learn, is just over 20 years old. It's been through one minor crash years ago, when it plowed into a snowbank on landing, but has been incident-free since. Aside from some paint flaking off on the underside of its wing, it looks to be in good repair. My son is impressed; he says it looks larger and sturdier than he imagined. I wonder how sturdy it will feel when we're in the air. The cabin is about the same size as the interior of a Volkswagen Bug. Carrying four grown adults would be a snug fit. Once our inspection is complete, my son squeezes into the back seat. Tess directs me to the primary pilot's seat on the front left. She climbs in through the door opposite and sits beside me in the right front seat, as the instructor normally does, behind a second set of controls.

So how do you turn on a Cessna 172? I'm somewhat familiar from the sim, but Tess directs me to a booklet stowed in a pouch beside my leg and observes as I read aloud through its checklist. First flip on the red **master**

switch, which lets power flow from the battery to provide electricity and enable the electric **starter**. Make sure the **beacon** light, a red flashing bulb atop the tail that warns people the airplane is operating, is switched on. If the airplane has been sitting overnight, Tess explains, you may need to turn on the fuel pump switch and gradually push the red mixture knob in for a few seconds until the gauge shows positive fuel flow, before turning it off again, to prime the engine.

Make sure the red mixture knob is all the way out, to cut-off, and push the black throttle knob in just a quarter of an inch. (On some aircraft, the throttle and mixture are vertical levers, but on the Cessna 172 they are push knobs that you move in or out with your right hand.) Either set the parking brake, tip the foot pedals forward to hold the brakes, or both. Look around and make sure the area is completely clear. Shout "CLEAR PROP!" out the window. Then place the key in what looks like a car **ignition** switch and turn it past Left, Right, to Both, all the way to Start. As the starter begins turning the propeller around sluggishly, firmly push the red mixture knob in full, waiting (and hoping) for it to catch. Ideally, if you've timed it right, the engine roars to life. I had to try twice for it to catch. Pull the throttle back so the propeller turns at just below 1000 RPM.

Per the checklist, next I flick on the white avionics switch and the GPS, radios, and other devices in the center of the instrument panel spring to life. The three of us each plug in and put on a pair of headsets that look like big green plastic earmuffs so we can hear (and be heard on) the intercom and the radio over the noise of the engine. It's time to taxi.

Taxiing is the first chance you get to use those foot pedals for real. I haven't mentioned it to Tess—I don't want her to think it's made me overconfident—but the sim has given me a basic idea what to do. Press the right foot pedal to turn right, left to turn left. Tipping either pedal forward with your toes applies the brakes for that wheel, which can also help you turn. Above all, go slow. At this point, the instructor is justifiably worried you will go careening into a ditch—or another parked plane. Later, you learn to keep the RPM low (700 will often do) to maintain just enough forward momentum, rather than riding the brakes, which can wear them out.

Before entering the runway, there is a **hold short line**—actually two solid yellow lines on the near side next to two dashed yellow lines on the far side—where we must stop (see Figure 14). This is where we do our **run-up**. Reading aloud again from another checklist, I make sure the controls are working and the instruments are correctly set. I press the brakes and rev the engine up to about two-thirds maximum power (1800 RPM in this Cessna) to check the engine gauges and the magnetos. I turn the ignition key to Left only, then to Right only, to make sure the engine runs smoothly on either (at this point I'm just following directions; I won't learn what this really means until later). Then I pull the throttle all the way out to idle, to make sure it doesn't just conk out when you do that. Lights on. Flaps set to the first setting of 10°, which is mandatory in many aircraft, but optional in this one. We are going to want that, Tess explains, because this is a pretty short runway.

The runway at Lincoln Park is 2,767 feet long and 40 feet wide—about the width of a small suburban neighborhood street. Several of my pilot friends later told me, "That's about the shortest runway I'd feel comfortable landing on," though before a year had passed, I would land on even shorter ones. The school advertises this as a plus, that learning to fly here means you will have the confidence to land most anywhere. And now Tess tells me that I will be doing the takeoff myself. Cool. I think. Right?

I know from the sim what to do. Line up on the centerline. Push the throttle full in. Dance on those rudder pedals to keep the nose centered down the runway. Keep one eye on the airspeed indicator, which would begin to move, or "come alive," when the plane's airspeed reached 40 knots. By now I knew that **knots** stands for nautical miles per hour. A **nautical mile (nm)** is a little bit longer than a normal **statute mile** and is used in aviation, as well as sailing, for reasons I'd only learn later. "Airspeed is alive!" shouts Tess as the needle rises. When the Cessna reaches 55 knots, or about 63 miles per hour, she tells me to pull back gently on the yoke. That's about the same speed as a car traveling on a highway, except this highway has a fast-approaching fence at the end of it. But that's already below us now, as I raise the nose just enough so it's about level with the horizon and let the speed build to 80 knots.

It all just happens, and like that I realize that I'm in a real plane, and I just really took off. To be honest, I don't like heights (my instructor admits, months later, that she doesn't like heights either), but there's an air of unreality as I simply focus on doing what I've done in front of my computer screen time and time again. In fact, the whole flight goes by with a feeling that this can't be happening, but it is. At one point, after gently banking out of turn, Tess tells me "You're a natural." It's a remark I am just sufficiently self-aware enough to realize is the kind of encouraging flattery an instructor would give any prospective student who isn't scaring them half to death.

I really must not be doing that badly, though, because halfway into the flight I realize we haven't heard a peep out of my son in the back seat. Has he somehow fallen out? "I'm fine," he replies over the intercom, displaying the kind of relaxed calm I wish I felt as I grip the yoke a bit more tightly than needed.

The dials in front of me are already familiar, and this is a big help. I can't imagine what it would be like to be seeing them for the first time, under these circumstances, and not knowing what they were telling me. I do, and it's a big confidence boost that I can control the plane the way I intend. Of course, landing is a whole other story.

On the car ride over my son asked me if I thought I could land a Cessna 172 based on my practice in the flight sim at home. I considered this seriously for a moment and said, "I know what I should do and what it should look like. But I don't have a feel for the plane and how it responds in real life. I would probably have a decent chance if I absolutely had to, but unlike in the sim the ground is hard and you don't get another chance if it doesn't play out the way you expect." So I am perfectly happy when Tess announces that she will land the plane, with my hands resting lightly on the yoke and my feet lightly touching the pedals to feel and follow what she is doing.

A single landing strip, like the one at Lincoln Park, is really two runways running in opposite directions. You always want to take off and land on the runway that points most directly into the direction the wind is coming from. Taking off into a **headwind**, in this way, adds the wind speed to your **groundspeed**, achieving the **airspeed** you need to get airborne more quickly, using less runway. Landing into a headwind means that your required airspeed on approach translates into a slower groundspeed, so you touch down more safely and take less distance to stop. In contrast, taking off or landing with a **tailwind** involves building up or winding down more energy, which may use up more runway than you have—not to mention the risk of colliding with aircraft taking off or landing in the opposite, *correct* direction.

The runway everyone is using, because it offers the most favorable wind, is called the **active runway**. At a small airport like this, you can determine it from which way the windsock is blowing or by listening to what other airplanes are doing over the radio. At a larger airport, Air Traffic Control (ATC) will tell you.

Directions in an airplane are based on the 360 degrees of the magnetic compass: 0° is north, 90° east, 180° south, and 270° west. Wind direction is defined by where it is blowing *from*: wind at 90° is blowing from east to west. Every runway (in each direction) is assigned a number based on the magnetic compass reading it points toward, which makes it easy to compare with the wind direction and select the runway that best faces into the wind. That morning, with the wind blowing from 20°, we took off toward the north from Runway 1 because it points approximately toward 10°. By the time we return, the wind has shifted to 170°, so now we need to land on the same strip of runway in the opposite direction, on Runway 19, which points toward 190°. These numbers are painted on either side of the landing strip, so as you come in to land on Runway 19 there's a large "19" facing you where the runway starts, which serves as an aiming point.

Lincoln Park has no control tower, so Tess has me announce our position over the radio, while looking and listening for anyone else in the process of taking off or landing. Our **call sign**, "Skyhawk Seven-Two-Niner-Juliet-Papa" (or "Niner-Juliet-Papa" for short), is based on our type of aircraft plus the plane's unique alphanumeric **registration** number (N729JP) painted on its side. All U.S.-registered aircraft start with N, so you leave that out. When we are sure everything is clear, I repeat Tess's instructions word for word and announce we are entering the **traffic pattern**.

The traffic pattern is the standard circuit for approaching or leaving an airport, whether it has a control tower or not. It's typically 1,000 feet above ground level, which translates to an altimeter reading above sea level you must know in advance. In our case, Lincoln Park is 181 feet above sea level, so the traffic pattern is set at 1,200 feet.

Because you take off or land on whichever runway has a headwind, each leg of the traffic pattern is defined in relation to which way the wind is blowing. Sometimes, due to terrain or airspace restrictions, the traffic pattern involves turns to the right. But most of the time, unless otherwise stated, each turn in the circuit is always to the left. When you take off, you either depart straight out or turn to the left, onto the **crosswind** leg. The next left will take you onto the **downwind** leg, flying in the same direction as the wind, parallel to the runway on your left. The next left is the **base** leg, cutting in toward the runway, and the last is **final**: lined up with runway and ready to land. (There's also an **upwind** leg, a jot off to the right, in case you're not ready to land and need to **go around** the circuit again.)

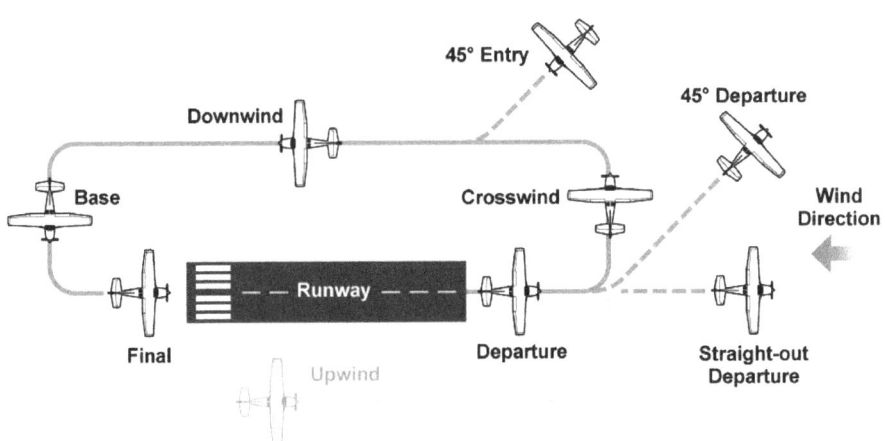

The basic elements of an airport traffic pattern.

An air traffic controller, in a tower, may instruct you to enter the pattern at any point, depending on where you and other planes are. But at smaller airports, without an active tower, you usually enter the pattern at a 45-degree angle to the midpoint of the downwind leg, with each pilot expected to communicate to the others where they are and maintain a safe spacing from them. Flying parallel to the runway on downwind, 1,000 feet up, allows you to visually check and make sure the runway is clear of obstructions, including other aircraft. Only then can you begin your descent and last two turns to land in the opposite direction.

The view on final approach to land, with the runway lined up before us, looks remarkably familiar from the sim. But the sensation of seeing the ground rushing to meet us, and the solid thump of our wheels touching down, is something no computer game can replicate. Back on *terra firma*, taxiing the plane to park, I regret that our flight is over so quickly and want to go up again. The fact that I've just been flying a real plane, and had at least some idea what I was doing, is exhilarating. The rising awareness of how much practice and skill is required to do it confidently and well is humbling.

Before we leave, I sign up for my next lesson.

CHAPTER 3

Medical

Now that I was determined to be a pilot, I needed to get a few things in order. There are three documents that any pilot must carry with them when they fly: a government-issued photo ID (such as a driver's license or passport), an **airman certificate** (a plastic card commonly referred to as a "pilot's license"), and a (paper) medical certificate. Before you earn your full license, a student license and a medical certificate are required to fly **solo**—on your own—with an instructor's permission. Until my first solo, I technically didn't need either, but I figured I should get the ball rolling so I'd have them ready when needed.

The **Federal Aviation Administration (FAA)** is the authority that oversees all civil aviation in the United States, including pilot training. Applying for a student pilot certificate is all done online these days via an FAA website called **IACRA** (Integrated Airman Certification and Rating Application). In fact, this is where all digital paperwork for new flying qualifications gets filed and processed throughout your aviation career. When I first registered on the site, it assigned me an FAA Tracking Number **(FTN)**. Not to be confused with the certificate number on my license, this is the personal identifier I'll use, forever after, whenever I sign up to take a new exam or checkride.

A couple of fun facts: You only need to be 16 years old to get a student license to fly solo, and 17 to take the checkride for your full license.[6] You can begin taking lessons with an instructor well before that, since there's no legal minimum. But the flight school does have to confirm that you can speak English, as part of the application process. Since 1944, English has been the official language of aviation worldwide, to ensure everyone can communicate with each other, and starting in 2008, proficiency became a requirement for nearly all pilots and air traffic controllers everywhere.[7] The U.S. is also a very popular place for students from Europe and elsewhere—where training regulations can be more costly and cumbersome—to learn to fly. For some, mastering English can be one of the biggest hurdles to overcome in pursuit of an aviation career.

With your student license in hand, there are a couple of different kinds of more permanent licenses you can go for, and because there's a lot of overlap in the initial training, you don't have to decide right away. Prior to 1991,[8] the only real option if you wanted to fly was a **Private Pilot License (PPL)**. That year, the FAA introduced the Recreational Pilot License, which requires less time but restricts pilots to flying in the local vicinity, during daytime in good visibility, and outside of controlled airspace without special permission. In 2004 it added the Sport Pilot License, which has similar restrictions and limits pilots to smaller, two-seat planes, but allows longer-distance flights. Like most students, I planned to go for the old-school PPL, which offers the most flexibility as well as the easiest path to further training if you want to pursue it.

Jumping through online bureaucratic hoops is hardly the most fun part of flying, but a few weeks later, after I was vetted by the Transportation Security Administration (TSA), I did get a neat little plastic card in the mail featuring an image of Orville and Wilbur Wright taking off at Kitty Hawk. With this in hand, I officially became one of over 222,000 student pilots in the U.S.[9] That might sound like a lot, but there's a catch: starting in 2016, student pilot certificates no longer have an expiration date. A lot of those students began their training but never completed it and are still on the books. Less than 40,000 students complete the written exam each year.[10] By some estimates, 80% of students drop out before earning their license.[11] I'll share some thoughts about why later.

Even before my card arrived in the mail, I feared I might end up as one of these statistics. The reason was something I had not seen coming: my medical history. There are three classes of medical certificates required to fly. Class I, for airline pilots, has very stringent requirements and must be renewed frequently: once a year for younger pilots, once every six months for those 40 or older. Class II is for non-airline commercial pilots for hire, and Class III is for private or student pilots—each with somewhat more forgiving health standards and longer expiration periods. I'd need a Class III, which for younger pilots is valid for five years, but for me (40 and above) has to be renewed every two years. The FAA has recently introduced a more lenient **BasicMed** program for private pilots of smaller aircraft that lets you extend the validity of your medical certificate through consultations with your regular doctor. However, you still need to pass at least one Class III medical exam to start.

The FAA designates certain physicians as **Aviation Medical Examiners (AMEs)**, qualified to issue pilot medical certificates. There are lists of them online, and you have to find one near you and request an appointment. This was not exactly easy during COVID-19, but I did locate one, a pilot himself, who was willing to schedule an examination. He directed me to another FAA website, MedXPress, that asked me to fill out an online form detailing my medical history, including all doctor or hospital visits over the past several years. While I wear glasses, I was in reasonably good health and figured I would have no trouble meeting the requirements. Without too much concern, I entered a recent trip to the doctor to test for possible COVID-19 symptoms (never confirmed, there were limited tests available at the time) as well as a kidney stone that flared up and passed about a year before.

His email back to me gave me a jolt. "Previous COVID-19 symptoms should be no obstacle, but the kidney stone may present an issue. Please send me full documentation of this and any prior kidney stone episodes." Uh oh. This had never occurred to me. With mounting alarm, I then did what I should have done in the first place and looked more closely at the FAA website about potentially disqualifying medical conditions. My heart sank. Yes, kidney stones can disqualify you, particularly if they are recurrent or unresolved. I wish I could claim this most recent incident had been my first experience with kidney stones. In fact, despite otherwise good health, there had been a string of them over the years going back to when I was 26—some more serious than others. So was that it? Was the dream over before it began?

Not quite. The FAA is mainly concerned that excruciating pain from kidney stones (which I can certainly testify to) could flare up suddenly and incapacitate a pilot mid-flight. They want to be aware of the condition, and they need assurances that it's not an imminent danger.[12] The AME can issue a waiver if they're convinced it doesn't stem from a more serious underlying condition and you aren't currently undergoing treatment. In the end, I needed whatever medical records I could gather, a letter from my regular doctor stating that I was fine for now, and a lengthy, detailed conversation with the AME about my previous symptoms and treatments. He signed off, but the FAA would have to review and approve my case.

As part of the exam, I had to pass a vision test as well. I've worn glasses since I was eight years old, and without them anything more than a foot away from my face is a fuzzy blur. When I joined the Army, I remember the guys who wanted to be helicopter pilots freaking out about passing the special medical exam. Their natural, uncorrected vision didn't have to be perfect, but it had to be pretty close.[13] The Air Force and Navy have similar requirements and, for many years, having laser surgery to improve your vision was a flat-out disqualifier (this has changed in recent years, and certain kinds of procedures are now allowed).[14] The fact that I'm nowhere near meeting any of these standards was always one of the things in the back of my mind that made me assume I could never be a pilot.

As far as the FAA is concerned, though, wearing normal prescription glasses or contact lenses is not a problem for private or commercial civilian pilots. Much like your driver's license, you can wear them for your vision test, and your pilot certificate will simply say you can't fly without them. LASIK or other corrective surgeries like the removal of cataracts are allowed as long as the results were successful. Color blindness can still be a showstopper, however, if it's serious enough. So can problems with depth perception, though apparently it is possible to get a medical waiver to fly with only one eye to see.[15] Wiley Post, who lost his left eye in an oil drilling accident in his native Oklahoma, got his license in 1928.[16] It prevented him from getting hired as an airline pilot,[17] but it didn't stop him from becoming one of the most famous air racing champions of the 1930s, making the first solo flight around the world, or pioneering high-altitude flying in the first pressurized flight suit.[18]

Like many people who have worn glasses for years, I'd let my prescription slip out of date. To make sure I met the standard for corrected vision, I paid a visit to the eye doctor and ordered a new pair, which I picked up the day before my appointment with the AME. This was probably poor planning on my part. As anyone who wears glasses knows, it takes a day or two to get accustomed to new lenses, making it a little difficult to focus. I passed, but I doubt it was with flying colors.

Besides color blindness and kidney stones, the FAA has a short list of conditions that can pose serious obstacles on the medical exam.[19] A history of epilepsy or unexplained seizures has long been a bar to getting a pilot's license.[20] Heart problems can be tricky; while a growing number of pilots do get approved after suffering a heart attack or undergoing coronary surgery, they have to satisfy the FAA that they've made a full recovery.[21] New advances in medical technology, as well as the desire to encourage pilots to seek treatment rather than hide problems, have gradually opened some new doors. Many pilots have been cleared to return to the cockpit after getting successful treatment for substance abuse or depression, including new anti-depressant medications.[22] However, some mental health conditions such as bipolar disorder or psychosis are still disqualifying because the FAA remains wary of the drugs used to treat them.[23] For a long time, diabetes requiring insulin was a big disqualifier, but recent advances in glucose monitoring have made it possible for even airline pilots to obtain special permission to return to duty.[24]

Though it comes as a surprise to many, plenty of pilots either learn to fly or are able to continue flying after the loss of an arm or a leg—including in commercial and military service.[25] One of the RAF's top fighter aces in the Battle of Britain, Douglas Bader, flew with two artificial legs after losing both—one above the knee, one below—in a prewar crash.[26] He was credited with 22 kills, and when he was later shot down and captured, he tried to escape so many times that the Germans put him in their special high-security prison at Colditz.[27] In 2008, an amazing woman from Arizona named Jessica Cox broke new ground by earning her pilot's license despite being born with no arms, adeptly operating the yoke and throttle with just her feet.[28] The ERCO 415-C Ercoupe she flies is a rather unique airplane designed in the 1930s that has no rudder pedals, with the rudder linked to the other controls via the yoke.[29]

In Jessica's case, the Sport Pilot License provided a pathway because, uniquely, it does not require a Class III medical—just a valid driver's license. I only learned that later. Had I realized this was an option at the time, I might not have been *quite* so worried that the medical exam would completely derail my hopes. If you want to learn to fly but face medical hurdles, so long as you can drive a car, there is a way.

That said, the FAA takes the medical aspects of flying very seriously. A decent chunk of the private pilot written exam is devoted to knowledge of medical regulations and risk factors. Being able to pass the medical exam is obviously important, at least for a standard license, but many risks can be more subtle. A lot of medical conditions or drug side-effects that are minor or at least manageable on the ground can cause much bigger trouble in the sky due to the effects of thinner air at higher altitudes.

Flying high brings many advantages. Airplanes encounter less drag and burn less fuel in thinner air, and can avoid bad weather below. But as mountain climbers know, the higher you go the less oxygen there is to breathe. Even at just 5,000 feet the **density** of the atmosphere is 17% less than at sea level, and by 14,000 feet, you get 41% less oxygen with every breath.[30] That's something we typically don't think about as passengers because airliners and private business jets have pressurized cabins, so the air we're breathing inside provides enough oxygen no matter how high up we are. FAA regulations require all commercial flights in the U.S. to maintain a cabin air pressure equivalent to no higher than 8,000 feet, which is enough to ward off most serious health effects. Still, the difference between that and sea level can be enough to cause your ears to pop and some people's feet to swell, and is a major reason why we often suffer from fatigue (jet lag) after long flights.[31]

Smaller planes like the Cessna 172, or older ones like most World War II bombers, typically are not pressurized at all. As a result, the dangers posed by flying at higher altitudes can be far more serious.

The initial symptoms of **hypoxia**—the lack of sufficient oxygen to the brain—vary by person. What's interesting though is that the symptoms for each person will be the same every time.[32] From crossing the high passes of the Himalayas from Nepal into Tibet at about 17,000 feet above sea level, I know that for me it's tunnel vision: my peripheral vision fades to black with any quick motion. For someone else it might be a change in skin color, a tingling sensation in the arms or legs, shortness of breath, a rapid heartbeat, sweating, headache, or perhaps most concerning, a sense of euphoria and overconfidence that can cause someone to ignore the danger they are in. In his novel *Bomber*, Len Deighton offers a macabre description of a pilot confidently riding an obviously doomed plane to his death, rather than bailing out, because his oxygen line had been severed, playing havoc with his judgment.[33]

The only solution for hypoxia is to descend and get down to an altitude where oxygen is more plentiful, or to breathe supplemental oxygen from a mask. In 1943, the world-renowned nuclear physicist Niels Bohr nearly died while being secretly evacuated from Sweden in a British bomber, to join up with the Manhattan Project after escaping from Nazi-occupied Denmark. He somehow neglected to activate his oxygen supply and fell unconscious. Fortunately, the pilot, hearing no response over the intercom, figured out what happened and quickly descended to a lower altitude, where the 58-year-old Bohr recovered—feeling, perhaps, like not such a genius after all.[34]

World War II bomber crews typically wore oxygen masks above 10,000 feet.[35] FAA regulations require any pilot flying an unpressurized aircraft over

12,500 feet for more than 30 minutes, or over 14,000 feet for any period at all, to use supplemental oxygen. Over 15,000 feet, passengers must be provided with oxygen, though it's their choice whether to use it. These altitudes might seem awfully high for someone training in a Cessna, but keep in mind they refer to sea level. If you're flying across the country and take off from Denver, you're already at 5,400 feet before you leave the ground. Since hypoxia can occasionally kick in as low as 5,000 feet, it's important to be aware.

Drugs, including alcohol, can seriously aggravate hypoxia by reducing the brain's ability to absorb whatever oxygen is in the blood stream. When I was crossing the Himalayas, one member of our party foolishly ignored warnings and went out drinking the night before. Not only did it leave him dehydrated, but he was basically in a stupor the whole bus ride over the mountain pass due to lack of oxygen. We all felt the effect of higher altitude, but for him it was far worse. Besides the obvious impairment drinking has on judgment and coordination, this side effect is a major reason why the FAA prohibits pilots from drinking alcohol at least eight hours before flying (most airlines require their pilots to abstain for twelve). Regardless, the acceptable blood alcohol limit imposed by the FAA is 0.04%—half the federal threshold for drunk driving.

Another similar danger is **carbon monoxide (CO)** poisoning. A byproduct of internal combustion, the CO produced by the plane's engine normally gets safely vented out through the exhaust system. In a smaller plane like a Cessna, with its single engine located right in front of you in the nose, a blockage or leak could easily channel toxic CO into the cockpit. You've probably heard about people who kill themselves (on purpose or by accident) by sitting in a closed garage and letting the car engine run. What happens is that the hemoglobin in our blood, which is meant to absorb and carry oxygen, absorbs CO much more readily, so the oxygen gets blocked, causing you to suffocate.

The initial symptoms of CO poisoning are similar to hypoxia but can take hold a lot more rapidly and prove deadly in short order. The solution is to close all the cabin heating vents from the engine, open all the windows to air out the cabin, and land as quickly as possible. Sometimes a leak might carry the scent of exhaust fumes into the cabin, but it could just as easily be odorless. For this reason, many pilots (including me) buy and carry readily available CO detectors in the cockpit with them when they fly.

You might think that breathing rapidly would get you more oxygen if you need it, but you'd be wrong. When you experience **hyperventilation** due to anxiety or panic, you expel more carbon dioxide (CO_2), lowering its level in your blood. This causes the blood vessels carrying oxygen to the brain to constrict and results in similar symptoms as hypoxia: rapid heartbeat, sweating, dizziness, even blacking out. For a passenger, this is an unpleasant but passing sensation at worst. For a pilot, hyperventilating can turn an already stressful situation into something more dangerous. Fortunately, once recognized, the solution is fairly simple: breathe slower, perhaps by talking aloud to yourself, or breathe into a bag (to restore some of that lost CO_2).*

Changes in air pressure due to altitude can also affect your sinuses, particularly if they're blocked by a cold. We all know the ear-popping you often have to do even in a pressurized airliner when it descends for landing. Based on her own horrible experiences, Tess warned me how painful this can be in an unpressurized plane with even a fairly mild stuffy nose, causing shooting pains across your face.

It's also important to know that even over-the-counter medicines, not to mention prescription drugs, can have much stronger side-effects than expected at higher altitudes. If you're taking something, you need to consult with an AME first to make sure it's okay. The FAA also maintains a website listing some common medicines and whether they are approved for flight. One day after getting a tooth filled at the dentist, I went there to check if Tylenol or Advil were alright; they were, but I couldn't just assume without looking.

---

*Another cause of very sudden hypoxia is experiencing high G-forces due to dramatic aerial maneuvers, which can make it hard or impossible for your heart to pump oxygen-laden blood to your brain. While jet fighter pilots have to worry about this a lot, if you're pulling super-high Gs in your little Cessna, your plane is probably going to fall apart before you do. It just wasn't designed for that.

Flying subjects us to conditions that humans are not well adapted to deal with, given our natural habitat on the ground. As passengers on a modern airliner, this barely occurs to us because we are largely shielded from them in a comfort-controlled cabin. The pilot of a small, single-engine airplane is not, and must often make complicated decisions while coping with them. These challenges are only compounded by other health issues. Suffice it to say, a pilot must always keep a close, critical eye on how their body is functioning, both on the ground and in the air.

For the moment, I was relieved to receive my Class III medical certificate from the doctor, and even more relieved a few weeks later when a letter from the FAA arrived confirming their approval. The letter warned me not to fly if I was ever experiencing any symptoms related to kidney stones, which prompted me to think carefully about the early warning signs I should look for and what I would do if I ever encountered them. Meanwhile, however, I was cleared to continue flying. But how is it, exactly, that we *can* fly in the first place?

CHAPTER 4

Aerodynamics

We're all used to riding in airplanes, but I imagine we all stop and wonder from time to time how in the world this heavy hunk of metal can possibly rise off the ground and stay suspended in midair without just falling down to earth. As I started my first real flying lessons, this became more than a matter of idle curiosity. Some of the ideas were a little hard to fully grasp at first, but they proved crucial to everything I would learn to do—and *not* do—in the cockpit.

The enigma of flight puzzled people for a long time, ever since they looked up in the sky and saw birds, and they began putting the pieces of that puzzle together well before the Wright brothers ever showed up on the scene. Back in 1809, George Cayley—an English gentleman-scientist who devoted his spare time at his various Yorkshire estates to inventing the seat belt, the tank tread, and the railroad crossing signal—first identified the four forces involved in heavier-than-air flight (as opposed to floating around in a balloon.)[36] They are lift, thrust, drag, and weight. They sound deceptively simple, but they interact in ways that a pilot needs to understand, anticipate, and control.

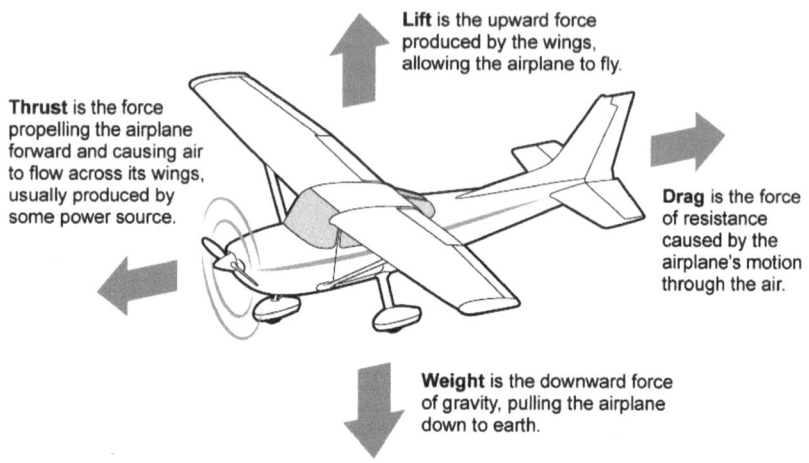

The four forces of flight

Let's start with **lift**, because this is what makes an aircraft different from everything else. Obviously airplanes have wings, which allow them to fly. But how, exactly? It all comes down to the difference in air pressure below versus above the wing, and there are different ways to conceptualize this. One way is **Bernoulli's Principle**. Take a tissue paper, place it under your lower lip, and blow hard and steady. What happens? Far from pushing the paper down, the stream of air along its top actually lifts it up. As the Swiss mathematician Daniel Bernoulli deduced in 1738, air moving at a higher speed produces lower pressure than air moving at a slower speed.[37] The higher **air pressure** below the strip of paper pushes the paper up, against the lower pressure above it.

The wings on an airplane are designed so that the air is forced over the wing at a faster speed than under the wing, creating a difference in pressure and therefore lift. You could say that the higher pressure below is pushing the **airfoil** (the name for such a surface) upward, or you could say the lower pressure above is sucking it upward. It's like a suction cup stuck to a wall:

AERODYNAMICS

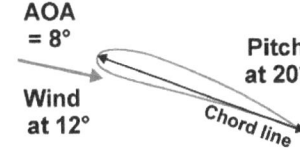

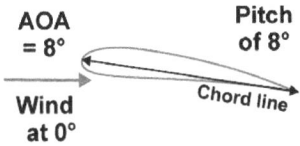

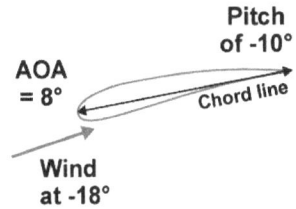

Angle of attack (AOA) is not the same as pitch. These examples show how an airfoil pitched up, level, or down could all have the same AOA due to its direction of travel and thus the angle of the relative wind.

Is the vacuum inside holding it in place, or the external air pressing against it? The answer is both, or rather, the interaction between them.

Wolfgang Langewiesche, who in 1944 wrote a landmark book about the art of flying titled *Stick and Rudder*, did not like the Bernoulli-based explanation—even though it's still what is found in the official FAA handbooks and included in the written exam. While admitting that it is technically true, he considered it irrelevant to the pilot's actual experience.[38] The wings, as he explained it, push the air down in front of them. According to **Newton's Third Law of Motion** ("for every action there is an equal and opposite reaction"), this pushes the airplane up.[39] The amount of air that slows down and bunches up below the wing depends on the **angle of attack**, which he regarded as *the* central concept to flying a plane.[40]

Angle of attack is the angle between the **chord** of the wing—the imaginary line from the center of its leading edge to its trailing edge—and the **relative wind**. Not its angle to the horizon (defined by the plane's **pitch attitude**) or to the fuselage (a design element called the **angle of incidence**), but to the way the air is blowing past it at that moment. If you are flying level, the relative wind is normally straight on; if you're descending, it's coming up from an angle below the plane; if you're climbing, it's coming from an angle above it. The greater the angle of attack, the more lift you have at any given speed.*[41]

The only problem is that angle of attack has a limit. At some point, usually somewhere between 15 to 20 degrees, the airflow going over the top will start to detach from the wing and swirl around it. The wing will cease to be an airfoil and become a mere hunk of metal hurtling through the sky. When this happens, it's called a **stall**. When most of us hear the word "stall," we think of a car engine sputtering out. A stall in aviation has nothing to do with the engine stopping; that's an entirely different problem. A stall occurs when a wing no longer produces lift because it has exceeded its **critical angle of attack**. As we will see, an airplane can recover from a stall and resume flying, but to do so the pilot must find a survivable way to reduce its angle of attack.

Besides angle of attack, the other factor that determines lift is speed. An airfoil only produces lift if air is flowing across it, and the faster that air is moving, the more lift is produced. Wind can help, but for an airplane this airflow is mostly the result of forward motion produced by **thrust**. Gravity can provide some forward thrust as long as the nose is pointed down, but sustained flight requires an independent source of propulsion, like a propeller or a jet engine. A jet delivers thrust directly, compressing air and then igniting fuel so that air expands rapidly, rushing out the back and—by equal and opposite reaction—pushing the engine forward, much like a balloon goes whizzing around the room when you release it and let the air out.

An airplane propeller seems just as straightforward—after all, we're all familiar with electric fans or ships' propellers. If you stand behind an airplane's propeller, you'll feel the air being blown back, which in turn pushes the plane forward. But for a pilot, it's important to recognize that the blades of a propeller are really another set of airfoils, like wings, but spinning through the

---

*This is why airplanes can also fly upside down. The way the wing is attached and curved may help produce lift in normal flight, but it's really all about how you position the wing relative to the airflow, whether right-side up or upside down.

air instead of flying straight through it. Like the wings, these spinning airfoils have their own angle of attack, which produces the equivalent of lift, though in a horizontal rather than vertical direction.

In the Cessna 172 and most other trainers, the angle (or pitch) of the propeller blades is fixed. For us, the proposition is straightforward: the more power we give the engine, the faster the propeller spins, and the more thrust it generates. More sophisticated airplanes often have a **variable pitch propeller**, where the pitch of the blades can be adjusted for different phases of flight. The optimal angle for the blades to take a bite out of the air on takeoff and climb isn't the same as for cruising level at different altitudes and air densities, and can impact both performance and fuel efficiency. Aviation author Walter Boyne compares adjusting the pitch of the propeller, by analogy, to shifting gears in a car.[42] The most common mechanism to achieve this is called a **constant speed propeller**, where the blade pitch is automatically altered, using oil pressure, to correspond to a target RPM set by the pilot.[43] Apart from a handful of potential questions on the written exam, new student pilots don't need to worry about this additional level of complexity at this point. It is, however, helpful to understand that the propeller is really an airfoil, which can be fine-tuned in this way.

In order for something to move through the air, the air has to get out of the way. This creates **drag**, as a counter to thrust. If thrust is greater than drag, the airplane will speed up. If drag exceeds thrust, it will slow down. If thrust and drag are equal—on the ground or in the air—the airplane will move at a steady speed.

Drag comes from a number of sources: from the resistance of the air to the shape of the airplane—parts like wing edges, struts, or nose—moving through it ("form drag"), from the friction of the air passing along the plane's surfaces ("skin drag"), and from different airflows disturbed by the airplane colliding into each other ("interference drag"). All of these forms of **parasitic drag** increase as the airplane's speed increases, requiring greater thrust to overcome. This is why, in level flight at least, the airplane can only fly so fast, even with maximum power.

There is another form of drag, however, that is inversely related to speed: **induced drag**. Remember, the lift created by the wings is a product of two things: angle of attack and the speed of the air flowing across it. Say you need a certain amount of lift to fly level, neither gaining nor losing altitude. The faster your airspeed, the lower angle of attack is required to produce that lift. The slower your airspeed, on the other hand, the higher angle of attack is required to produce enough lift to keep flying level. A wing with a higher angle of attack generates more lift, but also more drag. So the slower you fly, the higher angle of attack you need, and the more induced drag the wings produce. When an airplane is flying very slowly, like when it is coming in to land, you can find yourself "behind the power curve"—meaning that it takes as much or more power to fly slow as it can to fly fast, in order to overcome the induced drag caused by your higher angle of attack.

Fly slow enough and the angle of attack required will exceed its maximum, and the wings will stall. That's no problem if you're a few inches above the runway and you want the airplane to begin settling onto the ground. It's

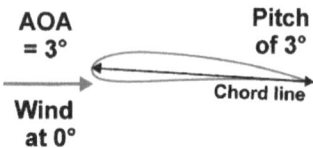

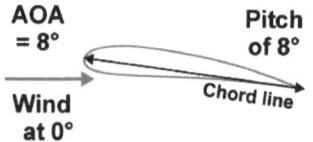

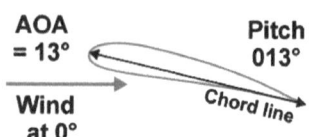

The faster an airfoil travels through the air, the less angle of attack (AOA) it requires to produce the lift required to fly level. The slower it travels, the greater AOA it requires to fly level—until it reaches critical AOA and stalls.

not an insurmountable problem 5,000 feet up, where you can put the plane's nose down to gain back speed from gravity and resume flying at a lower angle of attack. But at 100 feet—when you're coming in slow for a landing—you don't have the altitude to trade for speed before you end up hitting the earth. Every model of airplane has designated **stall speeds** with and without flaps (which alter the chord of the wing), both of which are typically depicted on the airspeed indicator. However, these numbers aren't actually set in stone, and the variability revolves around the relationship between lift and weight.

Lift is needed to counter **weight**. When lift exceeds weight, the airplane goes up in altitude. When weight exceeds lift, it goes down. When lift equals weight, it flies at a steady altitude. The airplane has an empty weight, but obviously its gross (loaded) weight can vary by how many people and bags are in the airplane and how much fuel is in the tank. As you fly you burn fuel, so the plane is going to be somewhat lighter landing than taking off. A heavier aircraft is going to have a higher stall speed and poorer performance overall, but that's just the tip of the iceberg.

The lifting force of the wings is not always directed straight up. When an airplane **banks** its wings to one side, a portion of the lift being produced by the wings gets diverted in a horizontal direction, causing the plane to turn to the left or right. But the vertical portion of the wing's lift is now reduced, and to avoid losing altitude the pilot must increase the wing's angle of attack, increase airspeed, or both to produce that much more lifting force to compensate. Another way of looking at this is that when banked, the wings must carry not only the weight of the plane, but also the force turning the plane in another direction. At a gentle bank of 20°, the resulting **load factor** is only 6% greater than the airplane's weight, but it goes up exponentially. At 40° it's 31% greater, and at 60° bank the wings are carrying twice the airplane's weight, often expressed as 2Gs. At 80° the load factor shoots up to 5.8Gs. Acrobatic planes are designed and strengthened to support such extreme Gs without the wings snapping off. A standard Cessna 172, on the other hand, can only safely sustain a load factor around three or four times its weight.

Even if your wings stay attached, that higher angle of attack required to sustain vertical lift can easily put a steeply banked airplane into a stall at a much higher speed than normal. Here's a simple calculation: in a steep turn, the stall speed of a plane increases by the square root of the load factor. In a 60° bank, the square root of 2Gs is 1.41, so without flaps, the stalling speed of a Cessna 172 rises from 48 knots to 68 knots.[44] This is called an **accelerated stall**. The most dangerous time for it to happen is when a pilot coming in at reduced speed to land accidentally overshoots the turn from base to final, then turns steeply at low altitude to try to line back up with the runway. For a variety of reasons that I'll explain more fully in the next chapter, this is called the "deadly turn."[45]

While lift is almost entirely centered on the wings, an airplane's weight is distributed unevenly along the length of the fuselage. The **center of gravity** (CG) is the point on which you could theoretically balance the plane on your fingertip and not have it tip forward or back. On most planes, including the Cessna 172, the CG is located forward of the main wings' center of lift. Without another force to balance it, the aircraft would be nose-heavy and tip over forward in flight. That counterforce is provided by the **horizontal stabilizers** on the tail, also known as **tailplanes**. They look like smaller wings, but they actually produce *negative* lift (partly due to the airstream coming back and down from the propeller), pushing the tail down to keep the nose from dropping. For that reason, the main wings actually have to produce enough lift to counter the weight of the plane *plus* the negative lift from the tailplanes keeping it stable.

Depending on how you've loaded the plane, the exact location of the center of gravity can vary, and in fact will shift slightly during flight as you expend the fuel from your tanks. A forward CG requires a greater downward force on the tailplanes to balance it, and a higher angle of attack from the main wings to produce that much more lift. A nose-heavy airplane will take longer to take off, fly more slowly, stall at a higher speed, and can be more difficult to level off when landing. But because the controls on the tail—the rudder and elevators—are farther from the center of gravity, they are able to exert more leverage, making the airplane more stable. A tail-heavy, aft CG requires less downward force on the tailplanes and can fly with a lower angle of attack. It will have better performance and have a lower stall speed. But the elevators and rudder on the tail will have less leverage, making the airplane less stable, and it could be much harder—if not impossible—to recover from a stall once you're in one.

Within certain parameters, laid out in the airplane's operating manual, these variations in CG might be noticeable but can be handled by the pilot. Beyond these limits, however, they can be extremely dangerous. There's a famous video on YouTube of a 747 cargo jet where the weight suddenly shifted aft on takeoff, causing it to point nose-up, stall, and crash to the ground in a giant fireball.[46] That's why one of the documents the FAA requires to be in the plane at all times—in addition to the airworthiness certificate, registration, and operating manual—is the **weight and balance** calculation, to show you're safely within those parameters. There is also a maximum weight that the aircraft is designed to carry, period, and it's surprisingly easy to exceed. An instructor and student can take off in a Cessna 172 with full fuel tanks, but throw two adult passengers and a dog in the back seat, not to mention luggage, and you may not have much weight allowance left for fuel at all.

In addition to the horizontal stabilizers, most airplanes have a number of other features designed to improve **stability**. A stable airplane wants to go back to the way it was previously flying, before the pilot or some other force pushed it in a different direction. Take the vertical fin on the tail, also called the **vertical stabilizer**. Without a tail fin, if a gust of wind knocked the nose to the left or right, there would be little to prevent the plane from starting to skid through the air sideways—with disastrous results. Instead, the oncoming airflow hits the exposed side of the tail fin, pushing the tail and nose back into alignment with the direction of travel. When banking into a turn, the airflow hitting the tail fin helps to rotate the nose into the turn, instead of away from it (which it would otherwise tend to do, due to the uneven drag produced by the control surfaces making it bank).[47]

When you look at most airplanes head-on, you'll notice a more subtle feature that adds to stability: their wings tilt up slightly, from the root to the tip. This is called a **dihedral**, and it comes into play whenever the plane starts sliding sideways through the air. Like so many things, it boils down to angle of attack—the way each wing meets the airflow. When both wings are upturned, the wing facing into the sideways airflow has a higher angle of attack, and thus more lift, than the wing facing away from it.[48] Take an airplane with its nose pointed straight ahead. If a patch of turbulence makes it suddenly bank to the right, its loss of vertical lift will cause it to start sliding "downhill," into the roll. With a dihedral, this sideways airflow gives the lowered wing more lift and the raised wing less lift, nudging them both back toward level flight.[49] On the other hand, if the airplane's nose is pointed away from its direction of travel, the sideways airflow will cause the upturned wings to bank, turning the plane to follow its nose.[50] Angle of attack—as you've probably started to realize—is everywhere, and it can be difficult to grasp, in large part because airflow can only be felt, not seen. But it's vital to understanding so much of what the airplane is doing, or wants to do.

Generally speaking, a stable airplane wants to keep doing whatever it was already doing and requires more consistent control inputs from the pilot to make it do anything different. That doesn't guarantee it was doing the right thing in the first place, but it does make it more predictable. That's a desirable quality in a trainer like a Cessna 172 or a commercial airliner. It's less desirable in a fighter plane going into combat, where you need to make bold and sudden changes in direction, at the slightest touch. If you look at a modern jet fighter like an F/A-18 or Su-27, their wings and tailplanes don't have any dihedral, since this would only resist and reduce their ability to bank and turn quickly. Instead, they are flat or even tilted down (anhedral). The ideal fighter is only just stable enough for a skilled pilot to fly without losing control.

I wasn't a skilled pilot yet, but I was learning a basic truth that instructors repeat over and over to students, until they get it: "The airplane wants to fly." You don't want to fight the forces at work, you want to direct and channel them. To do that, you need to master and use the controls.

CHAPTER 5

Controls

Most people imagine that the greatest achievement of Wilbur and Orville Wright, when they first flew in 1903, was figuring out how to apply the principle of lift to get off the ground. In fact, aspiring aviators had already been flying gliders for several decades, though with mixed results. True, the Wright brothers carefully studied their airfoils and made some improvements.[51] The development of small, lightweight internal combustion engines, such as those built by enthusiasts like Glenn Curtiss to turn bicycles into *motor*cycles, also made it finally possible to produce enough thrust to *stay* aloft, indefinitely.[52] But the brothers' real breakthrough—the thing that set them apart from their rivals and won them a patent—was their conceptualization of how to *control* an airplane in three-dimensional flight along three different axes, with a separate control assigned to each axis.[53] The basic idea behind these controls has remained the same ever since.

That's what I'm looking at here, as I sit in the Volkswagen-size cabin of my Cessna 172, though I hardly know it yet. Directly in front of me is a **yoke** that looks reassuringly like a steering wheel. If I turn it to the right or left while flying, the airplane will bank and turn in that direction. Unlike a car's steering wheel, I can also move the yoke forward or back. Pushing it forward will push the airplane's nose down, while pulling it back will pull the nose up (some airplanes have a **stick** instead of a yoke, which you push right, left, forward, or back, but the function is the same). At my feet are two **rudder pedals**. On the ground, as I've already mentioned, they turn the nosewheel for taxiing. In the air, they seem to awkwardly shove the nose of the plane left or right.

On the panel by my right hand is the black knob of the **throttle**. Pushing it in increases the speed the propeller spins, generating more thrust, while pulling it out does the opposite, which is all I really understand about the engine so far. The red knob next to it alters the fuel/air **mixture** for higher altitudes, but since we're flying relatively low and close to sea level, I don't really need to worry about that right now. Further to the right is a small white handle that goes down three notches, lowering the **flaps** to settings of 10, 20, and 30 degrees. Below the throttle is a mysterious device called a **trim wheel**, which I can rotate up or down, but is supposed to initially be set to "takeoff."

What exactly do these controls do that makes them so central to flying?

Most of us are used to driving a car. Unless you plunge your car off a cliff, you drive it in two dimensions and make turns left or right around a single vertical axis. An airplane moves in three dimensions, and the primary flight controls—the yoke and foot pedals—are linked to three control surfaces—the ailerons, elevators, and rudder—whose job is to orient the airplane on one of three different axes: longitudinal (the line running from nose to tail), lateral (wingtip to wingtip), and vertical (top to bottom). In other words, not a car.

Let's start with the yoke. Turning the yoke left or right drives a series of rods and cable pulleys connected to the **ailerons**, hinged extensions on the outer trailing edge of each wing. Turning the yoke right raises the aileron on the right wing, deflecting the airflow upward and reducing lift. At the same time, it lowers the aileron on the left wing, deflecting the airflow downward and increasing lift. The result is to rotate or **roll** the aircraft to the right around its **longitudinal axis** (from nose to tail). One wing dips and the other rises. As I explained in the last chapter, banking this way directs the lift from the wings in a direction other than straight up, causing the plane to turn (in this case, to the right), at the expense of potentially losing altitude.

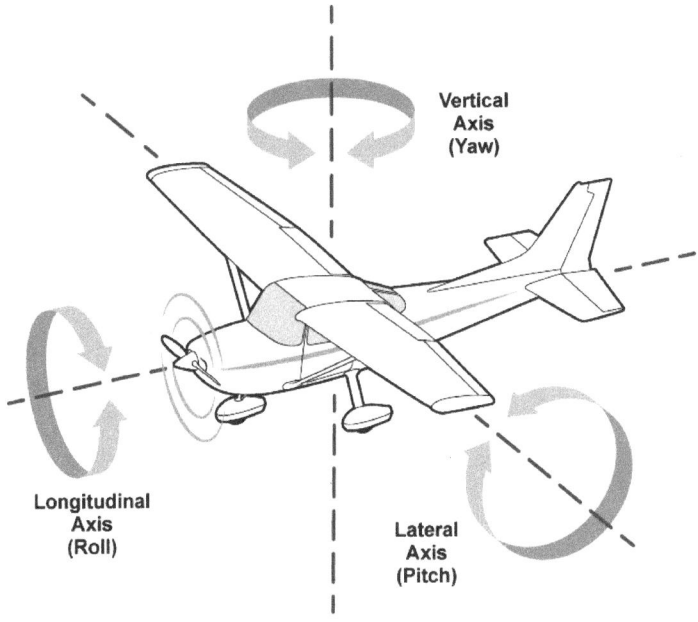

An aircraft's three axes of control.

This simple but crucial concept was the center of one of the earliest and bitterest quarrels in aviation history. Originally, the Wrights used wires to "warp" or bend the wings, to the same effect.[54] Other pioneers attached rotating wingtips.[55] Quickly, though, designers recognized that ailerons, which comes from the French word meaning "little wing," were the most effective and efficient solution.[56] When Glenn Curtiss—who discovered a new market for his lightweight engines in designing airplanes[57]—put ailerons on his wings, the Wright brothers sued him for violating their patent, which they claimed extended to any control surface.[58] Curtiss countered that this claim was overly broad, barring the way to further innovation and improvement.[59]

The acrimonious dispute raged for several years, making both parties miserable and holding back the country's progress in aviation until the U.S. government finally forced them to come to terms during World War I.[60] Meanwhile, the Europeans moved ahead regardless, either ignoring the Wright's patents completely or defining them so narrowly that they quickly became irrelevant.[61]

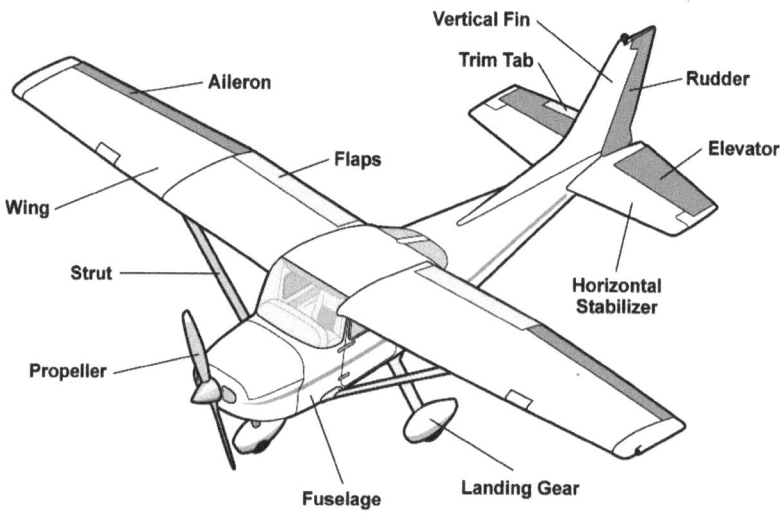

The key parts of a typical airplane, including its primary and secondary control surfaces.

A similar spirit prevailed in other dimensions as well. Pushing the yoke forward or back drives a similar set of mechanical cable pulleys that moves the **elevators**, hinged extensions on the trailing edge of the horizontal tailplanes. The Wrights originally put their elevators at the front,[62] but other designers soon moved them to the tail where they proved more effective and have remained, on most airplanes, ever since.[63] Recall that the tailplanes typically produce negative lift that balances the nose. Pushing forward lowers the elevators, altering the airflow to reduce that negative lift and tip the nose down. Pulling back raises the elevators, altering the airflow to increase that negative lift and tip the nose up. The result is to rotate the **pitch** of the airplane up or down around its **lateral axis** (from wingtip to wingtip).

It's tempting to think that pitching the nose up or down will simply *steer* the airplane up or down in altitude, but that's not correct. In fact, it can be disastrously wrong. In *Stick and Rudder*, Wolfgang Langewiesche wrote that the elevator control is best understood as an angle of attack lever.[64] By changing pitch, you raise or lower the wing's angle to the relative wind. And as we know, angle of attack is connected to both lift *and* speed. Pull the nose up, without increasing power, and the airplane may rise, but it will also slow—eventually causing it to lose lift and altitude. Put the nose down, without decreasing power, and the airplane may descend, but it will also speed up—eventually causing it to regain lift and altitude.

So how does an airplane gain altitude and keep it? The answer lies not in pitch, but power. It's easy to imagine that increasing power, by pushing the throttle in, will simply make the airplane gain speed, but that's not quite the case. To begin with, speeding up increases lift, unless the pilot lowers the nose to reduce the wings' angle of attack. The design of many airplanes, including the Cessna 172, takes this one step further. Push the throttle in and the increased downdraft from the wings, as well as the increased airflow (or **prop wash**) from the propeller, will push the tail down, raising the nose and trading greater speed for greater climb. To gain speed instead, you have to actively push forward on the yoke to stay level. Alternatively, pull the throttle out and the reduced downdraft and prop wash will allow the tail to rise, lowering the nose and causing the airplane to descend rather than slow down. To lose speed instead, you have to actively pull back on the yoke to stay level.

Langewiesche went so far as to say that the elevators control speed, while the throttle controls altitude—the opposite of what you might intuitively expect.[65] At the very least, pitch and power and altitude and speed are intertwined with each other, and you can't alter one without thinking about how it affects the others—an absolutely crucial thing to understand in order to safely fly a plane.

The pedals at your feet are connected via mechanical cable pulleys to the

rudder, a hinged extension on the trailing edge of the vertical tail fin. Pushing the right rudder pedal causes the rudder to move out to the right, altering the airflow and pushing the tail to left, thus rotating the nose to the right. Pushing the left pedal does the opposite. This movement is called **yaw**, and what you're doing is rotating the airplane around its **vertical axis**, which runs through it from top to bottom.

To be honest, it's easy to forget about the rudder—and a lot of pilots do, even after they've earned their license. For one thing, we're used to providing directional control with a steering wheel, not with our feet. For another, in normal flight a stable airplane like the Cessna 172 tends to automatically yaw in the direction of travel, without any rudder input. In fact, when you are traveling straight and you use the rudder to yaw the plane away from the head-on direction of the airflow, it can feel rather clunky. I have to admit that for my first several lessons, I barely thought about the rudder pedals at all, except for turning the nosewheel while taxiing on the ground and keeping the airplane straight on the runway while taking off.

Gradually, though, I began to appreciate that there are some situations where using the rudder becomes very important. Especially during takeoff and landing, at slower speeds, a single-engine propeller-driven airplane displays what are called **left-turning tendencies**, which cause the nose to want to veer off to the left. There are four main causes. The first is called **torque**. In most planes, the propeller turns clockwise from the pilot's viewpoint, and until you have sufficient airspeed for the wings and other control surfaces to grip the air and provide stability, Newton's law of equal and opposite reaction makes the body of the airplane want to rotate counterclockwise in response. This initially puts more weight on the left wheel, creating friction as long as you're in contact with the ground and pulling your nose left. You have to counter this with right rudder.

At the same time, as you put the power in for takeoff, the propeller produces a stream of airflow that swirls back around the fuselage in a corkscrew fashion. It can come up and smack the left side of your tail fin, pushing your tail right and your nose left unless you counter with right rudder. Eventually, as you gain airspeed, the **spiraling slipstream** expands out past your tail and the effect goes away.

The third left-turning tendency is called **p-factor**. Remember that the blades of a propeller are airfoils, like wings. When you are pitched up and climbing, the angle of attack of the propeller blades descending on the right side is greater than the angle of those same blades ascending on the left. They take a bigger bite out of the air, producing more thrust on the right side and pushing the nose to the left. As I became more familiar with flying, I began to notice that just after takeoff, in my initial climb, the plane tended to stray off course to the left unless I held in some right rudder.

The last left-turning tendency is called **gyroscopic precession**. When a force is applied to something that's spinning, like a propeller or a wheel, that force is actually felt 90 degrees further along in the rotation, at a right angle. It's a weird and counterintuitive thing, and there are plenty of videos on YouTube you can check out to see its somewhat bizarre effects. In any case, what it means is that when an airplane pitches down, that downward force exerts a force on its propeller from the right, pushing the nose left. This can happen to any airplane as it aims down toward the runway on final approach. But it's a particular issue on takeoff with **tailwheel airplanes**, the older-style airplane that—unlike the Cessna 172—rests back on its tail instead of forward onto a nosewheel. When the tail rises as it gains speed on takeoff, the nose rotates downward, adding gyroscopic precession to all the other forces shoving the nose to the left.

There's another reason why rudder control is particularly important when flying tailwheelers. On a tailwheel airplane, the plane's center of gravity is located behind the main wheels, which is why it leans back instead of tipping forward. When landing, or even taxiing, if the airplane gets out of line with its direction of travel, the tail can easily swing out and around, whipping the entire plane around in an abrupt circular **ground loop**. Ground loops are embarrassing, but at higher speeds they can also cause quite a bit of damage. In addition to gyroscopic precession on takeoff and the difficulty seeing over the upraised nose while taxiing, it's one more reason why tailwheel aircraft require additional training and a special endorsement to fly, and why practicing in a tailwheeler is a very good way for any pilot to learn not to ignore the rudder.

Jets don't experience the lateral forces caused by a rotating propeller, and multi-engine airplanes that have propellers are often designed so that they rotate in opposing directions, canceling each other out. With one propeller, however, the more powerful the engine, the stronger the turning tendencies that must be fought by using the rudder. For a Cessna 172, with an output of 180 horsepower, the effects are fairly mild, though noticeable enough for instructors to repeatedly mutter "MORE RIGHT RUDDER" to their students on takeoffs and landings—one of the oldest jokes in flight training. On the other hand, single-engine World War II fighters like the Spitfire, Corsair, or Mustang could have horsepower upward of 10 times that and were tailwheelers to boot. Their left-turning tendencies were so pronounced they could easily cause the airplane to veer off the runway and crash unless the pilot kicked the right rudder hard at the right times. I got a small taste of this trying my hand on these planes in *Microsoft Flight Simulator*, where it was a big challenge just to keep them on the runway, much less on centerline, once I powered up that monster engine and got rolling. Sadly, in real life, a not-insignificant number of new fighter pilots were killed in training, attempting to do just that.

Another time you *might* need to apply the rudder is in making a turn. In a **coordinated turn**, the tail follows the nose around the turn, with the airplane yawing toward the direction of travel. As I've mentioned, in a very stable aircraft like the Cessna 172, the forces acting on the tail fin tend to make this happen naturally. But it's possible, especially in a steeper turn, for the tail fin to need a bit of directional help from the rudder. If not, the turn can become "uncoordinated," with the plane either **skidding** to the outside or **slipping** to the inside of the turn. When the nose isn't head-on into the direction of the turn, the airflow begins to hit the side of the plane's fuselage, creating drag and causing it to slow. Since we know that a steep turn already increases the stall speed, this is the last time—especially if you're flying low and slow on approach from base to final—that you want to accidentally lose airspeed. Worse yet, an uncoordinated stall can turn into a spin, which I'll talk about more in the next chapter.[66]

There are times, though, when you *want* to turn the nose onto an angle from the oncoming airflow. One is if you're too high on final approach to land and want to purposely create more drag in order to descend more rapidly without gaining speed. The other is when you want to align the plane with the runway on landing despite a wind blowing across it at an angle (called a **crosswind**), without being pushed sideways. These maneuvers are called a **forward slip** and a **sideslip**, and they rely heavily on using the rudder. I'll talk more about how I learned to do them later. Suffice it to say, for now, that you can't just *steer* the plane with the yoke (or stick), you have to use those feet on the rudder pedals.

To summarize the primary controls: The yoke (or stick) rolls the airplane left and right around its longitudinal axis by moving the ailerons, and pitches it up and down around its lateral axis by moving the elevators. The relationship between pitch and power affects both altitude and speed. The foot pedals aid in rotating the airplane left and right around the vertical axis, as needed, via the rudder. Virtually every airplane in the world relies on these same controls, in one form or another.

The primary controls all work by deflecting airflow from its previous path around the plane, pushing the airplane in a new direction. As a result, their effectiveness depends very much on airspeed. The slower the airspeed, the less airflow there is to deflect, and the more control input is required to alter the airplane's direction. At very low airspeeds—while landing, for instance—the controls can feel "mushy" and sluggish.

The larger and faster the airplane, however, the more force is required for the control surfaces to deflect the onrushing air. Pilots of some World War II bombers and early airliners, which had only mechanical controls like the Cessna's, often had to exert a great deal of strength to wrestle with the yoke—a major reason they had a co-pilot to take care of other tasks.[67] Today, big aircraft like the 747 use hydraulics (pressurized fluid) to help the pilot overcome this,[68] while even more advanced airplanes like the Airbus 320 and the F-16 are **fly-by-wire**, with the controls sending digital instructions via computer to the hydraulic actuators that do the work.[69]

The Cessna 172 is small enough that mechanical connections with rods and pulleys do just fine. Not only are they lighter and cheaper, they also work regardless of whether the engine or the electrical master switch is on. If these systems fail entirely in the air, turning the yoke will still move the ailerons; same for the elevators and rudder. For the most part, fairly gentle inputs are all that is needed.

In addition to these primary controls, many airplanes have secondary controls that, while less essential, assist the pilot and improve performance. The Cessna 172 has two: trim and flaps. The first of them, trim, is specifically designed to reduce the fatigue from constantly handling the controls.

When you walk around and examine the tail during the pre-flight inspection, you will notice a small, hinged metal surface inset into the trailing edge of the right elevator. This **trim tab** can be raised or lowered by turning the **trim wheel** in the cockpit. Doing this changes the default position of the elevators, including when the yoke is at rest. Say you are holding the yoke back to keep the airplane's nose raised to a certain pitch to either climb or remain level. Rolling the trim wheel—and the trim tab—down will automatically deflect the elevator up, allowing you to release the back pressure on the yoke previously needed to hold it there. Rolling the wheel up would do the opposite, pushing the nose down. In a properly trimmed plane, you should be able to take your hands entirely off the controls, at least for a little while, and continue flying straight and level.

Not only does **trim** give your arms a rest, it also helps control the plane more precisely. Since pitch determines speed at any given power setting, setting trim is often called "trimming for speed." Once you are trimmed and level, increasing the throttle will cause you to climb while decreasing the throttle will cause you to descend—all at the same constant speed and angle of attack. When Navy pilots are trained to land on an aircraft carrier, this is the method they use.[70] It's entirely possible to fly a Cessna 172 safely, from takeoff to landing, without ever touching the trim wheel. But a good pilot will know how to use trim to reduce workload and control the aircraft more efficiently.

More advanced airplanes sometimes have additional trim settings for the rudder and even the ailerons. The former can be used to counter left-turning tendencies during takeoff and climb, while the latter can offset a horizontal imbalance in loading. For faster airplanes like airliners and fighter jets, metal panels called spoilers or speed brakes can be deployed from the wings or fuselage to add drag and quickly slow the plane, usually for landing. A small, relatively slow airplane like the Cessna 172 does not require these additional features and isn't equipped with them.

I've used the expression "hinged extension" to describe a number of control surfaces, and avoided the somewhat more intuitive word "flap," because in aviation **flaps** only refers to one specific device. You've probably seen the flaps come down while looking out the window of an airliner as it prepares to land. Flaps come in many different forms, but they are basically a surface on the inner trailing edge of the wing that can be extended and lowered. This changes the shape of the wing, adding lift and increasing drag. Lowered flaps are sometimes called a **dirty** or landing configuration. When landing, they allow you to descend toward the runway at a steeper angle without gaining speed. They also reduce the airplane's stall speed so you can safely approach and touch down at a slower airspeed than without them. Many aircraft also deploy at least some degree of flaps on takeoff to reduce the length of runway needed, though for the Cessna 172 this is optional and up to the pilot's discretion. In normal flight between takeoff and landing, on the other hand, you want to make sure the flaps are raised, putting the wings into what is called a **clean** configuration, which reduces drag and allows the plane to fly much faster.

Like trim, flaps are helpful but not absolutely necessary. Airplanes during World War I, and even some World War II trainers, did not have any flaps. You can take off and land a Cessna 172 without using flaps, though you need to realize how it will handle differently and have different performance limits. The lever to extend or retract the flaps in a Cessna is connected to them by an electric motor, so unlike the other controls, if the electrical power goes out, they will be stuck in place and you won't be able to move them—something to keep in mind in an emergency landing.

Describing how a plane flies, and the controls used to fly it, can be done in a few pages. But getting a "feel" for it took some time and practice. So now, let me take you along with me on a typical early lesson to show how all these different pieces I've been describing actually come together, in the air, for a student learning to fly.

CHAPTER 6

Maneuvers

I arrive at the airport alone this time, something I'm getting used to as autumn turns to winter. My son is back in school now, and in any event, he has grown bored by the repetitive nature of my lessons. The school's receptionist hands me the airplane's keys and I go out to do the pre-flight inspection on my own, trying to keep my gloves on as much as possible in the biting breeze. Poking around the outside of the plane in the stinging cold is no fun. The inside, at least, is already warmed up from another student who just finished a solo flight earlier that morning. I wonder with vague envy what it must be like to be that far along in your training.

My instructor, Tess, comes out to join me when the airplane is ready to fire up. We taxi to the opposite side of the runway from where the wind is blowing and, as always, I gulp down a slight sense of nervousness as I position for takeoff. I'm gaining a better sense of when control over direction shifts from the nosewheel to the rudder, as airspeed picks up headed down the runway, and the weight on the wheels grows light and floaty as lift from the wings begins to develop. In the colder, denser air of winter, the Cessna 172 actually lifts off the ground on its own before I can pull back on the yoke. In fact, I have to press the yoke forward slightly to keep the nose from pitching above the horizon as I build up to a safe climb speed of 80 knots. I'm also more aware of the need to keep my right foot gently pressed on the rudder pedal to prevent the nose from drifting to the left during the climb.

The air today is not nearly as calm and smooth as during my first discovery flight. Occasional gusts of winds cause the airplane to dip and bank without warning. At first the lurches feel alarming, but I soon learn that the plane quickly corrects itself with only modest inputs from me on the controls. This is only mild **turbulence** and riding out the choppy air is no more dangerous than driving a car down a bumpy road.

Full throttle on the Cessna 172, for takeoff and climb, reaches around 2700 RPM, though that can vary depending on altitude and air temperature. Once we level off at our desired altitude, I'll pull that back to around 2300, a typical setting for cruising.

We're heading north, as we usually do, away from the busy airspace around Newark, across the alternating ridges and lakes of northern New Jersey to a practice area called the Onion Fields, a flat and open stretch of farmland just across the New York border. God bless the people who live there, because they must hear small airplanes buzzing overhead all the time, repeating over and over again the basic maneuvers required to demonstrate effective control of an airplane and earn a pilot's license.

Tess walked me through most of these maneuvers on my discovery flight and we've been practicing them ever since, with her giving me a steady stream of feedback and suggestions on how I'm doing. There's no set order to this ballet, but today, entering the area at an altitude of 3,500 feet, we'll begin with **steep turns**. But first—as always—we must start by making two clearing turns, 90 degrees left, then 90 degrees right, to make sure the area is clear of other aircraft. Next, I pull the throttle back slightly to slow to below **maneuvering speed**, around 90 to 95 knots, so our abrupt movements won't put undue stress on the airframe. Ready?

Steep turns means turning at a roughly 45° bank through a full 360-degree circle. We do one steep circle to the left, then level off and immediately go into an opposite steep circle to the right. At first this seemed rather straightforward, even if seeing the horizon tilt that abruptly made me a little squeamish. After a few lessons, however, I'm starting to appreciate that the real trick isn't banking at such a steep angle but maintaining a steady altitude (without gaining or losing more than 100 feet in either direction) and a steady speed (without gaining or losing more than 10 knots) for the whole way around, as the formal standards require. A steep bank reduces the amount of vertical lift from the wings. To compensate, I need to raise the wings' angle of attack by pulling back on the yoke (some instructors recommend throwing in some nose-up trim to help). This will in turn increase drag, slowing the plane, just as the increased load factor on the wings is causing the stall speed to invisibly rise—which means I will need to push the throttle in a little to increase power and maintain speed.

As I bank to the left today, I start pulling back on the yoke a tad too soon—just as I'm rolling into the turn—causing the plane to rise almost 100 feet before I'm a quarter of the way through. "Watch your altitude," Tess intones, though I already see it. I spend the rest of the turn pushing forward on the yoke and fiddling with the throttle, struggling my way back down to my initial altitude. As I finally come around and level the wings out of the turn, their vertical lift is suddenly directed upward again. I have to keep pushing forward on the yoke to avoid popping back up into a climb—but only just for a moment, as I immediately enter my turn to the right.

Because of the plane's left-turning tendencies, which increase with angle of attack, the turn to the left didn't require any rudder. But now the turn to the right needs some firm right rudder to point the nose in the direction of the turn and avoid slipping through it sideways. This time I somehow catch the bank, pitch, and power just right, and instead of struggling up and down I find myself in a steady, even graceful 45° bank to the right, all the way through the turn. When I reach my initial heading, I once again push forward on the yoke to avoid popping up as I roll the wings back to level. "That one was better," nods Tess approvingly.

Now that we're straight and level again, Tess tells me to transition to

slow flight. I pull the throttle back to 1500 RPM and lower the first stage of flaps. Normally this would cause me to descend, but instead I pull back on the yoke—gently at first, then with increasing pressure—to keep from losing any altitude. The airspeed starts falling, fairly quickly. At 80 knots I put in the second stage of flaps and at 70, the third. At 60 knots, with the needle still descending, I push the throttle back in to around 1900 RPM to stabilize at 55 knots. All of this takes place in a matter of several seconds, with my right hand darting from the throttle to the flaps and back and my left hand pulling with increasing strain on the yoke. Eventually, once my right hand is free again, I'm able to relieve this pressure by adjusting the trim wheel.

The purpose of slow flight is to learn, at a safe altitude, how the plane will handle as it comes in for a landing, at a speed barely above stalling. The nose is pitched up, creating a different view, or **sight picture**, out the front windshield than normal. With the airflow over them significantly reduced, the controls feel "mushy," the airplane wobbly and sluggish. When Tess tells me to turn left to a new heading, I do it slowly, at no more than 10° bank, nursing the nose of the plane in the desired direction. Moving any more abruptly could increase the load factor and induce a stall. When she tells me to climb, I push the throttle full in, but with my flaps still down full, I'm barely able to coax the airplane into a gentle climb and still maintain my airspeed.

If I want to go back to normal flight, I have to push the yoke forward after adding the throttle, to stay level and gain some speed first, before gradually lifting the flaps in stages. It's a fragile dance, barely above stall speed, requiring just enough patience combined with just enough urgency—exactly the combination I would have to exercise if I needed to go around again instead of completing my landing. Each stage I raise the flaps reduces drag and allows the plane to go faster, but also reduces lift and raises my stall speed. Suddenly "dumping" all the flaps at once to try to quickly climb again is a mistake that, on go-arounds, has gotten more than one person killed. So we practice—over and over again—at a height of 3,500 feet, where a mistake, even a stall, has room to be fixed.

Instead of smoothly recovering from slow flight, that's exactly what we'll do next: intentionally provoke a **power-off stall**. We do this for two reasons: first, to experience what it feels like to flare and stall the plane on landing, and second, to practice recovering from a stall if it happens prematurely, on final approach. We start by descending in slow flight, with RPM at 1500, down to 3,000 feet—just as if we were coming in to land and that was ground level. When I reach that altitude, I level off and pull the throttle all the way out to idle. Airspeed bleeds off, and gradually I have to pull back harder and harder on the yoke, as far as it will go, to maintain altitude. The nose is pitched up, above the horizon, and the airplane's **stall horn**—a device which warns of a dangerously high angle between the wing and the relative wind—rises from a low warble to a frantic blaring.

The plane wallows unsteadily through the air, though it stays generally on course. In the cold, dense air, my Cessna 172 remains suspended in this state, with the yoke pulled back almost to my chest and the stall horn screaming, for an excruciatingly long several seconds. Then the nose suddenly lurches down on its own as the wings stall and lose lift. Immediately I release my back pressure on the yoke and let the nose fall—don't fight the stall—while pushing the throttle in full to maximum power. Remember, to break the stall I need to regain airspeed to get sufficient air flowing smoothly again over the wings. Dipping the nose does that, but it should last only a moment before I pull the yoke back to level and lift the first stage of flaps. With power to max, I gradually let the airspeed build, allowing the next two stages of flaps to be lifted one at a time and the aircraft to climb back to its original altitude.

The next maneuver, the **power-on stall**, is harder. This simulates what could happen if I pitched up too steeply on takeoff. Starting in normal, level flight, I pull the throttle back to idle—without adding any flaps. I pull back on the yoke to avoid losing altitude. Then just as the airspeed falls to 55 knots, I add full throttle and pull the yoke back even more to pitch up into the sky, as if I'm taking off in a rocket ship. The steep upward angle feels unnatural and alarming. No longer able to see the horizon over my nose, it feels like I'm going to flip over backwards.

A less fanciful problem is that, by pitching upwards at full power, I've just increased the left-turning tendencies of the propeller. Normally Tess suggests using a cloud overhead as a visual reference to keep the nose pointed straight up. But today is mostly clear, so I can only assume the nose wants to veer off to the left, which I must counter with firm right rudder. The stall horn blaring in my ears, the plane begins to buffet for a moment, as though I'm driving over an uneven gravel road. Then finally the nose gives way slightly—far less noticeably than in the power-off stall—and I immediately release the back pressure on the yoke and let the nose fall, down to slightly below the horizon. The throttle is already at full power and the flaps are already up, so with airspeed building again, I can quickly recover and—at a safer pitch, this time—resume my climb.

Let's say I put in too little or too much right rudder and the nose was off-center, in one direction or the other, as I reached the crest of the power-on stall. One wing would drop first, and I would start to enter a **spin**. A spin happens when the wing on one side becomes more stalled, or stalls sooner, than the other, causing it to drop first. As Langeweische explains,[71] in normal flight when one wing dips, its downward motion increases its angle of attack to the relative wind, which produces more lift, while the rising wing opposite decreases its angle of attack, reducing lift. The effect of both—normally—is to cushion the roll. But when the dipping wing is already stalled, increasing its angle of attack only deepens that stall. Meanwhile, the other wing, by rising, reduces its angle of attack, to the point where it may actually un-stall itself and regain lift. The result is a terrifying process called autorotation, where the airplane topples over to either the left or the right and keeps toppling, filling your front windshield with a dizzying vision of the ground and sky—mostly the ground—doing cartwheels.

Your natural driver's instinct, at this point, is to turn the yoke hard against the direction of the spin, to try to re-level the wings. But the ailerons only work by altering the airflow over the wing, and there is no smooth airflow over the wings—they're stalled, though one is more stalled than the other. To stop the spin, you need to stop the stall. The go-to emergency acronym is PARE: Power, Aileron, Rudder, Elevator. Pull the throttle all the way out to idle, keep the ailerons *neutral*, push the *rudder*—not the yoke—hard against the direction of the spin, and push the nose down, into the dive, in order to regain speed.[72] It takes some concentration and practice to fight your natural instincts to do otherwise.

At safe altitude, the Cessna 172 recovers fairly readily from a spin. After a few moments of terror-inducing cartwheels, the rudder levels the wings into a dive—no longer stalled because of your rising airspeed—which you can exit by pulling back on the yoke. Typically you lose between 500 and 1,000 feet in altitude. Some aircraft—including some trainers—do not recover nearly as easily and are not authorized for intentional spins. Recovery from a full spin isn't a formal part of training for a Private Pilot License, but it is required for aspiring flight instructors.[73] Regardless, when I practiced power-on stalls there were several times when I misjudged my rudder input and began to enter a spin and had to recover from it. Of course, if you are 300 feet off the ground, on takeoff or a turn to final approach, all the spin recovery technique in the world won't save you, so the real point is to recognize the signs of an impending stall and prevent one before it happens.

Now that steep turns and stalls are behind us, Tess has me move on to **ground reference maneuvers**. These are done about 1,000 feet above ground level, so I first need to reduce power and descend. The basic idea here, once I level off, is to maneuver in the air around objects on the ground, while adjusting for the effect of wind direction.

When you take off into a headwind, you get off the ground faster, because it adds to your airspeed. But once you are airborne, a headwind slows your progress from point to point on the ground, because you're fighting the wind the whole way. The opposite is true of a tailwind. If the wind is blowing perpendicular to your plane's heading (a **crosswind**), you will be gradually pushed to the side along with it, so your path over the ground below ends up being diagonal. From whatever angle the wind is blowing, you're like a swimmer caught in a river's current.

To swim across the river in a straight line, you must swim at an angle *into* the current or be swept off course. On a windy day, an airplane must do the same thing, **crabbing** its nose into the wind to compensate for the drift. From the vantage point of the cockpit, it can appear as though you are flying diagonally across the ground, crawling sideways (like a crab) in your desired direction. (Some quick vocabulary here: **heading** is the direction the airplane's nose is pointed; **course** is the direction you want to go; the difference between them is the **wind angle. Ground track** is where you end up going, relative to the world below, whether you planned to or not.)

One of the simplest exercises for putting this into action is the **rectangular course**. Flying at 1,000 feet above ground, Tess identifies a large field of crops with roads on each side. The smoke rising from a distant smokestack, she points out, indicates that the wind is coming from the northwest. Entering from that direction, I fly each leg of the rectangle, crabbing into the wind as needed to stay on course. What I'm doing, Tess explains, is flying a traffic pattern around an imaginary runway and learning how to point the nose slightly into the wind to prevent being accidentally pushed too close or too far from the airport. I'm also getting a feel for how a headwind can slow me down compared to the ground, while a tailwind at my back can push me much faster along—which if I'm not prepared for can easily cause me to overshoot my turns.

Turns around a point require applying these same lessons in a more subtle, continuous fashion. It sounds simple: pick out a feature on the ground—a house, a road intersection, a tree—and do a full circle around it either to the left or the right, maintaining the same distance, altitude, and speed. Just remember that the wind is going to constantly be pushing me to one side. If I hold a steady bank, the path I trace on the ground will end up being a wandering spiral, as I am pushed downwind. To correct for this, when the wind is to my back I must bank more steeply in order to cut the turn short. As I curve around back into the wind, I must make my bank shallower to stretch the turn out over the same distance, until I get back to where I started.

That's the theory, but it requires constant gradual adjustment, and it's easy to lose track of exactly how far I've gone around the circle. A more intuitive (and complementary) approach that Tess suggests is to pinpoint the object I'm circling out either my left or right window, just under my wing, and try to hold it in the same place as I turn, adjusting my bank as needed. But I've found that looking out the side window makes it difficult to sense the plane's pitch, especially in a bank. It's all too easy to pitch slightly upwards without noticing, gain unwanted altitude, and lose airspeed—or the opposite: pitch a little too nose-down, lose altitude, and accelerate. The reminders from Tess will be not slow in coming: "Watch your altitude! Watch your speed!" So all the way around the turn, I keep darting my eyes back and forth between different reference points and instruments, making sure not to stay fixated too long on any single one.

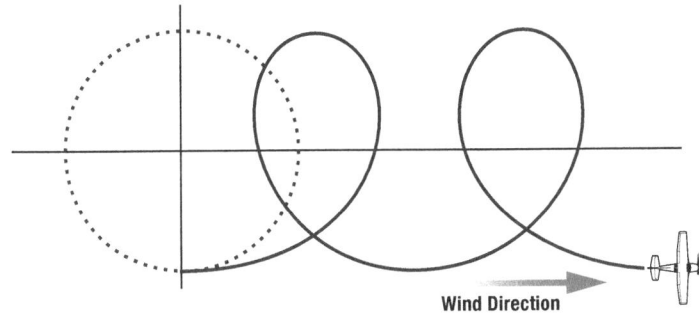

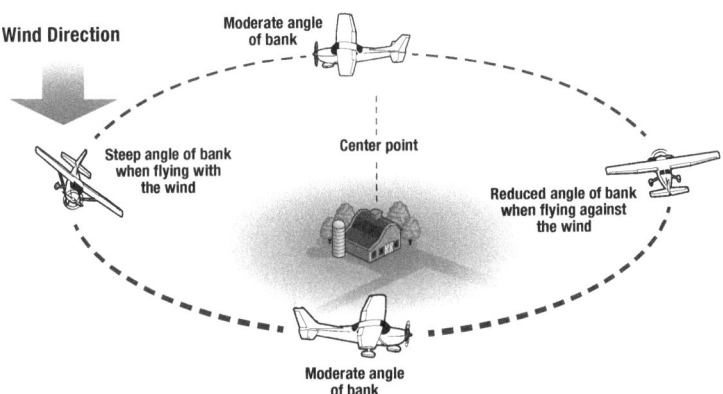

An airplane turning at a constant bank will be pushed by wind (top). To correctly make a "turn around a point," the pilot must learn to adjust bank through the turn to compensate for the wind (bottom).

S-turns are alternating half-circles extended back and forth along some linear feature like a road or, in my case today, a tree-lined canal running across the Onion Fields. As I cross the canal for the first time, with the wind at my back, I begin to bank more steeply to keep from being pushed too far away, keeping the same point on the canal at the tip of my left wing. As I turn around left to face the wind again, I moderate my bank to stretch the turn out, since it will take me longer to get back. Approaching the canal again, I level the wings and look left and right to make sure I'm crossing at a right angle. Then I begin a right turn, gently at first since I'm still heading into the wind, but growing steeper as the wind begins pushing me back toward the canal. I level off, cross the canal, and repeat again. All the while I'm keeping a close eye on my altitude and speed, and adjusting pitch and power to hold them steady.

Each of these basic maneuvers—steep turns, slow flight, power-off and power-on stall, and ground reference maneuvers—must be performed to standard on the final checkride to receive my pilot's license. But to be honest, that's beyond the scope of my imagination at this stage. More importantly, by practicing them in each lesson, I'm getting a "feel" for flying the plane—how it behaves, and how to get it to do what I want. Perhaps most crucially, I'm developing an intuitive sense of where the airplane will be one second, three seconds, 10 seconds from now. I'm also gaining a sense of how my actions, at the controls, can change this—or prevent unwanted changes from developing further.

As Tess and I climb away from the Onion Fields to return to Lincoln Park, I realize that controlling the plane's movements is starting to feel more natural, requiring less conscious thought. This frees my mind up for other tasks, such as listening and communicating on the radio, looking for other aircraft, or just figuring out where the heck I am. There's no lack of things to think about when piloting an airplane, but I'm no longer gripping the yoke like a life-preserver. And that's a start.

CHAPTER 7

Instruments

Throughout all these maneuvers, as you probably noticed, I was constantly referring to the instrument panel in front of me to keep track of my airspeed, altitude, heading, and other vital information.

As an airline passenger, I imagine that like me you've sometimes stolen a glance inside the cockpit just as you board, only to be intimidated and overwhelmed by the array of gauges, switches, and lights covering nearly every surface. The systems used to operate a modern airliner are indeed complex, but that complexity can also be deceiving. In virtually every airplane—from the simplest trainer to the most sophisticated jet fighter—there are typically just *six* primary instruments that are the focus of the pilot's attention. Someone used to flying a Cessna 172 can sit down in the pilot's seat of a 747, and amid all the other screens and knobs and devices, promptly recognize the information these six instruments are conveying—though it's likely to be presented via a single digital screen rather than separate dials.

Up through World War II, these primary instruments were often scattered in different places across the panel. Since then, their arrangement has become increasingly standardized, regardless of the airplane's make or origin, in what's dubbed the "six pack": two rows of three dials each, directly in front of the pilot. In the center of the top row is the attitude indicator, or artificial horizon. To its left is the airspeed indicator, and to its right, the altimeter. On the bottom row, from left to right, are the turn indicator, the heading indicator, and the vertical speed indicator. The relatively recent introduction of **glass cockpits** (digital display panels instead of the traditional **"steam gauges"**) has led to new, more integrated forms of presentation, as I'll explain, but the information being presented is recognizably the same.

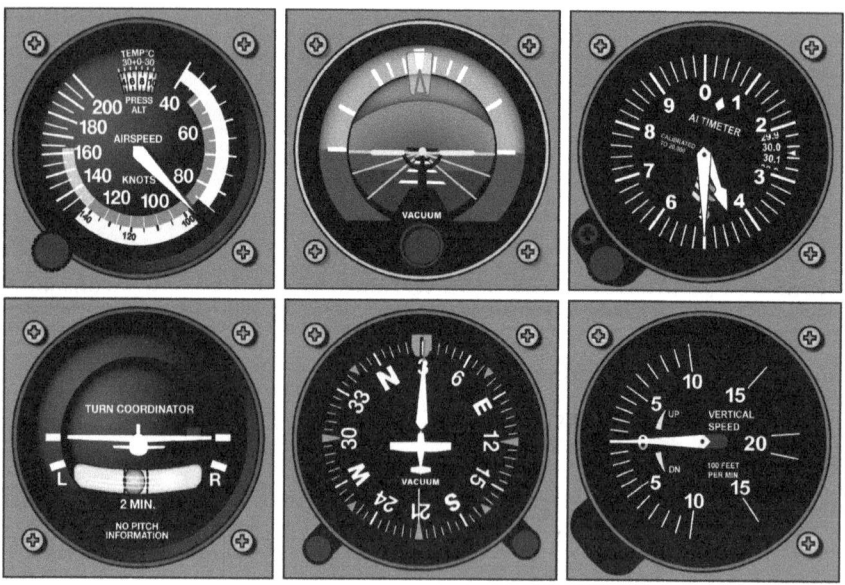

The standard "six pack" of cockpit flight instruments: airspeed indicator (top left), attitude indicator (top center), altimeter (top right), turn coordinator (bottom left), heading indicator (bottom center), and vertical speed indicator (bottom right).

A pilot must not only be able to read these six instruments but understand how each of them works. As an economist, I constantly deal with numbers—GDP, unemployment, inflation—that most people tend to assume can be taken at face value. Over the years, I've come to appreciate that it's not that simple. Only when you understand where the numbers are coming from, and what exactly is being counted, can you recognize their limitations and what they might be hiding. The same is true in a cockpit. Three of the main instruments—the airspeed indicator, altimeter, and vertical speed indicator—operate based on readings of air pressure. The other three—attitude indicator, heading indicator, and turn coordinator—rely on gyroscopes. They are all rather ingenious devices, capable of conveying a great deal of useful information. But they can also mislead the unwary.

Let's start with the **altimeter**, which looks like a clockface with the "minute" hand indicating increments of 100 feet, the "hour" hand for 1,000 feet, and either a little arrow or a third, thinner line for 10,000 feet, together telling you how high in the sky you are. Well, technically it doesn't quite do that. What the altimeter does do is measure the outside air pressure and compare it to an air pressure you've set for sea level, in order to *estimate* how high you are. Inside the altimeter is a sealed metal packet able to expand and contract like an accordion. This is called an aneroid (sealed) wafer and contains air at the "standard" sea level pressure of 29.92 inches of mercury (in/Hg). That packet is surrounded by a chamber filled with air piped in from a **static port** on the outside surface of the airplane. Air pressure decreases with altitude. So when the airplane climbs, the lower air pressure in the outer chamber allows the little accordion to expand because of the higher air pressure inside pressing outwards. This expansion turns the hands on the face of the gauge to indicate a higher altitude. The opposite happens when the airplane descends: the rising pressure of the outside air in the chamber presses the little accordion closed, turning the hands to indicate a lower altitude.

Assuming it's reasonably accurate, the figure the altimeter displays is altitude *above mean (average) sea level*, or **MSL**. It tells you nothing about how high the airplane is *above ground level*, or **AGL**. An airplane flying at 5,000 feet MSL over terrain with an elevation of 3,000 feet is only at 2,000 feet AGL—and the altimeter won't tell you that. When entering a standard traffic pattern at 1,000 feet AGL, the equivalent altitude in MSL on the altimeter will vary by airport, depending on elevation—information you have to know in advance.

Accuracy cannot be assumed, however, even for MSL. In real life, air pressure at sea level varies all the time with the weather. It might be higher or lower than 29.92, and it might change throughout the day or as you fly from place to place. On a high-pressure day, an unadjusted altimeter set to 29.92 sitting at sea level would show the airplane *below* sea level; on a low-pressure day, it would show the aircraft well above it. That's why there's a knob on the altimeter to adjust the dial to reflect the air pressure at sea level for that time and place. If you're getting ready to depart a small airport and don't know it, you can just set the dial for the known elevation of that airport. As you fly from place to place, hours pass, and weather changes, you have to regularly update your altimeter setting based on weather reports from nearby airports, received over the radio. If you don't, the estimate of your actual altitude might be way off. If the current altimeter setting is 28.92 and you've left it set at 29.92 (one inch too high), you will be 1,000 feet lower than you think you are—or Air Traffic Control told you to be. The lower air pressure in the atmosphere, overall, has fooled you into thinking you are higher in altitude, but you're not. An easy way to remember this relationship is the refrain: "From low to high, you're in the sky; from high to low, watch out below."

All of this assumes "standard" temperatures: 15º Celsius (59º Fahrenheit) at sea level, decreasing by 2ºC (3.5ºF) every 1,000 feet in altitude. When it's warmer out, the rate at which air pressure decreases with altitude slows, causing the "bands" to widen. A difference in air pressure that "normally" corresponds to 3,000 feet might now be 3,500 feet, or more. The opposite occurs in colder weather: the bands compress. The reading on your altimeter, despite being correctly adjusted for the latest reported air pressure at sea level, might say 3,000 feet when you're really only at 2,500. There's no way to adjust the altimeter for this, and Air Traffic Control doesn't expect you to—you just need to be aware of it to avoid any nasty surprises. There's a rhyme for this too: "From cold to warm, free from harm; from warm to cold, watch out below."

Whenever airplanes fly above 18,000 feet MSL into what's called Class A airspace, they turn their altimeters back to the standard setting of 29.92. Altitudes above this level are always reported in terms of "flight level" with FL200 corresponding to a reading of 20,000 feet and FL300 to 30,000 feet *at this setting.* Why? Flying at this altitude, you're above all but the highest mountains. Figuring precisely how high you are above the ground is less important than having the *exact same altimeter setting* as all other aircraft, no matter where they might be coming from, so you don't accidentally hit them. When airplanes descend below 18,000 feet again, they resume using the current weather-based altimeter setting from the nearest airport so they can safely approach and land.

More complicated than you thought? Yeah. Now take the **airspeed indicator**. It looks like the speedometer in your car. But rather than measuring how fast your wheels are turning, it too measures differences in air pressure. Behind the face of the gauge is a chamber, much like in the altimeter, connected via the same static port to whatever the outside ambient air pressure is. Inside it there's another metal accordion, or diaphragm, but instead of being sealed this time it's linked to the **pitot tube**, an L-shaped metal device that—at least in the Cessna 172—hangs from the underside of your left wing. The front opening on the pitot tube channels the impact pressure, from the air rushing past the plane in flight, into the diaphragm causing it to expand. The faster the airplane is going, the greater the difference in pressure, the more the diaphragm expands, pushing the gauge's needle farther to indicate higher airspeed.

The relationship between these pressure differences and airspeed are only calibrated to be truly accurate at sea level on a hypothetical **Standard Day**: air temperature of 15ºC and air pressure of 29.92 in/Hg. If either of these is different—because of the weather or because you're flying at a higher altitude—the change in air **density** will throw things off so that **true airspeed (TAS)** no longer matches **indicated airspeed (IAS)**. In fact, they usually don't match. As a rule of thumb, TAS is 2% faster than IAS for every 1,000 feet in altitude. So typically, if you're flying at 5,000 feet and your airspeed indicator says 100 knots, you're really making 110 knots. If it's a hotter day than normal, you'll be faster still—because there's much less pressure difference for the instrument to measure from the impact of the warmer, thinner air. Some aircraft have an outside ring on their airspeed indicators, which can be adjusted based on **pressure altitude** and temperature to find TAS. Others, with digital cockpit displays, compute and display it automatically.

It's important to understand when "true" airspeed matters, and when it doesn't. TAS is mainly useful for planning purposes: when you want to calculate how long it will take to fly from one place to another, adjusting your true airspeed for the wind to find ground speed. But the lift that allows an airplane to fly depends, not on speed per se, but on air pressure—the very differences in pressure that *indicated* airspeed is measuring. So regardless of altitude or temperature, you *fly* the airplane based on indicated airspeed, and you *plan* the flight based on true airspeed.

That's why the main numbers on the airspeed indicator still show *indicated* rather than true airspeed, even if it's not really an accurate measure of exactly how fast you are flying through the air.* On most modern airplanes, these "speeds" are depicted on the airspeed indicator as colored arcs (see Figure 15). A white arc runs from V_{S0}, the stalling speed with full flaps (40 knots for a Cessna 172) to V_{FE}, the maximum safe speed for flaps to be fully extended (85 knots). These are the safe operating speeds for when the plane is configured for landing. A green arc, indicating the safe operating speeds for normal flight, runs from V_{S1}, the stalling speed with flaps up (48), to V_{NO} (128), the maximum speed for normal operations. Beyond this is a yellow arc, which is safe only as long as you are flying in smooth air. It's also a warning that you are approaching the red line at V_{NE}, the **Never Exceed Speed** (163), beyond which the airplane might not hold up under stress. Not all airplanes have these colored arcs, and you have to commit these speeds—which are different for each model of airplane—to memory in any case, but they are a helpful reference point when you glance quickly at the airspeed gauge.

The **vertical speed indicator (VSI)** is a clever device that actually measures the difference in air pressure between moments in time. It also has a

---

*You can think of it this way: To generate the same differences in air pressure (in terms of IAS) required to fly, an airplane must fly faster (in terms of TAS) in thinner air than it must fly in denser air. But it is the IAS, shown on the airspeed indicator, that determines how the airplane will fly.

small metal accordion, which is linked to the static port and reflects the outside ambient air pressure. This sits in a chamber that is also connected to the static port, but through a restricted opening, which in effect introduces a delay. When the airplane goes up in altitude, the smaller diaphragm is exposed to the lower air pressure immediately, while at first, the larger chamber still has the higher air pressure from the starting altitude. This causes the little accordion to shrink, moving the needle to show a rate of climb. If the aircraft levels off, the chamber will eventually catch up to the diaphragm, causing it to expand again, and the needle will go back to show level flight. The opposite occurs if the plane descends in altitude. The comparison between "now" and "then" isn't perfect: the needle tends to jump immediately in response to any altitude change, but the steady "leak" from the chamber means it equalizes only gradually, possibly after the airplane has already leveled off. It's important to keep this lag in mind when trying to stop a climb or descent, to avoid overshooting the mark. But the VSI is an important tool for regulating the speed of a climb or descent, and also for recognizing unwanted changes in altitude that might be too gradual to notice quickly by glancing at the altimeter.

What would happen if the static port, on the side of the plane, became blocked or damaged in some way? The altimeter and vertical speed indicator would no longer function because the air pressure inside them would remain unchanged. Impact pressure from the pitot tube would still move the needle on the airspeed indicator, but without changing ambient air pressure as a basis for comparison, the reading would become inaccurate if you climbed or descended. In this event, there's an alternate static port which the pilot can activate from the cockpit panel.

On the other hand, if only the pitot tube were blocked, the first two instruments would work just fine. Depending on how it was blocked, though, your airspeed indicator would either get stuck in place, read zero, or start acting like an altimeter (going up or down with altitude, rather than speed). One of the most common ways for this to happen is for the pitot tube to become blocked by ice. That's why, even in the Cessna 172, there's a switch in the cabin to turn on a heater in the pitot tube to melt any ice that might form. Aside from the heater, however, none of these three **pitot-static** instruments require either the engine or the electrical system to be on in order to function.

The same cannot be said for the next three instruments, which rely on **gyroscopes**. These work on the basis of the phenomenon of **rigidity in space**. When an object is spinning—like a bullet fired from a rifle or a football thrown by a quarterback—it wants to remain spinning on that same axis. A gyroscope holds a spinning disk within three frames that are free to move in any direction, so that regardless of how the object where it is mounted (such as an airplane) tilts or rotates, the disk stays upright in its original orientation.

Take the **attitude indicator**. In its case, an engine-driven vacuum pump sucks air through the instrument, causing the gyroscope's disk to spin on a horizontal plane. When the airplane banks left or right, or pitches up or down, the gyroscope remains oriented to the earth below, along both axes. So a horizontal bar or image connected to it can function as an **artificial horizon**, with markings to show degrees of pitch or bank. Pitch up 10º and the displayed "horizon" rotates down, so that "airplane" depicted at the gauge's center rests on a marking in the "sky" above it that reads 10º. Bank right 10º and the displayed "horizon" slants to the left, so that the "airplane" appears to be banking right and the markings above it rotate to indicate 10º. One glance tells you if the aircraft is pointing up or down, wings level, turned on its side, or even upside down, whether or not you can see anything outside your window.

The **heading indicator** works the same way but on a different axis. This time, the vacuum pump causes a disk to spin on a vertical plane. On the face of the gauge is the miniature outline of an airplane, which always points up, surrounded by a rotating disk marked with the directional 360 degrees of the compass. When the airplane turns to the left, for instance, the resistance of the gyroscope to turn in the same direction moves gears that cause the disk to rotate to the right and the heading indicated at the top of the gauge to advance to the left. It's very intuitive, as if you are the miniature airplane, with all the points of the compass laid out around you, extending out in every direction.

The problem is that mechanical friction, as well as the earth's rotation, will introduce the same forces of gyroscopic precession we encountered before with the propeller and its left-turning tendencies, which can cause the indicated heading to drift off its correct alignment. Every 30 minutes or so, the heading indicator has to be reset to the airplane's **magnetic compass**, which in the Cessna 172 is located on the dashboard above.

So why not just use the magnetic compass in the first place? Because of the way a compass floats in its housing filled with liquid (usually kerosene), it only gives an accurate reading when the airplane is in straight, level, and steady flight. When turning to or from a southerly direction, the compass tends to lead the change in direction; when turning towards a northernly direction, it tends to lag; and when turning away from due north the compass can initially move in the *opposite* direction to the turn, before following behind. On a heading of east or west, an airplane gaining speed will deflect the compass direction to the north; slowing down will deflect it to the south. (As a history buff, I remembered these rules—which can appear on the pilot's written exam—by thinking of the American Civil War. Initially, the South *led* the fighting and won several battles, while the North *lagged*. But eventually, the North's war effort *accelerated*, and the South's *decelerated*.)

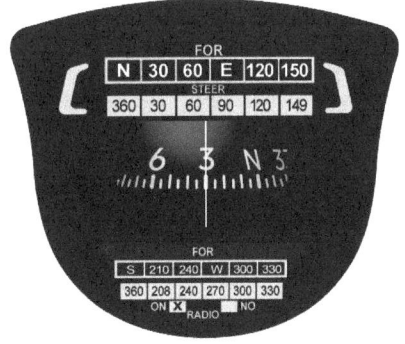

The heading indicator (left) compared with the magnetic compass (right). Note the reversed directions on the magnetic compass (N appears right of 30°, whereas it actually requires a turn to the left), which makes the heading indicator more intuitive to use. The series of numbers above and below the magnetic compass are corrections for magnetic deviation.

Another reason it can be tricky to use the airplane's magnetic compass is that its directions appear to be reversed. Let's say you want to turn from 30º (north-northeast) to a heading of 60° (east-northeast). On the heading indicator's directional disk, you can clearly see that 60º is to the right of 30º and requires a turn to the right. But when an aircraft changes direction, it rotates around the floating compass, and the markings you see on its back side turn in the opposite direction. In other words, on the back side of the magnetic compass, 60º is to the *left* of 30º. It would be easy for a pilot to glance at this and think, without really thinking, that they need to turn left, only to be baffled when the compass reading rotates in the other direction. For all of these reasons, the gyro-based heading indicator is more stable and easier to use at a glance, even if it needs to be regularly reset to the more trustworthy, but more finicky, magnetic compass.

Last but not least, the **turn coordinator** measures movement left and right, along the same axis as the heading indicator, but is focused on the characteristics of the turn itself, rather than the change in direction that results. This time, an electric motor causes the gyroscope inside to spin, instead of the engine-driven vacuum pump. The spinning vertical disk is constrained, however, so that any yawing motion left or right translates, via gyroscopic precession, into a twisting motion. This causes the wings of a miniature airplane on the face of the gauge to appear to bank in the direction of the turn. This motion, however, does *not* depict the actual bank of the airplane (which is shown on the attitude indicator), but its rate of turn. (You'll notice that when you turn while taxiing on the ground, the wings on the turn coordinator will tilt because you're rotating the plane left or right, even though the wings themselves remain level.) There are marks next to each "wing" indicating straight flight, as well as a **standard rate turn** of 3º per second, which equates to a full 360-degree circle every two minutes. Many instructions from Air Traffic Control—for instance, to circle rather than proceed to land—assume the pilot will make a standard rate turn, so it isn't completed too soon or too late.

Below the miniature airplane is an **inclinometer**, which consists of a black ball suspended in a slightly curved, liquid-filled tube. In normal flight, gravity causes the ball to rest in the center, and in a coordinated turn (with the nose moving in the direction of the turn, with the tail behind it), the ball will remain centered. On the other hand, if the turn becomes uncoordinated and the airplane begins to slip or skid, centripetal force will push the ball to one side or the other. The pilot must "step on the ball"—push the right rudder pedal if the ball is leaning to the right, the left rudder pedal if it's leaning left—to bring the nose and tail of the plane back into alignment. In other words, the ball tells you when you need to use the rudder to correct unwanted yaw.

The turn coordinator is probably the least familiar instrument to a new pilot, but it's actually one of the oldest. Wilbur and Orville Wright invented the very first flight instrument when they tied a piece of yarn to the front of their 1902 glider to show if it was slipping or skidding relative to the airflow so they knew when to apply the rudder.[74] Without any gyroscopes, however, Charles Lindbergh's *Spirit of St. Louis* had only an inclinometer to try to ensure straight and level flight throughout his landmark 33-hour solo crossing of the Atlantic in 1927.[75]

There's a lot of contingencies built into the system. If the engine or vacuum pump go out, the turn coordinator will still work as long as the battery holds out. The attitude and heading indicators, on the other hand, need engine power but don't require electricity. The magnetic compass and inclinometer rely only on the basic laws of physics. During one of my lessons, the heading indicator started spinning uncontrollably and wouldn't stop. Though it was far from ideal, I used the magnetic compass to find our way back. Although each instrument serves a purpose, the others—if you appreciate how they work—often leave enough clues to fill in the gap.

As I mentioned before, on some aircraft the arrival of new technology has enabled all six of these instruments to be combined on a single digital screen in front of the pilot, called the **Primary Flight Display (PFD)**. I didn't have this in my real-life Cessna, but I became familiar with it on *Microsoft Flight Simulator* (see Figure 9). Typically, the entire screen is filled by an artificial horizon, sometimes with a 3-D computerized depiction of the terrain ahead.

There are markings indicating current pitch and bank, as well as a moveable marker showing whether the "ball" is centered. On the left is a moving vertical scroll of numbers showing airspeed, including the usual colored ranges. On the right is a similar vertical scroll showing altitude, and usually some sort of arrows indicating the current rate of climb or descent. At bottom center is a rotating heading indicator that shows the compass direction where the nose is pointed.

The cockpit also has numerous engine gauges, which I'll go into later when I talk about how the engine works. But there is one, and in some aircraft two, engine gauges that I can't pass over now, because they are essential to flying the plane. The **tachometer** can be located anywhere, but in the Cessna 172 it's right under the "six pack." It measures propeller RPM, which with a simple fixed-pitch propeller is directly controlled by the throttle. I quickly came to learn the Cessna's RPM settings for different phases of flight (2500 or higher for climb, 2100 to 2400 for cruise, 1700 to 2000 for descent, around 1500 or so when coming in to land). In fact, after a while I started to be able to recognize them just by listening to the engine's sound, with only a quick glance at the tachometer to confirm.

With an adjustable pitch/constant speed propeller, this becomes two gauges. One shows **manifold pressure**. This is the amount of air entering the engine to fuel combustion, which is directly controlled by the throttle and correlates to the power the engine is producing. The tachometer, on the other hand, still measures propeller RPM, but that is now determined by a combination of the engine's power and the setting of the **prop lever**, or "blue knob."[76] The Cessna 182, the slightly larger, more powerful big brother of the 172, has one. Some newer single-engine airplanes, like the popular Cirrus SR22, mechanically integrate the throttle and prop lever into a single power control.[77] Others, like the Diamond DA42 NG, go one step further, using a digital computer called a **FADEC** (Full Authority Digital Engine Control) to automatically optimize the fuel/air mixture as well as propeller pitch, via the same power lever.[78] I didn't have any of these in the cockpit of my Cessna 172, but if you see a blue knob, or a manifold pressure gauge, now you know what it is.

In a "glass cockpit," the engine gauges are usually shown on a second digital screen, called a **Multi-Functional Display (MFD)**, which frequently also shows navigational maps and flight planning information. The MFD is usually located to the right, or in a larger cockpit with a PFD for each pilot, in the center of the instrumental panel (once again, see Figure 9).

Many of the devices I've described may seem exotic, but there's one instrument you may not realize was born in the cockpit which you might even be wearing right now: the wristwatch. In 1904, the Brazilian-born aviator Alberto Santos-Dumont approached one of his friends in Paris, the jeweler Louis Cartier, with a problem. Men at that time carried pocket watches, but he needed both hands free to operate the controls of his experimental aircraft. Cartier designed for him one of the first men's wristwatches,[79] beginning a long association with aviation that remains evident in luxury watch advertisements to this day.[80] Almost all airplanes now have a clock (or more formally, a chronometer) with a stopwatch embedded in the instrument panel to time maneuvers and aid in navigation.

Now you know your way around a cockpit and the useful information each instrument provides. But what happens when you can't see anything outside of your windows, and the instruments are all you have? Can you still fly the plane, blind? Let's find out.

CHAPTER 8

Hood

At some point in my lessons, Tess turned to me mid-flight and took out "the **hood.**" This can take the form of a restrictive visor, but in our case, it was a set of plastic eye protectors with the top half fogged over, commonly referred to as "**foggles**" (though like Kleenex and Xerox, Foggles is actually the name of a particular brand of such glasses). She took the controls for moment to allow me to put them on over my regular glasses. Like a horse wearing blinders, I now could see the instrument panel in front of me and nothing else.

One of the first rules you learn as a student pilot is *don't fly into a cloud*. You are learning to fly according to **VFR**, or Visual Flight Rules. This means steering clear of any clouds (exactly how far, by regulation, depends on the designated airspace) and not taking off at all if the **cloud ceiling** is too low (clouds covering more than half the sky, less than 1,000 feet above ground) or the visibility too poor (less than three statute miles). Part of the reason is that if you can't see other aircraft, and they can't see you, you could collide with them. But mainly it's due to the risk of **spatial disorientation**.

The inner ear is a funny thing. The liquid sloshing around inside it helps us keep our balance, but it's meant to work hand in hand with our other senses, particularly sight. When we don't have any visual references, it can play all sorts of tricks on us. Close your eyes next time you're taking off in an airliner and try to interpret what the airplane is doing. Chances are you will end up feeling like it's banking to one side, only to open your eyes and find the wings perfectly level—or vice versa. You might even get the sensation it's tipping over backward when it's actually leveling off from a climb. There's all sorts of fascinating science and terminology behind this, but the gist of it is that when you can't see, your sense of balance doesn't know what the hell is going on.

In the early days of aviation, instruments were extremely rudimentary, and pilots flew by visual reference or—if that wasn't possible—"by the seat of their pants." In other words, they tried to *feel* which direction the plane was moving based on their sense of physical momentum. A lot of pilots who flew into clouds—especially airmail pilots, who were expected to deliver their cargo regardless of weather—lost their sense of up and down and got killed crashing into the ground. In the years immediately after World War I, the average life expectancy of the first U.S. Postal Service pilots was 900 hours of flying.[81] They dubbed it the "Suicide Club."

At least one U.S. Army aviator thought he could change this. Jimmy Doolittle is best known for the audacious carrier-based bombing raid on Japan that he organized to retaliate for Pearl Harbor, immortalized in the book and film *Thirty Seconds Over Tokyo*,[82] but he deserves at least as much fame for becoming the first person to fly solely by reference to instruments. After World War I, he worked closely with Elmer Sperry, an inventor who developed some of the first modern gyroscopes to help naval warships steer and aim their guns more accurately in rolling seas.[83] In 1929, Doolittle covered the cockpit of his Army biplane with a tarp hood and using early experimental versions of the instruments I described in the last chapter—including the first artificial horizon and heading indicator—successfully took off, flew, and landed at an airstrip in Long Island completely blind.[84] Another Army pilot, a flight instructor based in California named William C. Ocker, worked with Sperry to introduce the gyroscopic turn coordinator and made the first instrument-only cross-country flight the following year.[85] Pilots could now fly through clouds without getting killed—as long as they were properly trained.

Pilots today can qualify to fly using **IFR**, or Instrument Flight Rules, which allows them to fly through all but the very worst visibility situations. However, you need to earn an **instrument rating**, a process at least as demanding as earning your private pilot's license in the first place. Even to get their initial license, student pilots must still perform at least three hours flying "under the hood" to gain at least some familiarity with relying on instruments, in case they find themselves unintentionally flying into **IMC (Instrument Meteorological Conditions)**—one of the most common causes of aircraft accidents and fatalities.

So, on with the foggles. Some students are tempted to peek by raising their head or glancing out the sides, but that defeats the whole purpose: to gain confidence that the instruments are actually telling you all you need to know to fly the plane. Once I'm ready, Tess gives me a series of instructions to perform, using only the instruments to guide me. Turn to a heading of 270°. Now reduce speed to 90 knots. Climb to 4,000 feet at this airspeed. Now descend at a rate of 500 feet per minute while turning to a heading of 30°, and level off at 3,200 feet. Some find this uncomfortable; I found it a fun and interesting challenge. I also found it developed my ability to fly the plane more precisely, even after the hood came off.

Learning to fly proficiently based only on instruments takes a great deal of discipline, and a lot more than three hours of practice. There are specific procedures to follow, as well as errors to avoid, and the challenge of multitasking—talking on the radio, not getting lost, dealing with other problems—makes it that much harder. At least three famous episodes stand as tragic warnings of how deadly it can prove for the overconfident and underprepared.

In 1930, the Post Office under President Herbert Hoover awarded U.S. government airmail contracts to a select group of airlines by region, to boost their development.[86] After he was elected, Franklin Delano Roosevelt decried what he saw as a corrupt sweetheart deal. In February 1934, he abruptly canceled the contracts and ordered U.S. Army pilots to carry the mail instead.[87] Two of the most famous men in America, Charles Lindbergh and former World War I fighter ace Eddie Rickenbacker—then the head of Eastern Airlines—publicly blasted FDR's decision, warning that Army pilots were not trained, nor their airplanes equipped, to fly under instrument-only conditions, and that the results could prove deadly.[88] So they did. Over the next few weeks, amid bad fog and severe snowstorms, there were 66 crashes that killed 12 pilots.[89] President Roosevelt was forced into a rare and humiliating climbdown and restored the system of mail contracts. The enmity bred by the incident between FDR and Lindbergh endured and festered through the start of World War II.[90]

In February 1959, budding rock'n'roll star Buddy Holly along with fellow performers Ritchie Valens and "The Big Bopper" J.P. Richardson were doing a winter tour across the rural Midwest. To avoid another long, frozen bus trip to their next gig, they chartered a small plane out of Mason City, Iowa.[91] The weather was technically VFR, but a night flight with low clouds and few lights on the ground meant the pilot would need to rely heavily, if not entirely, on his cockpit instruments for reference.[92] The 21-year old pilot had 711 flying hours, including 52 hours of instrument training, but had so far failed to earn his instrument rating, and he was unfamiliar with the older type of artificial horizon installed in this particular airplane.[93] Within minutes of taking off, witnesses saw the plane make two steep turns to the north, then its lights descended and disappeared. The wreckage found the next morning told the story: the plane hit the ground at high speed at a steep bank, nose-down.[94] All four aboard were killed, a tragedy that inspired the song "American Pie," with its refrain "the day the music died."[95] Authorities concluded that the crash was caused by an overconfident pilot falling prey to spatial disorientation after underestimating the risks.[96]

John F. Kennedy Jr., his wife, and sister-in-law were killed in July 1999 after taking off at dusk from Caldwell (also known as Essex County Airport), just a few short miles from my own airport at Lincoln Park in northern New Jersey.[97] After the sun set and low clouds moved in, he lost all sense of direction over the dark and featureless water off Martha's Vineyard, unknowingly entered a spin, and crashed into the ocean. A number of other factors—pressure to arrive at a wedding, a foot injury, and neglecting to call for help—

likely contributed, but ultimately it was spatial disorientation that turned trouble into tragedy. JFK Jr. had recently started his instrument training, and his flight instructor even offered to accompany him on the flight, but he declined. When conditions worsened, he pressed on. It was a series of decisions that, cumulatively, proved fatal.[98]

For all too many pilots, their first encounter with poor-visibility conditions can end up being their last. This is where I found *Microsoft Flight Simulator* surprisingly helpful. Even as my real-world lessons progressed, I continued flying on *MSFS 2020* regularly. I began one of the "bush trips," a pre-set itinerary of flights that started in Croatia and continued down the Adriatic Coast to Greece in a Cessna 172. When I arrived at the end, on the island of Santorini, I decided to keep going all the way clockwise around the entire Mediterranean, logging over 100 hours of virtual flight time and over 100 virtual takeoffs and landings. I always flew with "real weather" on, which meant that some days I was grounded by cloudy or stormy or foggy conditions. But occasionally I braved the virtual elements in ways I wouldn't risk doing in real life—and walked away from it with some valuable experiences.

I remember very clearly my first virtual takeoff at night, on a flight from Santorini across the Aegean Sea to the island of Kos. The clouds were overcast but high, and conditions were technically VFR. Taxiing and taking off from the well-lit runway presented no challenge. But the moment I pitched up to leave the runway, all I could see was black nothingness. Even sitting in front of my PC at home, the feeling of complete disorientation was sudden and alarming.

Then, after a few moments of confusion, my eyes looked down to the instrument panel in front of me, which was equipped with a digital display. Everything I needed was there. The artificial horizon showed that my wings were level and I was pointed slightly up in a gentle climb. My airspeed was stable at 80 knots, and I was steadily gaining altitude. For all I could see outside I might be at the bottom of the deepest ocean, but the instruments painted a clear picture of a flight unfolding as normal. They became my world, with the blackness around me all but disappearing from my awareness, as if it were veiled by foggles. Through the entire half-hour flight, I only spotted a few tiny points of light, as I passed a small island to my right, until the bright thin line of a runway gradually emerged from the darkness ahead and I landed at my destination.

This and other experiences in the simulator taught me that there are really two very different ways of flying a plane. When I fly in VFR conditions, all of my senses are fully deployed. I'm looking around, "feeling" what the airplane is doing, and selectively checking my instruments—altitude, airspeed, heading, vertical speed—to confirm that I'm right. In fact, they say that when flying VFR, you should spend at least three-quarters of your time looking outside, to spot other aircraft and maintain situational awareness, rather than burying your head in the cockpit.

But the moment the foggles go on—or I fly into a cloud in the sim—the instruments become my entire world, to the exclusion of every other sensory input. My eyes snap immediately to the artificial horizon on the attitude indicator. It replaces the view out my front windshield, which is the whole reason it sits top and center, and becomes the centerpiece of a disciplined scan from the attitude indicator to each instrument in turn, and back again. Every other glance goes back to the artificial horizon, to make sure I'm not tilting in some unexpected direction. If I sense the airplane going faster or slower, rising or falling, turning, or even spinning around, I completely ignore it, and focus on the instrument panel like I am playing a video game.

Flying regularly in the simulator at home also gave me some exposure to using **autopilot**. At first, I thought autopilot sounded like cheating, and it's true that none of the training required to become a private pilot involves learning to use one (the simple autopilot unit in my own practice Cessna was broken and labeled "inoperative" the whole time). In fact, making smart use of autopilot—which dates back to the early years of aviation—is an important part of flying many modern aircraft. Lawrence Sperry, the son of gyroscope pioneer Elmer Sperry, demonstrated the first autopilot in 1914 at a flying exposition in Paris, using his father's devices to keep his plane flying straight and level while he waved his hands in the air.[99] As the gyroscopes suggest, using autopilot is, in a way, an extension of instrument flying, except that the instruments actually do the flying, based on the parameters you input. Managed properly, autopilot can fly steadier and more precisely than any pilot can do manually, especially over a long period of time.

Autopilots vary in complexity. The simplest might allow you to set and follow a certain heading or maintain your current altitude. More advanced models allow you to climb or descend to a desired altitude at either the vertical rate (feet per minute) or airspeed (knots) you select. The most sophisticated let you program in an entire **flight plan**, guiding the plane from waypoint to waypoint and automatically adjusting heading to the wind to stay on course. Except in airliners, most autopilots do not control the throttle, so engine power must be adjusted manually throughout flight. If you tell the autopilot to descend at a certain rate and don't pull back the throttle, the airplane will speed up. If you tell it to climb at a certain rate and do not add throttle, the airplane will slow down. If you instruct it to climb at a certain airspeed, whether it will actually begin to climb, and at what rate, depends on whether you add sufficient power.[100]

The thing to *always* remember about autopilot is that, like any computer, it does exactly what you *tell* it to do, not what you *want* it to do. If you tell it to climb too fast and do not add enough throttle, the airplane will pitch up steeply until it stalls—and the autopilot will not try to recover. It's just trying to follow your instructions. The first thing to do when the airplane does something unexpected while on autopilot is to *turn the autopilot off*, and fly it manually, until you can figure out why. Most planes have a big red button right on the yoke so the pilot can disengage autopilot in an instant.

Later on my virtual Mediterranean adventure, I departed out of Sardinia at night, to head across the sea to Tunisia. After takeoff I turned on the autopilot for my Cessna 172 to follow a pre-programmed course based on an IFR flight plan. A short while later, amid flashes of lightning, I realized that the planned route was taking me straight into the heart of a violent thunderstorm. I immediately flipped off the autopilot to seek a way around, only to find myself in instrument-only conditions, flying blind while getting knocked about by turbulence. Again, I shut out the scene outside and focused solely on the instruments displayed in front of me—particularly the attitude indicator and the altimeter. Since I was over the ocean, I knew that as long as I stayed high enough—and made sure the barometer setting on my altimeter was correct—I wouldn't crash into anything. Once the situation stabilized, I entered new instructions to hold this safe altitude and fly due south. After an hour of staring intently at the screen, the winds calmed and I could see a clear sky of stars out the window. Eventually the lights of the Tunisian coast came into view.

The FAA recognizes the value of flight simulators, allowing students training for their instrument rating to use them, instead of a real airplane, for up to half of the flight hours required—though it has to be an FAA-certified mock-up of a cockpit, not your home PC setup. While my PC-based experiences clearly didn't count for such training, and certainly didn't prepare me to fly in real-life instrument conditions, they did teach me to *trust the instruments*. I think that's why, when I put the foggles on in the real plane, I didn't feel panicked or disconcerted. I felt comfortable that if the instruments indicated I was flying straight and level at 3,500 feet, that's what was happening.

Of course, it helped to know that my instructor was sitting right next to me, with a clear day's view out the window. Flying into a real bank of clouds, alone, was a very different proposition, and I didn't intend to try that anytime soon.

CHAPTER 9

Navigation

When I finally took the foggles off, after each session of "hood practice," Tess's first question to me was: "Okay, where are we?"

I had no idea, of course, because I had just been blindly following her instructions for the past half hour. And the view 3,000 feet over northern New Jersey, especially in winter, is one vast expanse of tree-covered ridges with identical lakes between them. Figuring out where you are—and where you want to go—is the next step in learning to fly: navigation.

The methods involved in aerial navigation have evolved in three main stages over the years, and pilots still utilize all three. The earliest, which dates back to those "seat of the pants" air mail routes, is a combination of **dead reckoning** and **pilotage**. (Some pilots and instructors refer to it as "ded reckoning," with the DED short for "deduced." In fact, this appears most likely to be a neologism that came about in the 1930s. The original term, always "dead," dates from the days of sailing ships, at least as early as the 1600s, and may refer to the practice of estimating speed—and distance traveled—by reference to a piece of flotsam lying dead in the water.)[101]

Whether dead or deduced, reckoning begins with plotting a planned route on a map, which in aviation is called a chart. Since the 1930s, the FAA publishes a series of maps for VFR flying called **sectional charts**, which carve the continental United States into 37 rectangles, each named for a major city, depicted on a scale of 1:500,000 with one inch equivalent to about eight miles. The charts show major terrain features (rivers, highways, towns, and cities) and elevations (ranging from low greens to tall browns) as well as potential hazards to aircraft, such as tall smokestacks or power lines. They also show every airport, large and small, including basic information such as their elevation, radio frequencies, runway length, and—very important—whether they have a control tower or not. Last but not least, the charts show the regulated airspace around each of these airports and across every inch of the country in between. The charts are regularly updated every couple of months so all the information on them is current.

Putting aside airspace rules for a moment, let's say I wanted to fly a straight route from Cincinnati's main airport to John Glenn Columbus International, both on the same chart. I'd start by using a ruler to pencil a line between them, then use a protractor to measure the angle between that route and the closest vertical line of longitude, crossing the chart from north to south. That angle, which works out to be 55°, is my **true course**—true in reference to north, south, east, and west on this or any other map, defined by the earth's axis of rotation.

Though true course is the direction I want to go across the map, there are at least two, possibly three reasons I can't just follow this heading to my destination. I have to adjust for the direction the wind will push me, the difference between "true" and magnetic north, and any known inaccuracies of my magnetic compass. I also can't just read my airspeed indicator to tell how long it will take to arrive. We already know that indicated airspeed isn't true airspeed, which depends on air density. We also know that the wind can speed me up or slow me down in reference to the ground below. So before I can even climb into cockpit, I need to roll up my sleeves, take out some data charts and a calculator, and get to figuring.

The **Winds Aloft** report, which I can obtain online or by phone, will tell me the expected wind direction and speed at my planned cruise alti-

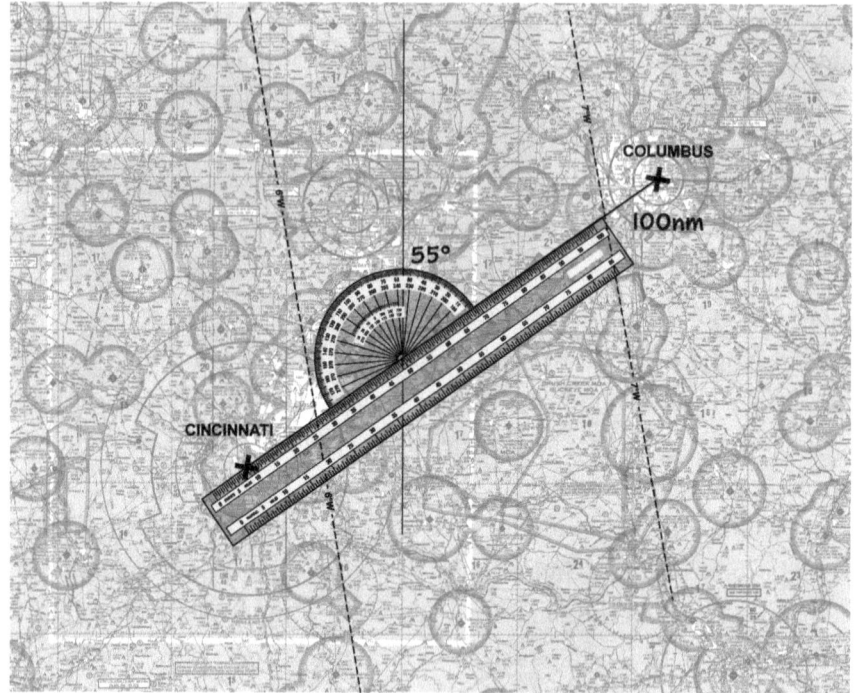

Using a pilot's protractor to determine a route's course and distance on a sectional chart. The two dashed lines highlighted from the chart indicate magnetic variation, for converting courses or headings from true to magnetic.

tude. Today the wind at 4,500 feet is forecast at 19 knots from 229° (the southwest). This particular report always gives wind directions in reference to "true" north, so it's consistent with my true course. The report also indicates that the forecast temperature at that altitude is 17°C. Since "standard" temperature is 15°C at sea level minus 2°C for every 1,000 feet, or 6°C, this temperature is +11°C above standard. The altimeter reading for Cincinnati today is 29.96 (just slightly above the standard 29.92). For many years, pilots used a special **E6B** slide rule to calculate the resulting **density altitude**. These days I plug the temperature, pressure, and planned cruising altitude into a handheld electronic calculator that performs the same functions and retails for $69.95 from a pilot supply store online. It tells me that because it's a warm day, at 4,500 feet MSL the airplane will perform like it's flying in thinner air at 5,700 feet—over 1,000 feet higher. When I look this up in the aircraft's **Pilot Operating Handbook (POH)**, I have to extrapolate somewhat from the tables, but I can estimate that with power set at 2300 RPM, my true airspeed (TAS) will be 110 knots, and I will burn 7.5 gallons of fuel per hour.

Entering the forecast wind speed and direction, along with my own TAS and intended course, into the E6B calculator will also tell me how far the wind will push me off course and how I need to compensate. Because the wind today is almost directly behind me, the wind angle is only 1°, which means my true heading should be 56°, just slightly to the right. The strong tailwind will propel me along faster towards my destination for an estimated groundspeed of 128 knots. On the chart, I can measure that the distance from start to finish is 100 nautical miles. Factoring in my initial climb (slower speed at higher power) and final descent (similar speed at lower power), I can calculate the total time (49 minutes) and fuel (roughly 8.5 gallons) I expect the entire flight to take.

If I fly a heading of 56° based on my instruments, however, I'll miss my mark. That's because the earth's magnetic field does not precisely match up with its axis of rotation, and the magnetic north pole, which my compass gravitates towards, is not located at the geographic north pole. The difference between true north and magnetic north—called **magnetic variation**—depends on where you are located. Dashed red lines, called **isogonic lines**, crisscrossing the sectional chart tell you what the variance is. Around New York, on the East Coast, the isogonic lines bend 13° to the west, and this number must be added to the **true heading** to get the **magnetic heading**. Around Los Angeles, on the West Coast, the isogonic lines bend 12° to the east, and this must be subtracted from true heading to get magnetic heading. Our trip, from Cincinnati to Columbus, passes between the 6°W and 7°W lines. That means to fly a true heading of 56° (and thus a true course of 55°, given today's wind), I need to follow a magnetic heading of 62° on my heading indicator, after setting it to my magnetic compass. (The magnetic north pole tends to migrate around, from year to year, which is one more reason why the FAA has to regularly update its sectional charts.)

Sometimes, when a magnetic compass is installed in an airplane, the metal parts and electrical equipment nearby pull the needle slightly away from magnetic north. This is called **magnetic deviation**. The mechanics, when they do their required regular inspections, note the observed deviations on a card placed next to the compass. Typically, the deviations are no more than a few degrees, which makes little difference on a short journey.

This method of dead reckoning—estimating the heading needed to follow a certain course, based on the weather and aircraft performance—can be broken up into multiple legs for a longer or more complicated route, with each leg calculated based on its own inputs. This is how Charles Lindbergh planned and flew his journey across the Atlantic in 1927.[102] He knew that, compounded over such huge distances, an error of just a few compass degrees could easily put him hundreds of miles off course.[103] Even if he ran the calculations correctly, an unexpected wind could have pushed him as far north as Norway or as far south as Portugal, or slowed him down so much that he ran out of fuel before making land.[104] As it turned out, his luck held, and he arrived right on target over the west coast of Ireland a few hours sooner than expected.[105] But you can easily understand, now, the risks that were involved.

Lindbergh was flying over the featureless ocean, which made it impossible for him to check his progress until he made landfall somewhere. Fortunately, flying over land we have many more opportunities to validate our dead reckoning estimates and adjust accordingly, by reference to known landmarks. This process is called **pilotage**. It could involve breaking a straight route into legs, each with an easily spotted checkpoint on the ground, like a bridge, quarry, or road intersection—or an alternate airport, where you could land in the event of a problem. Or it could mean designing your route to follow a river, highway, or railroad (giving rise to the old joke among VFR pilots: "Sure, I fly IFR: I Follow Roads"). At each checkpoint, you can compare your location and time of arrival with your projections, and alter either your plans or your flight to reflect that. Of course, this requires relatively clear visibility to do.

Whenever the foggles came off, my first priority was to try to use pilotage to identify where I was. When you're lost, I was instructed to follow the six Cs: Confess to yourself that you don't know where you are, Circle so you don't wander farther off course, Climb to get a better view of the area, and Conserve fuel by reducing power and flying slower. Sometimes I was able to identify a place I recognized, like the bridge leading to a small island in the middle of Mohawk Lake. Of course, if all else failed I could move on to the next two Cs: Communicate with ATC and Comply with their instructions. I could ask ATC to find me on their radar and give me a **vector**—a heading to follow—to a known location. Fortunately, however, I had another option before doing this. I'm talking about the second stage of tools developed for pilots to find their way: radio navigation.

In the Cessna, to the right of my "six pack" of primary flight instruments are two dials called **Course Deviation Indicators (CDIs)**, one on top of the other. They look kind of like heading indicators, with a ring of 360-degree compass markings that can be rotated using a knob called an **Omnidirectional Bearing Selector (OBS)**. Inside the ring, the top one has two white needles, one vertical and one horizontal, that look like a crosshair, while the bottom one has only the vertical needle. To their right, in the center of the cockpit above the power controls, is the **radio stack**, which has two frequencies (**COM1 and COM2**) dedicated for verbal radio communication, but also two other frequencies (**NAV1 and NAV2**) for radio navigation. With these tools, I can readily find my location, follow a path to or from a known spot on the map, and even—if I got my instrument rating—find my way to land safely through a veil of clouds.

In 1929, when Jimmy Doolittle made his first "blind" flight based solely on instruments, he used a radio beacon to find his way back to the runway to land. Over the following decades, radio beacons (on the ground) and receivers (in planes) became a new way of navigating that didn't depend on educated guesswork or readily recognized landmarks. Tune in the correct frequency on a **Non-Directional Beacon (NDB)** and turn the airplane until the vertical needle becomes centered on the corresponding gauge, then follow it to its source. If Lindbergh had access to radio beacons, once in range he could have picked up a known location along Europe's coastline and made straight for it, rather than wondering and worrying that he might miss a landfall that was just out of sight.

There are still a few NDBs around the U.S., and many overseas, but starting in the 1960s most were gradually replaced by a more versatile radio beacon called a **VOR**, which stands for VHF omnidirectional range. On the ground, a VOR looks like a small building surrounded by a circular array of antennas, sometimes with a kind of cone on top. It sends out a rotating signal that allows the receiver to determine which magnetic direction, or **radial**, they are on relative to the station. The station itself is marked on the sectional chart, surrounded by a large circle showing the radials extending in every direction. Sometimes the VOR also has **DME** (Distance Measuring Equipment) that will give distance to the station as well. A **VORTAC** is just a station co-located with the U.S. military's separate but similar TACAN direction-finding system.

Let's go back to where I took off my foggles. I'm circling and climbing but can't see any clues to where I am. So, at Tess's prompting, I look on my map and identify some VORs in the general vicinity. The higher I am, the better chance I can pick up their signal at longer range. I select two (named Huguenot and Sparta), find their frequencies from the sectional chart (116.1 and 115.7), and enter them into NAV1 and NAV2 on my radio stack. "Before you do anything else," Tess interjects, "you need to confirm that you've tuned in the correct VORs." To do that, I pull out a tiny knob next to NAV1 and listen carefully for a Morse code signal, which I can compare to the series of dots and dashes printed next to the Huguenot VOR on my sectional chart. Six short BIPs followed by four longer BEEPs—H U O. That's it, that's a match. I then do the same for the Sparta VOR on NAV2.

"Now tell me where we are," Tess says. Holding the chart pinned to the yoke in my left hand, I reach over with my right to the OBS knob on the top CDI, in the center of the instrument panel, and use it to rotate the compass ring until the vertical needle is centered with the dial displaying the word "FROM." Initially it shows "TO," so I need to turn it halfway (180 degrees) around until the needle is centered again showing "FROM." The top of the compass ring now reads 15, which means I am currently somewhere on the 150° radial FROM the Huguenot VOR. On the chart, I draw a line—as straight as I can—from the VOR through the 15 marked on the surrounding circle and beyond. It's a handful, considering I have to fly the plane and look out for other traffic at the same time.

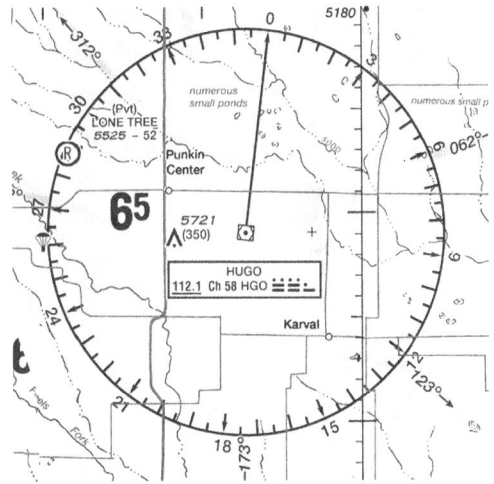

A VOR displayed on a sectional chart, surrounded by a circle showing the radials extending in every (magnetic) direction.

The Course Deviation Indicator (CDI), with the OBS knob at bottom left. This CDI is tuned to the 210° radial leading FROM a VOR, which the needle shows is off to the left.

Next I turn the OBS on the bottom gauge until its vertical CDI needle is also centered and displaying "FROM." This is my radial FROM the Sparta VOR, and I can draw a similar line on the map away from that VOR station. (If the plane only had one CDI, I could do each reading in sequence; that works too.) I show Tess the chart and point to where the two lines intersect: "That's where we are." Amazing Grace. I once was lost but now am found, was blind but now I see.

"Good job," replies Tess. "Now fly us to the Huguenot VOR." Since that frequency is already tuned on NAV1, I reach over and use the OBS knob to turn the CDI dial halfway around until the vertical needle is centered with the gauge now displaying "TO." The compass reading on top of the dial is the magnetic course I must fly to reach that VOR—the reciprocal (180-degree opposite) of the radial FROM that VOR. It's very close to 33, or 330°, the opposite of the radial we were on (150 + 180 = 330). I begin banking the plane to turn and follow that direction.

As I fly, I need to keep the vertical CDI needle centered to stay on course. If it drifts to the left, I have wandered off to the right and must jog over the left to get back on that radial. The opposite is true if the needle sways to the right. That's why it's called a Course Deviation Indicator. Keeping the needle centered, Tess warns me, is not as simple as following that heading. I might have to adjust my heading to compensate for wind, which I may only be able to sense from being blown off course. If the needle gets way off, and my only goal is to reach the VOR—as opposed to approaching it *on a particular radial*—I can always turn the OBS to re-center the needle and follow the new indicated course. "But try to follow the needle," she urges, "because staying on a specific radial is important practice for when you learn to fly IFR."

As I approach the Huguenot VOR, the radials converge at the station and the distance between them gets smaller and smaller. The needle starts swinging more wildly now, so much there's hardly any point in chasing it. Almost above the VOR, we've entered the "zone of confusion," where we're too close for the needle to give a helpful direction. "Look down," Tess points, and there below us, on the top of a wooded ridge, I spot the small white domed structure of the VOR station itself. As I look back to the CDI, I notice the indicator has silently flipped from "TO" to "FROM." We are now on the 330° radial FROM the station, and we can follow that radial away from it just as we followed the "TO" reading to reach it.

"It's vital to keep the TO and FROM indication straight," Tess cautions, as I enter a new FROM heading to follow out from Huguenot toward our next destination. The CDI has no idea what direction you're going or wish to go, only what radial you are on. Center the needle on FROM and it tells you the magnetic course from the VOR to you, and beyond. Center the needle on TO and it tells you the opposite, the course you must follow to get to the VOR. Get them switched—try to follow a FROM reading to the VOR, or a TO reading away from it—and not only will you head in the wrong direction, but the Course Deviation Indicator will be reversed: chasing the needle to the left or right will take you farther *away* from the desired radial, not towards it. This is called **reverse sensing**, and it's a pilot error, not an equipment error.

It's possible to form entire routes as a series of handoffs from one VOR to another, until you reach your destination. In fact, that's exactly what many IFR flight plans are. Common legs from one VOR to another are often designated as **Victor airways**, a kind of highway in the sky, depicted as straight, light blue lines on the sectional chart. When following a Victor airway, it's important to keep your eyes out for other aircraft (either VFR or IFR) that might be doing the same. Their convenience, as a method of navigation, can also make them crowded.

Other kinds of radio beacons, such as **ILS (Instrument Landing System)**, can help guide aircraft onto the correct glideslope to land on a designated airport runway, in low visibility, often using a nearby VOR as a starting point. That's where the horizontal line on the gauge comes in, to follow the correct path of descent. But this is a subject pilots learn for their instrument rating, and I don't have to worry about that now.

Ask a pilot these days where they are, and they probably won't search for a landmark out the window or tune in a VOR. Even in a small plane, they'll look at a digital map display in their cockpit or on an iPad strapped to their lap. They've moved on to the third stage of aerial navigation, which makes use of the **Global Positioning System (GPS)** and wireless data streaming. Most people are familiar with GPS—a system of orbiting satellites providing location-finding data for receivers anywhere on earth—from the digital map screens that are fast becoming ubiquitous in cars. Similar, but far more elaborate, navigational apps in the air are giving pilots loads of new options besides VORs or even ILS to find their way across the sky and back down to earth.

So starting in January, I made an investment that paid off big time. I bought an iPad Mini equipped with GPS, which I dedicated solely to flying, and subscribed to *ForeFlight*, one of a variety of high-powered pilot apps. I also bought a Sentry, a small plastic device that looks like a garage-door opener and, when stuck on your plane's backseat window with a suction cup, receives all sorts of information from a wireless network called ADS-B and feeds it directly into *ForeFlight*.

The main screen of *ForeFlight* is a world map similar to Google Earth, which can be zoomed in or out with your fingers. You can select layers from street map to satellite imagery to—most importantly—full sectional charts for the entire U.S., seamlessly patched together into a single map. Touch the symbol for any airport on the chart and a panel showing detailed airport information pops up, such as traffic patterns, radio frequencies, and telephone numbers, plus in most cases a taxi and runway diagram—all of which you would normally have to physically carry with you in your flight bag. It also shows the latest airport weather report and forecast. Additional map overlays display a ton of weather information, from radar and satellite images to winds and temperatures aloft to hazardous weather warnings.

Amid all of this, the GPS places your location on the map as a blue dot or, if you are moving, as a miniature airplane pointing in the direction of travel. You can turn on features that show distance rings, your maximum glide distance (if you lost engine power), and a track of your route so far. You can even see where you are taxiing on the airport diagram when you have it open. At the bottom of the screen, while flying, you can find your current altitude, heading, and groundspeed—though notably not your airspeed, which it has no way of knowing. All the flight data is recorded, and you can go back and review the entire flight over a 3-D terrain map, along with graphs showing all the key metrics over time.

Prior to flying, you can create flight plans with the touch of a finger, selecting known waypoints like airports or VORs, or any other coordinates you choose on the map. The flight plan will automatically do the "dead reckoning" calculations I described earlier based on available weather data, giving you a recommended magnetic heading as well as an estimated flight time and fuel burn. When you do fly, the planned route is shown as a bold colored line across the map, and you can see how accurately you are following it—and how close you are to any restricted airspace—with a quick glance at your iPad. It almost feels like cheating.

When you use *ForeFlight* at home, all of this data is delivered via your Wi-Fi internet connection. When you climb in the cockpit and lose your internet connection, the same data gets accessed via the Sentry or some similar device using a network called ADS-B. Starting in 2020, the FAA mandated that all aircraft flying in airspace that would normally require a **transponder** —a device that transmits location, identification, and altitude data to Air Traffic Control—must also be equipped with built-in **ADS-B Out**, which transmits even more data via a wireless communications network that gives ATC a more complete and detailed view of what is happening than their traditional radar.

While it's not required, aircraft that have an **ADS-B In** device like a Sentry also get access to all that data from ground stations, ATC, and every other aircraft transmitting ADS-B Out. In effect, it's like Wi-Fi in the sky, at least for specific apps. Not only can you view the latest live weather on your iPad screen, you can also see *other traffic*—most of the planes around you—depicted live on your chart as well. Suddenly the map in your *ForeFlight* screen is populated with blue arrows showing the altitude, speed, and heading of other aircraft which you need to look for and avoid—and which turn yellow or even red if you're getting too close. It's like a miniature Air Traffic Control sitting in your lap.

The conventional approach, of course, is to physically install these features in the form of an advanced ADS-B and GPS-enabled avionics suite, with glass panel map displays, into the cockpit of the plane itself. It has become more and more common for small private aircraft to boast the kind of digital technology that only recently has become standard on top-end airliners. (One version of the Cessna 172 I flew in *Microsoft Flight Simulator* had standard "steam gauges" like the one I flew in real life; the other had a Garmin G1000 "glass cockpit" with all the bells and whistles.) The advantage of an installed system, compared to *ForeFlight* on an iPad, is that it can be connected to the plane's autopilot to automatically fly each leg of a flight plan per instructions. But these systems typically cost at least $20,000, and often many times that. My training Cessna had no fancy avionics, and utilizing the autopilot (had it worked) wasn't in the lesson plan. But for just over $1,000, an iPad with *ForeFlight* strapped to my lap provided 90% of the same functionality for my purposes.

One great feature of *ForeFlight*, which really sealed the deal for me, is that it can connect and interface with *Microsoft Flight Simulator*. After downloading and activating a simple program like *Flight Events* onto my PC, *MSFS* could send the data from my virtual flights to *ForeFlight* via Wi-Fi, making it display that I was flying over the Andes or in Kuala Lumpur getting ready to take off. Not only is this a fun feature, it gave me a lot of practice using *ForeFlight* to plan flights and navigate en route, while exploring all of its capabilities, so that by the time I brought my iPad with me into the real cockpit, it was as comfortable as an old shoe.

Back in the day, the task of navigating could be so consuming that many airplanes devoted a separate crew member to it. All of this new technology in the cockpit has made it easier, but can also become a huge distraction. It's all too easy to bury your head scanning traffic on your iPad, while missing the small kit plane or glider with no electronic footprint coming right at you. As in so many areas of life, digital technology is improving our visibility and expanding our horizons at the cost of bombarding us with more and more information to process. The days of making back-of-the-envelope estimates of heading and airspeed, or even following a radio beacon, may not be over, but they are certainly changing. It's a prime example of one of the main things I discovered during my year learning to fly: while the fundamentals of flying remain the same, the *experience* of flying is undergoing a profound transformation.

CHAPTER 10

Charts

No matter what method or technology you're using, the key to successful navigation is preparation: knowing the airspace and the landscape you're flying across as well as possible. That means spending a lot of time with maps. Whether planning a flight or in the midst of one, the sectional chart is the pilot's guide to the world outside the cockpit. The chart—either paper or digital—helps me identify what I am seeing and alerts me to what I'm not. A smart pilot always keeps one eye out the window, one eye on the instruments, and one eye on the chart. If you've noticed that this adds up to three eyes, you're catching on.

A sizeable part of the written exam is devoted to working with navigational charts: identifying what is on them, plotting courses across them, and interpreting their implications for your flight plan. Using charts is so central to what a pilot does that it's worth digging deeper into what's on them, and why. Describing a map in abstract is difficult, so I highly recommend that as you read this chapter, you go to a website like Skyvector.com and zoom in on the part of the world where you live, or at least part of the United States you're familiar with (turn off all the additional layers, leaving just the map itself).

What do you see? At first glance, it looks a lot like a topographical roadmap, with lower elevations in green and higher ones graduating to tan or brown. Built-up urban areas are shown as blocks of yellow. Large roads and highways can be seen as light gray lines but aren't nearly prominent as they would be on a roadmap. Lakes, rivers, coastlines, and railroads are readily visible, just as they might be from the air.

The most prominent features of all are the airports, depicted as blue and magenta dots sprinkled across the map. The little icons themselves convey a lot of information. Blue means the airport has a control tower (at least part of the time); magenta means it does not. A star on top means the airport has a lighted **beacon**; tick marks around the outside indicate that refueling is available. Inside most dots are small white lines showing the general direction of paved runways. For major airports with much larger runways, those lines have outgrown their dots and appear by themselves, outlined (typically) in blue.

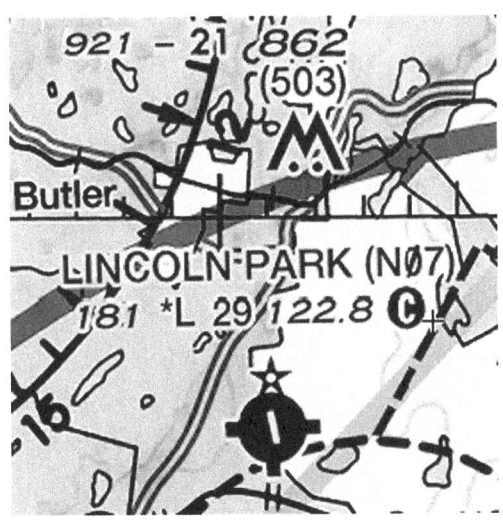

A small portion of the sectional chart showing information about Lincoln Park Airport and a few nearby obstacles.

Next to each airport are a few lines of text, giving its name, code, and a few bits of important information. Every airport has a unique code. Most have a four-letter code assigned by the **ICAO** (International Civil Aviation Organization), which may be similar but is distinct from the three-letter IATA (International Air Transport Association) airport code you see on your airline tickets and baggage tags when traveling. For instance, the ICAO code for Chicago's O'Hare airport is KORD, while the IATA code is just ORD. ICAO codes for airports in the Continental U.S. (excluding Hawaii and Alaska) always begin with K. The very smallest airports don't have an ICAO code and are assigned an ID by the FAA, typically a combination of three to four numbers and letters. Lincoln Park's code is N07.

The first number on the second line shows the airport's elevation. For Lincoln Park, this is 181 feet above sea level. An "*L" indicates the airport has runway lights for night operations, but with some limitations that you might need to research beforehand. The next number shows the length of the longest runway in hundreds of feet—in this case 2,900 feet. Finally, 122.8 is the Common Traffic Advisory Frequency, or **CTAF**, the designated frequency for aircraft to communicate with each other directly, in the absence of ATC. Other airports might include additional frequencies for talking to the control tower or getting the weather report. Say you suddenly had to divert to an airport you aren't familiar with; all this information is immediately at your fingertips, right next to it on the sectional chart.

Take a step back now and look at the bigger picture. The entire sectional chart is divided by thin black lines of **latitude** (running horizontally east and west) and **longitude** (running vertically north and south). Between them, they appear to form perfectly square boxes, but this isn't exactly the case. The horizontal bands of latitude are exactly parallel to each other and represent regular angular intervals from 0° at the equator to 90° at the North or South Poles, forming ever-smaller rings as they get closer to those poles. On the sectional chart, each line of latitude signifies half a degree. Between them, along the vertical lines of longitude, are 30 tick marks that each signify a "minute" of latitude (for a total of 60 minutes for every degree).

Because the earth isn't perfectly round, the length of each minute of latitude—the distance between each tick mark, north and south—isn't exactly

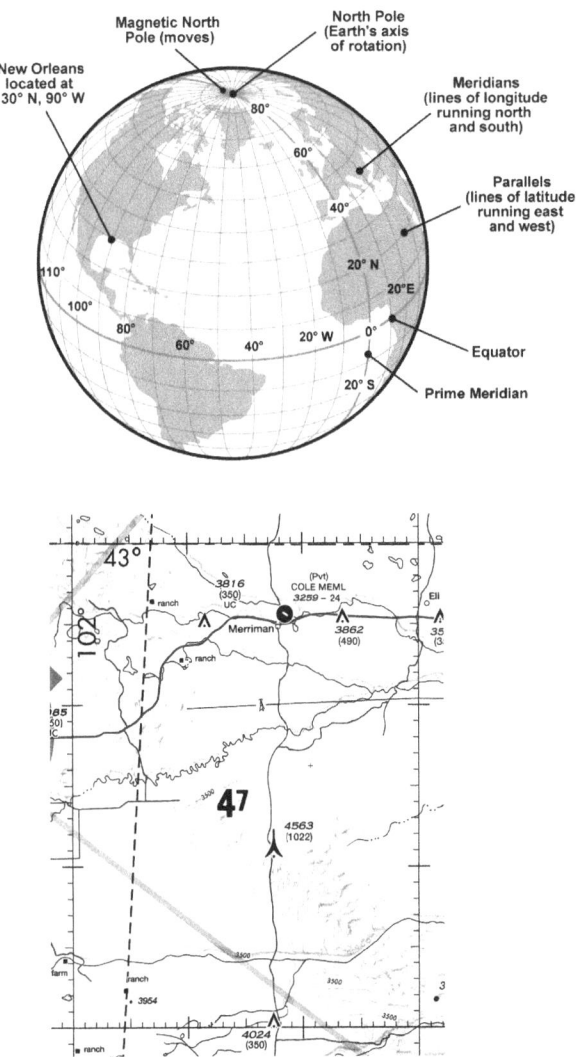

Lines of latitude and longitude as they appear on the globe (top) and the sectional chart (bottom). The number "47" at the box's center indicates that the highest obstacle inside that box is 4,700 feet MSL.

the same, but it's very close.[106] The agreed standard is 6,076 feet.[107] *This is the definition of a nautical mile.* Sixty nautical miles equals one degree of latitude, or 1/90th of the distance from the equator to the pole. The fact that nautical miles and knots derive directly from the dimension of the earth itself is why both ships and aircraft use them to measure distance and speed when navigating across that globe, as opposed to more arbitrary man-made measurements like statute miles or kilometers.[108] And the fact that each tick mark of latitude, north or south, equals a nautical mile means that, if needed, you can measure distance solely by reference to the chart itself.

Lines of longitude are a bit different. Rather than forming rings parallel to the equator, they radiate from the poles, in a 360° circle, dividing the earth into slices, like the wedges of an orange. Alternatively, you could see the equator as a circle divided into 360°, with lines of longitude running from it to converge at both the North and South Poles. The line running through Greenwich, England is defined arbitrarily as the starting point, or Prime Meridian (0°). Lines of longitude west of it are designated as 0-180°West, all the way to the other side of the world, while lines of longitude east of there are designated 0–180°East, all the way around to the same point.

Just like latitude, each line of longitude on the sectional chart signifies half a degree. And the 30 tick marks between them, along the horizontal lines of latitude, similarly signify minutes. But while lines of longitude are equidistant from each other, they are not parallel. The distance between them narrows as they converge at the poles and widens as they move towards the equator. As a result, a minute of longitude—the tick marks running east and west—can be of variable distance, and does not equal a nautical mile.

Any spot on Earth can be identified and located by reference to degree, minutes, and—if necessary—seconds of latitude and longitude. For instance, the Great Pyramid of Giza stands at 29°58′45″N 31°08′03″E, while the ruins of Machu Picchu are located at 13°9′48″S 72°32′44″W. Because of the curvature of the earth, the shortest distance between them, when depicted on a flat surface, isn't defined by a straight line but by an arc. For much shorter journeys—the kind a student in a Cessna 172 might be taking—the difference is hardly noticeable, and we typically just draw a straight path between two locations on the same sectional chart.

One of the most important things to know, whether planning a flight or in the air, is the elevation of the ground and any obstacles in the area. Besides the chart's color shading, the elevation of nearby airports provides some clue, along with the pinpoint height given for some hills. The chart also highlights certain hazards, like radio transmission towers, that could pose a danger to aircraft. For instance, just north of Lincoln Park, the chart shows two overlapping, inverted Vs—most likely cell phone towers. The smaller number above them, in parenthesis, shows that this group of obstacles rises 503 feet above ground level (AGL). The larger number, without parenthesis, indicates this is equivalent to 862 feet MSL. As long as you fly above that altitude—ideally with some room to spare—you should safely avoid them.

There's another way to make sure you're in the clear, at a very quick glance. Each "box" formed by the chart's lines of latitude and longitude features a large blue number near its center. The one closest to Lincoln Park, for instance, says "20." This means that, for this entire sector, the highest any terrain or obstacle reaches is 2,000 feet MSL. For pilots planning a safe cruising altitude, or encountering poor visibility, knowing this "floor" can be extremely helpful.

What is a safe altitude? The general principle is that you should be high enough to make an emergency landing if the engine fails—a particular concern if you are crossing over a body of water. It's instinctive to fear heights, but in an airplane, altitude is normally your friend. The higher you are, the more time you have to respond to a situation before hitting the ground, and the farther you can glide to a safe landing spot. At the very least, you need to stay well clear of any tall objects like hilltops, buildings, or towers. Over a congested area—including those yellow areas on the chart—the rule is to stay 1,000 feet above the tallest obstacle within a 2,000 feet radius of the aircraft, unless making an approach to land. Elsewhere, the rule is to stay at least 500 feet AGL, and in no event closer than 500 feet to any person, vehicle, or structure—including boats on the water.

Terrain and obstacle awareness is no joke. While many accidents happen when pilots lose control of their aircraft, like in a low-level stall or unrecoverable spin, according to the FAA about 40 each year—about half of them fatal—involve pilots flying straight into something on the ground. The term for this is **Controlled Flight into Terrain (CFIT)**.[109] You might think this would mostly occur at night or in poor-visibility conditions, but all too many collisions occur on clear sunny days. Typical culprits include high-voltage electrical wires or thin antenna towers, which can be difficult to see until it's too late. Sometimes pilots are just carelessly flying too low; other times they simply forget about an obstacle in the vicinity, especially on takeoff or landing, or get pushed into it unexpectedly by a strong tailwind or crosswind. It usually boils down to lack of situational awareness, which often has its roots in lack of preparation.

Perhaps the most unfamiliar and confusing aspect of the sectional chart, for new students, is its depiction of airspace. All around the various airports you will see lines—some of them straight, others curved, some blue, some magenta, some solid, some shaded, others dashed. The larger, busier, and closer the airports, the more cluttered and confusing it can seem. Two-digit numbers appear scattered everywhere. It looks like a code only the fully initiated can read.

Well, let me initiate you. It's not really as complicated as it first seems. There are seven main types of airspace, A through G, often referred to by their names in the phonetic alphabet (Alpha, Bravo, etc.). But it basically boils down to this: Class A stands for high in the Air, Class G stands for close to the Ground; there are three kinds of towered airports, large (Class B), medium (Class C), and small (Class D); and Class E stands for Everything Else. Each category of airspace has its own rules and regulations, with A being the most restrictive and G the least.

One thing that's vital to understand is that the chart is like the blueprint of a building. While it depicts airspace in a flat two dimensions, that space really exists in 3-D with floors and ceilings as well as walls.

That's why Class A (Alpha) doesn't appear at all on the sectional chart. I've already mentioned it before: it's everything above 18,000 feet MSL up to Flight Level 600 (a reading of 60,000 feet at a standard setting of 29.92 in/Hg). This is where the airliners and executive jets cruise, and it requires IFR clearance—and an instrument rating—to fly in. As a beginning pilot, I won't

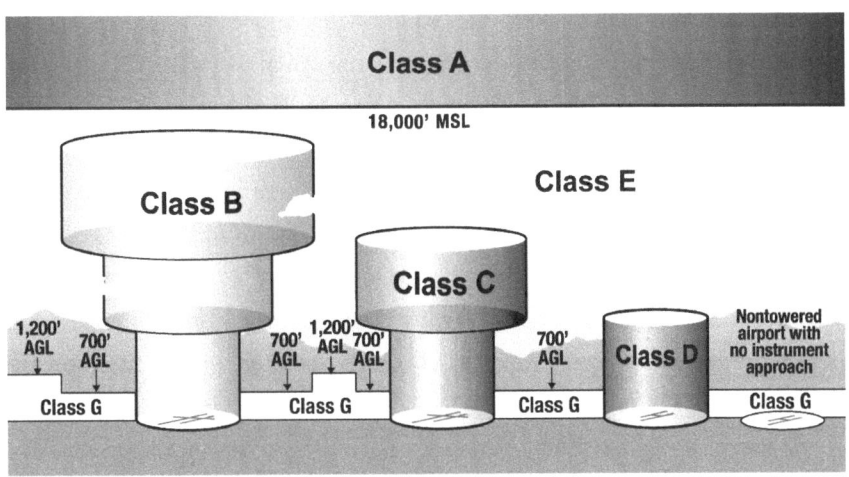

Classes of airspace and their typical arrangement (not to scale).

be going there, I just need to know it's up there.

The largest airports in the country—think JFK or LAX—are surrounded by Class B (Bravo) airspace. In its simplest form, on the sectional chart, this looks like a series of three to four solid blue concentric rings around the airport itself. Figure 7 shows an example: New Orleans' Louis Armstrong International Airport (KMSY). In fact, these "rings" are really layers, arranged like an upside-down wedding cake. The innermost ring starts at the surface and might top off as high as 10,000 feet AGL. The next ring starts a little higher—at perhaps 2,000 feet AGL—up to the same ceiling. The next begins a bit higher, and so on. Aircraft can fly above the ceiling *or below* any of these "shelves" without entering the highly restricted Bravo. What they can't do is avoid the thin, solid magenta circle 30nm from the airport in all directions called the **Mode C Veil**, which requires all aircraft inside it to use an altitude-transmitting transponder (and now, ADS-B Out as well), for Air Traffic Control to track.

In reality, every Bravo airspace is different, with slices taken out of it, added, raised, or lowered to reflect the surrounding terrain and approach paths. The result, on the chart, often looks less like a neat set of rings and more like the jumbled outline of stained-glass window. Each piece is bordered in solid blue and has two numbers inside, one over the other, like a fraction. The top number shows the ceiling in hundreds of feet MSL, the lower one the floor. For instance, 70/30 means that particular slice of Bravo airspace starts at 3,000 feet MSL and goes up to 7,000 feet. Note that while these floors and ceilings are determined by AGL (height above the ground) they are shown on the chart in MSL (altitude above sea level) so pilots can compare them directly to their altimeters to know where they stand. It's one more reason to make sure the altimeter is set to the correct barometer reading based on the airport's latest weather report.

If you're flying anywhere near a Class B airport, you need to know the dimensions of each piece of the Bravo you might encounter, or at least be able to refer to it quickly. For instance, Lincoln Park is located under an outer ring of Newark's Bravo that starts at 3,000 feet MSL. Departing to the north, towards the Onion Fields, we had to level off with the altimeter at 2,500 feet until we were clear of it, before resuming our climb. Heading south, we had to stay below 3,000 feet while avoiding the edge of the next closer ring that begins at just 1,800.

Medium-size regional airports like Albany (KALB) or Des Moines (KDSM) aren't as busy, so their Class C airspace is simpler and less restrictive. It also looks like an upside-down wedding cake, but with just two layers, up to about 4,000 feet AGL. The larger top layer, which has a radius of 10nm, only goes down to around 1,200 feet AGL. The inner core, which has a radius of 5nm, goes down to the surface. On the chart this looks like two concentric rings outlined in solid magenta instead of blue. As with Class B, numbers translate these floors and ceilings into MSL for pilot reference. Unlike most Bravos, the top of the Charlie is often low enough even for smaller airplanes to fly over it entirely, at a normal cruising altitude, but they must have a transponder and ADS-B Out to fly either in or over it. Fresno Yosemite Int'l (KFAT), near the top of Figure 8, offers a good example of Class C airspace.

The airspace at Class D airports—smaller airfields that are still busy enough to have a control tower—is simpler still. The Delta goes up to about

2,500 feet AGL and extends out 4nm. Its boundaries are marked by a dashed blue line, and its ceiling in hundreds of feet, translated to MSL, is printed in brackets. Lemoore Naval Air Station in the lower left corner of Figure 8 is a good example. Because its elevation is 228 feet, its ceiling is 2,700 feet MSL. Passing aircraft can easily avoid it entirely by flying over it. If they do enter the Delta, unlike a Bravo or Charlie they're not required to have a transponder or ADS-B Out, just a working radio to talk to the tower.

Sometimes Class D airports can be found nestled underneath the outer shelves of Class B or C airspace. South of Lincoln Park, Essex County (KCDW) and Morristown (KMMU) are both located right underneath the Newark Bravo, which starts just above them at 3,000 feet MSL. For that reason, we could never fly over their Delta airspace, only through or around them.

The Class B, C, and D airspace around towered airports takes up only a relatively small portion of the sky below 18,000 feet. Outside their marked boundaries, most of the airspace is Class E, with Class G closer to the ground. This is the free range, where you're not expected to look to Air Traffic Control for instructions. Golf usually starts at the surface and goes up to either 700 or 1,200 feet AGL, where it gives way to Echo. There are a handful of places out west where Golf still goes all the way up to 14,500 feet MSL, but they are very few and very remote. To be honest, there isn't much practical difference between Echo and Golf, except Golf has somewhat looser VFR minimums, at least during the day.

When I first started looking at sectional charts, I was perplexed by the shaded magenta bands—some circles, other forming irregular shapes—that seemed to stretch across every part of the map. You can see several of them in Figure 8. They were so prominent I figured they must mean something important. In fact, all they signify is this: inside the bands, closer to various airports, Golf airspace only goes up to 700 feet AGL, while outside of them, it goes to 1,200. The lower threshold, with its slightly stricter VFR minimums, is there to provide more safety margin for aircraft doing instrument approaches. At some non-towered airports, Echo airspace goes all the way down to the surface for this same reason, and this is indicated by a dashed magenta line or circle. Visalia (KVIS) in the bottom right corner of Figure 8 is a good example of this. For a pilot flying VFR in good visibility, these boundaries between Echo and Golf airspace are of no real significance.

There are two other types of "special use" airspace that appear frequently on charts and merit an explanation. In Figure 8, in the lower left and the far right, you can see some irregularly shaped boxes bordered by magenta line with hatch marks on the inside. These are **Military Operations Areas (MOAs)**. You don't require any permission to fly through them, but you do need to be alert that encountering fast-moving aircraft is a real possibility and keep a sharp eye out for them. One time when I was driving across the remote Scottish Highlands, I got buzzed out of nowhere by two RAF Tornado fighter-bombers on practice maneuvers, about 50 feet overhead. I thought the world was ending and nearly drove off the road. You wouldn't want a jolt like that while flying along in your Cessna.

If the hatched lines were blue instead, that would make it a **Restricted Area**. If it's active (and sometimes they aren't), you need explicit clearance to enter because there could be missile testing, artillery firing, or a sensitive military installation. Details on each MOA and Restricted Area that appear on a chart—such as floors, ceilings, and when they are active—can be found on its margins.

I'll talk more about the rules and procedures for flying in different types of airspace—particularly around towered airports—when I actually encounter them in my lessons. For now, I just want to explain what you're seeing on the chart.

In the last chapter I described what VORs and Victor airways look like on the VFR sectional chart. Pilots flying IFR use a different set of charts, where these and other instrument-based waypoints—along with the peak obstacle elevation for each sector—are featured much more prominently, against a mostly white background. After all, when flying IFR you don't really expect or need to see the ground features below you. Nor do you need to see all the airspace boundaries around airports in quite as much detail, since your flight plan has been cleared in advance and you are normally in continuous contact with ATC throughout the flight. What IFR pilots do need to carry with them, in addition to charts, are pages called **approach plates** that describe and map the procedures for landing at a given airport, based only on instruments. These sorts of materials are beyond the scope of what new student pilots learn in their initial training, but it's helpful to recognize what they are when you see them.

The sectional chart provides just enough airport information to serve in a pinch, but to plan well and operate safely, a pilot needs some additional materials on hand. The **Chart Supplement**, also known as the **Airport/Facility Directory (AFD)**, is a series of small books published and regularly updated by the FAA that presents detailed information on all airports in a given region, including runway lighting, services available, contact numbers, and a small sketch of the runways and general layout. A full-page **taxi diagram** of the airport—with each **taxiway** labeled by name—can be downloaded from the FAA's website for free and is considered essential to have on hand in the

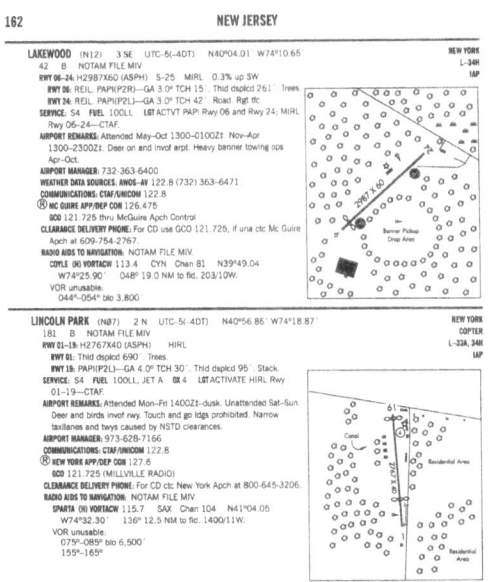 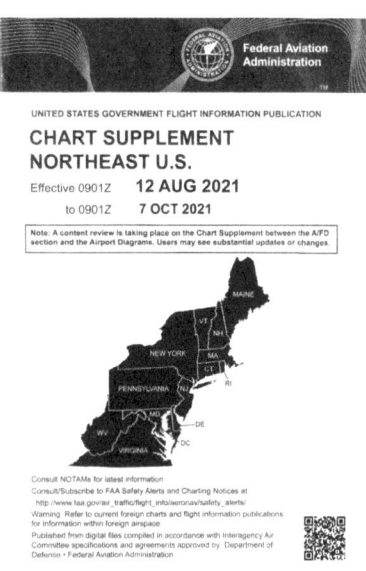

An example of airport information provided in the Chart Supplement.

cockpit for both departure and arrival. At Lincoln Park, we had only one taxiway, which ran beside our only runway, but at airports that are only modestly larger, it's all too easy to get confused and go the wrong way.

Navigating on the ground can be as complicated, and require as much attention, as navigating in the air. The most important reason to use a taxi diagram—and why many instructors insist on it—is to avoid a **runway incursion**. That's when a plane enters or crosses a runway either without clearance from the tower, or—at a non-towered airport—without taking due care and alerting other aircraft over the CTAF (common frequency). Sometimes the pilot misunderstands ATC's instructions or doesn't ask for clarification. Sometimes they try to remember complicated taxi instructions instead of writing them down. Having a taxi diagram and drawing out your planned route can avoid confusion and mistakes. It can highlight when the planned route crosses another active runway, so you can confirm whether you have clearance to cross it or need to hold short and await permission. Many taxi diagrams draw attention to "hot spots" where collisions or incursions have occurred in the past, to be extra wary of. Of course, you don't want to have your head so buried in the diagram that you forget to look outside and see what's happening around you.

Between one or more sectional charts, multiple taxi diagrams, a flight plan, and a Chart Supplement booklet, that's a lot of paper in the cockpit. A cluttered cockpit can become a real hazard in itself. If you've ever tried to unfold or refold a map while driving, imagine trying to do it while flying a plane—in the daytime, much less the night. Drop a piece of paper or pen and go rummaging around the rudder pedals for it? It's been known to happen. Even Lindbergh nearly had his map flutter out the window of the *Spirit of St. Louis*, when the wind grabbed it off his lap over Nova Scotia.[110]

You can begin to appreciate, perhaps, how helpful an app that places all of this information onto a single iPad screen can be. An **"electronic flight bag" (EFB)** like *ForeFlight* not only reduces the sheer bulk of material you have to lug onboard, it lets you manipulate them with a swipe of the finger. *ForeFlight* can even pinpoint where you are on the airport's taxi diagram when

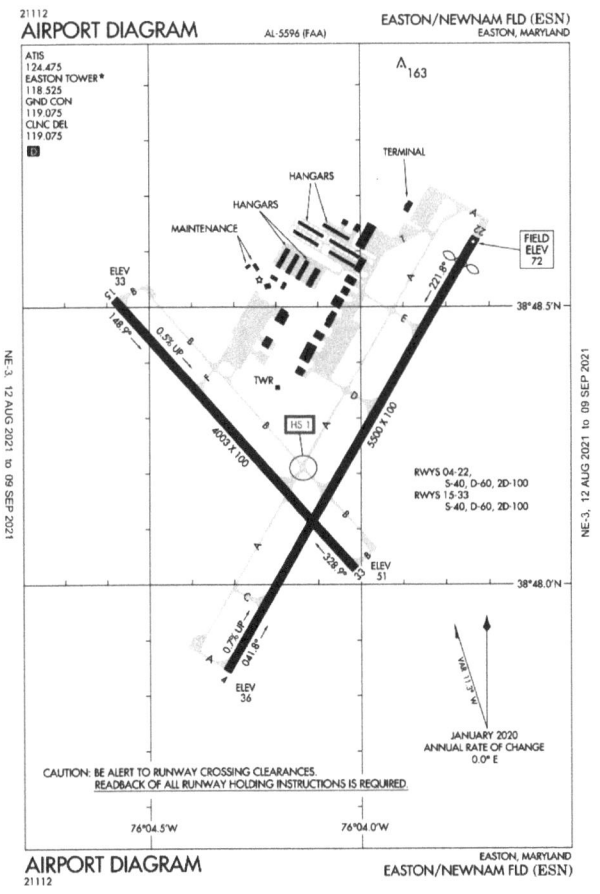

An example of an airport taxi diagram.

you have it open. Accessing all this information on a small screen can take some getting used to, and it's still advisable to carry some paper backup in case the battery runs out or your iPad overheats. But more and more pilots—amateurs and professionals—are deciding it's the way to go.

If you want to learn to fly, it helps to love maps. Time spent learning to read and understand them is time saved in the cockpit scratching your head while under pressure. But as much as a sectional chart can tell you about your planned route, it can only offer a static picture. And many of the conditions you'll face on that route are anything but static—especially the weather.

CHAPTER 11

Weather

Most of the map overlays on *ForeFlight* relate to weather, and for good reason. Aviators sail through the air much as mariners sail across the sea and are subject to the same forces of nature. Before I learned to fly, I never truly appreciated just what a central role weather plays in aviation.

We all get annoyed, and maybe even roll our eyes in skepticism, when an airline flight gets delayed or canceled due to "bad weather." It just seems hard to believe that a little wind or rain could get in the way of such a massive, modern machine. But adjusting to weather—and avoiding unsafe weather hazards—remains a critical aspect of every flight. For smaller planes, it's even more important. As my flying lessons progressed, I grew used to waking up to find my session that day canceled due to high winds, low clouds, or freezing conditions. I soon learned to schedule three lessons each week in the hope that just one might pan out, and eagerly scan the weather forecasts for clues as to whether we could fly.

How weather works and where to find out about it are topics that make up a sizeable part of the written exam. Studying for it didn't turn me into a meteorologist, but I'll try to sum up the most important things I learned. Then in the next chapter, I'll share an experience—fortunately a "virtual" one in the sim—that drove home some of the less obvious risks that weather can pose.

Our weather comes from the sun. Light from the sun warms the earth, air, and water, but it doesn't do it evenly, and the uneven distribution of heat drives movement. A good example of this is coastal breezes.[111] The earth heats and cools faster than water; as a result, water is always playing catch-up. In the morning, the sun's rays warm the earth, and the earth in turn warms the air above it. That warming air expands and rises, leaving an area of lower pressure over the land. Meanwhile, the air above the water, just offshore, remains cooler and denser for some time, resulting in relatively higher pressure. The difference in pressure causes the air near the surface to blow from the ocean onto the shore (a "sea breeze"). Later, after sunset, the land rapidly cools. The air above it cools as well and, becoming denser, sinks to form an area of higher pressure. In contrast, the water holds on longer to the heat it gradually absorbed through the course of the day. The air above it remains warmer and less dense—an area of lower pressure. The air near the surface, always flowing from high pressure to low, now blows from the shore out to sea (a "land breeze").

Coastal breezes and similar weather cycles can be localized occurrences. But whether it's hot or cold, sunny or rainy can depend on weather systems that span the continent. Much like along the coast but on a far larger scale, huge bodies of air called **air masses**, often spanning many hundreds of miles, are affected by and take on the qualities of the land or water beneath them. The air mass that forms over an arctic tundra will be cold and dry. One that forms over a tropical sea will be warm and moist.

The character of these air masses themselves, and the boundaries between them, create areas of higher and lower air pressure. Gradations in pressure are shown on weather maps by curvy lines called **isobars**. Just as contour lines on a topographical map connect points of equal elevation, isobars connect points of equal air pressure. Air flows from high pressure to low pressure, and the closer the isobars—the steeper the differences in pressure—the faster it moves. Because of the inertia caused by the earth's rotation, however, it doesn't follow a straight line. The **Coriolis force**—the same momentum that supposedly makes water swirl down a drain in Australia in the opposite direction it does in the U.S.[112]—causes the air flowing from a center of high pressure in the northern hemisphere to rotate around it in a clockwise direction, or what is called an anti-cyclone. That means the air flowing into a low-pressure area rotates around it in counterclockwise direction, or a **cyclone**. These directions are reversed in the southern hemisphere (hence the legend of the drain, accurate or not).

Water is constantly evaporating into the atmosphere. The warmer the air is, the more moisture it can contain in the invisible, gaseous form of water vapor. When air cools, that capacity is reduced, and any excess moisture will **condense** out and become visible as tiny droplets of mist to form either dew, fog, or clouds. As more and more water vapor condenses, the droplets in suspended clouds become larger and heavier until they fall to earth as rain. The more moisture the air is carrying, the higher the temperature at which its carrying capacity will be exceeded, called the **dew point**. If the air temperature is close to its dew point, you know that just a small drop in temperature—either on the surface or as you go up in altitude—will push the **relative humidity** over 100% and begin wringing water droplets from the air.

Now we can start to see the implications for those air masses whirling around, moving from high pressure to low. The denser (and often colder) air in a high-pressure zone sinks and spreads outward, meeting no resistance. There is nothing to force it upward or cause any moisture in it to condense. An area of high pressure, as a result, will typically enjoy clear skies.

In contrast, all the air being sucked into a low-pressure zone causes different air masses to converge, forming **fronts**—a term invented during World War I by meteorologists envisioning cold and warm air masses clashing like armies and battling it out.[113] If there's a cold air mass to the north and a warmer air mass to the south, the winds swirling around the low-pressure center will create a surge of southward advancing cold air—a cold front—

along a line to the west, and a surge of northward advancing warm air—a warm front—along a line to the east. Various fronts often radiate like this, counterclockwise, around a low-pressure zone. And just like when enemy armies meet, they create a lot of action.

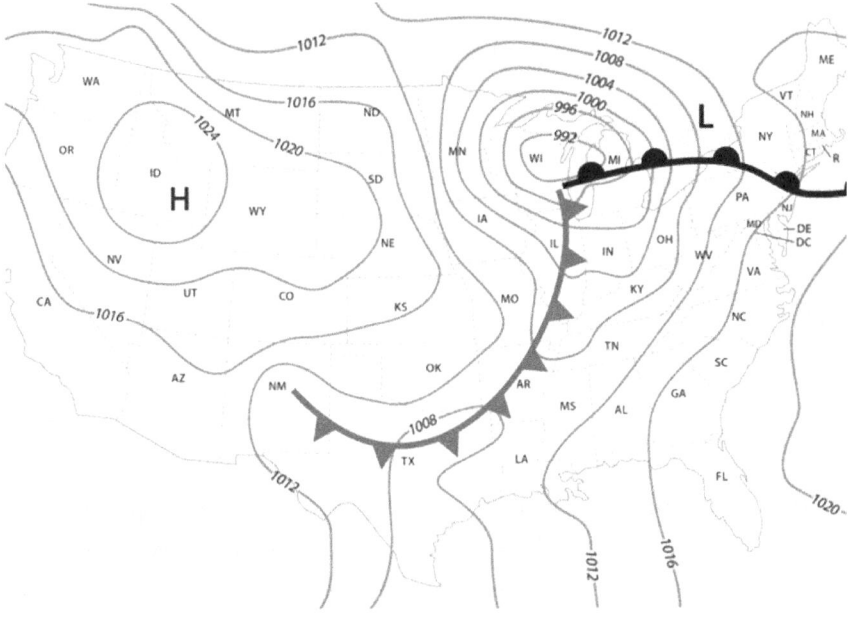

In this weather map, the wavy "contour lines" are isobars, showing lines of similar air pressure. Note the high-pressure area over Idaho, and the low-pressure area over Wisconsin. The thicker spiked line is a cold front, while the thicker bumped line is a warm front. Both are moving in a counterclockwise direction around the low-pressure area. The closer the isobars are, the stronger the wind is likely to be.

The advancing air in a warm front will tend to slide over the colder, denser air it is overtaking. As it rises fairly gently, it will cool and the moisture it carries will condense into clouds, which can often produce showery rain. The advancing air in a cold front typically moves twice as fast, because of the greater pressure difference, and drives a wedge *below* the warmer, less dense air it's overtaking, forcing that warm air rapidly upward. The stage is set for an intense thunderstorm.

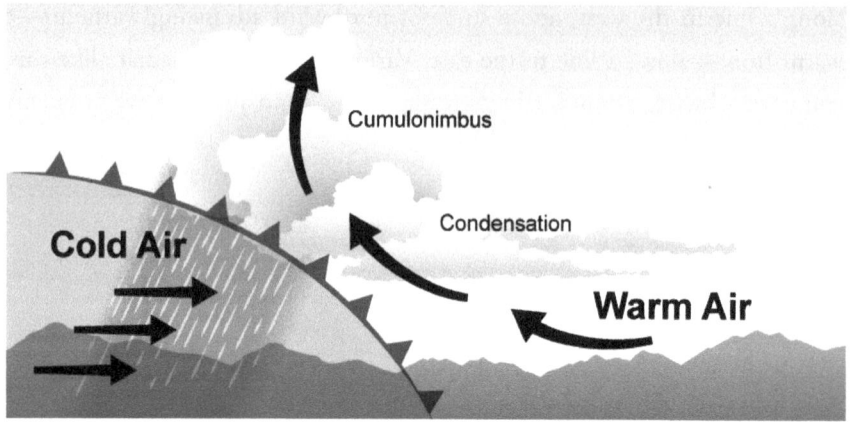

The formation of a line of thunderstorms, as an advancing cold front pushes warmer, moister air upwards where it condenses.

A thunderstorm may be awe-inspiring, even a bit refreshing, from the ground, but it presents major hazards to aircraft. It is produced by the rapid uplift of moist air, forming billowing clouds that can ultimately tower up to 40,000 feet in the sky. Eventually all this condensing moisture begins to fall as heavy rain, accompanied by strong downdrafts of air. The rapidly rising and falling air generates electrical charges that take the form of lightning and thunder. The main threat to aircraft isn't bolts of lightning, however, it's the turbulence and **wind shear** (sharp changes in wind direction and speed) that can surround the thunderstorm for many miles in each direction. Inside the storm cloud itself, it's not unusual for an airplane to be thrown higher by an updraft, only to get hammered down by a severe downdraft, causing it to gain and then lose thousands of feet in altitude in a few seconds. One particularly dangerous phenomenon are **microbursts**, strong downdrafts that, when they hit the ground, spread off in every direction. Approaching a microburst, a plane might encounter a 20-knot headwind, which suddenly transforms into a 20-knot tailwind as it reaches the other side, resulting in a 40-knot drop in airspeed. A plane encountering this while flying low and slow on final approach could easily stall out and crash. The strong updrafts in a thunderstorm can also cause rising moisture to freeze into golf-ball size chunks of ice, called **hail**, which then fall to earth and do serious damage to aircraft in their way. Airliners can often avoid all but the very tallest thunderstorms by flying above them, but smaller and lower-flying aircraft don't have that option.

You can often anticipate what kind of conditions you'll encounter in the air by taking note of the clouds. White, fluffy cotton-ball type clouds, called **cumulus**, are a sign of unstable conditions, with air rising and falling and churning about. They could be the precursor of coming thunderstorms, but more frequently indicate bumpier air along with good visibility. Flatter, featureless sheets of **stratus** clouds, on the other hand, are a sign of stable conditions with little vertical air movement, which means a smoother flight but also poorer visibility. One possible reason for stable air could be a **temperature inversion**. Normally air temperature falls as you go up in altitude, but a layer of warmer air aloft can trap cooler air below, along with tiny particles of pollution, creating a thick blanket of haze. Sometimes when you're flying above an inversion, you can see a clear line between the hazy layer below and the clearer air above, like oil and water refusing to mix. Although each air layer itself is smooth and stable, pilots have to beware of possible wind shear when climbing or descending from one to the other.

A more localized hazard to pilots is **fog**. Fog is just a cloud that forms close to the ground, and the key is always dew point: either the air temperature falls to the dew point, or moisture gets added to the air and raises the dew point to the air temperature. For instance, take the most common type, called radiation fog. Overnight, the ground radiates away the heat gained during the day, and the cooler ground cools the air just above it. That air would normally circulate, but if there is hardly any wind, or the area is sheltered from wind (such as in a valley), the cooling will be concentrated and any moisture will condense into either dew or fog. When the sun rises, the ground and the air next to it will eventually warm up, causing the fog to "burn off."

A very similar thing happens with advection fog, when wind blows air from a warmer surface (such as a lake) onto a colder one (the nearby shore), cooling it to below its dew point; in this case, fog will keep being generated until the wind subsides. In upslope fog, wind blows air up the side of a mountain slope, causing it to cool as it rises and creating clouds that cling to—and possibly obscure—the higher terrain. Steam fog, the curling wisps you can sometimes see over a lake or river, is produced when warmer water evaporates into the air above it. The additional moisture raises its dew point to meet the air temperature. Precipitation or frontal fog works the same way, except the additional moisture comes from evaporating rainfall being added to the air. Ice fog takes place when even tiny amounts of moisture are added to extremely cold air, causing it to condense out into ice crystals suspended in the freezing air.

One reason fog is so dangerous to pilots is that it can be deceptive. Viewed from above, you can easily see through the thin layer to the ground. Come down to land, and you start looking through the fog crossways, making it much thicker and impossible to see. Fog often forms at night, which can make it hard to know it's even there, blocking your view. (I came to appreciate this from the times I set *Microsoft Flight Simulator* to real-time weather at night, then altered the time setting to daytime, revealing all the hidden fog banks hugging the ground.) These dangers are why, though somewhat tedious, it's important for pilots to be able to identify all the different circumstances that can cause fog to form, and why dew point—which I certainly never heard of before—plays a prominent role in all aviation weather reports.

The formation of ice on the airplane's surfaces in cold weather conditions is another major hazard, which I'll go into in more detail next chapter.

So now that we know what to look for, where do we find the weather information we need? The traditional answer, when preparing for a flight, is to call for an official weather briefing. In the U.S., calling 1-800-WX-BRIEF and providing your location will direct you to the local Flight Service Station (FSS), an air traffic facility run by Leidos, a company contracted by the FAA. You give them your aircraft type, time of departure, route, and cruise speed and altitude, and the live agent provides you with a personalized run-down of all the various weather information relevant to your flight. If you call within six hours of departure, you can request a Standard, comprehensive briefing;

prior to that, they can give you a heads-up Outlook Briefing that you will then need to update before departing. You can call anytime for an Abbreviated Briefing that either serves to update the first one or clarify specific questions you have.

You can also go to www.1800wxbrief.com to get a computer-generated briefing instead, which can be read online or printed out. I personally like this better because I don't have to worry about writing down everything the live briefer is saying, which can be a lot. If there's anything I don't understand, or need more information on, I can always call up the phone number for an Abbreviated Briefing as a follow-up. Besides its map overlays, *ForeFlight* also has the ability to prepare a weather briefing—in many ways more graphically sophisticated than the online FSS one—based on the flight plan you've already built in it.

A printed weather briefing can be quite lengthy; the one I generated for my checkride ran to some 60 pages. It typically includes weather maps much like those you might see on the TV news, depicting the broader weather systems at work; current condition reports (**METARs**) and forecasts (**TAFs**) specific to each airport along the planned route; an evaluation whether or not the route is flyable by VFR; the **Winds Aloft** data for various altitudes en route; **AIRMETs**, warnings issued by weather authorities about possible low clouds, turbulence, or icing in certain locations; **SIGMETs** warning of more severe weather conditions including thunderstorms, sand or dust storms, or volcanic ash; and any recent **PIREPs**, reports from other pilots actually encountering such conditions in-flight. While they technically aren't weather, the briefing also includes **NOTAMs,** notices of relevant runway or taxiway closures, as well as **Temporary Flight Restrictions (TFRs)** due to special events such as sporting events, rocket launches, military exercises, or visiting VIPs.

Some of these items can appear in abbreviated code. While apps like *ForeFlight* automatically translate them into plain English, students taking the written exam are expected to be able to decipher them and tell whether the conditions they indicate are VFR or IFR. METARs, for instance, are snapshots of current weather at an airport that are issued hourly, usually just before the hour. Here is an example:

KORD 132051Z 13009KT 10SM BKN036 OVC050 17/15 A2989

This says that at Chicago O'Hare Airport, on the 13th of the month at 2051 Zulu (3:51 p.m. local time), winds are from 130° (southeast) at nine knots, and visibility is 10 miles or more, with a layer of broken clouds (covering more than half of the sky) at 3,600 feet above ground, and another layer of overcast clouds (covering the entire sky) at 5,000. The temperature is 17°C and the dew point is close behind at 15°. The altimeter setting for air pressure is 29.89. Since the cloud ceiling is above 1,000 feet and visibility is greater than three miles, these are VFR conditions, though the narrow spread between the temperature and dew point should alert you to the possibility of fog as the evening air cools.

All official times in aviation, including in weather reports, are given in **Zulu time**, or **UTC** (Coordinated Universal Time)—otherwise known as Greenwich Mean Time (GMT) —to avoid confusion as airplanes cross from one time zone into another. That in itself can be confusing, at least to new pilots, since recalling what time it is in London is hardly intuitive at first. Where I was flying, in New Jersey, it meant subtracting five hours (or four during daylight savings) to get the local time.

TAFs (Terminal Aerodrome Forecasts) are weather forecasts for the next 24 to 30 hours, issued four times a day (at 0000, 0600, 1200, and 1800 Zulu time). They and PIREPs (pilot reports of weather) are published using similar—though not identical—codes as METARs, which you must be able to interpret. Here's a PIREP:

PWM UA /OV RKD260020/TM 2257/FL060/TP C402/TB LGT CHOP

It's for the area near Portland International Jetport in Maine, and UA means it's routine, not urgent. The pilot of a twin-engine Cessna 402 reports that at 2257 Zulu (6:57 p.m. local time) he encountered light chopping turbulence (a kind of rhythmic bumping, with no change in altitude) at 6,000 feet. The exact location was 20 miles west of KRKD (Knox County Regional Airport) on a bearing of 260°. As long as you know what each section of the code is supposed to be about, it's not hard to read, but it does take some practice.

Many of the items in the weather briefing feed directly into the flight planning calculations I described in Chapter 9. They might prompt you to revise your plan for greater comfort, speed, or safety—or decide against taking off altogether. Most of this information can be found independently, either in *ForeFlight* or online, but receiving a complete weather report ensures that nothing gets overlooked.

After taking off, there are a number of ways to obtain updated weather information in flight. Obviously, if you have *ForeFlight* (or a similar app) and an ADS-B In receiver, it can be streamed onto your iPad. However, the most important way—one that is required if you're contacting ATC—is to tune in the **ATIS** on your secondary radio frequency (COM2). The ATIS, or Automatic Terminal Information Service, is a regularly updated recording which basically reads aloud the current weather report, or METAR, for that airport, identifies the active runway, and calls attention to any other critical information, such as runway closures. It's worth noting that unlike the Winds Aloft report, the wind direction given by the METAR and ATIS is magnetic, not true, which means it can be compared directly to the magnetic headings implied in the airport's runway numbers. Each ATIS update concludes with a phonetic alphabet designation from Alpha to Zulu (e.g., "inform ATC you have ATIS Information Juliet"), which you must repeat when you contact ATC so they know you have the latest weather information.

You can find the ATIS frequency next to the airport on the sectional chart. Many smaller, non-towered airports have an **AWOS** or **ASOS** instead, which is essentially the same thing except that it won't identify the active runway. This you'll have to infer from the reported wind direction and confirm by listening over the regular radio frequency to other aircraft taking off and landing.

Some of the smallest airports, like Lincoln Park, don't have any weather broadcast at all. If there's no one already in the pattern, this can make arriving there something of a guessing game. We'd listen to the ATIS at Caldwell (KCDW) a few miles to the south, expecting it might be similar, but the hilly terrain often proved that hope wrong. We would also overfly the field above the traffic pattern, trying to spot the windsock 1,500 feet below, but that could be tricky. Some airports have arrowhead-shaped tetrahedrons or T-shaped wind tees, which can be more easily spotted from the air, but we did not.

If you have serious questions or concerns about the weather, or need help navigating around it, it's possible to call up a Flight Service Station (where you got your original pre-flight briefing) while in flight. The frequency for doing this can either be found in the Chart Supplement or on *ForeFlight* at a touch of the screen. It's a bit like "phoning a friend" on *Who Wants to Be a Millionaire?* Sometimes, printed next to a VOR on the sectional chart is a frequency for contacting FSS. You can tune it in and radio your message, and they talk back to you—oddly enough—over the VOR navigational frequency. With cellphones and iPads available, hardly anyone ever does this anymore—so, of course, the examiner asked me all about it on my final checkride.

There's an old saying among pilots that it's "better to be on the ground wishing you were in the air, than in the air wishing you were on the ground." We all nod our heads in agreement but, from time to time, we all find ourselves in the latter situation. So to impress the point, let me tell you a story about my worst encounter with hazardous weather—which fortunately for me, wasn't real.

CHAPTER 12

Luck

In his book *Ferry Pilot*, Kerry McCauley relates some advice his uncle gave him when he started his flying lessons:

> *"Every pilot has two bags, an experience bag and a luck bag. When he first starts out his experience bag is empty and his luck bag is full. Every time the pilot survives doing something stupid or dangerous, he takes a little out of the luck bag and puts it in the experience bag. The trick is to fill the experience bag before the luck bag runs out."*[114]

Flying on a home flight simulator like *MSFS 2020* can be an enjoyable diversion as well as reasonably good practice, but every once in a while, things can turn downright harrowing. And when that does happen, it can leave a lasting impression that hopefully makes a difference.

As the year 2020 came to close, I had just over 12 hours of real-world flying time. In *Microsoft Flight Simulator*, though, I was close to completing my nearly 10,000 mile, 100-hour journey in a Cessna 172 around the entire Mediterranean, starting and ending in Croatia (see the map in Figure 11). In the last week of December, I flew a simulated flight from Venice over the Julian Alps to land in a snow-covered Klagenfurt in southern Austria. I'd driven the same route in real life a year earlier and wanted to see if I could spot some of the nearby sights I had visited, before recrossing this southeastern spur of the Alps into Slovenia and then back down to my original starting point.

My trek along the Po Valley in northern Italy, using real-time weather, had been mired in winter fog, often grounding me for days before I could continue. Now, just after arriving in Klagenfurt, a cold front swept in, bringing with it a major snowstorm. For several days, every time I logged on, Klagenfurt's airport was enveloped either in heavy snow flurries or a thick blanket of fog, with visibility measured in feet rather than miles. Every few hours I checked the METARs on skyvector.com for any sign of change. The colored dots on its map remained either red or purple, signifying IFR conditions at both Klagenfurt and my intended destination, Ljubljana. So near to my goal, I grew more and more impatient, but the weather wouldn't let up.

Finally, on New Year's Eve the dots changed color. Klagenfurt showed green, indicating VFR with a cloud ceiling above 3,000 feet AGL and visibility up to five miles. At first, Ljubljana was blue, indicating Marginal VFR with clouds at least above 1,000 feet AGL and visibility up to three miles, but then it turned green as well. Taking off and landing seemed possible. But what about the mountains between? *ForeFlight* did have global cloud overlays, and it looked like the clouds topped off at 8,000 feet MSL or so. It might be possible to fly "**VFR over the top**," above the mountains and the clouds—if the cloud cover was broken enough in both places to get above them, and then get back down safely again.

When I logged on, the situation looked somewhat encouraging. To the south, my intended route of travel, the clouds lay low and dark, obscuring the mountains I would need to fly over. But the clouds over Klagenfurt itself were higher, with a few reasonably large patches of blue indicating holes I could use to climb above them. The temperature, however, was -4°C on the ground. For every 1,000 feet I climbed, I could expect it to grow -2°C colder. I realized that staying clear of clouds the entire flight would be a matter of life or death, not just because of visibility but because of **icing**.

When the temperature is below freezing (0°C), any visible moisture that makes contact with the airplane's surfaces can freeze and form ice. The problem isn't necessarily the weight of the ice itself (though that can alter the aircraft's center of gravity, making it either nose- or tail-heavy), but that ice alters the shape of the aircraft's surfaces, disrupting the airflow over it. Even a modest amount of ice on the wings can reduce lift by 25 to 30% and lower the critical angle of attack—at which the plane will stall—by full eight degrees (from around 18 degrees down to 10). Ice on the propeller—which, remember, is really just a spinning wing—can significantly reduce the amount of thrust it produces. The airplane must fly at a higher speed, but is less capable of achieving that speed. At the same time, ice on the windshield and windows can obstruct visibility.

Frost has a similar effect, but its causes are somewhat different. Frost is basically dew that has condensed (often overnight) as the air cools, but under freezing conditions. During winter, my instructor Tess often found frost on our plane in the morning and had to scrape it off before we could fly. Even a small amount of frost can disrupt airflow, reducing lift, lengthening the distance needed to take off, and raising the aircraft's stall speed. If you ignore it, you can be in trouble. But once you scrape it off, the problem is solved.

Structural icing, on the other hand, can form in flight, and rather quickly. The key thing is, it requires visible moisture. Even on an extremely cold day, well below zero, you can fly safely so long as you stay clear of clouds, fog, rain, or snow. I frequently did just that during my real-life lessons through the winter, as long as there was clear weather. Even when the temperature is above zero, however, you can still encounter liquid raindrops that are supercooled from falling through freezing temperatures above and will freeze on contact with your aircraft. This is called **freezing rain** and can be extremely dangerous.

I recognized, up front, that if this were real life, I would not have departed Klagenfurt under these conditions. Flying around the local area, well below the cloud cover, would probably have been alright—I had flown in similar winter weather in my lessons over New Jersey. But flying through a hole in the clouds, then up and over the cloud-covered mountains, hoping to find another hole to land at the other end? No. Too many things would have to go just right, and too many things could easily go wrong. But this was a flight sim, and the worst thing I could injure was my pride. On that basis, I figured I'd give it a go.

Klagenfurt is already 1,500 feet above sea level and is surrounded by hills about 1,000 feet higher. So there wasn't that much room between those hilltops and the cloud ceiling looming at about 4,500 feet MSL. Nevertheless, my short trip to the north to revisit the pilgrimage church at Maria Saal, the Roman ruins on Magdalensberg, and the medieval castle at Hochosterwitz (the inspiration for Disney's Snow White Castle) was neither dangerous nor difficult. When I returned to the vicinity of Klagenfurt, the clouds over the mountains further south were still low and imposing, but a clear patch of blue sky was visible through a large break in the clouds straight to the east.

I started climbing steadily through that opening, over the River Drava and the Völkermarkt Reservoir, gradually leaning the fuel mixture to retain full power. At 7,000 feet, passing above the first layer of clouds, I began turning to the south. There was a higher layer, but plenty of space between, and it appeared to thin out ahead. However, as I came around the southwest, to rejoin my original course over the mountains, the puffy clouds below piled up higher and higher, forcing me to continue climbing to stay beyond their reach. In a short while, I was at 12,000 feet, with an air temperature of -11°C. I was clear of the clouds, but just barely, with the chilly winter sun glinting in my windshield. To give myself a margin of error, I slowly inched up another 1,000 feet to 13,000 MSL, nearing the Cessna 172's maximum operating ceiling.

At this altitude, with the fuel mixture leaned out by almost half, the power produced by its ignition with the thinning air was just enough to maintain a steady cruise. The towering Julian Alps, reaching over 8,000 feet tall but shrouded entirely from sight, were well below me. The brooding silence of the cotton-like clouds, whose very touch could freeze, was broken only by the labored humming of my single engine. Some turbulence stirred up by the mountains below shook the plane, as if to remind me that I remained in the material world. So far, so good.

The first sign of trouble was a small, crystalline tendril of ice in the corner of my windshield, reaching quietly outwards. A wave of unease spread with it, through my gut. I swear I had not touched the edge of a cloud. Could it be a glitch in the simulation? Or wisps of mist too thin for me to make out and avoid? I looked out my left and right cabin windows. Yes, there it was: a frosty film of white, beginning to form on the leading edge of both wings. I craned my (virtual) neck to look out the rear window and saw it on the tail fin and tailplanes as well.

There are two kinds of ice that form on an airplane's surface.[115] Tiny droplets of moisture freeze almost immediately, building up to form a milky white, crusty coating called **rime ice**—similar to what you might find accumulating along the inside edges of your kitchen freezer. Rime ice tends to break easily and fall off in chunks if weakened. When larger droplets such as freezing rain hit the plane, they spread out and then freeze. The result is a strong, solid sheet of **clear ice**, which is much more dangerous. While clear ice is smoother, its disruptive effect on airflow is much greater. It is also heavier, and a lot harder to weaken and remove. The ice forming on my airplane at 13,000 feet was almost certainly rime ice, but it was a still a problem.

My first response was to abandon getting back to my planned course and turn immediately south toward Ljubljana. I was already halfway across the mountains, and although I couldn't see it yet, both *ForeFlight* and the weather radar on my in-sim G1000 indicated that the skies were clear just east of my destination, only 15 nautical miles away. If the icing grew no worse, I could maintain my altitude for another 10 minutes or so, reach that clearing, and descend to safety.

Other, more sophisticated aircraft typically have some sort of anti-icing system that helps prevent or eliminate ice.[116] Most airliners, for instance, pipe hot air from their jet engines into the wing's leading edge, as well as the engine casing itself, in order to warm them and melt whatever ice has formed.

Other aircraft have expandable rubber "boots" on the leading edge of the wings and tail, which can be rapidly inflated to break the ice and knock it away. Some have tiny openings on their wings and other surfaces that squirt de-icing chemicals onto them, causing ice to melt away (you've probably also seen such chemicals being sprayed all over an airliner, perhaps as you were waiting before taking off in a winter snowstorm). The Cessna 172 has … none of these. You just have to be smart and avoid icing conditions.

I wasn't feeling very smart at that point. The minutes passed like hours, and though I couldn't see it, I could tell the ice buildup was getting worse. The airplane was slowing and had to pitch nose-up to provide more lift to maintain its altitude. Far from pulling back on the yoke, however, I had to push forward, presumably because the ice on the tail was making it heavier, or perhaps creating more negative lift. The plane was still flyable, but with a forbidding blanket of clouds still stretching out before me, time was running out.

I glanced down and suddenly noticed that the airspeed on the digital display was showing zero. Altitude and other indicators appeared to still work. I thought for a moment, then it dawned on me: aha, the pitot tube is frozen. That, at least, I could do something about. I flicked the panel switch to turn the pitot heat on, and in a few moments, the airspeed reading came back to life.

This minor victory behind me, I realized that time had run out. The nose was pitched up, the stall horn was going off, and despite all this, I was starting to lose altitude. I was going down into the clouds, like it or not, and I could only hope that all the additional moisture wouldn't turn me into a solid brick of ice on the way down. I pushed forward on the yoke as hard as I could, to get the nose down and build up speed, and plunged into a world of gray blindness.

It was like riding an out-of-control toboggan down a hill in a blizzard. Turbulence buffeted me from every direction. My children strolled in and saw me gripping the yoke tightly, eyes glued to the screen. I told them I was probably going to crash. My only hope was to control my descent to keep airspeed above stalling, while staying clear of any mountains below. Luckily, the artificial horizon on my glass cockpit panel was enhanced to show the terrain ahead, and I could see that I was following a valley down, with steep slopes on either side. According to the map in *ForeFlight*, this valley threaded its way between two of Slovenia's tallest mountains, Storžic (6,995 feet) to west and Grintovec (8,392 feet) to the east, before spilling onto the plains below, barely a mile or two from Ljubljana's airport.

The airport's elevation is 1,300 feet. As I reached the mouth of the valley, I passed 2,000 feet MSL—just 700 feet above ground—and could still see nothing. Then—at 1,900 feet—a band of gray sky appeared, just out the corner of my eye, over the trace of a darker landscape below. And even more astonishing: electric lights, in two converging rows ahead to the left. The lights of the airport runway.

I wasn't sure if I could level off in altitude, but in the denser air it seemed that I could. The temperature was just above freezing but I had no expectation that the ice on my airplane would melt quickly, if at all. I couldn't climb. I had one shot to land the plane, straight in; there would be no go-arounds.

In real life, I'd be declaring an emergency to the tower over the radio. On the sim, the quiet was unnerving. As I got closer, nose high, it became harder to see the runway through the ice obscuring my front windshield. (I later learned that turning the cabin heat on might have helped melt it, but I had barely noticed the ice was there while descending through the clouds, since I couldn't see much of anything anyway.) I planted myself over what I hoped was the runway, cut the power to idle, and hoped to touch down in one piece.

Bump … bump …

The Cessna gradually slowed to a halt, and I turned the engine off. Had it been real life, I would have gotten out of the plane and kissed the ground. As it was, I sat in front of my computer screen trembling, completely exhausted by the 15 minutes that had passed since I first noticed ice starting to form in the corner of my windshield. An inspection outside showed thick patches of ice encrusting both wings, the tail fin, and tailplanes (Figure 10). *If there is a virtual luck bag, I had just made a hefty withdrawal from it.*

What did I put back in my experience bag?

First, I learned that *weather is no joke*. Reading about it in a textbook, or even in a pre-flight briefing, weather can seem remote and abstract. As airline passengers, we've become used to flying through terrible weather, and it always seems to work out alright. Before jet airliners were introduced that could fly above most weather, however, being a passenger was a lot riskier proposition.[117] Even today, the airlines put a lot more planning into how to handle the weather than most of us realize—partly for comfort and fuel consumption, but also for safety. Winds, temperature, air pressure, and moisture affect nearly every aspect of flying, from aircraft performance to choosing a route. And as my near disaster over the Alps demonstrates, an encounter with a weather hazard such as icing can turn a routine flight into an intense brush with death in a matter of minutes. I read later that George McGovern, the Democratic nominee for President in 1972, piloted a B-24 bomber on raids across the very same mountains in World War II, and he said that between the weather and the murderous anti-aircraft fire, weather scared him more.[118]

Second lesson: *plan for the worst, not the best*. Crossing the Alps, I knew that the combination of clouds and freezing temperatures presented an icing risk. But my plan to avoid it left little or no room for error. Since this was the flight sim, I don't regret giving it a go to see what happened, but I wouldn't want to wind up where I did in real life. I thought that the clouds would top out at 8,000 feet; instead, they forced me to 13,000. That put me near the limits of the Cessna's performance, where any loss of lift or thrust due to ice would be most problematic. I hoped that I could find a clear patch to descend over my destination, and might well have done so; but I had no safe "Plan B" if anything—ice, engine trouble, mountain turbulence—forced me down sooner. I was lucky that my glass cockpit gave me a picture of the terrain below, despite being encased in the clouds, so I could follow the valley on my runaway descent. I was lucky that the weight on my tail wasn't enough to prevent me from forcing the nose down, rather than going into an unrecoverable stall. I was damn lucky I could level off in the thicker air when I finally caught sight of the runway. There was too much reliance on luck, not enough credible backup plans.

The third lesson, however, was *never give up*. Once the ice formed and began pulling me down, I could have thrown up my hands, switched off the PC, and called it all a mistake best forgotten. Instead, I used the tools at my disposal, took my best shot—and it worked. Recognizing why the airspeed indication suddenly went dead, and flipping on the pitot heat to fix it, may not seem like a landmark moment in my flying career, but it was. If I could solve one problem, maybe I could solve the rest. It reminded me of what Mark Watney, the astronaut who survived being left behind on Mars, told his students at the end of the film *The Martian*:

> *At some point, everything's gonna go south on you and you're going to say, this is it. This is how I end. Now you can either accept that, or you can get to work. That's all it is. You just begin. You do the math. You solve one problem and you solve the next one, and then the next. And if you solve enough problems, you get to come home.*[119]

It was a lesson that, before this tale is done, would help me make it home for real.

CHAPTER 13

Engine

Any pilot who wants to come home safely has to be keenly aware of their airplane's limitations. The reason my Cessna 172 could fly only so high, and no higher, on my virtual flight over the Alps comes down to its engine and how it works. When I first started my flying lessons, I admit that I tended to take the engine largely for granted and not think about it very much. After all, most of us drive cars all our lives without really understanding how the engine and its various parts function, or so much as glancing at the engine gauges. If it breaks down, for any reason, the car just rolls to a stop, and we can figure it out then. If an airplane's engine malfunctions, on the other hand, there aren't many places in the air to pull over. So it's a lot more important to appreciate the engine's limitations from the very start and be able to identify and respond to problems the moment they begin, before they grow worse.

The Cessna 172's engine is located just in front of the cabin, separated from it by the controls and instrument panel as well as a firewall. It consists of four strong metal **cylinders**, arranged on either side of a metal crankcase. Inside the cylinders are **pistons**, which are propelled forcefully downwards by a controlled explosion of fuel and air—ignited by one or more electric spark plugs—then pushed back upwards by the release of exhaust gases and the force of the opposing piston. This rapid, "reciprocating" motion up and down, back and forth, turns a crankshaft, via connecting rods, which turns the propeller in front of the engine. The number of times the propeller shaft turns each minute (between 700 and 2,700) is the engine's RPM, displayed on the tachometer. So these mini explosions are taking place between five to 23 times per second in *each* of the four cylinders. Their combined output is 180 horsepower, or the power needed to move almost 50 tons one foot in one second. (No, it's not quite like having 180 horses harnessed to the front; horses can actually pull almost 15 horsepower when working hard.[120] And of course the horsepower is not pulling the plane itself, it's spinning the propeller.)

The air to enable all this combustion comes in through a box-like opening at the bottom of the nose, where it gets filtered. The throttle, in the cockpit, controls a valve that determines how much air is allowed in. Push the throttle full in for maximum power and the valve opens wide. Pull it back to idle and the valve nearly shuts, letting in a much smaller amount of air. The amount of oxygen molecules that actually does flow in, at any given setting, depends on the outside air density: the lower the air pressure, the warmer the air, and the higher the humidity, the less oxygen gets piped into the engine.

This is the main reason the Cessna 172 and other aircraft with "naturally aspirated" engines can only fly to a limited altitude. The thinner the air, the less combustible oxygen is being fed to the engine, even if the fuel flow is adjusted to match. As the airplane climbs higher, maximum power will gradually be reduced, until there isn't enough power to produce the excess lift required to climb any higher. A supercharger—which the Cessna 172 doesn't have—is basically an air compressor that boosts the density of the air flowing into the engine, even at higher altitudes. They are often powered by a turbine turned by the engine's escaping exhaust gases, making them a **turbocharger**. Planes with turbochargers can climb to higher altitudes without losing as much power. A turbocharged piston airplane is not to be confused with a **turboprop**, which is basically a jet engine whose thrust is used to turn a propeller instead of shooting straight out the back.

At some point, either before or after reaching the engine, the incoming air will be mixed with fuel. Many older airplanes, including some Cessnas, have a **carburetor**. This device uses a narrower section of the intake tube, called a Venturi throat, to force the air through it at a faster speed. We know from Bernoulli's Principle that air moving faster has lower pressure, and that lower pressure sucks and vaporizes fuel from a feed into the airstream *before* it passes through the throttle valve. The cockpit's mixture control regulates how much fuel is available from that feed, to determine the ratio of fuel to air reaching the combustion chamber.

One potentially very serious problem is that the lower pressure of the air rushing through the Venturi throat, together with the vaporization of the fuel, causes a sharp drop in temperature, by as a much as 70°F. On a humid day, even if the outside air temperature is *well* above freezing, this sudden cooling can cause the moisture in the air to condense and freeze, forming chunks of ice that can partially or entirely block the flow of air and fuel to the engine, making it sputter and fail. One early sign of **carburetor ice** can be an unexplained drop in RPM. To solve this, the pilot can flick a switch to direct heat from the engine to the carburetor to melt and break up the ice. The engine will make all kinds of nasty noises until the ice is gone. Why not keep **carburetor heat** on all the time, then? Because warming the air flowing into the engine reduces its density, which—absent ice—we already know diminishes the engine's power.

Inside each wing of a Cessna 172 is a 28-gallon fuel tank, for a total of 56 gallons, of which 53 are usable. The engine runs on blue-tinted 100LL **avgas**, and I'll explain what that means when we get into the combustion chamber. Because the Cessna's high wings are above the engine, fuel normally flows by gravity down to the engine. If, for some insane reason, you try to fly a Cessna upside down, the engine will sputter and cut out as the fuel stops flowing (there are videos online of people trying this, because of course there are). Low-wing aircraft require a fuel pump to push fuel to the engine, but the 172 does not, though it does have an auxiliary electric fuel pump when gravity alone isn't doing the job. Occasionally, it's necessary to turn the fuel pump on while pushing the mixture knob in for a few seconds to **prime** the engine—feed a small amount of fuel into it—before starting the plane, especially in cold weather.

The fuel tanks have vents to allow air to flow in to replace expended fuel; otherwise a vacuum would form, creating suction and preventing the rest of the fuel from flowing down. When the tanks are not full, moisture in that air can gradually condense and contaminate the fuel, which is why it's important to sump each fuel tank as part of the pre-flight inspection. Since the clear water is heavier than blue-tinted avgas and they refuse to mix, the water will be resting on the bottom of the tank and can be drawn out until none is left. Otherwise, the water could reach the engine and cause it to fail.

After leaving the wing tanks, fuel flows through pipes running down both the forward and rear door posts on either side, before coming together at the fuel selector knob, on the cabin floor. Here, the pilot can select whether to draw fuel from the left tank only, the right tank only, or both at the same time (the usual choice). The fuel then proceeds past a reservoir tank and the auxiliary fuel pump to the fuel shut off valve, on the lower part of the cockpit instrument panel. Pulling this out will immediately cut off all fuel flow to the engine, in the event of a fire or other emergency. At this point, the fuel line passes through the firewall and through the fuel filter (which further screens out water and other contaminants) to be used by the engine. All of these collection points, near the belly of the airplane, must also be sumped before each flight.

Just like newer cars, the Cessna 172 I flew had a **fuel injection system** instead of a carburetor. An engine-driven pump pushes fuel through a "control unit," also called a fuel/air servo, which essentially replaces the carburetor and meters out fuel based on the pilot's throttle and mixture settings. That fuel is then introduced directly into the cylinder head, alongside the air coming from the intake and throttle. This significantly reduces the chances of the air and fuel flow freezing during flight, but can sometimes make it harder to start the engine on hot days, due to vapor lock—more an annoyance than a real danger.

The action inside the cylinder takes place in a four-step—or "four stroke"—process. First, an intake valve opens to allow fuel and air into the chamber, just as the piston is pulled down, sucking them in. Second, the piston is pushed upwards, compressing the fuel/air mixture. Third, one or more **spark plugs** ignites the compressed fuel and air, causing them to rapidly expand and push the piston downwards. Fourth, an exhaust valve opens, just as the piston pushes upwards again, expelling the burned gasses out the top of the cylinder. The process then begins again, and repeats many times per second. The opening and closing of the intake and exhaust valves is triggered by rotating bumps along the camshaft, a metal rod parallel to and turned by the piston-driven crankshaft.

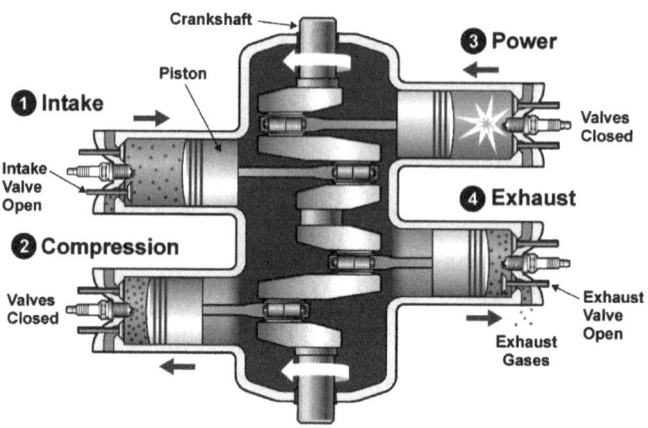

The four strokes of a piston engine.

I said "one or more" spark plugs fire, and I need to explain. Every cylinder has two spark plugs, though only one is required. Attached to the engine are two **magnetos**, little magnet-driven generators. When the propeller shaft turns, the magnets rotate, producing an electrical current. This current is what fires the spark plugs, igniting the fuel/air mixture. Each magneto is connected to its own spark plug in each of the four cylinders, so that if one of the two spark plugs fails, the engine will keep firing on the other.

Now we can understand what's happening when I do a magneto check during run-up, just before takeoff. By turning the **ignition** switch from Both to R, I ground the left magneto and disable it. The engine, now running on only the right magneto and its spark plugs, should lose no more than 150 RPM (usually more like 50). Same thing when I turn the ignition switch to L and disable the right magneto. If the engine fails, or sputters, on either setting, I know one of the magnetos isn't functioning properly. If turning the switch to R or L does not produce any reduction in RPM at all, that could spell a different problem: it's possible that one of the grounding wires isn't working. If that is the case, even when I turn the ignition off one of the magnetos could still be live. The engine could stay on, or it could restart without warning and injure someone.

The magnetos fire the spark plugs and keep the engine going when the propeller is already turning, but how does the engine start in the first place? The Cessna 172 has a 24-volt **battery**, which when the red battery switch is turned on supplies power to an electrical **starter**. When I turn the ignition switch past Both to Start, this starter begins turning the propeller. This activates the magnetos and fires the spark plugs, and—so long as fuel is being supplied for combustion—starts the engine, which now turns the propeller, and the magnetos, under its own power. The ignition switch can then be set back to Both. It is entirely possible to start a Cessna's engine without using the electric starter, by having someone hand-turn the propeller like in the old movies. When the pilot yells "Contact!" it simply means that the magnetos are live and no longer grounded, so turning the propeller could start the engine. **Hand propping** an airplane like this can be dangerous, and requires both caution and experience. It's probably smarter to just get your starter fixed.

Side by side with the red battery switch is another red switch, which turns on the **alternator**. These two switches are typically turned on or off at the same time and together are often called the **master switch**. The alternator is another kind of generator, which uses field coils instead of permanent magnets, but like the two magnetos it too is driven by the engine and produces an electrical current. It provides all the electrical power for the interior and exterior lights, pitot heat, flaps, and some gauges, and—when the white avionics switch is also turned on—to the radios, transponder, and GPS systems as well. If the engine isn't running, or the alternator is broken or turned off, these systems can still function by drawing on the battery's power, though not for long. On the other hand, when the alternator is running, part of its electrical power initially gets diverted into recharging the battery.

To the left of the yoke is an **ammeter**, which shares a dial with vacuum pressure (for running the gyroscopic instruments) and shows electrical current flowing into or out of the battery—an important thing to keep an occasional eye on. When I first get in the aircraft and turn on the master switch before starting up the engine, it will show a negative reading because I'm drawing power from the battery. Once I start the engine and the alternator is generating electricity, the gauge should initially give a positive reading, indicating that the battery is being recharged, but eventually go back to zero. If the engine is running and the ammeter still reads negative, that means the alternator isn't working and I'm still drawing power from the battery—which will eventually go dead. On the other hand, if I'm well into the flight and the ammeter still reads positive, the battery may be getting overcharged, which could cause it to catch fire or explode.

Note that in a Cessna 172, the ignition system (magnetos and spark plugs) and the electrical system (battery and alternator) are *completely independent systems*. In an automobile, they are not: its spark plugs are fired by the car's battery, which is then recharged by the engine, via the alternator. In the Cessna, they are fired by the magnetos, which are driven by the propeller turning. If the battery or alternator fail (or if I turn them off) and the rest of the plane's electrical power goes completely dead, the engine will keep *itself* running. In his book *Ferry Pilot*, Kerry McCauley tells the story of losing his alternator and eventually his battery while taking a Cessna 210 across Africa and flying all night with no radio, no GPS, and only a flashlight to read his instruments. His engine kept going, though, for 1,800 miles until he reached his destination.[121]

Back inside the cylinder's combustion chamber, the main challenge is the intense heat being generated, along with mechanical power. If the heat becomes too great and isn't dissipated, two things can happen. First, hot spots may develop within the cylinder that ignite the fuel and air too early, before the spark plug fires. This is called **preignition** and pushes down on the piston out of sync with the cycle, causing wear and damage. Second, instead of a burning smoothly, the fuel/air mixture can explode all at once, slamming the piston down too violently instead of giving it an even (if split-second) push. This **detonation**—which is the same thing as "engine knocking" in cars—can damage the pistons and even cause them to break. Depending on their severity, preignition or detonation can either take a long-term toll on the engine or destroy it in a few minutes. Regardless, at some point it will eventually give out.

The Cessna 172 relies on several methods to prevent this from happening. The first is the exhaust system, which removes a great deal of heat along with the burnt gases. The second is the fuel itself. Higher octane gasoline can withstand greater compression without detonating.[122] That's why one solution to "engine knock" in your car is to fill it with premium 91/93-octane gas at the pump instead of regular 87-octane. "100LL" avgas means 100-octane with low lead—basically a super-premium gasoline, which is why in 2021 it cost over five dollars per gallon, compared to just over three dollars for the regular gas you put in your car. The person responsible for establishing 100-octane fuel as an aviation standard was none other than Jimmy Doolittle, of instrument-flying fame, just prior to World War II. His farsighted decision gave the Allies an often-overlooked advantage, allowing their fighter planes to get better performance with less wear and tear than the 89-octane Germans or the 87-octane Japanese, despite their having equally powerful engines.[123] Jet fuel (called "Jet A"), which is also commonly sold at airports, is a kind of highly-refined kerosene.[124] It has an octane of just 15.[125] In a jet, fuel doesn't need to be compressed, just burnt. If you accidentally put jet fuel in a piston airplane, however, the engine would start but quickly begin detonating and shake itself apart.[126]

Having a **rich** fuel/air mixture—one with a slightly excessive amount of fuel that doesn't get burned—can help keep the engine cooler. It can also, however, gradually leave a buildup of lead and other gunk on the spark plug heads, interfering with ignition. On the other hand, an overly **lean** mixture—with too little fuel relative to air—can contribute to overheating. Leaning the mixture just the right amount, using the "red knob" in the cockpit, is more of an art than a science. One method is to use the **EGT** gauge, which shares a dial with fuel flow to the far left of the instrument panel and measures the temperature of the airplane's exhaust gases. As you lean out the mixture, the temperature will rise until it peaks and starts coming down again. Bring it back to peak and just a little more, so it's slightly "rich of peak."[127] Other, less precise methods involve listening to the sound of the engine (it will start to run rough when you've leaned too much) or watching the effect on RPM—though this last trick won't work with a constant speed propeller. If you want to watch a group of old pilots get into an argument, ask them whether it's better to run slightly "rich of peak" or "lean of peak," in terms of engine wear and fuel efficiency. They'll bring out their charts and theories and debate it passionately for hours.[128]

Another important factor in cooling the engine, much like in an automobile, is **oil**. Oil is kept in a sump, or pan, beneath the Cessna 172's engine, with a maximum capacity of eight quarts. The oil level must be checked as part of the pre-flight inspection, to make sure there's a minimum of five quarts to take off. When the engine is on, it drives a pump that distributes this oil to all the moving parts of the engine. The oil constantly lubricates those parts, reducing friction and the heat it generates, and also absorbs heat and carries it—along with stray particles of soot, dirt, or metal—back down to the sump. Along its route, the oil passes through a cooler where the heat can radiate away, as well as a filter that removes any contaminants it picked up.

Among the rest of the engine gauges, on the left, is a combined gauge showing **oil pressure and temperature**. In the Cessna 172, oil temperature is the main indication we have of the engine as a whole overheating, for whatever reason (some other aircraft also have a gauge for cylinder head temperature). If oil temperature is too low, it's usually because the engine has just started and needs to warm up, which can take a few minutes, prior to takeoff. If it's too high, a quick glance over to oil pressure will tell whether it's due to insufficient oil supply to the engine, perhaps because of an oil leak. If not, the best ways to reduce oil (and engine) temperature would be to reduce power, slightly enrich the mixture, and increase air flow over the engine.

That last is important because, of all the factors I've mentioned, airflow is the most important way the engine stays cool. Automobile engines are primarily liquid cooled: water or some other cooling fluid circulates through the engine via pipes, absorbs heat, and carries it back to the radiator to be released. Many early airplanes, including World War II fighters, had liquid cooled engines. The Cessna 172, in contrast, is air-cooled. Outside air enters the engine cowling via two openings on either side of the propeller, like nostrils, providing direct cooling. Of course, this works better on cold days than hot ones. Nevertheless, if the oil temperature gauge is rising, increasing airspeed—and airflow over the engine—can help. Because you want to reduce (or at least refrain from increasing) power at the same time, this normally means reducing the rate of climb, leveling off, or even descending a bit. Some higher-powered aircraft, like the Cessna 172's slightly bigger cousin the 182, have cowl flaps that must be opened on taxi, takeoff, and climb to increase airflow and keep engine temperature under control.

When aircraft do descend, it's important to keep that hot engine from cooling too quickly, however. Sudden, large reductions in power can lead to **shock cooling**: the metal parts of the engine can contract unevenly, due to the rapid temperature change, causing damage. Valves can get stuck, and cylinders and pistons can even crack. The more powerful the engine, the more thought the pilot must give to planning a gradual descent and power reduction that the engine can handle.

One of the most common things pilots encounter, from time to time, is called **running rough**. Rather than a steady, smooth sound, the engine crackles and rumbles and vibrates and coughs, though the propeller still turns. You never want to take off with the engine running rough, and it may even prompt you to abort a takeoff in progress. Often, however, the problem is caused simply by the mixture being too rich or too lean, which can be easily adjusted. It might also be due to a buildup of lead from the fuel on one or more of the sparkplugs. If you're still on the ground, revving up the engine to around 1800 RPM for a few minutes while learning the mixture can often burn the lead off. If that doesn't work, the sparkplugs may be faulty and need to be replaced.

Another possibility is a faulty magneto, making its spark plugs spark a bit out of time with the engine cycle. This can be checked by turning the ignition switch to each magneto to see if the rough-running is tied exclusively to one or the other. If that is the problem, and you're already in the air, it's possible to fly on the one good magneto until you can land and get the other one fixed. If you haven't taken off yet, no flying today: the plane needs to go to maintenance.

Despite being someone who was never mechanically inclined, I found learning about the aircraft's engine quite interesting. Dials and gauges that my eyes once glossed over took on new significance, imparting information that, if noticed, could identify trouble early so I could nip it in the bud. And at a time when people were arguing bitterly about COVID-19 and the just-finished presidential election, I found studying something stubbornly objective like how an engine works rather soothing. You can't argue with an airplane engine. It either provides the power you need to fly, or it doesn't. Facts, as they say, don't care about your feelings.

Facts were certainly piling up. Aerodynamics, navigation, weather, airplane mechanics, human physiology, rules and regulations—I knew sooner or later I would be tested on my knowledge of all of them. To become a pilot, I had to take and pass the pilot's written exam.

CHAPTER 14

Exam

If at any time you've found the material in the last few chapters tough going, like a rush of information coming at you, then you'll understand why I, like most student pilots, was in no hurry to take the private pilot written exam. Occasionally Tess asked me how my studies were going and confided that in her case, she put off taking the exam so long that her school finally put their foot down: there would be no more flying time until she took it (which she promptly did and passed). I assured her I was making progress, even though it felt sometimes like tackling a mountain.

Covering every subject I've described and more, the exam consists of 60 multiple-choice questions, with a minimum grade of 70% (a maximum of 18 wrong) required to pass. A passing score is valid for two years; if you don't pass your final checkride within that time, you need to take the written test all over again.

Most of the online ground schools, including the Sporty's course I was taking, sign off on the endorsement required to take the exam after you demonstrate you're ready by passing a couple of practice tests. To prepare, Sporty's provides a library of over 1,000 practice questions gleaned from prior exams. After completing all the instructional videos, I tried my hand at some of the test questions and quickly realized that answering many of them would require a whole new level of study effort. It's one thing to recall the definition of dew point after watching a few videos, quite another to be ready to calculate the expected base of clouds given the dew point and surface temperature.

Nothing on the written exam is actually that complicated (to find the cloud base, subtract dew point from temperature, divide by 2.5, and multiply by 1,000), there's just a lot of it. It can be hard to know where to begin, or to feel like you're making any progress. Since I wasn't on any strict timeline, I decided that I would take the test when I felt ready and not stress too much about it in the meantime. Instead, I tried to learn just one thing per day, however small. This meant not just glancing at it, but really getting it down. Monday I might memorize when you're required to pack a parachute (when you intentionally pitch up or down more than 30° or bank left or right more than 60°, unless you're doing stalls or spin training with an instructor). Tuesday I might commit the standard weight of fuel, for weight and balance calculations, to memory (six pounds per gallon). I bought the *ASA Private Pilot Test Prep* book, which was loaded with these sorts of tidbits as well as more practice questions, and started cherry-picking my way through it bit by bit.

At first there was no rhyme or reason: I grabbed discrete topics I figured would be relatively straightforward to remember and get under my belt—simple things, like the number of GPS satellites needed to determine your position (four), or the speed limit when flying under 10,000 feet MSL or in Class B airspace (250 knots). Speed limit, did you say? Yes, in addition to the rule I just mentioned, aircraft are also restricted to 200 knots within a 4nm radius of a Class C or D airport up to 2,500 feet AGL, or underneath the shelf of Class B airspace, unless instructed otherwise by ATC. Since the very maximum safe speed of my Cessna 172 was 163 knots, this wasn't really of any practical concern to me in the air. But, like so many other odd bits of information, I did have to know it for the test.

Gradually, I moved on to subjects that were more complicated or required more rote memorization. I struggled a bit to wrap my mind around the difference between air pressure and air density, at first. I remember stamping my feet in the cold waiting for my daughter to finish her ice skating lessons, while reciting to myself all the various ways the magnetic compass can lead or lag, the ten types of clouds, and the six types of fog. I put off memorizing the VFR restrictions for each different category of airspace for as long as possible, but eventually I just had to sit down and do it. One by one, through December into January, the pieces fell into place.

After whittling down the knowledge topics, I turned my attention to the work problems. Many of them involved maps and flight planning. The exam might ask you, for instance, to determine the magnetic heading to fly from one airport to another, given a certain wind direction and speed. This requires measuring the true course with a protractor, adjusting it for the wind angle, and converting from true to magnetic direction based on the nearest isogonic line. Or instead, you might be asked to calculate your expected time of arrival, on the same journey, based on true airspeed and wind. It wasn't rocket science, but practice helped me identify and avoid stupid but common mistakes, like adding when I should have subtracted, and get familiar with using the correct function buttons on my electronic E6B calculator, which I'd be allowed to use on the exam.

One important category of calculation problems on the exam is weight and balance. While I understood the concept, up to this point I had no experience running the actual numbers; Tess had taken care of it. So I took a few evenings to learn how it works. Consider a seesaw (next page). The force exerted by any object placed on the board depends not only on its weight, but its distance from the pivot point. A lighter object farther from the pivot can balance a heavier object that is closer to it. This distance is called **arm**, and the product of weight times arm is the object's **moment**.

In an airplane, arm is defined in reference to an arbitrary point, called the **datum**. In the Cessna 172, for instance, the datum is the firewall between the cockpit and the engine. Every point in the aircraft where weight can be added—the front seats, back seats, baggage compartment, fuel tanks, etc.—has an arm from that datum. By multiplying the weight and arm, you get the moment for each. The empty airplane has its own weight, arm, and moment, which has already been determined. Adding up the total moment, then dividing it by the total weight, gives you the aircraft's fully loaded center of gravity, as a distance from the datum. Comparing this weight and CG to the parameters in the aircraft's operating handbook (POH) tells you if the airplane is safe to fly or not. Exam problems might ask you how much fuel you can carry to remain within limits, or how much the weight and CG change due to fuel consumption, before landing. It's really just basic spreadsheet work, multiplying and adding across a table. But once again, practice with various types of problems makes perfect.

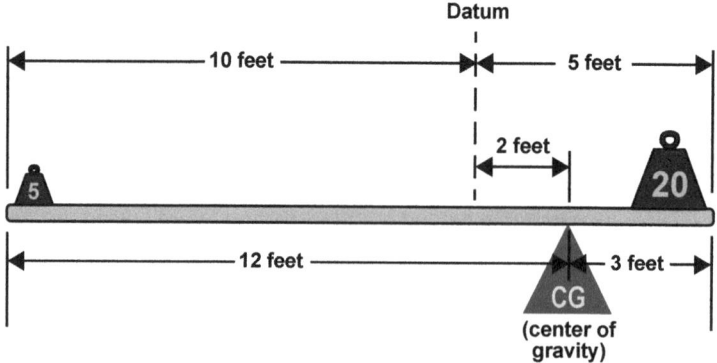

Using an arbitrary datum to calculate center of gravity

Sometimes I picked up a trick that made a hard problem a lot easier. One type of practice problem I struggled with at first shows you a CDI tuned to a certain VOR and asks where it implies you are located on the map. After twisting my brain in pretzels for a while, I discovered a video on YouTube that demonstrated a very simple process of elimination.[129] On a blank sheet of paper, draw a circular compass ring, then reorient it so the direction displayed on the CDI (in the case below, 210°) is on top. By drawing a vertical and horizontal line, divide it into four quadrants. If the CDI reads "TO," cross out the upper two quadrants; if it reads "FROM," cross out the lower two (if it shows a red-and-white-striped off sign, you must be located *on* the horizontal line). Next, whichever direction the needle is pointing, cross out the remaining quadrant on that side (if it's pointed straight, you must be *on* the vertical line). The remaining quadrant is where you must be—in this case, somewhere between 210° (SSW) and 300° (WNW) from the VOR, regardless of which direction the plane is flying. As the French say, voilà!

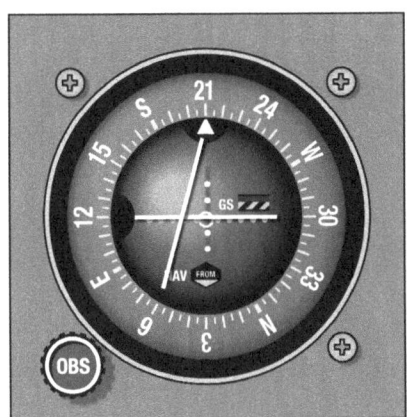
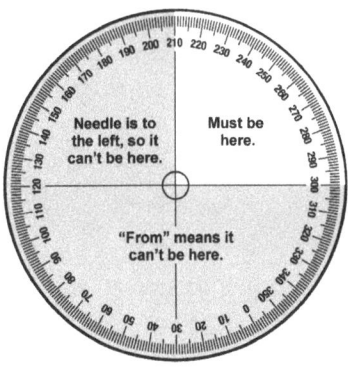

Deducing where you must be on the sectional chart from a VOR reading.

Perhaps the craziest type of problem on the exam involves some of the charts used to calculate minimum required takeoff or landing distance (on the next page). Solving one is like playing a game of Chutes and Ladders. You start with the outside air temperature and draw a line vertically, until you hit the curve for the correct pressure altitude. Next you draw a line horizontally across until you hit the next curve, then follow it down until you reach the aircraft's loaded weight. You continue horizontally from there until you hit the next curve, which you follow down until you reach the correct headwind speed. Depending on whether there's a 50-foot obstacle or not (pay attention to the question!) you follow another curve up. Where you end up shows how long a runway you need to safely take off. There's also a very similar chart for landing. To get the right answer, you must draw the lines very precisely, then peer at the tiny conclusion until you go cross-eyed. I hoped I wouldn't get one of those on test day.

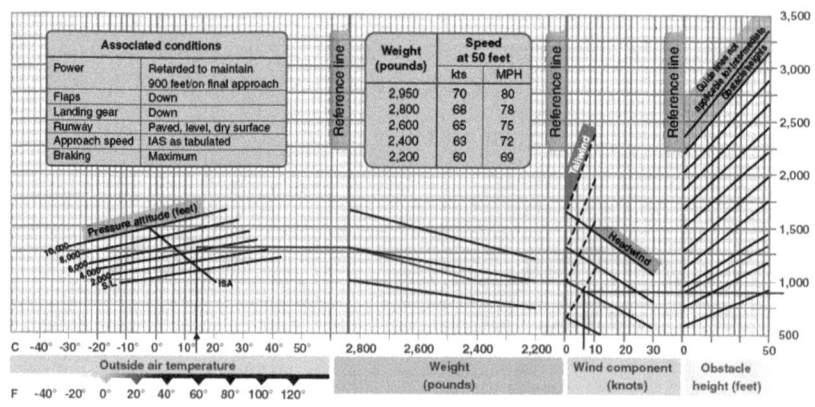

Example of a chart for determining minimum takeoff distance required, for use on the written pilot's exam.

The maps, diagrams, and illustrations for these and other problems are found in an official FAA booklet called the *Airman Knowledge Testing Supplement*. If you buy a test prep book, it usually comes with a copy of this booklet for use with your practice questions. As far as I could gather, as long as it was up to date, this was the *exact same* booklet and the *exact same* exhibits that the questions would refer to on the actual exam. If the exam asked me to decipher a METAR, TAF, or PIREP, there was an excellent chance it was going to be one of the examples already printed in the booklet. Same if it asked me to read an altimeter, interpret a CDI, or identify an airport sign. If that was the case, it would be well worthwhile to study and know every single item in the booklet and be prepared in advance to answer questions about them, would it not? I certainly thought so.

This got me to thinking. When you study for the SAT, you know that the practice questions—including ones from prior year exams—may be good preparation, but the questions asked on the exam itself will all be entirely new. But in many states, when you take a written driving exam, the exam questions are drawn from a pool that rarely changes from year to year, and the practice questions reflect this. When I applied for a driver's license in China, they were explicit that the questions on the test would come from a book of 800 or so questions you could study in advance. That was still a lot to study, but a useful thing to know. So which was it, I wondered? Would the questions I faced on the exam be similar or *identical* to the ones I was now studying? Everything I saw and heard hinted there was a great deal of carry-over from year to year, which implied that many questions were a known quantity. But ask as I might, I couldn't get anyone to give me a straight answer.

In the end, I concluded it didn't matter, for two reasons. First, even if the questions were not identical, they were almost certainly going to be very, very close and cover the exact same ground. Second, I realized that I wasn't learning this material solely to pass a test, but because I needed to know it as a pilot. There are programs offered that help students cram for the written exam over a weekend, and I imagine this involves simply memorizing answers to anticipated questions. But while this might help nab me a passing grade, it wouldn't help me *understand* all the subjects I would eventually need to understand to get through the rest of my training.

By now, I had worked through the whole test prep book, including the practice questions. As January turned to February, I started on the Sporty's online question bank. Over the course of several evenings, I worked systematically through each one—more than a thousand in total. I didn't refer to the prep book for answers, and if I got one wrong, I marked it down and moved on. By the end, I had about 200 questions that I got incorrect. I then went over each of these to figure out what the right answer was and why, taking note of any common errors I tended to make. Eventually, I narrowed the list down to 30 questions or so that were giving me the most trouble, though by now I knew them almost by heart. It was time to try a real practice test.

Sitting at my kitchen table, I gathered my calculator, pencils, scratch paper, and transparent overlays (it's not allowed to draw in the exhibit booklet you use for the exam, so I figured I should get some practice using the marker and transparencies they give you instead). I had two and a half hours to answer 60 questions, multiple choice. So many of the questions looked and felt familiar, by this point, that I was able to complete the test in just 30 minutes. I then went and did each one over again, fresh, to make sure I got the same answers, which took another half an hour. At the one-hour point, I hit submit, and received my first score: 100%.

I had another practice test to do before Sporty's could endorse me, but I figured it was time to schedule the exam. You do this online through the website faa.psiexams.com, and I already knew my flight school at Lincoln Park was an authorized test center. I booked a slot for the following week, paid my fee, and notified the school I'd be coming in. I also took my second practice test online (another 100%) and printed off the endorsement certification I would need when I showed up.

The day arrived and I was feeling reasonably confident. If you've ever taken any kind of standardized test at a testing center, you know the drill. They carefully checked my ID (even though they knew very well who I was) and led me into a well-lit back room with a cubicle and a computer. I logged on, read through some initial instructions, and hit "begin" to start the timer. Right off the bat, I understood why I never could get a straight answer to my query regarding the question bank: The testing program sternly warns you that you are not allowed to reveal anything about the questions on the exam, or a 10-ton weight will fall on your head and a pit of snakes will open up beneath you. So, sorry, I can neither confirm nor deny whether my suspicions proved true.

What I can say, though, is that nothing on the exam felt unfamiliar or unexpected. It was, as Yogi Berra said, déjà vu all over again. As I've indicated, if you know the material, you don't need the full time to finish. Taking my time, I completed every question in 45 minutes, then went back to the beginning and did them all over again, like new, which took me another 30. None of my answers changed. Finally, I took a deep breath, hit "submit," and went outside to hear my score printing on the computer printer at the reception desk. Abbie, the flight school owner, looked up and confirmed with a smile what I had hoped was true: I passed with 100%.

If you don't pass with a perfect score, quite frankly, it's no big deal. When your result prints out, it shows which subject areas you got wrong answers in, and you're expected to review them with your instructor, who has to sign an endorsement to that effect before you take your checkride. You present your exam report on the checkride, and the examiner must ask you about the areas you got wrong to make sure you fixed the gaps in your knowledge. I heard many people say that it's good to do as well as you can, because walking into the checkride with a solid written exam score starts you off on the right foot. While the examiner can't cut you any slack, they'll probably assume you know your stuff pretty well and may be inclined to give you the benefit of the doubt.

If you fail the written exam, it's not the end of the world either. Your instructor has to go back and review your deficient areas with you, and sign another endorsement that you're ready to retake the test. You can keep doing this over and over again as many times as you like, though each time you have to pay a new exam fee.

In 2021, 90% of people taking the private pilot airplane written exam passed, with an average score of 83%.[130] To be fair, I had a couple of advantages. Most importantly, I had all the time I wanted to prepare. That's a luxury that some—including young people trying to get their license as quickly as possible so they can advance toward a career in aviation—don't always have. I'm a CPA (Certified Public Accountant), so I've tackled hard tests before. But to be honest, if I had walked into this one unprepared, I would have flunked, no doubt. The range of subjects it covers is so broad, and was so new to me, that it took a couple of months—and a fair bit of head-scratching—to absorb enough to be confident, even with multiple choice.

Apparently, the FAA recommends that students take the written exam later than I did, after their first solo cross-county flight. I'm glad I had some flight hours under my belt first, so it wasn't all just theory learned from a book. But I'm also glad I took it when I did, for the same reason I've laid out all these subjects in the first half of this book. Maybe I just like knowing what I'm getting myself into. Passing the written exam also gave me a big boost of confidence—which was good, because in the months ahead, I sure would need it.

CHAPTER 15

Instructor

As soon as that exam grade came off the printer, I noticed a subtle shift in how my instructor saw me. I had not yet soloed (flown the plane by myself, without the instructor onboard), so I had not passed that major threshold to being a real pilot. But I was a serious student now, one who had shown himself willing to put in the effort required to earn my license, not just take a few lessons for fun. My instructor had more experience, and a lot more to teach me, but we spoke the same language now. In fact, I was starting to realize that, though she was much farther along than I was, we were both relative newcomers to the world of aviation.

Not that I gave it much thought, but I suppose my image of a flight instructor, before I began taking lessons, was that of a hoary old veteran, imparting the craft and wisdom seasoned by decades of flying to wide-eyed greenhorns such as myself (or reckless hotshots, like in the movie *Top Gun*).[131] This image was reinforced by all the tales I read from pilots who learned to fly on their father's knee, figuratively but sometimes literally, before they were old enough to drive. In fact, with a few notable exceptions, most **Certified Flight Instructors (CFIs)** are relatively young pilots just starting out in their careers, who are building the flight hours they need to qualify for their dream job with the airlines.

Flight hours—I began hearing those magical words shortly after taking my first lesson. Soon afterwards, I ordered a pilot's **logbook** from online. When it arrived, Tess and I sat down and inscribed each of my previous lessons into its lined pages, like entries in a bank checkbook. By the time I passed my written exam, I had exactly 18.3 hours, including 2.2 under the hood and 5.0 **cross-country**, entered into my logbook. From that point on, no lesson was deemed complete until the latest hours were logged and added to the tally.

The path to becoming a CFI, or anything else, begins exactly where I was now: earning a Private Pilot License (PPL). There are two routes to do this, labeled Part 61 and Part 141 for the different FAA regulations that lay out their requirements. I was in a **Part 61** program, which is part-time and flexible, and follows a tailor-made curriculum. You fly when you can and advance when you are ready. Part 61 technically requires a minimum of 40 hours total flying time to take your final checkride for a license, but usually takes somewhat more than that to complete all the other standards, like solo cross-country flights, night flying, and getting all the maneuvers down right. **Part 141** is a more intensive, full-time program with a fixed, FAA-approved lesson plan and a rigorous schedule. It is more like going to school. Because it meets more demanding FAA requirements, a Part 141 program requires a slightly lower minimum of 35 flight hours, though there are often more hours of formal ground instruction compared to Part 61. Smaller flight schools like mine are usually Part 61, but many larger schools are either Part 141 or offer both options.

Earning your PPL is a huge step, but it doesn't mean you can suddenly do anything you want in the air. For one thing, you can't be paid for flying: passengers can pitch in their share of the fuel, rental, airport fees, and other expenses, and you can fly for certain charitable activities, but otherwise you're on your own dime. The initial license only permits you to fly a single-engine airplane. Even then, you'll need **endorsements** in your logbook from a CFI to fly one that is tailwheel (as opposed to nosewheel), **complex** (with flaps, a constant speed propeller, and retractable landing gear), or **high performance** (with an engine over 200 horsepower), certifying that you've received the required additional training. Without an **instrument rating**, you can only fly VFR, not IFR. If the plane weighs over 12,500 pounds or is powered by a jet engine, you'll also need to earn a **type rating** specific to that model of aircraft. Obviously, this leaves quite a few steps between getting your PPL and jumping into the cockpit of an airliner.

For plenty of people, flying is a hobby and they earn whatever ratings or endorsements they feel they need to do the kind of flying they want. A work colleague of mine, for instance, went out and got a single-engine seaplane rating, because he thought learning to take off and land on water would be a fun and interesting challenge. A PPL has no expiration date, but every two years you do need to do a **flight review**—basically a refresher lesson with a CFI—to continue exercising its flying privileges. Earning a new rating can be an appealing alternative because it sets the clock back to zero for your next flight review.

For someone on a professional path, the next step is a bit clearer: they need to earn a **Commercial Pilot License (CPL)**, which will allow them to fly for hire. To qualify, they need to rack up more flying hours: a cumulative total of 190 hours if participating in a Part 141 course, or 250 hours if receiving more loosely structured Part 61 instruction. It's normally expected that this will include earning an instrument rating along the way. The training pilots specifically do for the CPL builds on the basics they learned for the PPL and takes those skills to the next level, with a certain number of hours devoted to flying a complex airplane and solo night flying (which are not part of the PPL curriculum), as well as longer-distance cross-country flights. There's another, more rigorous written exam covering similar subjects in greater detail, and another checkride evaluated to higher, more exacting standards.

At this point, our newly minted commercial pilot has a couple hundred flight hours. Unless they are very lucky and have latched onto some sort of airline or military scholarship, they likely have paid for all of this training out of their own pocket, to the tune of at least $80,000.[132] They are legally permitted to fly for hire, but still have very few immediate job options. They may or may not have earned a **multi-engine airplane rating**, which they almost certainly will need going forward. In fact, it's quite possible they still have never flown anything yet besides a Cessna 172. Somewhere along the way, they may or may not have earned a college degree, which major airlines will strongly prefer if not formally require.[133] Most importantly, to get hired by any airline they now normally need 1,500 flight hours, the amount required to qualify for an **Airline Transport Pilot (ATP)** license.

This **1,500-hour rule** is actually fairly new. Before 2013, pilots with only a CPL and the requisite 250 hours could potentially get hired as a first officer (co-pilot) by one of the regional airlines (which operate shorter routes under contract for the major brand-name airlines and serve as a stepping stone to working for one). While flying as second-in-command, they would be building their hours to eventually qualify for their ATP and move into the captain's seat.[134]

That all changed in the wake of the 2009 crash of Colgan Air Flight 3407, a two-engine turboprop being flown for Continental Connection.[135] The accident, which killed all 49 people aboard and one more on the ground outside of Buffalo, New York, was attributed to relatively inexperienced pilots bungling their response to a stall warning, prompting the FAA to require *all* airline pilots, including entry-level co-pilots, to hold an ATP.[136] The new rule was and remains controversial, with critics pointing out that both pilots of the crashed plane had over 1,500 hours, and still would have qualified to fly. Many argue that placing the focus on time-building, often in smaller, cheaper aircraft, instead of on more relevant training can actually be counterproductive.[137] Regardless, the forceful regulatory response to this crash—which at the time I'm writing, was the last major U.S. commercial airline crash in over a decade[138]—has had a huge impact on the entire marketplace for pilots.[139]

In short, it's contributed to an already growing shortage of qualified airline pilots. The sudden shutdown in travel due to COVID-19, resulting in an onslaught of airline layoffs and early retirements, disguised this reality for a brief period. However, the long-term trend is quickly making a comeback:

steadily rising demand for air travel, worldwide, is creating more and more slots for pilots to fill.[140] Meanwhile, the barriers to entry for new pilots hoping to fill these slots have been rising higher than ever before, in terms of both time and money.[141]

During the Cold War, the Air Force provided an affordable, if highly competitive and demanding, path for many into the cockpit. After leaving active duty, military pilots often transitioned straight into the airlines; even now, under the new rule, they require just 750 hours—half the normal requirement, which they likely already have—to qualify for an ATP. But military downsizing, along with the rise of unmanned drones as a combat weapon of choice, has meant this route is available to fewer and fewer people.[142]

These days, many aspiring airline pilots who can afford it, or are willing to take on student debt, opt to attend university-sponsored programs. Purdue, Embry-Riddle, Baylor, and Auburn host some of the best known in the country. These schools combine a bachelor's degree in aviation with a Part 141 curriculum that takes them through their PPL, instrument, and CPL training, and even to multi-engine before graduation.[143] One advantage is that graduates can qualify for a provisional ATP once they reach just 1,000 hours, and many airlines have forged alliances with top schools to channel students into their pipeline.[144] This potentially gives students a big leg up, because the sooner they can lock in that airline job, the sooner they lock in their seniority.[145] And when it comes to airlines, seniority—the date you were hired—is everything. It determines which aircraft and routes you get to fly, where you are based, when you get promoted from first officer (co-pilot) to captain, when you can take vacation, and—if business slows down—who gets laid off and who stays. So once a pilot gets their commercial license, it becomes a giant race to log whatever hours they still require for their ATP, while somehow earning a living in the process.[146]

Some of the jobs available to "low-hour" pilots include taking skydivers up for jumps, pulling advertising banners, and flying sightseeing tours, but these tend to be seasonal. Ferrying aircraft long-distance (even across oceans, typically for delivery to a new owner) can be one way to build a lot of cross-country miles in one go but gigs tend to be intermittent. All of these entry-level jobs—along with pipeline surveillance, aerial photography, and bush-flying outdoor adventurers to remote locations—tend to be with small local outfits where personal connections are key to hearing about, much less landing, a spot.[147] Although flying cargo doesn't require an ATP, all but the smallest cargo operators usually require new hires to have around 1,200 hours, so it doesn't fit the bill.[148]

For many, that leaves working as a flight instructor, at least for a time, as the most plausible path forward.[149] Getting a CFI certificate is much like earning another rating, though I'm told that many consider it the toughest. There are two written exams, one focused on teaching methods and the other on aviation knowledge. Aspiring CFIs spend training hours both on the ground preparing lesson plans and in the air giving mock lessons, as well as getting accustomed to sitting on the right side of the cockpit, before taking a final checkride. The whole process takes five to six months and around another $10,000.[150]

When a CFI takes a student up for a lesson, the instructor is allowed to log those hours as **Pilot in Command (PIC)**. PIC normally means the pilot is in sole command of the controls, but flying lessons—where the student is usually in direct control of the airplane, under the CFI's supervision—are a special case. And this is why working as an instructor is, for many, a very efficient and attractive way to rack up lots of hours quickly.

From the start of my training to the end, all but one of my flight instructors were women, as were all of their bosses. But this is far and away the exception. As of 2021, women account for less than 15% of student pilots in the U.S. and not quite 8% of CFIs. Only 6% of all licensed pilots in the U.S. are women, and less than 5% of airline pilots. Those numbers have been rising in recent years, but very slowly. Still, the demographics favor a rising role for women: the average age of female pilots in the U.S. is 36, compared to 44 for men.[151]

When Tess and I first met, she had been teaching as a CFI for just over two months and had 360 flight hours. As the daughter of an airline flight attendant, she had known many pilots as family friends growing up but wasn't sure she wanted to go into aviation until she completed college and realized her chosen field—fashion—was not for her. Her father offered to finance her pilot training if she made the decision right away. So, to his surprise, she quit her job the very next day. She got her PPL under Part 61, switched over to Part 141 to complete her instrument rating and CPL, then went straight into her CFI training. COVID-19 had just started, so she knew all the other low-hour jobs were being filled by laid-off pilots, and instructing was really the only way to go. The last I talked to her, while writing this book, Tess had reached 1,350 hours after about a year and a half of teaching and had just begun the process of applying for a job as a first officer (co-pilot) for a regional airline.

The good news, for pilots like Tess at least, is that the airlines have been really struggling and competing to fill their open pilot slots, which means the long journey may be worth it in the end.[152] Before COVID-19 hit, senior pilots with major U.S. airlines were talking about getting emails offering them jobs in China—where foreign pilots make up 10% of the rapidly expanding workforce—for upwards of $500,000 a year.[153] Even newer pilots, starting off in the regional U.S. airlines that serve as feeders for the majors, were benefiting from the bidding war, with entry-level salaries more than doubling in a few short years from $22,000 up to almost $50,000.[154] Airlines that once charged pilots for their initial ATP and type rating training were now providing it for free, along with signing bonuses.[155] And those same airlines were reaching even further down the pipeline to open their own flight schools, or make early "pre-hire" offers to pilots still working on their hours.[156]

From a student's perspective, there are several implications worth keeping in mind. When you take your first discovery flight, the CFI is like God: They know everything about flying a plane, and by comparison you know nothing. In fact, most CFIs are at a relatively early stage in their careers and are still developing as pilots. They have studied hard and demonstrated their ability in important ways, but they have not "seen it all," and there are still many things outside the realm of their experience. If the engine were to fail on takeoff, for instance, there's a good chance this hasn't happened to them before, either. Purely in terms of flying skills, each CFI has their own strengths and weaknesses. Not all of their landings are perfect. The same goes for their ability to perceive, conceptualize, and articulate what you are doing as a student, and how to improve. That's why it can be helpful, every once in a while, to take a lesson with another instructor to get a different perspective on your flying skills. I would eventually get a chance to do that.

Soon after starting my lessons, I happened across a short satire called *CFI! The Book*, by Alex Stone, a tongue-in-cheek, fictionalized account of the misadventures of a flight instructor. The antics at the low-budget flight school in Florida—including a student who can't speak English and never shows up, and another who has over 400 hours and still hasn't soloed—made for some hilarious, if somewhat alarming, reading. "They're the [ones] who really made the job exciting," Stone writes lovingly of his students, "the ones who tried to kill me."[157] Aside from the (hopefully exaggerated) horror stories, though, the book's crazy tales helped make my own CFIs feel, well, a bit more human. "I was at 632 now," the narrator relates, "hopefully 632.4 by the end of this flight. Ask any instructor how many hours they have, and they can tell you down to the tenth. The highlight of my day was when I got home and totaled up my logbook for the day. Each day getting closer and closer to having enough flight time so that I wouldn't have to do this anymore."[158]

My own flight school experience was nothing like the book, and Tess always did a great job. But looking at things from a CFI's perspective—even a somewhat twisted one—helped me appreciate a few things that, in the end, made me a better student. Just as my instructor was starting to see me as a serious and committed student, I was starting to see the CFI less as a task master to please and more as a partner I was working with to improve my skills and understanding. That meant that, while her input was invaluable, there were some things I'd still have to figure out for myself.

The biggest of these was mastering *exactly* how to land an airplane.

CHAPTER 16

Approach

I knew from the start that landing would be one of the toughest hurdles I'd have to overcome in learning to fly. Still, after scoring so well on the written exam in mid-February, I couldn't help feeling like the next big step, my first solo, was right around the corner. Little did I realize that—due partly to my own learning curve, and partly to factors beyond my control like weather—it would be a frustrating two and a half more months before I would reach that milestone.

A pilot's first solo almost always consists of a quick lap around the traffic pattern, lasting only a few minutes between takeoff and landing. You practice this over and over again with the instructor on board—as many times as it takes—until they have *zero* doubt that you can handle it on your own. The key, of course, is having your landings down pat.

There are two phases to landing. The first phase is the **approach**, and second is the **round out** and **flare**, just over the runway. Tess had already talked me through the process many times. The standard approach begins on the downwind leg, flying parallel and in the opposite direction to the intended runway. The runway out your side window should be about half a mile to a mile away—close enough to glide to if the engine failed, but not crowded too close. On a high-wing airplane like the Cessna 172, the runway should be about halfway up the wing strut, when looking out the side window. On a low-wing airplane, it should be near the wing tip.[159]

Lincoln Park has no control tower, so on entering the downwind you announce your presence there over the radio, look to confirm that the runway is clear, and pull back the throttle on the Cessna to about 2000 RPM to slow down to between 90 and 100 knots, while maintaining the traffic pattern altitude of 1,200 feet MSL (about 1,000 feet above the ground).

📡 *Lincoln Park Traffic, Skyhawk Seven-Two-Niner-Juliet-Papa, left downwind, Runway One-Niner.*

When you come **abeam** (or alongside) the numbers at the start of that runway—your intended landing spot—you pull the throttle back to 1500 RPM and put in the first stage of flaps, while continuing to fly straight ahead, opposite to the direction of landing. The nose should start to dip and the plane descend, but I often found it took some firm forward pressure on the yoke to get the descent started. The goal on this last stretch of the downwind is to have the Cessna descending at a steady 500 feet per minute (on the vertical speed indicator) and 80 knots (on the airspeed indicator), though you might have to adjust both pitch and power to get this right.

When the runway numbers are about a 45-degree angle behind you, out the side window, you begin making a 90-degree turn onto the base leg cutting in towards the runway, and announce that turn over the radio:

📡 *Lincoln Park Traffic, Skyhawk Seven-Two-Niner-Juliet-Papa, turning left base, Runway One-Niner.*

Around the same time, add the second stage of flaps. The additional lift may make you **balloon** upwards a bit, so you need to keep the yoke pressed forward to resist this and keep the descent steady. The additional flaps should slow the plane to around 70 knots. At this point, you need to look towards the runway to get a feel for whether you are coming in too high, too low, or just right. If the runway looks too flat, you're too low and need to add some power and arrest that descent a bit. If the angle looks too high, you need to take out power and make sure you're pitching down.

Very soon—and you don't want to overshoot—it's time to make the last turn onto final, so the runway is lined up straight in front of you. Announce over the radio that you're "on final" and put in the last stage of flaps, which should slow the Cessna to 65 knots. For the rest of the way in, you need to adjust pitch and power as needed to stay on a steady **glideslope**—the path of descent that will reach the runway—by holding the runway numbers steady in your front windshield as an **aiming point**. Meanwhile, you must use the ailerons and, especially as the aircraft slows, the rudder to stay lined up with the runway's centerline horizontally. Sometimes on calm, smooth days, this can take almost no adjustment at all—you slide right in, on speed and on target. On more gusty, bumpy days, it can take constant adjustment and readjustment all the way until you're coming in right over the runway's threshold. Speed is as important to monitor as altitude: If you get close to stalling, you won't be able to safely manage your descent, and if you come in too fast, the airplane will **float** and refuse to set down onto the runway.

The ideal glideslope for all airplanes is usually a 3-degree angle from the runway, which corresponds to a descent of roughly 300 feet per nautical mile. There are all sorts of rules of thumb to calculate this, but beginning pilots are mainly taught to rely on a remembered sight picture—what the runway looks like from that angle. The recommended approach speeds are different for each type of airplane; the ones I've given are for the Cessna 172 but are typical for small trainers. In lieu of anything else, the rule-of-thumb speeds for most airplanes are 1.5 times the flaps-down stall speed (V_{S0}) on downwind, 1.4 times on base, and 1.3 times on final. Because the 172 has a fairly slow V_{S0} of 40 knots, the approach speeds are a bit higher to add in more margin of error.

There is a point, as you near the numbers, that you have the runway "made" (you can glide there even without any power). At this moment, at least with the Cessna 172, you pull the throttle all the way back to idle. You don't want to dive—which will cause you to pick up too much speed—but you do want to let the nose drop and bring you down. At about 10 feet off the runway, gently pull back on the yoke to level off. You are now in **ground effect**, where the influence of the ground on the surrounding airflow will give you additional lift, so if you pull back too much—due to a natural fear of striking the runway—the plane can easily balloon upwards. If that happens, the last thing you want to do is overreact by pushing the yoke forward too hard, which can slam the plane down on its front nose gear and cause it to bounce repeatedly back and forth between the nose and rear wheels—a dangerous blunder called **porpoising**. Gentle adjustments will do.

If you round out correctly, you end up in slow flight over the runway, with the power to idle, same as when practicing power-off stalls. That's exactly what you're trying to do: bleed off speed until the airplane settles and either stalls or nearly stalls a few inches above the ground. Basically, you want the airplane to run out of energy and stop flying just as you touch down—and before you run out of runway. Jason Schappert, a 30-something flight instructor and entrepreneur who has turned himself into something of a guru on YouTube, prefers the term "transition" (to slow flight) rather than "flare," which to him suggests too dramatic a nose-up attitude.[160] But you do want to gradually pull back on the yoke to hold off landing as long as possible and land on your rear wheels first, before letting the nose settle (tailwheel planes have their own techniques).

If anything is wrong at any point in this entire process—if you're too high or too low, too fast or too slow, or too far off centerline, or things just don't feel right—you can always **go around**. Put the throttle in full, stay level for a moment to gain speed, and gradually—definitely not all at once—take out the flaps in stages to climb back for another try, same as if you were recovering from slow flight in practice maneuvers.

This was the plan. In reality, it took lots and lots of practice. For one thing, while Lincoln Park only has one strip of runway, I had to land on it from either one direction or the other—Runway 1 from the south or Runway

19 from the north—depending on which way the wind was blowing. That meant getting to know two different approaches equally well. As the map I've sketched on the next page shows, both approaches at Lincoln Park have left-turning patterns—Runway 1's to the west and Runway 19's to the east—but each has its own characteristics to remember, and I never knew which I'd be able to practice, based on the wind, until I showed up that day.

For another, Lincoln Park presented an unusually tough nut to crack. Months afterwards, I came across the blog of an experienced pilot who called the little airport "the worst I've flown out of, ever, and I've said this time and again."[161] His animated description of its 2,767-foot-long, 40-foot-wide landing strip and the obstacles around it gave me a wry chuckle: "Runway 1/19 is like landing on a carrier without a tailhook. Runway 1/19 has turned the Solid Male to Jell-o."[162] My flight school's website put a somewhat more positive spin on it: "When you learn to fly here, you'll be able to handle most public-use airports in America."[163] Any way you put it, this wasn't the easiest place for a beginner.

Runway 19 is the easier of the two. You enter it either by turning left after takeoff and then taking another left just over a small lake, or on a 45-degree angle to the downwind leg after circling around to the southeast. The downwind leg flies over a suburban neighborhood east of the airport that's very flat and follows a long straight road north, parallel and opposite to the runway. After starting my descent abeam the numbers, I aimed at a noticeable bend in the road to the right, just ahead. As soon as it began to disappear under my plane's nose, I knew it was time to turn left to base. On base, I aimed straight towards a small tree-covered hill just north of the airport, while craning my head left towards the runway to gauge my height. Turning left once more onto final, I had a clear view of Runway 19 just beyond a patch of several greenhouses hugging the ground before me. The moment I reached the small road separating those greenhouses from the airport, I knew I had the runway made and could pull my throttle to idle and come in gently to land.

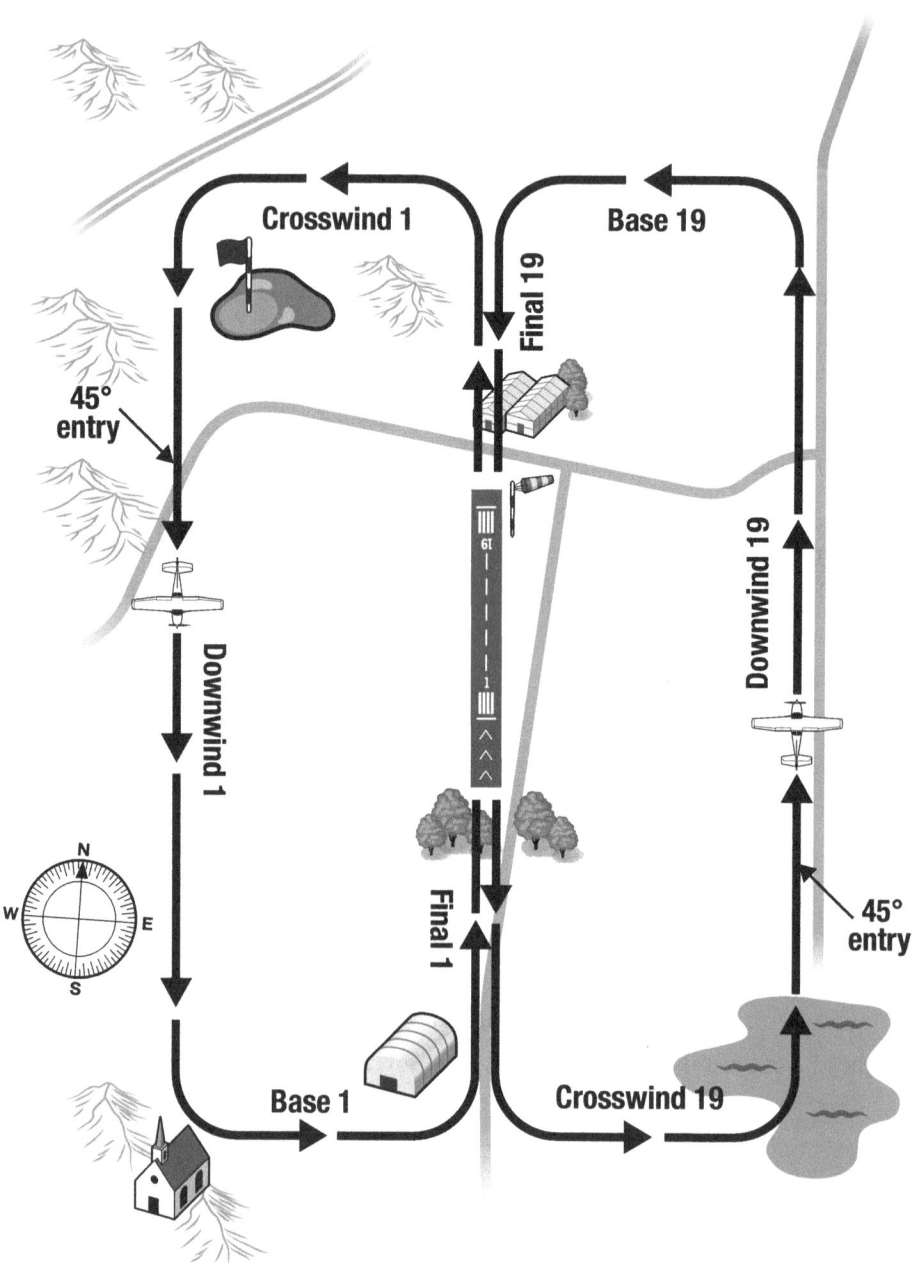

Diagram of the traffic pattern and approach for each runway direction at Lincoln Park (N07).

The approach to Runway 1 is trickier. The downwind leg runs west of the airport, along—and about level with—the 1,000-foot-tall ridgeline to the west and north. To enter the pattern, you have to either turn left after takeoff and head directly towards the ridge while climbing or drop in from over the ridge onto the 45. There are no linear roads to follow here, only a golf course below, so to align myself on the downwind I aimed at a church perched prominently on another ridgeline straight ahead to the south. I'd begin my descent abeam the numbers, aiming still more intently at that church. There is a white tent-like structure—a small sports facility—along a road running south of the airport, and when I passed it on my left, it was time to turn left onto base. If you don't turn promptly, before reaching the railroad tracks, you'll trespass into the Delta airspace belonging to Caldwell Airport to the south. On final, the base of the runway is obscured by a tall 50-foot stand of trees. You have to come in right over them, then cut the power and swoop down to land past the **displaced threshold**.

A displaced threshold, marked off in white arrows or chevrons (see Figure 14), indicates a part of the paved runway that can be used to begin a takeoff, but not a landing. Because of some obstacle to safety (like trees blocking the approach), you must land farther on, past the white threshold bar, where the runway numbers are placed. Other sections of pavement marked out in yellow, called **blastpads** or **stopways**, cannot be used either to takeoff or land, though you can use them to taxi into position or come to a halt after landing. Many runways have some combination, which means you don't really have the full length of the runway to land on.

At Lincoln Park, Runway 19 has a relatively short 95-foot displaced threshold, to give planes space to clear the road just in front of it, but you land fairly close to where you start your takeoff. (You still have to be careful. Tess told me that one plane coming in too low thumped the top of a FedEx van on that road with its wheels. There were no injuries or damage, but the driver must have gotten an awful fright.) The tall trees blocking the approach to Runway 1, on the other hand, pushed the threshold back a full 690 feet. A plane clearing those trees has to continue descending over this stretch of runway before reaching the numbers, leaving less than 2,100 feet of remaining pavement to round out, touch down, and brake to a stop. This is actually about twice the length of a modern aircraft carrier's flight deck, but yeah, no tailhook.

As you can tell, every detail of these approaches is ingrained into my mind. They had to be. In his YouTube videos, Jason Schappert frequently says, "A perfect landing begins with a perfect traffic pattern."[164] In other words, the more predictable and steady your entire pattern, the earlier you make corrections, the more likely you end up coming in over the runway at the right place and the right speed to make the right touchdown. Practicing each approach over and over again develops a kind of slideshow in a pilot's mind of what a correct approach should look like. Am I too high or too low? Too fast or too slow? Is it time to make the next turn? Am I lined up correctly or drifting due to wind? Each element of that slideshow—the landmarks and aiming points, the sight pictures out of the front windshield, the readings on the instruments, the changing hum of the engine's RPMs, even the subtle awareness of time ticking away—serve as prompts, a reminder of what you should be looking for, and what you should be doing, to stay on track for landing.

When student pilots can't get into the air, they often practice by **chair flying**. If you ever come across someone sitting on a park bench, with their eyes closed and feet propped up, operating imaginary controls and mouthing radio calls, they might be a lunatic—or they just might be learning to fly. I did it too, every spare moment I could grab, quietly visualizing and acting out each moment of my approach and landing. The problem with chair flying is that you can only practice what you can remember, and there's nothing to test if you've done it right. For that, in lieu of real landings, you need a flight simulator.

For me, this is where *MSFS 2020* proved amazingly useful. Many schools have complex, FAA-approved flight simulators to help students practice their landings. My school owned one that looked like a life-size cockpit on moving stilts, with a sticker price of over $70,000. I tried it once, on a day when the weather didn't cooperate with our plans to fly, but I wasn't inspired to use it again. The internal cockpit layout was highly authentic, and probably excellent for instrument training, but the outdated graphics only rendered generic stick trees against a plain brown landscape, making it difficult to judge distances and interpret my surroundings. In contrast, the photorealistic graphics and satellite imagery in *MSFS 2020* were not only breathtaking, but detailed and accurate. All of the features I looked to in real life—the hilltop church, the tent-like sports facility, the bend in the road ahead—were visible and easily recognizable in the sim. They might not be *exactly* the same (the greenhouses looked more like warehouses), but it was darn close. Especially after I downloaded a free user-created, handcrafted mod for Lincoln Park itself, it was almost like being there.

Weather permitting, I might be able to get in one real-world lesson a week, and complete five to six practice patterns. Which approach I could fly depended entirely on the wind that day. That kind of intermittent practice can make for halting progress—and growing frustration. In *MSFS*, I was able to practice those same approaches every day, as many times as I wished, in whichever direction I chose, in an environment that looked uncannily like the real thing. I could change the wind, the weather, or the time of day. I could take screenshots of my sight pictures at each stage of the approach, to look at later. If I wanted, I could download free tools that tracked and analyzed my approach, round out, and flare, and scored whether I landed on centerline and how hard my wheels touched down in g-forces. None of this could replace the real thing, but it helped me stay in practice, think through problems, and get a lot more out of my actual time in the air.

The immersive quality of this experience got kicked up a notch when, for Christmas, I bought myself the new HP Reverb II VR (Virtual Reality) helmet and hooked it up to *MSFS*. I won't say it was perfect—the graphics resolution was a bit lower and prone to stutters. Since I wear glasses, I needed to buy special prescription lens inserts. Even then, the distance between my eyes is about a millimeter smaller than the helmet could adjust, which made it tricky to focus. Because I now had a helmet over my head, I had to grope around at first for the yoke, throttle, flaps lever, and other controls on my desktop, which I could no longer see. But it was worth it, because the *feeling* of sitting in the cockpit, in virtual reality, was absolutely surreal. Instead of flipping between pre-set views, I could crane my neck to look around the next turn, or quickly glance *down* at the instruments and then back up again, as I did in real life. It also created a sense of physical motion, as the airplane banked to turn or leveled off over the runway, that even a wide-panel computer screen simply could not produce.

That was important, because getting used to the sensations of landing wasn't easy, especially with such a short and narrow runway. On final approach, the 40-foot-wide landing strip looked pencil thin, and I often joked that it felt like trying to land on a sidewalk. Just as I neared its threshold, the runway always seemed to come rushing at me like a freight train. One moment I was aiming for it ahead, the next I was right on top of it, trying hard not to mentally fall behind. An instant later, leveling off over its surface, I was anxious to touch down before running out of runway—a feeling gratefully relieved by the thump of the wheels onto the pavement. I never actually missed the runway or ran out of room to stop, but the rush of events felt both daunting and disconcerting.

I'll bluntly admit that I struggled with landings. It takes a lot of nerve to point an airplane at the ground, and a lot of patience to figure out how to set it down just right. The next several weeks would put both my nerve and my patience to the test.

CHAPTER 17

Landing

I joked to Tess that learning to land at Lincoln Park reminded me of a line from the Ben Stiller comedy *Dodgeball,* when the grizzled, half-crazy old coach agrees to teach the struggling team the secrets of the game. "If you can dodge a wrench, you can dodge a ball," he declares, before throwing a metal wrench at a player's head, knocking him sprawling on the floor in agony.[165] Twisted, yes, but there *is* a kind of logic to it. If you can handle the toughest thing anyone can throw at you, everything else should be a breeze.

There's a lot going on when you land a plane, and the biggest challenge is untangling it all. My difficulty wasn't making the same mistake (coming in too high or too low, too fast or too slow) with any consistency, but feeling like I didn't know—at least with any confidence—what I was doing right or wrong each time. Even when a landing went well, I wasn't always sure how much of that was my doing versus my instructor's timely, if subtle, inputs to ensure we landed safely.

Faced with a complex, frustrating problem, it can often be best to break it down into its component parts, so that's what I tried to do. First, there was the challenge of learning to control the plane's altitude and speed on approach, in order to stay on a safe and steady glideslope. Second was the vertical challenge of leveling off at the right height over the runway. Third was the horizontal task of keeping the airplane aligned on the runway's centerline, from final approach to touchdown. Finally, there was intimidation factor of landing at such a small airfield.

To remove this last factor from the equation, at least for the time being, Tess took me to some other nearby airports that have larger runways. Morristown (KMMU) was closest but was usually very busy and required Tess to constantly interact with the control tower. I liked Sullivan County (KMSV) the best. Perched in a quiet corner of upstate New York, it has a runway that is 6,298 feet long and 150 feet wide—over twice as long and almost four times as wide as Lincoln Park's. With no tower to preoccupy us, we could run through the pattern as many times as we liked until it was time to head home.

Unlike our home base, Sullivan County also has a **PAPI (Precision Approach Path Indicator)**, one of several types of visual guidance systems that help pilots tell if they're coming in too high, too low, or just right on final approach. The PAPI, illustrated below, is a set of four lights next to the runway which turn from white to red depending on your angle to the runway. Four red lights means you're low, four white means you're high, and two red two

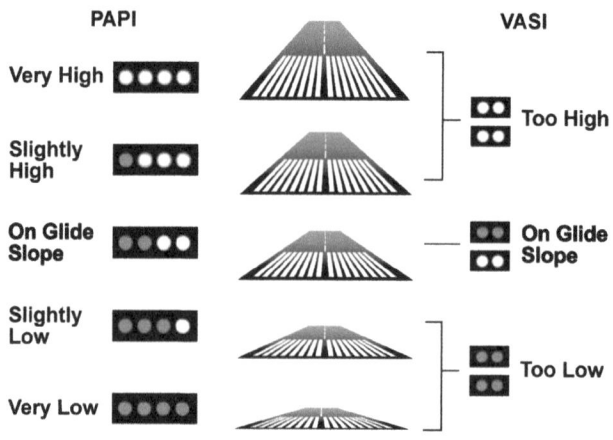

Two systems (PAPI and VASI) commonly used to provide vertical guidance on runway approach.

white means you're on the 3-degree glideslope. Some airports have a similar device instead called a **VASI (Visual Approach Slope Indicator)** consisting of two sets of lights, one on top of the other. If the top row is red and the bottom is white, you're good to go.

After banging my head against a wall at Lincoln Park, landing at Sullivan came as a welcome relief. Dodging a wrench, it seemed, really did teach you to dodge a ball. "Oh, now *this* I like!" I laughed to Tess as we glided in at a measured, almost relaxed pace towards a runway that looked more like a four-lane highway than a sidewalk, with two white and two red lights winking steadily at me on the PAPI. It felt like aiming at the broad side of a barn. The runway was so lengthy that I could put any worries about floating too far and running out of room aside and focus entirely on my technique—which needed plenty of focus at that point. In fact, once we did touch down there was plenty of runway left to do a **touch-and-go**. Rather than slowing down and exiting the runway to taxi back, as soon as my wheels were down I put the throttle in, lifted the flaps, and took right back off again. Touch-and-goes can save a lot of time while practicing, but were strictly prohibited back at Lincoln Park, where there was only just enough runway to come to a full stop.

At the end of every lesson we came back to Lincoln Park to land, which gradually became less and less intimidating. After a while, I began to notice that the alarming sensation I once felt there on final approach, of the runway suddenly rushing up at me, had gone away. Almost imperceptibly, the world seemed to have slowed down to a more manageable pace. It reminded me of my experience learning to drive a car as a teenager. I still vividly remember the evening when our instructor had our carload of nervous students take turns driving onto the interstate highway for the very first time. When I merged into the stream of traffic, it was absolutely terrifying. *Everything was moving so fast*, a confusion of bright lights and speeding metal, that I was convinced the slightest misjudgment would send me smashing into the cars hurtling around me. After only a couple more tries, though, my brain started learning to cope with this sensory onslaught rather than being overwhelmed by it. These days when I drive down the highway, I feel like I have plenty of time to see and react to what's going on around me. Something like this seemed to be happening now, as I got used to landing a plane.

I was also starting to get the sight pictures fixed in my mind, so I could tell at a glance if I was too high or too low on approach. I learned to recognize the perception of **sinking**, relative to the runway ahead, that takes place if you are descending too fast, and the perception of rising if you aren't descending fast enough. And finally, after dozens of landings, I began to realize that 2,000 or so feet of runway really did leave enough room to land, as long as I came in over the numbers at the correct airspeed. The handful of seconds between leveling off and touching down no longer felt like time desperately running out.

Sometimes, though, my progress felt like two steps forward, one step back. You know how it is: when you begin learning something, you respond to it naturally at first, relying on your intuition to just do your best. Then as you improve, you start overthinking it and messing up. Around this time, I began reading Wolfgang Langewiesche's classic *Stick and Rudder*, a book I've mentioned earlier. It gave me plenty to think about, much of it helpful. But as we all know, a little bit of knowledge can be a dangerous thing.

Langewiesche insists that, especially on an approach to land, you should control the plane by using *pitch for speed, power for altitude*.[166] A number of instructional videos say the same thing.[167] This can seem counterintuitive, but as I explained in Chapter 4, it's true because it's how angle of attack works. Armed with a new awareness of this insight, I came to my next lesson prepared to put it into practice. On final, if I was exceeding my target airspeed I lifted the nose up, and if I was slipping below it, I pushed those nose down. Meanwhile, I tried to manage my rate of descent—whether I would fall short of the runway or overshoot it—entirely with the throttle.

Things did not go well. My final approaches—which had been nice and stable—that day felt odd and uncoordinated. I could tell Tess was dismayed that I seemed to suddenly be having such a tough time, after so much improvement.

I went home, gave it some thought, and practiced more on *MSFS*. What was I doing differently than before? Then it hit me. In concentrating so much, and so abstractly, on pitch and power, I was forgetting to focus on what was right in front of me: *my aiming point*. First and foremost, I needed to visualize myself flying towards a fixed point at the start of the runway, usually the numbers; only then could I make the adjustments needed to put myself and keep myself on the right glide path. Langewiesche was right, of course: I couldn't just point the nose and expect the airplane to follow. If I was sinking on that glide path, my first instinct should be to add power, just not pitch up; if I was rising, I needed to take power out, not just pitch down. And I could never alter pitch up or down, to keep my aiming point centered, without anticipating how it would affect speed. But I needed to always aim first, otherwise how would I even know where I was going? My own rule became *aim the plane where I want it to go, but always adjust power accordingly*. And for me, it worked. On my next lesson, Tess was relieved to see I had somehow gotten my mojo back.

I mention this because it's a hotly debated topic among pilots. Everyone seems to have their own way of internalizing the complex feedback loop between pitch, power, speed, and descent, and explaining it to themselves. What's more, different kinds of airplanes respond differently.[168] For a student hearing competing interpretations, it's easy to get confused about what is already one of the most stressful and challenging parts of flying. It took me some time—and some stumbles—to find a way that worked for me.

While my approaches were looking good, the round out and flare—those last few moments before landing—still felt shaky. I always ended up safely on the ground, but I didn't feel *in control* of what was happening. After pulling the throttle back and swooping down low over the runway, I knew in theory what I should do, but my sense of control evaporated and I just held the yoke back in the hope—fortunately, always fulfilled—that the plane would land itself. Vertically, I had only the vaguest notion whether I had leveled off too high (risking an eventual hard thump onto the runway, when I lost lift) or too low (threatening to bounce or smack right into it), and fearing the ground, I tended to err on the high side. To stay on centerline, Tess would periodically urge "more right rudder" but in those last few moments I couldn't honestly tell whether the nose was yawing to one side or the other.

Tess could offer observations and suggestions, but she couldn't sort out what was going on inside my mind—only I could do that. Practicing in *MSFS* could only take me so far. I had landed in the sim hundreds of times, but somehow the sensations of those final few seconds before touchdown felt different and stranger in real life.

March turned out to be an extremely windy month, with many lessons canceled. As I struggled to come to grips with my landings, my schedule seemed to hit every bad day on the calendar. At one point, there was a nearly three-week stretch when I repeatedly went to bed hoping to practice the next day only to wake up disappointed. Time between lessons gave me time to think, which was frustrating because I wanted to put my thoughts into action to see if they worked. But time to think could also prove fruitful, with insights often coming from unexpected sources.

That spring, my eight-year-old daughter signed up for a baseball team. It was her first experience playing. I took her out to buy a glove, a bat, and a ball, and we went down to the patio behind our apartment building to practice throwing and catching. She found it very difficult at first, so I started off easy, tossing her light ground balls to scoop up. She fumbled them like mad to begin with, but gradually learned how to stay low and center her body in front of where the ball would bounce. She still flinched, though, whenever I tossed the ball straight at her to catch.

At that moment, my heart opened, and I saw myself in her. To my daughter, the ball was unpredictable and a little scary—much like landing the airplane was for me. To me, on the other hand, the ball had a logic I had learned to intuit and anticipate. Even when the ball was coming straight at my face, I could calmly lift my glove to intercept it. Seeing her go through the same tough time I was gave me a different perspective on my own abilities. It made me more patient and sympathetic, but it also gave me hope. This gap between us—there must be a way to overcome it. And if I could help her over this hurdle, maybe I'd learn something that was relevant to my own situation.

As we practiced, I saw my daughter working furiously to make sense of the ball. Her brow furrowed in concentration as she formulated ideas where the ball would go, watched them go wrong, grew frustrated, and recalibrated. It was a process of trial and error, partly conscious, partly unconscious. Improvement came in fits and starts. Sometimes several practice sessions went by with little visible progress—then the next day, out of nowhere, a breakthrough, and a smile. Patient repetition, almost imperceptibly, was starting to transform a blur of motion into a more coherent picture, prompting a more confident and effective response. When we started, I had been tempted to say that I could catch the ball "without thinking." But as I watched her come to grips with it, I came to appreciate there was a lot more going on than I was aware of. We weren't turning her brain off, we were turning it on. We were training it to see and respond to the world in a completely new way.

Tossing the ball back and forth, I started to think about the amazing range of skills—thousands of them—that human beings master in this way. Swimming, riding a bicycle, playing a musical instrument, skiing, ice skating, dancing the tango, speaking in sign language, performing brain surgery, typing, tying our shoes—each of them involves elaborate, split-second perception, information processing, and coordinated response. Many of our skills we learned so young that we have only a dim recollection of how we acquired them. Instead, they just seem *natural*. By the time we reach a certain age, we tend to stop learning new skills, and rely on the set that we have. What's more, we tend to assume that the skills we possess are naturally the most important ones, and that anyone who struggles with them must be clumsy or slow-witted. Only when we try to teach someone these skills, or go out of our well-set ways to learn a new one for ourselves, are we reminded that these really aren't *attributes*, but *disciplines*.

Learning a new skill is a humbling experience. That's true in the narrow sense that we get frustrated and are forced to admit that there's something we're not seeing, not getting right. But it's also humbling in a broader sense, by showing us the limits of the little worlds we create for ourselves and believe we have mastered. "There are more things in heaven and earth," Hamlet tells

Horatio, "than are dreamt of in your philosophy."[169] Indeed. The world was filled, I now saw, with people—some of them, like Tess, much younger than me—who could do things that I could not, because they had learned to see things I could not. But as my daughter showed me, it was possible, with patience and determination and practice, to learn to see them too.

So what was I not seeing, in those last moments of flight, or what was I seeing wrong? Some useful clues came from watching YouTube videos online. Landings are a challenge for almost every student pilot, so there are plenty of videos out there. For instance, landing left of centerline is a very common problem,[170] one that I was experiencing. Often the problem is not enough right rudder,[171] but in my case, at least part of it was a lot simpler. Because I was sitting on the left side of the cockpit, I tended to assume that I should align my sight picture, in flight and while taxiing, slightly to the left of the runway's centerline. The videos revealed this as a misconception.[172] The view out the front windshield is essentially the same from either seat, and the centerline should run straight ahead from your body. I confirmed this by switching from seat to seat in the sim, and while parked in the real plane. Here was at least one mistake identified, and hopefully fixed.

Other videos dealt with the tricky question of knowing exactly how high to level off over the runway. Unsure, I tended to err on the high side, float for too long, and touch down harder than I'd like. One video in particular by Rod Machado provided a very helpful tip that reinforced and expanded on something Tess had told me. In between his signature dad jokes, Machado highlighted how there is a certain moment, about 10 feet above the surface, when the runway appears to suddenly widen to the edges of your vision. This "runway widening effect" is the cue to level off.[173] You can't look *at* it, you can only look *for* it, because it's a function of your peripheral vision. It happens in a flash, so I'd have to respond quickly, but at least now I knew what to keep my eyes out for.

After a long, frustrating delay, I finally got back into the air on Tuesday, March 30, and spent two hours doing nothing but traffic patterns at Lincoln Park. Some of the tips helped, but I still found those final moments, right over the runway, a confusing muddle. There was something I just wasn't seeing. So on my last go, rather than trying again I asked Tess to fly the pattern, from downwind to landing, while I filmed it with my iPhone from my usual pilot's seat. I felt a little lazy being the passenger, but maybe, viewing it again, I'd be able to spot something I was missing.

It was one of the smartest moves I made. The recording, which I watched, paused, and rewound over and over again, let me to step back from the moment and analyze each phase of the approach and landing in detail. In particular, it became apparent that, at the end, there were *six vital seconds* (by my count) that defined the last moments of flight, which were causing me so much confusion. The first three seconds—one, two, three—comprised the **round out**, starting with pulling the throttle back to idle as the airplane neared the threshold, and ending with flying level about 10 feet off the ground. The next three seconds—four, five, six—consisted of the **flare**: gradually pulling back on the yoke as the speed bled away, increasing the angle of attack to the point of stall, while keeping the nose straight and centered, until the wheels touched down. I knew that's what happened, but I had never paced it out like this before. These two stretches, consisting of three seconds each, gave me a template. These seconds could pass in a blur, I realized—*or they could be utilized*, if my brain knew what to look for and how to respond.

My next flying lesson was scheduled for a little over a week later. In between, I took my family on a driving vacation to upstate New York, a welcome getaway from our COVID-restricted routine. As is typically the case, the kids chattered away in the back seat until everyone, including my wife, dozed off to sleep as the miles passed uneventfully by. Left to my own devices, I occupied myself mentally rehearsing those last six seconds of flight, over and over again, as though I were flying the plane instead of driving the car. I thought through not only what I should do, as those six seconds ticked by one by one, but what I expected to see, what I should look for. And what soon became clear to me was *I wasn't looking in the right place*.

Approaching on final, my eyes were fixed—aside from quick glances down to the airspeed indicator—on my aiming point, which was usually the runway numbers. As I neared the threshold, and cut the throttle, those numbers slipped beneath the nose of the airplane, leaving me to readjust my eyes … where? The instructional videos said I should look up, towards the end of the runway, but I realized that in the first three vital seconds I often continued to look down, just over the nose, in an attempt to gauge how high I was from the ground. When I finally lifted my eyes, for the last three seconds, they didn't really have a focal point. They just kind of glazed over as I went into the flare, until I felt that fortunate thump of the tires.

As I drove along the interstate, I tried replicating this, to examine its implications. I stared down right over the car's hood and attempted to drive straight within my lane. I managed to, but it took a lot of anxious concentration and jittery steering. Then I looked up, staring blankly out at the horizon; I could barely drive this way either. Where did my eyes naturally rest, while driving? The answer was: on the road ahead, somewhere between the halfway point and the horizon. If I simply aimed at this point, where the road lay ahead, and made gentle adjustments to the steering wheel, I would naturally stay centered in my lane, without having to frantically look down to confirm.

Of course, driving a car I didn't have to worry about my front end yawing to the left or right, or how high I was above the road. But the sight picture in the iPhone video I took, in those last three seconds, looked remarkably like driving a car *slightly above* a road. On takeoff, I knew how to use the rudder pedals to keep the plane centered along that "road," even as the wheels began to lose their grip on the pavement below. Wasn't keeping the nose aligned during round out and flare nearly the same, in reverse? Yes, the controls would be "mushy," because that's how the airplane behaves in slow flight—but I had practiced slow flight, in the sky, many times.

As for the flare itself, another YouTube video I came across both echoed what had been troubling me and pointed to a new way of thinking about it. In it, Charlie Gasmire, the genial, bearded guy who hosts Airplane Academy, talked about the tendency, once over the runway, of pilots "just giving up on it, pulling the power, and waiting for it to stop." You become, as he put it, "a passenger in your own cockpit"—exactly the feeling I was trying to overcome. "I think we need to shift our mindset on landings," he offered, "to less of just kind of being something that happens and more of an intentional flight maneuver." The nature of this maneuver, he explained, is to hold back and burn off the airplane's remaining energy as you "intentionally feel for the ground with the main tires."[174] This image—of allowing the wheels time to seek out and find the runway beneath them—resonated with me, and I practiced visualizing it in the car as I counted down those last three seconds before touching down.

In the process, another more amusing image sprang to mind. As Mama told The Supremes (and Phil Collins), "You can't hurry love."[175] As most of us learn the hard way, you can't seduce someone by throwing yourself into their arms. If I wanted my contact with the runway to feel like a kiss, I had to treat it like one, and play hard to get. ♪ *You gotta trust, give it time, no matter how long it takes* ♪. The idea gave me a chuckle, but it actually made some sense, and was easy to remember at an otherwise tense moment.

Our trip to upstate New York took us through Hammondsport, a small town on the southern end of one of the finger lakes that aviation pioneer Glenn Curtiss had called home. We visited a museum with life-size, flying replicas of his early airplanes, and the field where he made the country's first public flight on July 4, 1908. More than curiosity drove me there. I felt a kind of kinship. The earliest aviators, like Curtiss, didn't know what they were doing either. In their case, they had no one to help teach them. They had to go up in the air and figure it out for themselves. Some got themselves killed in the process, but enough succeeded to begin a chain of instruction, from one person to the next, that eventually led to me. My stumbling efforts were heir to their own, a promising thought that gave a much-needed boost to my spirits.

Thinking back to the practical task before me, I knew I had made some worthwhile discoveries of my own. I would at least have a lot more concrete things to think about, look for, and hopefully respond to in those vital final six seconds of flight. As we drove back home from our family vacation, I eagerly looked forward to putting them into action on my next lesson, in the first week of April.

It was a breakthrough. As I crossed the threshold of Runway 19 and pulled the throttle back to idle, I self-consciously raised my eyes to the second half of the runway, prying them away from the ground below. I allowed the airplane to descend until the runway suddenly widened, then leveled off, imagining I was driving down the highway with the "road" stretching out straight before me. With increasing back pressure on the yoke, I played "hard to get" (humming Phil Collins in my head), counting down the final three (or so) seconds until the wheels gently found the pavement. I was able to do this several times, on repeated circuits around the pattern, much to Tess's relief and satisfaction.

Most important of all, those final six seconds before landing now felt to me like a conscious maneuver, with a clear method and objective, instead of an anxious blur. I was no longer a passenger in my own cockpit. I was flying the plane all the way down to the runway, rather than letting it fly me.

The capstone of the day came at the very end. As I made my last final approach, another plane was waiting patiently at the hold short line for takeoff. After I smoothly flared and touched down, the pilot—a complete stranger to me—broke in on the radio, unprompted, to say two words.

"Nice landing."

He had no idea how much that meant to me.

CHAPTER 18

Solo

By early April, I had nearly 30 flying hours in my logbook. I searched on Google to find how many hours students typically take to solo, and the answer somewhat dismayed me. "The average," one website reported, "is around 15 hours but it isn't uncommon to solo after just 10 flight hours."[176] Was something wrong with me? Maybe I just wasn't very good at this.

I reflected, though, that I probably shouldn't read too much into this. First, some instructors initially focus on getting new students through their first solo, before moving on to other topics. With Tess, I had spent multiple hours flying cross-country, learning to navigate by VOR, and working "under the hood" before starting to focus on landings. Second, learning to land on a smaller runway was a tougher challenge, but well worth it. Third—and most importantly—I reminded myself that for me, at least, this was not a race. At some point I would be on my own, reliant on my own skills; for now, I should value the time with my instructor, to bring those skills up to where they needed to be. I resolved that if I ever felt unsure or uncomfortable about something, I would speak up and get it fixed instead of trying to paper over it to bolster my pride, or in pursuit of some arbitrary deadline. If becoming a proficient, safe pilot took some more time, so be it.

With my landings looking and feeling a lot better, I knew that—finally—my first solo really was just around the corner. You usually need a nice day with calm wind, however, for the instructor to sign off. As it turned out, such days were not to be had for the next several weeks, at least not when I was scheduled. We could still fly, and practice landing in more challenging conditions, but my "big moment" kept getting postponed.

What I got instead was an introduction to handling **crosswinds** and **gusts**. Normally you want to take off or land into a headwind, but you can't count on the wind to be perfectly aligned with the either direction of a given runway. Some airports have multiple runways set up in different directions to maximize the chance of that, but often the wind has a **crosswind component** blowing sideways across the runway's length. For instance, a 10-knot wind coming from 45 degrees to the right equates to a seven-knot headwind and a crosswind pushing you at seven knots to the left. A 10-knot wind from 60 degrees to the right equals a five-knot headwind and a nearly nine-knot crosswind pushing you to the left.

Gusty days have irregular, changeable winds. The wind might be fairly calm for a while, then you get hit with a 10-knot blast from some direction, lasting just a few moments. If you're in the process of landing, the crosswind component could knock you off track from the runway while the headwind component could boost your airspeed, causing you to float down the runway farther than expected—and then suddenly lose lift when it goes away. Landing on a very gusty day can take constant and sometimes urgent adjustments all the way down, without taking anything for granted until the wheels are securely on the ground.

Even when taxiing, pilots must take care when facing crosswinds and gusts: a strong crosswind, at just the right angle, can even lift one wing and tip over a small airplane like a Cessna 172. The rule on taxiing is: "Climb into the wind, dive away from it." If there's a crosswind blowing from the plane's front (called a quartering headwind), turn the yoke towards it, so the ailerons counter any asymmetric lift. For a **tricycle-gear airplane** (with a nosewheel), the elevators can be held neutral, but for a tailwheel airplane, the yoke should be pulled back. For a quartering tailwind from the rear, for either type of plane, the yoke should be turned away from the wind while pushing the yoke forward. Since taxiing can involve many turns and changes in direction, relative to the wind's direction, the yoke's position may have to be frequently altered to counter it.

Takeoffs with a crosswind, within safety limits, begin with the yoke turned all the way into the direction of the wind. As the airplane builds up speed, the ailerons become more effective and this can be gradually eased; but depending on the windspeed, some deflection will still be needed to keep one wing from gaining lift before the other. Once the plane is airborne, the crosswind will try to push it to the side, away from the runway, and the pilot should respond by crabbing the nose into the wind as necessary, just as in ground reference maneuvers. It's good practice to stay on track with the runway, in part so you could abort and land in an emergency, but also because Air Traffic Control might expect you to maintain that course until told otherwise.

Landing with a crosswind requires, first and foremost, an awareness of how it will affect flying the pattern. It will push you sideways on downwind, either towards or away from the runway unless you crab to compensate, and on base can become either a headwind slowing you down or a tailwind speeding you up. The latter can easily cause you to overshoot your turn to final. On final approach, you'll be pushed sideways again and will need to crab. Some student pilots find the sensation of crabbing on final—pointing your nose at an angle to the runway and following a diagonal descent down—disconcerting. I always found it kind of fun, and oddly intuitive. What I did find awkward was one final maneuver that takes place in those last few seconds before touchdown, when you have so much else to think about: the transition to a **sideslip**.

You could counter a crosswind by crabbing all the way down and landing diagonally, but that puts a lot of lateral stress on the tires and landing gear, which can damage them. So instead, just as you level off a few feet above the runway, you must also execute a kind of pirouette from the crab angle to a

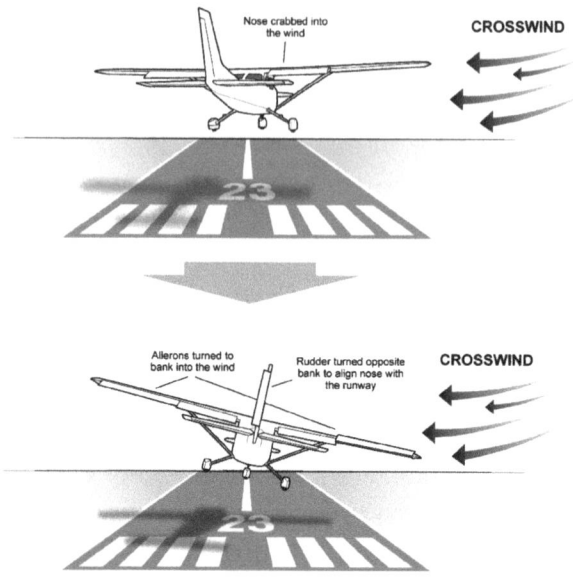

The pirouette from crabbing (top) to a sideslip (bottom) when landing with a crosswind.

sideslip. Say there's a crosswind coming from the right. To enter a sideslip, you turn the yoke to the right, dipping the right wing into the wind. At the same time, you press your foot on the left rudder pedal, yawing the nose in the opposite direction (to the left) to align it straight with the runway. This ungainly positioning forces the plane to "slip" sideways against the wind, countering the wind's push and holding it steady, albeit tilted, over the runway. As you flare and lose lift, the right wheel should touch down first, followed by the left and then the nose. It can be a lot to manage, even for an experienced pilot. Not only does the flare already demand a fairly sensitive touch, but the degree of the sideslip—the dip of the wing and the rudder pressure to bring the nose forward—depends entirely on the pilot sensing, and countering, the sideways push of the wind. Add some sudden wind gusts, and it gets decidedly tricky.

Search for "crosswind landings" on YouTube and you'll find enough videos to churn your stomach and make you vow never to board an airplane again. Long after they get their license, pilots are always practicing crosswind landings or wishing that they had. Crosswinds play a prominent role in the **personal minimums** that the FAA encourages pilots to set for themselves, when deciding whether or not to fly, to avoid getting in over their heads. Tess and I were practicing in crosswinds of around 5 knots, gusting occasionally to 10, which are considered light to moderate. The Cessna 172 is "rated" for a 15-knot crosswind component, which means that's what the manufacturer's test pilots confirmed it could handle. I've heard pilots tell stories of landing one in a 30-knot crosswind, but I suspect they needed a change of underwear afterwards.

Meanwhile, I practiced incessantly at home, awaiting a calmer day for my long-awaited solo. This is where *MSFS*, especially with the VR helmet, truly came into its own. Every day I flew three pattern circuits, from takeoff to landing, for each approach, for a total of six. I came to notice some slight differences in performance—the Cessna 172 in the sim was a few seconds slower in the climb than in real life—but they were of little consequence compared to the immersive, repetitive experience it offered. To my wife's somewhat annoyed bemusement, I practiced each radio call aloud, on each leg, until it became a barely conscious reflex. I came to know, second by second, what sight picture to expect and what the instruments should read at each stage of flight. I was ready.

Monday, April 19. The evening before, I had checked out the weather forecast for my scheduled lesson the next morning. It looked perfect: clear skies, calm winds. This was it. I woke up, dropped the kids at school, and prepared to depart for the airport. Then my cell phone rang. It was the receptionist at the flight school. "We've had some trouble with the registration on the airplane," he informed me, "and are waiting for a fax from the FAA. We can't fly today."

I was, in a word, crushed. You know the cartoon meme of Grandpa Simpson shaking his fist at the sky, with the newspaper headline "Old Man Yells at Cloud"? That was literally me. I told myself I was overreacting, that even though the weather forecast looked crummy for the rest of the week, the delay was only temporary. But after all the weather delays over the past month and a half, it just felt like the last straw. I didn't blame the school—these things happen—but it did get me thinking seriously about an idea that had been kicking around in the back of my head since the very start, when I reached out to that flight school in Florida. Perhaps I could go somewhere sunny for a week, pack in as many flying hours as possible, and make some more consistent progress before returning home to pick up where I left off. The woman I spoke to back then thought it was a bad idea, and I was glad I followed her advice—up to a point. But now, I wasn't so sure.

I talked it over with my wife and—to my lasting gratitude—she gave her consent. Then I called my instructor, Tess, to discuss the situation and get her advice. She was very supportive and encouraging, and suggested I call her former Part 141 flight school in Scottsdale, Arizona. It's a large operation, she explained, turning out dozens of new pilots each month, but I'd definitely get a chance to fly every day. The opportunity to see a different side of the pilot training business appealed to me—at worst, if I didn't like it, I could call it off and come back home. I'd only lose a week that I might lose anyway due to weather. I had some frequent flyer miles that I hadn't used due to COVID-19, and I wouldn't have to commute all the way to New Jersey for each lesson, so the additional expense didn't work out to be that much. So I gave the school a call, and by that afternoon they were sending me a quote and asking me when I could start. After consulting my wife and the airline schedule, we picked a date: not that coming Sunday, but the following one, May 2. The plan was that I would take two three-hour lessons each day, for six days. My flight training was about to get turbocharged.

I didn't cancel my remaining lessons in New Jersey, though, and a week later the weather was looking good for Thursday and Friday, the days right before my planned departure to Arizona. When I headed to Lincoln Park on Thursday morning, April 27, the wind was calm and the gray layer of overcast just high enough to safely allow flying in the pattern. Tess and I went up and flew a few circuits together, taking off and landing to the south on Runway 19, the easier of the two approaches. They went smoothly, so we shut down the engine and went inside for her to fill out the required endorsements to solo. I had already completed the required pre-solo take-home written exam several weeks ago, which verified that I knew important specifics like the airport's traffic pattern altitude and radio frequency and the V-speeds for the Cessna 172. So she only needed to sign one last entry in my logbook, authorizing me to fly solo in a 172 for the next 90 days.

I walked back out to the airplane, climbed in, and started it up, for the first time on my own. The thing I remember most was the silence—apart from the clamorous racket of the engine, of course. After I taxied and did my run-up at the hold short line, I glanced over at the empty seat next to me and my heart skipped a moment's beat. But oddly, the sight was also reassuringly familiar, because I had seen the exact same thing every day under my VR helmet. In fact, as I announced my departure on the radio and moved out onto the runway, it felt strangely like I was doing it in *Microsoft Flight Simulator*, in VR. "You've done this before, dozens of times," I muttered to myself. I stopped for a second to grab my iPhone and take a picture looking down the runway—a big moment to remember. Then I pushed the throttle in full and, dancing on those rudder pedals to stay pointed straight, gained speed until I lifted off the runway.

Tess was standing on the taxiway taking a video. When I watch it now, the takeoff looks so simple and uneventful, but that very fact brings a warm glow to my heart. I was scared but not scared. I was ready. I had flown this traffic pattern over and over again every day in the sim, as well as many times with Tess under much more challenging conditions. There is, in short, not much to say about the flight. It unfolded just as I expected, from start to finish. Some people report surprise at how buoyant the airplane feels with no instructor onboard, how it seems to zing off the runway on takeoff, but the warmer weather, with its lower air density, must have canceled that out for me. Before I knew it, I was abeam the runway numbers on downwind and routinely beginning my descent. On landing, as I flared over the runway, I started to balloon slightly but avoided overreacting, adjusted the back pressure on the yoke, and touched down gently a few moments later. Announcing that I was clear of the runway, I taxied back for another takeoff. After my third takeoff and landing, I returned to the parking area and cut the engine as Tess came over to show me the videos on her phone. We took a few photos to commemorate the occasion, then resumed our normal lesson together.

The next day also happened to have good weather, so when I arrived Tess sent me up solo again. This time, there were other aircraft in the pattern, also practicing takeoffs and landings, so my radio calls were for more than just good form. I had to listen and watch for where the other planes were located, and there were several times I had to slow down or extend the downwind leg to give them room to land and clear the runway. When another plane is landing ahead of you, you should wait to begin your descent not when *you* pass abeam the numbers, but when you pass *the plane ahead of you* on their final approach. That meant deviating from the standard pattern you might be used to and adjusting it to accommodate the other traffic. It was another step in developing the confidence that I could actually fly the plane in real-life conditions.

Flying your first solo is a landmark in any pilot's life, filled with pride and a sense of real accomplishment. But as I came to realize, that first solo often marks the point where many student pilots begin to lose their drive and energy, and end up quitting. I talked to so many people who, when they heard I was learning to fly, told me, "I took lessons a while ago, and I even soloed, but I never got my license."

I can understand why. After all, with your first solo you have achieved what you initially set out to do: fly an airplane by yourself. On reaching the top of this huge peak, you then gaze out over the wide horizon and see stretching before you ... many more peaks to climb, none of which seem anywhere near as thrilling, but look just as difficult. It's a bit deflating, really.

For some, flying their first solo becomes a kind of false dawn, a sense of accomplishment that later gives way to regret that they didn't press on. Fortunately, I didn't have time to rest on my laurels or dwell on what lay ahead. My week at a flight school in Arizona was already booked, which meant I had a plane to catch.

CHAPTER 19

Bravo

I could still feel the warm breeze of the desert when I arrived after sunset at the Best Western hotel on the edge of the airport in Scottsdale, Arizona. On top of my first solo flights, the last several days had been a flurry of activity, making preparations to depart. The school forwarded a list of items I would need, and I gathered them into a "flight bag," a.k.a. a blue backpack I could fit in the backseat of the plane. Pilots wear headsets with earphones and a microphone to use the radio while muffling the engine's noise. Up to this point, I had simply borrowed my school's, but now I needed to order a set of my own. I also ordered a small flashlight with white and red lenses in case we ended up doing any night flying. I wasn't sure whether *ForeFlight* would be allowed but packed my iPad anyway, along with the Sentry, plus my calculator, protractor, an extra kneeboard for writing, and extra batteries for everything.

The school had me get the maps for the Phoenix area—both the sectional chart and a larger-scale **Terminal Area Chart (TAC)** for the immediate vicinity of the city's international airport—as well as the regional Chart Supplement (AFD) book covering all the airports in the Southwest. They also sent a link to a website providing very detailed descriptions of the various practice areas we would be using along the city's outskirts.[177] The night before I left, I spent a few hours on *Microsoft Flight Simulator* flying out of Scottsdale Airport to these practice areas, as well as some other nearby airports. This proved to be time well spent. It became clear to me, pretty quickly, that the crowded airspace around Phoenix would take some real concentration to successfully navigate.

Up to this point, I had spent nearly all my time flying in relatively unhurried Class E or G airspace, out of non-towered airports, in which we were never expected to talk to Air Traffic Control (ATC). While New York City's three main airports—Newark, LaGuardia, and JFK—have some of the busiest airspace in the world, we almost entirely avoided it by flying to the north over rural New Jersey and upstate New York. Though it isn't strictly required, like most aircraft we still used a radio, transponder, and ADS-B Out to communicate and signal our presence to other traffic. Flying in these less restrictive areas—which make up the vast majority of lower-altitude airspace over the United States—relies mostly on listening and looking out for yourself. It's not the Wild West, but more akin to arriving at a local intersection posted with stop signs, where each driver is expected to know the rules of the road and take their turn.

Towered airports, on the other hand, and the Class D, C, and B airspace around them, are more like a busy city intersection at rush hour with a traffic cop directing each car where to go and when. Tess had taken me to Morristown, a nearby Class D airport, to practice landings. But she had handled most of the conversations with the control tower, and we had stayed well clear of Newark's highly restricted Bravo airspace above and next to it.

A CFI who I later met told me, "In my experience as an instructor, student pilots who train at non-towered airports are afraid of towers, while those who train at towered airports are afraid of non-towered ones, because there's no one to tell you what to do." I was in the former camp, and arriving in Arizona, I suddenly found myself in the deep end of the pool. Scottsdale (KSDL) itself is a Class D airport, with its own control tower, at least during daylight hours. Nearby are *eight* other Class D airports, all of them wedged under and around the jigsaw puzzle-shaped Bravo airspace of Phoenix Sky

Harbor (KPHX), the eighth busiest airport in the country (see Figure 20). To reach some of the practice areas meant crossing the Bravo from one side to the other and back. That was a lot of towers to talk to, and a lot of complicated airspace to figure my way around, starting the moment I got into the cockpit.

Before heading to bed that first night, I took a walk along the street running beside the airport, past some hangers to the parking lot of the flight school I'd be showing up to the next day. All was quiet, for now. Outside a glass-walled administrative building an old Stearman biplane, in yellow and blue U.S. Army Air Corps colors, hung suspended in mid-flight from a glass atrium ceiling. During World War II, thousands of brand-new enlistees learned to fly in Stearmans before shipping out for duty overseas, in intensive training programs crammed into a few short weeks. Now I was about to embark on my own "crash course," at least for the next few days. I wondered if I was up to it.

When I arrived at 8:30 a.m. the next morning, the school was already bustling. Several students—not one of them over 30—were busy preparing for their morning flights. The school had two practice simulators, one of which was already in use. Through a door down the hall, I could see an instructor teaching a classroom full of aspiring CFIs. Celine, the young office manager who had contacted me by email over the previous few days, greeted me dressed in a well-pressed pilot's uniform complete with epaulettes, which contrasted with her soft-spoken tone. She ushered me into her office to look over my logbook and handed me a copy of the flight school's own customized, 200-page textbook. She paired me up with Brian, a 20-something instructor with a blond crewcut, and informed me that the two of us would begin with a knowledge review session on the ground, followed by a three-hour evaluation flight after lunch, to see where I stood.

The ground review session proved useful (I'll say more about it later), but all I could think about was getting into the air. By 1:00 p.m., the sun was beating down mercilessly, and the airport was a hive of activity. Brian and I met behind the school and strolled over to one of three Cessna 172s parked on the nearby tarmac. He watched me do my pre-flight check, spot-checking me with a few questions, and then I hooked up my Sentry and *ForeFlight*, which would help me keep track of the lay of the land. At this point back home, we would just hop in the plane, start it up, and—after quick call out on the radio—take off. But this was a towered airport, so before anything else I had to tune in the ATIS frequency (118.6), take down the weather information, and adjust the altimeter accordingly. Only then could I radio the **Ground** controller on 121.6 for permission to taxi. All radio calls follow the same pattern: who you are talking to, who you are, where you are, and what you want:

> *Scottsdale Ground, Skyhawk Four-Eight-Two-Mike-Kilo, at the flight school ramp with ATIS information Oscar, requesting taxi to the active runway.*

To make sure I didn't stumble, Brian had me rehearse this to him before I pressed down the radio button, on the yoke, to make the actual call. Then I waited a moment to hear ATC's reply:

> *Skyhawk Four-Eight-Two-Mike-Kilo, proceed to hold short Runway Two-One via Alpha.*

I then repeated this information back to Ground. Without this exchange, we were not allowed to pass the dashed Movement Area line on the tarmac, which separated our parking area from the taxiways. I consulted the printed taxi diagram on my lap to confirm that I knew the indicated route to the active runway via Taxiway Alpha. As I began to taxi, I continued monitoring the ground frequency in case of further instructions, and for good reason: Several times I was instructed to halt until other traffic could pass. There were dozens of planes making their way to and from the runways: sleek corporate jets, small trainers (like mine), a red aerobatic biplane, and even some kind of jet fighter (which caused even my instructor to crane his neck for a better look). I performed my run-up while waiting in line, and eventually took my position at the hold short line (solid yellow lines closest to me, dashed yellow lines on the far side) marking the entrance to the runway. Now I could change the frequency to 119.9 to contact Tower.

📡 *Scottsdale Tower, Skyhawk Four-Eight-Two-Mike-Kilo, at Alpha One-Fife, holding short Runway Two-One, southwest departure to the Bravo Transition.*

I was telling Tower we were ready to depart and where we intended to go after taking off, so they could direct us on our way. Keeping with radio protocol, I kept my transmission as concise as possible and said "niner" and "fife" rather than nine and five to avoid being misheard. Tower briefly acknowledged our presence, then we waited.

While we waited, I had a moment to visualize what was happening all around me. Scottsdale's Delta (Class D) airspace reaches out in a circle, four nautical miles in every direction, from the ground to 2,500 feet above it. Since the airport's elevation is already 1,510 feet above sea level, that meant it tops out at 4,000 feet MSL on the altimeter. On the chart, displayed in Figure 20, this area is marked by a blue dashed circle just north of central Phoenix. A jot to the northwest, almost touching it, is another blue dashed circle defining an almost identical Delta airspace next door, at Deer Valley (KDVT). The airspace around and directly over these circles is relatively more relaxed: Golf closest to the ground, and then Echo above it.

But above that, looming over everything like the canopy of a large tree, are various "shelves" of Bravo airspace belonging to Phoenix Sky Harbor, with each distinct sliver outlined in solid blue lines. Its ceiling is constant at 9,000 feet MSL, but its floor descends like a series of steps, from an outermost layer at 8,000 feet MSL, dropping down to 6,000 directly over much of Scottsdale Airport, then to 5,000 to the southwest, in the direction we were taking off. One layer of Bravo shelf even rests directly on a corner of Scottsdale's Delta. Over Sky Harbor itself, just a few miles farther, the Bravo comes all the way down to the surface, effectively blocking our path to the south.

That left some room to maneuver around the area without talking to a control tower, but not much. To enter Scottsdale's Delta—or any of the other nearby Deltas, for that matter—does not require formal clearance, but it does require two-way radio communication with Tower first, which means hearing them say your call sign back to you. Ideally, that's done at least 10 miles out, though here that could be tricky, depending on what direction you are coming from. If you intend to land, Tower will tell you where and when to enter the traffic pattern—it could be downwind, base, or straight in, depending on their convenience—and eventually give you final landing clearance. If you're just passing through, Tower might give you a direction or altitude to follow, or some area to steer clear of. It might tell you to circle, if things start to get too crowded.

What happens if you screw up or don't comply? Think of it like a traffic ticket. Typically, the controller will give you a telephone number to call after you land. (Everyone else, listening to this request, will be thinking to themselves "Uh oh, you're in *trouble!*") Like a traffic ticket, the penalty depends on how serious the infraction was and how many others you have. Your license could be suspended or revoked, or you could be fined. If you have a good record, you might be let off with a warning or required do some remedial safety training. There are only two instances in which a pilot is allowed to break the rules, any rule: to prevent a collision, or in the case of a genuine emergency. This isn't an all-purpose excuse, however. Once you are safely on the ground, you may be required to write the authorities a letter explaining your actions and the reasons for them.

So there I was, holding short of the runway, listening to the controllers in the tower talk to about a dozen other airplanes overhead, waiting next to me on other taxiways, and coming in to land. I had to keep a careful ear out for our call sign, however, because in a few minutes I abruptly heard the following:

📡 *Skyhawk Two-Mike-Kilo, cleared for takeoff Runway Two-One, maintain runway heading.*

Once you get clearance at a busy airport, it's a narrow window. You don't dawdle. Quickly repeating the information back, I rolled right out to the centerline of the runway and, without stopping, pushed the throttle in full and began my takeoff.

At an elevation of 1,510 feet, it might seem like Scottsdale isn't that high. But with the temperature at 35°C (95°F), the density altitude was over 4,000 feet, compared to nearly sea level back home. Furthermore, I was flying a 172R instead of a 172S, with an engine producing 160 horsepower rather than 180. I could feel all of these differences as the airplane gained speed down the runway. Back home, the Cessna vaulted itself off the runway at 55 knots, and I usually had to put forward pressure on the yoke to keep the nose from pitching too high. Here I had to apply some actual back pressure to coax the plane off the ground. As the airspeed approached 80, my normal climb speed, Brian warned me to let the nose down further and climb at 90. That would gain altitude more slowly but create more airflow over the engine to cool it. I noticed that the oil temperature gauge was already pressing the upper boundary between green and red. In this environment, it would be all too easy to overheat the engine.

📡 *Skyhawk Two-Mike-Kilo, proceed on course, frequency change approved.*

That was Scottsdale Tower telling us we no longer had to hold the runway heading in our climb, and could proceed on our way and leave their radio frequency. We weren't out of their Delta airspace yet, but they knew where we were going, and were helpfully giving us a head start on contacting ATC at Sky Harbor.

As I explained in Chapter 10 on Charts, Class B airports are the largest and busiest in the country. Like other Bravos, Phoenix's airspace is shaped like an elaborate upside-down wedding cake, with multiple layers and specific slices cut out or added to reflect the standard approaches to its runways. The purpose of all of this is simple: to keep you and your little Cessna well out of the way of the many airliners that are taking off and landing. To enter Bravo airspace requires not only two-way radio contact, as with Class D and even C airports, but explicit **clearance** from Air Traffic Control. You have to ask for permission to enter, and if you don't belong there, they won't give it. Student pilots flying solo need a special endorsement from their instructor to enter a specific Bravo, and some of the busiest Class B airports, such as Newark, don't allow it at all.

An airplane could fly right over to top of Phoenix's Bravo at 9,000 feet MSL, but since we started off underneath its outer shelves that wasn't a feasible option. We could stay under and around it, but that would be quite a detour. Fortunately, there is a special air corridor set up to allow VFR aircraft like us to go safely through it (make a Bravo **transition**), without obstructing the airport's main traffic—as long as we got clearance first.

I was in Echo airspace now, leveling off at 4,000 feet MSL, under the Bravo shelf, with Phoenix's landmark Camelback Mountain to my left. I tuned in 120.7 on the radio to call Phoenix Approach. Unlike a Class D airport, at a Class B or C airport you don't contact Tower directly. You contact **Approach**, on its own frequency, to talk to a different air traffic controller who—like the Ground controller telling planes where to taxi—doesn't have to worry about clearing planes to take off and land. If you're passing through, you'll probably just keep talking to Approach until you leave the airspace, but if you intend to land, Approach will hand you off to Tower, on its own frequency, when you're within sight of the airport. If you're departing a Class B or C airport, Tower will clear you to take off, then hand you over to Departure (yet another controller) to direct you on your way. This more complex arrangement, compared to Class D, simply reflects a division of labor among controllers to handle the busier traffic in and around a Class B or C airport. In fact, the largest Class B airports like Phoenix typically have several Approach, Departure, and even Tower frequencies for different sectors.

📡 *Phoenix Approach, Skyhawk Four-Eight-Two-Mike-Kilo, at Piestewa Peak, 4000, request Bravo Transition to the South Practice Area.*

Piestewa Peak, a small mountain directly north of Sky Harbor, is a VFR waypoint, marked on the sectional chart with a small red flag. That means it's a known reference point for ATC on their radars, so by mentioning it, along with our altitude, they would know exactly where we were.

I wish I can say I made this announcement confidently and well, but at this point I was nervous as hell. We weren't talking to some tower that patiently handles clueless student pilots all day—this was Air Traffic Control at one of the busiest airports in the country, and we were asking permission to fly straight over its main runways. We were a mere 1,000 feet below one Bravo shelf, and if I kept flying our current heading, would soon run smack into another one. What's more, the frequency was alive with what sounded like dozens of call signs being shouted back and forth. I strained carefully to catch any mention of my own—which, since I was in a brand-new plane, was still unfamiliar to my ears.

📡 *Skyhawk Four-Eight-Two-Mike-Kilo, squawk 3242, ident.*

At a Class D airport, controllers may have a handful of aircraft to handle in their vicinity at any given moment. At a Class B, there could be dozens of blips on their radar, so to go anywhere within 30 nautical miles of a Class B airport—inside the solid magenta circle called the "Mode C Veil"—requires an altitude-transmitting transponder and ADB-Out, to help ATC track them all. Since takeoff, already inside the veil, we had our transponder on and set to "**squawk**" (transmit) the default VFR code 1200. Now Approach was telling me to enter a new code, 3242, into my transponder and press the "Ident" button, which would cause my radar blip to light up for a few seconds on their screens and make me easier to find. They don't always tell you to press Ident, and you shouldn't unless they do. Because this was my first time to the dance, and I wasn't expecting this instruction, I stumbled and had to ask Brian what code they had said. He told me, I repeated it back to them, entered it into the transponder, and hit Ident.

This was *not* clearance. This was just processing the request. To avoid entering the Bravo prematurely, Brian told me to begin a turn to the right, circling over Piestewa Peak. While keeping half my mind on the turn, and neither gaining nor losing altitude, the other half listened frantically to the radio chatter for my call sign, fearing I could miss it. Then I heard:

> 📡 Skyhawk Four-Eight-Two-Mike-Kilo, cleared into Bravo airspace via the east transition, altimeter 29.94, climb and maintain 4500.

First I had to repeat that back to them, then I had to remember it, then I had to do it. My brain was already fried from the tension. Unsure of myself, I had to check with Brian to make sure I had really heard the magic word "cleared." Yes, I had. So I finished my turn and aimed straight over the end of the two busy runways, while climbing to my new altitude.

It's actually very, very cool to fly directly over a Boeing 787 airliner as it takes off or touches down a few thousand feet below you. Small aircraft need to be careful around large jets, not only due to their speed (about twice the speed you're going), but also the **wake turbulence** created by their passage. Wake turbulence is caused by eddies of air, called **wingtip vortices**, generated around the tips of an airplane's wings as they produce lift. These disruptions spread behind and below the path of that airplane, especially if it's large and (relatively) slow on takeoff or landing, and can create a real hazard to smaller aircraft that get caught up in them. But flying above the airliners, we were well clear of their descending wake and could enjoy a truly memorable view.

I had to keep listening hard for my call sign, because during the transition, ATC might warn you to look for aircraft transitioning from the other direction—perhaps a mere 500 feet above or below you—or give you a new altitude. About midway across they had me change to a new frequency, as I entered a new sector to the south. Finally, however, I heard:

📡 *Skyhawk Four-Eight-Two-Mike-Kilo, squawk VFR, altitude restriction lifted, frequency change approved.*

That meant I was clear of the Bravo, as far as they were concerned, and could proceed as I wished. But first I had to repeat those instructions back to them, and then change my transponder code back to 1200.

Whew! We were barely 20 minutes into the flight, and I felt ready to land and call it a day. I could already tell that my time in Arizona was going to be a wild ride.

CHAPTER 20

Arizona

My first three days in Arizona fell into a pattern: three hours of ground school in the morning, followed by three hours of flying in the afternoon. When Celine first told me I'd be reviewing their textbook with Brian, from front to back, it crossed my mind to object—after all, I had come all this way for the flying weather—but I bit my tongue. They obviously had a system, and as a new student, I had to earn their confidence. As it turned out, I found the ground sessions very worthwhile. Since he knew I had scored 100 on the FAA written exam, the conversation focused on identifying and filling the holes in my knowledge. I came to appreciate that it's one thing to recognize answers from multiple choice, quite another to fully explain a subject in my own words, as I eventually would have to do on the oral portion of the checkride. We covered a third of the book that first morning, then completed the rest over the next two mornings for a total of nine hours of one-on-one ground school. It wasn't what I had planned, but in truth, I was glad I did it.

As we broke for lunch on the first day, Brian showed me a wall full of info packets, copied from the POH of each airplane in the school's fleet, that could be used for planning purposes. Each day, by our scheduled flight time, I was expected to prepare the weight and balance sheet for whichever plane we were assigned. I had done these types of calculations on the exam, but this was my first time doing them in actual practice—typically over a hurried meal of chicken salad and crackers from the Best Western's lobby pantry. By the end of the week, I felt like an old pro at it.

The ideal time to fly in the desert is early morning before the heat sets in. By the time we took off each afternoon, the air was usually a little turbulent. Over the practice area, we regularly encountered patches of thermals—columns of warm air rising off the desert floor—which made it difficult to maintain a steady altitude. It took a bit to get used to flying in a very different climate, at a different elevation, in a slightly different model of airplane. Understandably, most people learn to fly in only one part of the country, then get a rude shock when they fly somewhere else. Experiencing and contending with this new environment was, from my perspective, one more benefit of this Arizona trip.

Each day we practiced the standard maneuvers, tedious as they sometimes felt: slow flight, stalls, steep turns, S-turns, turns around a point. We transitioned though the Bravo multiple times, so it became, if not routine, at least less terrifying. We knocked out the last of the three required hours of flying "under the hood" by instruments, which I had begun with Tess. We also practiced landings at several different airports in the Phoenix area.

After spending so much time and effort on my landings back home, I was feeling pretty confident, especially considering the much larger runways I had to work with here. I was in for a surprise. On the very first day, near the end of my initial evaluation flight, we headed to Deer Valley Airport, which was supposed to be less busy than Scottsdale. After getting the ATIS and contacting Tower I was directed to join the downwind approach to Runway 25L. Everything was going great on final until, crossing the runway threshold, I pulled the throttle back to idle and put both hands on the yoke to round out and flare. "What are you doing?!" Brian yelled, which rattled me and probably produced a bumpier landing than usual. As we taxied off the runway to a full stop, he explained to me that on landing, I should never take my right hand off the throttle. That meant I needed to learn how to control the yoke with my left hand alone.

Tess had mentioned this as *desirable,* but had never insisted on it. Still, I saw Brian's point. If anything happened on landing that forced me to go around, a hand on the throttle, instead of two on the yoke, might make a split-second difference between success and failure. I resolved—as if I had any choice—to land one-handed from now. Initially I found it difficult, for two reasons. First, the force I had to exert to push the yoke forward or back, with my left arm alone, was more than I was previously accustomed to. Second, when I put both hands on the yoke I felt centered on it, like a driver behind the wheel of a car. With only one hand, at first, I felt vaguely off-center. It was an awkwardness I would have to overcome; in the meantime, it didn't do any wonders for the smoothness my landings had only recently acquired.

A few days later, at a small non-towered airstrip out in the desert, Brian introduced me to another important landing technique, the **forward slip**. When you are coming in too low on final approach, the solution is fairly straightforward: put in the throttle, not to climb, but to level off while retaining speed, until you reach the correct angle to the runway where you can resume your normal descent. You often have to add more power than you'd think, because the flaps are fully down, creating a lot of drag, but as long as you're assertive and keep a close eye on the airspeed indicator, it works. If you're coming in too high, on the other hand, you need a way to descend more quickly without gaining unwanted speed. Sometimes pulling the throttle out to idle and just gliding down is enough. But sometimes it's not.

To show me another alternative, my instructor had me come all the way around base to final *without* beginning my descent. As I turned to final, we were *way* too high even to glide down without power, without gaining a ton of airspeed. So instead, Brian had me kick the right rudder in *full,* yawing the nose away from the runway. To prevent from turning that way, however, I turned the yoke (and the ailerons) almost full to the left. It was the same maneuver as a sideslip on crosswind, but instead of putting myself back *in line* with the runway by countering the wind, I was purposely turning the side of my aircraft to the entire airflow while forcing it to keep traveling straight ahead. This created a lot more drag, which would have slowed the aircraft, so I push the yoke hard forward to lower the nose and descend. My airspeed remained steady as I dropped like a stone. It looked and felt like I was riding down in an elevator, for just long enough to wonder whether I could get off. But the unnatural posture I had forced the plane into, against its own inclinations, was also my salvation. As soon as I reached the proper glideslope and saw the runway from the expected angle, all I had to do was release the controls back to their normal position to "step off" the elevator and let the plane fly again like it wanted to. From there, the landing went surprisingly like normal.

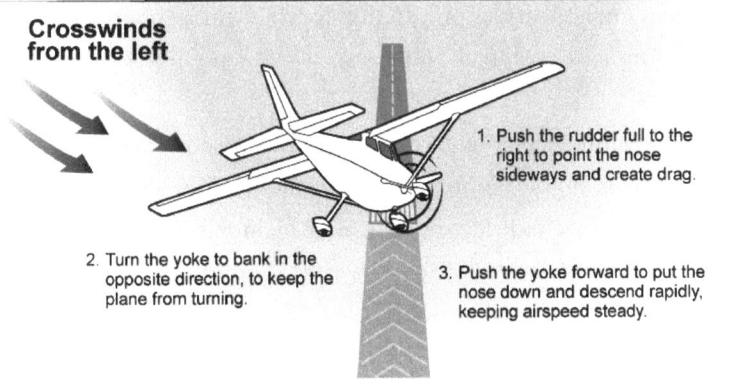

The forward slip, a method to quickly lose unwanted altitude, without gaining unwanted speed, on approach to land. If there is any crosswind, that's the direction you want to bank into.

In his memoir *Flight of Passage*, which chronicles two teenage brothers flying coast-to-coast in a Piper Cub in the 1960s, author Rinker Buck often referred with awe to his older brother forward slipping to land on a tiny runway. In Rinker's eyes, it was like pulling a rabbit out of a magic hat, and testament to his brother's astonishing natural skills as a pilot.[178] The Bucks were the kind of boys who learned from their father (an old Stearman pilot from the war) before they could shave, and in many ways I envied them.[179] The forward slip was a pretty nifty trick, and I enjoyed it a lot. But I recognized it would take a lot of practice to do confidently and well.

Besides flying one-handed, Brian also emphasized another discipline: in-flight **checklists**. Back home, I had certainly followed the lengthy checklists for conducting my pre-flight inspection and run-up before takeoff. But once in the air, we tended to focus on learning the most common procedures by heart. This made sense, in a way, because the Cessna 172 is a simple aircraft and the in-flight checklists are quite brief. The Climb Checklist in the POH, for instance, consists solely of confirming airspeed, throttle, and mixture. The After Landing Checklist has but one entry: "wing flaps—up." But, Brian emphasized, it's important to establish the *habit* of using checklists even when they might seem unnecessary, as preparation for flying more complex aircraft, where it is all too easy to forget and miss a vital step—like lowering your landing gear.

Some of the more elaborate checklists involved responding to emergencies, such as a fire or engine failure, which I would practice a great deal more back home prior to my checkride. But the most memorable experience, along these lines, was a real-life emergency that we heard unfold over the radio. We were holding short for takeoff at Scottsdale when suddenly over the Tower frequency we heard another Cessna 172 in the air declare "**Mayday! Mayday! Mayday!** Engine out." Everyone immediately went silent so the controller—who was understandably flustered—could communicate with the pilot. The anxiety in her voice reflected her powerlessness. She told the pilot he was clear to land, but he replied, with mounting tension, that he could not make it and was intending to land on a road. He gave the rough vicinity of where he was going down, then stopped responding. The controller announced she was dispatching emergency services to the site and, as no one could do anything more to help, Tower went back to directing normal traffic. Later I saw on the news that the pilot did successfully land on a road north of Phoenix without damage or injury.[180] His plane had run out of fuel—a surprisingly frequent cause of accidents.[181] He had rented it and was told by the owner that it had enough fuel for a two-hour flight, but apparently flew too far[182]—a good reminder to take pre-flight planning and inspection seriously.

There were moments of comedy, as well. Setting out one day, I finished my start-up, called Ground, and received permission to taxi. But when I released the brakes and revved the engine to move, the plane refused to budge. Looking frantically around, I saw out my window that the wheel chocks—wooden blocks preventing the tires from rolling—were still in place. We never used chocks at Lincoln Park and they weren't on any formal checklist, so I had plum forgotten to remove them. When the propeller is spinning, you can't just hop out of the airplane to do something—that's a big safety no-no. You have to shut the whole thing down and go through the entire start-up procedure again. Brian called ATC and let them know we weren't ready to move, kindly omitting the reason. He let me stew in my embarrassment until we were ready to go again, when with a grin he reassured me: "I've done it myself. It happens to everyone."

Brian was even younger than Tess, and that created a somewhat curious dynamic between us. There were times when he sharply corrected me, and I'll admit that I instinctively—if quietly—bridled at being scolded by someone half my age. But the fact that I remember those corrections over a year later suggests that they served an important purpose, by getting my attention. For his part, I sensed that Brian treated me with, if not respect, at least consideration due to my age—I wasn't some 17-year-old kid who needed reminding to take flying more seriously. For my part, I reminded myself that true respect had to be earned. After all, I could easily get both of us killed by doing something stupid, and that left no room for coddling my feelings.

The days in Arizona were rewarding but stressful. The first few evenings, I walked back to the Best Western and took a few laps in the pool to unwind the tension and relieve the heat. The glass-walled airport building with the Stearman on display contained a nice restaurant with an outside balcony where I could watch the corporate jets, as well as other student pilots, come and go. It was strange but thrilling to be so focused on flying, from dawn to dusk. Normal life seemed so far away.

On Wednesday night, however, there was no time for relaxing. We had completed reviewing the entire textbook that day, so I had no ground session the following morning. Instead, I had two cross-country flights scheduled for the next day: one in the afternoon, the other at night, both accompanied by my instructor. I was given the airports, but the route and all the planning were up to me to figure out. Meanwhile, I had to fill out the school's own pre-solo exam so I could be approved to do solo flights once I returned—standard stuff, but time-consuming.

Back in my hotel room that evening, I spread the sectional chart out on a table to consider my options. You can see the environs and the route I chose in Figure 21. The daytime flight would take me to Marana (KAVQ), a small airport on the outskirts of Tucson, about 80 miles southeast of Phoenix, then to Coolidge (P08) on the way back, before returning to Scottsdale. The night flight would go to Marana and then straight back. Otherwise, the two routes were virtually identical.

Interstate 10, which connects Phoenix and Tucson, offered the most obvious path to follow, one that should be easy to see day or night. As much as I might like to avoid it, the Bravo transition directly over Sky Harbor provided the obvious route to link up with I-10 on the south edge of Phoenix. I figured this was intentional, and expected. Further along the way, I identified several landmarks about 10 to 20 miles apart—a couple of other airfields, some major highway intersections, and a few prominent terrain features—which I believed I'd be able to spot from the air, in order to verify I was on course and on time. I marked down the frequencies of nearby VORs in case I got lost, but for this flight at least, I thought it would make most sense to rely primarily on old-fashioned pilotage, aided by my dead reckoning estimates.

To start those estimates, I needed to select a **cruising altitude**—the height in MSL that I would climb to and maintain for most of my flight en route. When pilots file an IFR flight plan, ATC assigns them a cruising altitude in the round thousands. To avoid them, VFR pilots are expected to stick to cruising altitudes midway in-between, at the 500-mark. Flying VFR to the east, between 0° and 179° magnetic, you should cruise at any *odd-numbered* thousand plus 500 feet (e.g. 3,500, 5,500, 7,500); flying west, between

180° and 359°, at any *even-numbered* thousand plus 500 (e.g. 4,500, 6,500, 8,500). From these options, I needed to choose two cruising altitudes (one there and one back) that were low enough to reach quickly, high enough to stay safely clear of terrain, and—ideally—enjoyed favorable winds.

I'd have to wait to get the winds the next morning, but barring any big surprises, I made some provisional choices. On the way down, I planned to climb to 5,500 feet MSL as soon as I could get out from under the 5,000-foot Bravo shelf. I would fly the way back at 4,500 feet. That should keep me a safe 1,000 feet above any obstacle directly along my planned route, but I noted that there were some mountains to either side that either reached or exceeded these elevations. Though they could serve as helpful landmarks, they could also be hazards if I didn't take care, especially at night. Even during the day, mountains affect the air around them, producing strong updrafts, downdrafts, and turbulence—invisible hazards that make "mountain flying" its own special category of training. I didn't expect to fly close enough to them for this to be a factor, but it was important to be aware.

I marked down the elevations for the airports at Marana and Coolidge, as well as their traffic pattern altitudes, so I would know how to plan my approaches. I noticed that both airports had right instead of left traffic patterns for certain runways, an important thing to remember. Neither of the two airports had control towers, and after leaving the Bravo I would be traveling almost entirely through Class E airspace. That meant, once south of Phoenix, I wouldn't have to deal much with Air Traffic Control. But I still needed to mark down the CTAFs, or common traffic frequencies, for both airports as well as their AWOS (the non-towered equivalent of ATIS) frequencies to get the latest available weather information when I arrived. Just in case, I also noted the radio frequencies for several airports—Chandler (KCHD), Casa Grande (KCGZ), Eloy (E60), and Pinal (KMZJ)—that I would be passing en route, and for Flight Service and the regional ATC center as well. Most of these could be found on the chart, but having them closer at hand couldn't hurt.

Hopefully I wouldn't get lost or need to deviate from my planned route, but you never know. With this in mind, I spent some time familiarizing myself with the general area, especially any nearby airspace restrictions. Just south of Marana is Saguaro National Park. While it's not strictly a rule, aircraft are strongly requested not to fly lower than 2,000 feet above any national park or nature preserve. Further south is a Class D airport at Ryan Field, and more significantly, a co-joined Class C airspace around Tucson International and Davis-Monthan Air Force Base. There is a large MOA (Military Operations Area, bordered by a magenta hatched line) to the southwest, extending down to Mexico, where border agents conduct air patrols. There's another large MOA just northeast of Coolidge—used by pilots from Luke Air Force Base training in F-16 and F-35 jet fighters—that includes a small sliver of blue hatchmarked Restricted Area which is prohibited to enter. Unless I got myself way off course, these should not be a concern.

This was about all I could do before going to bed. I had to wait until the next morning, within six hours of takeoff, to call Flight Service for my weather briefing. It turned out to be typical Arizona weather: clear skies, with no notable weather hazards except for some light turbulence. There were no temporary flight restrictions to pose any unexpected difficulties. High afternoon temperatures were expected to translate into high density altitudes, which meant longer takeoffs and slower climbs but faster cruising speeds. I noted down the Winds Aloft, METARs, and TAFs to use in my flight planning calculations.

"Flight plan" actually refers to two related but different things: one you can file with the authorities, the other you take with you into the cockpit. You can file a formal flight plan with FSS either by phone or online, typically when you get your weather briefing. Pilots flying IFR must file a flight plan, because that is how they get route clearance from ATC, but for VFR, it's entirely optional. The main reason to do it is that if you go missing, someone will start looking for you, and have some idea where to look. After you've filed, you then call FSS to "open" the flight plan right before takeoff. You have to remember to call them back and "close" it once you land—or let them know that you've been delayed. If they don't hear from you within 30 minutes after your expected arrival time, the authorities will start calling around, and eventually launch a very expensive and very pointless search and rescue operation—for which you will receive a very large bill. In this case, there was no real need to file a flight plan because my flight school knew exactly where my instructor and I were going and when we should be back, and would sound the alarm if we didn't.

Whether or not they file it, nearly all pilots carry a flight plan with them to use as a reference in the cockpit. It can be entered into *ForeFlight* or an onboard avionics system, but for training purposes today, we were doing it old school, with everything condensed onto a single sheet of paper (below) that Brian would review prior to our departure and I would hold on my lap en route. In addition to vital airport information, it listed each leg of my intended journey with the calculated course, heading, groundspeed, distance, flying time, and fuel burn for each. After receiving the weather briefing, I

The pen-and-paper flight plan for the first leg of my day cross-country flight, from Scottsdale (KSDL) to Marana (KAVQ).

spent the rest of the morning furiously figuring and rechecking the calculations for each. Every detail mattered. Back home, the magnetic variation was 13°West, which needed to be added to find magnetic heading. Here, the lines on the chart showed 10°East, which had to be subtracted—a small but vital difference. I added the required 30 minutes reserve fuel, plus some, to confirm that we carried enough fuel for the entire trip. Finally, I computed the weight and balance, along with the minimum takeoff and landing distances, for each stage of the route.

Time was quickly running out as my 1:00 p.m. flight time approached. I had worked on each piece of this puzzle in preparing for the written exam, but this was my first time putting it all together in real life, seeing all the elements come together into something real. While I couldn't take *ForeFlight* with me into the cockpit on this trip, before leaving I did enter the flight plan into the app to make sure all my pencil-and-paper calculations matched up reasonably well. Hurrying out the door, I stuffed the folded sectional chart, marked with the route, along with printed-out taxi diagrams for each airport in my flight bag. I marched over to the school, where Brian quickly reviewed my preparations, and we were on our way.

I don't want to say the cross-country flight was an anti-climax. But it was nowhere near as stressful as the pre-flight preparation. Taxi, takeoff, and even the Bravo transition took place without a hitch. Before I knew it, we were leveling off at 5,500 feet, with the sun-bleached Arizona desert spread out before us. I-10 proved ridiculously easy to follow, and each checkpoint was visible for miles ahead. The standard was to reach each checkpoint plus or minus three minutes the calculated time, and we hit each one on the head. Soon Brian stopped spot-checking and pulled his seat back to enjoy the view.

By now, Brian was starting to trust my flying abilities more and our conversation became more easy-going. As we flew over Pinal Airpark, and began our descent towards Marana, he leaned over and snapped some cell phone photos of the dozens of airliners parked on its taxiways for storage, in the dry desert sun. After many tedious hours practicing maneuvers and tense sessions mastering landings, flying had become an adventure again. For the first time, the anxious concerns of learning to fly fell away, and I found myself on a majestic sightseeing tour over a wondrous landscape. For months, I had been intent on the task in front of me, with barely a chance to look around, driven by the desire to prove—if only to myself—that I could do it. That gave me a sense of accomplishment, to be sure, but this … this was *fun*.

Something that awaited us at Marana made it even more fun. When I was 12 years old, my parents took me to White Stallion Ranch outside of Tucson. I learned to ride a horse, stayed up late playing poker, and came away with a treasure trove of memories. The previous February, just before COVID-19 broke out, I brought my own wife and children back to White Stallion, almost 40 years later, for them to have the same experience. They loved it. Now, as I taxied back for takeoff from Marana, I told Brian what I had discovered while planning the flight: the ranch is located just next to the airport. I could even see it as we came in to land. Brian suggested that before turning back north we take a pass to catch a better view of it, as close and as low as we could without annoying anyone on the ground. I leapt at the chance. As we circled overhead, careful to maintain a safe distance, Brian offered to take the controls for a moment so I could take a few photos to send my family back home. There it was: the corral, the bungalows, the riding trails—all from a perspective I never expected to experience.

It gave me a lot to think about as we flew home, back up I-10, past an uneventful stop at Coolidge, and on towards our reentry to the Bravo. To be honest, I didn't know what to expect from coming to Arizona. I signed up out of frustration at the chronic delays that had stood between me and my first solo, but that had worked out before I left. Yet I had still come, with little more than a gut feeling that a bout of serious flying would do me some good. And I now realized that it had, in two ways. First, flying with a different instructor, in a different environment, under a very different learning regimen, had revealed a lot to me about my strengths and remaining weaknesses as a pilot, and pushed me in the direction of fixing those weaknesses. Second, on this flight, I finally saw all the pieces—airspace, maneuvers, weather, navigation, landings, knowledge of the machine, knowledge of myself—come together in a way that gave me growing confidence that I could soon be ready to do this myself.

I didn't have a lot of time to ponder these things, however, because the moment we landed in Scottsdale, we realized that we had only an hour before our night cross-country was scheduled to begin. The sun was setting, and I had to run back to my hotel room to call for a quick weather update and run all the new calculations for the next flight. At that moment, I would have sorely loved to soak in the pool for a bit. Instead, I grabbed a candy bar as my dinner and trudged back to school in the gathering darkness, revised flight plan in hand.

The words of Robert Frost's poem came to mind.

But I have promises to keep,
And miles to go before I sleep,
And miles to go before I sleep.[183]

CHAPTER 21

Night

There are three requirements for night flying that must be completed before getting a Private Pilot License, and we planned to knock them all out in one evening. First, you have to fly three hours at night. Second, those hours must include a cross-country flight of over 100 nautical miles. Third, you have to make 10 night-time takeoffs and landings to a full stop. All of these are done alongside an instructor; only the commercial license requires you to fly solo at night.

But what exactly is "night"? There are three different criteria, depending on why you are asking. The method I made up to remember them was the phrase "LIGHTS (self-explanatory), CAMERA (recording flight hours), AC-TION (carrying passengers)":

- LIGHTS: From sunset to sunrise, aircraft are required to turn on their navigation lights for night-time recognition.

- CAMERA: Pilots can log "night" hours from the end of **civil twilight** at dusk to the start of civil twilight before dawn. Civil twilight takes place after sunset and before sunrise when the sun is no more than six degrees below the horizon, creating enough light to perform normal daytime tasks. The precise times vary by location and day of the year and used to be published in almanacs, but now can be quickly looked up online.

- ACTION: To carry passengers during the period from one hour after sunset to one hour before sunrise—when real darkness prevails—a pilot must be current: They must have performed three takeoffs and three full-stop "night" landings during that same period of darkness in the past 90 days.

To log three night hours, we needed to make sure we departed after civil twilight at Scottsdale for May 6, 2021, which was 7:40 p.m., 25 minutes after sunset. For my 10 night takeoffs and landings to count for my requirements, I needed to do them at least an hour after sunset, but we knew by the time we reached Marana that would no longer be an issue.

You might think that flying in the dark with its diminished—or at least significantly altered—visibility would require an instrument rating. It does not. Any pilot with a private license can take off and fly at night under otherwise VFR conditions, and can take passengers along if the recent takeoff and landing requirements are met. Still, flying VFR at night is a very different experience than during the day, and not to be taken lightly. Many of the same sensory illusions that can throw pilots off when blanketed in clouds are present at night, plus a few new ones. The required night training for a PPL is really more about orienting new pilots to the challenges than qualifying them to go right out and tackle them on their own. Even after earning their license, a prudent pilot might be well advised to invite a CFI or instrument-rated pilot along for the ride as they gain more experience night flying.

To begin with, our eyes see differently at night. At the back of our eyeballs are two kinds of receptors: **cones** and **rods**. Cones, which are grouped near the center, are adept at perceiving detail and color. When we focus on something during the day, we are relying on our cones; at night, the cones are far less effective. Rods are more evenly distributed across our retinas. They are quick to pick up motion, including on the periphery of our vision, and are more sensitive to low levels of light. (To remember this, I told myself that "rods help you spot a mugger about to hit you on the side of the head with a rod.") Rods are what we rely on for night vision, and this has some important implications. At night, we have a blind spot at the center of our vision which grows larger with distance and are better at seeing things if we look at them somewhat off-center. In the dark, we are much better off letting our eyes rove around picking up contrast and motion than trying to stare intently at any one object.

It takes about a half hour for our rods to become fully sensitized to the dark, and even a brief moment of exposure to bright light can spoil everything. You know exactly what that's like if you've ever been blinded by oncoming high-beam headlights or someone flashing them in your rearview mirror while driving. So when we arrived at the school, we kept the lights down low and I used a small flashlight to conduct my pre-flight inspection. Once we got into the cockpit, I'd switch its white lens to red, which is less disruptive to the rods. Although the instruments all have backlighting, I'd try to keep them dimmed to a minimum as well, to avoid glare on the windshield.

This time, my pre-flight inspection included checking the **navigation lights** on the airplane's wingtips and tail to make sure they were working. The light on the left wingtip (from the pilot's point of view) is red, while the one on the right is green. There's a white light on the back of the tail fin, along with a red flashing beacon light. The latter should always remain on (day or night) whenever the master switch is on, to warn that the aircraft is in operation.

This arrangement of lights, which is the same for all aircraft large and small, helps pilots quickly identify which direction an airplane they encounter at night is moving (see Figure 24). If you see only red and white lights, you're looking at the left side of an aircraft moving to the left. If you see only green and white lights, you are seeing the right side of an aircraft moving to the right. The wingtip lights are usually shielded so if you see the plane from the back, moving away from you, you only see the white tail fin light. But if you see green on the left and red on the right, beware—the other plane is coming straight towards you.

Many planes (including the Cessna 172) have white flashing strobe lights, also called anti-collision lights, on the tips of each wing as well. They are supposed to be turned on while in flight from takeoff to landing, day or night, to make the aircraft more visible to other traffic. While taxiing at busy airports, however, they are usually turned off to avoid distracting other pilots. As a result, turning them on or off is often part of the immediate pre-takeoff and post-landing checklists.

I also tested the taxi and landing lights on the forward edge of the left wing, though I did this from inside the cockpit to avoid damaging my night vision. These are basically white spotlights that shine down, at different angles, on the ground below to help illuminate it. The FAA advises flying with the landing lights on at lower altitudes, day or night, to make yourself that much more visible to other traffic. But landing lights technically aren't a required piece of equipment, even for night flying, and it's entirely possible to land without them solely by using the lights on the runway as reference. Much like wing flaps, they are helpful but not absolutely essential.

The airport was relatively quiet at this hour, so once we were ready there was little delay in getting permission to taxi and take off. I must admit, I was nervous about what flying at night would be like. From night flying on *MSFS* at home, I knew how that first moment on takeoff, when you pitch up and momentarily lose sight of the runway below, could be weirdly disorienting. So I felt a fleeting twinge of "What the hell am I getting myself into?" as I pushed the throttle in and began hurtling down the runway. To my surprise, though, I didn't find it disorienting at all. Perhaps I was growing more comfortable relying on the instruments in front of me; but I suspect it was also due to how brightly the lights of the city below illuminated the entire area, making it easy to keep my bearings. Even after we passed through the Bravo, and began crossing the desert to the south, the string of lights from the I-10 expressway presented a clear path to follow.

Flying at night, of course, was still a very different sensation. One of the trickier illusions is known as a **false horizon** in which light patterns on the ground, a partially illuminated cloud bank, or the backlit slope of a hillside can be mistaken for the level horizon, with potentially disastrous results. The antidote is to make consistent reference to the attitude indicator's artificial horizon instead of putting sole trust in your visual impressions. Another common phenomenon is **autokinesis**, when staring too long at a light will make it appear to move. This can be avoided by keeping your eyes in regular motion. Since there was so much to look at and take in along the journey, this was easy advice to follow.

I made note, along the way, of how pilotage works differently at night. Some features that stood out very prominently and made great checkpoints in the sunlight, such as a large quarry, were now blanketed in total darkness. In contrast, a playing field that was indistinguishable from the rest of suburbia during the day was now awash in lights and visible from many miles away. Picacho and Newman Peaks, which straddled I-10 and stood like a welcoming gateway to my destination on the day cross-country, now loomed as invisible dangers should I forget their presence.

Even entire airports could hide in the dark, unless you gave them a little help. To save electricity and assuage neighbors, many smaller airports have systems that allow pilots to turn on their runway and taxiway lights only when needed, by clicking your microphone button over their designated CTAF radio frequency a certain number of times. We tuned in Eloy Municipal as we passed by and gave it a try. Three clicks, in quick succession, and a black patch of ground suddenly blossomed into a fully lit airport. Five more clicks and the lights grew brighter. Seven more, brighter still. A timer would eventually turn them all off again.

One thing I soon wished I had was a headlamp. I had seen these curious devices, designed to be strapped to one's head, advertised in Sporty's catalog when I was shopping for a red lens flashlight. I thought they looked a bit ridiculous, like you were pretending to be some sort of surgeon in an operating room, so I passed. About halfway down to Marana, I already regretted that decision. Holding the yoke with one hand while consulting and making notes on your flight plan and chart with the other is hard enough; holding a flashlight to illuminate them with a third hand is something else.

Thumbing through these pilot catalogs often reminded me of my time in the military. Some of my more bemusing memories from serving in the Army involve the mail-order catalogs and stores on base that sold an endless array of doodads and gizmos that promised to make your life easier in the field. It was like a candy store. You could spend your entire paycheck on them if you wanted. In my experience, though, the old 80/20 rule prevailed: 80% of the merchandise would end up sitting in your closet, while the remaining 20% were must-haves and worth every cent. I now saw that I had woefully misjudged the headlamp and, ridiculous looking or not, it would be going on my wish list for next Christmas.

It wasn't long before I could see the rotating beacon at Marana in the distance ahead and began my descent. As I've mentioned, a little star above the airport icon on the sectional chart means the airport has a lighted beacon, which usually operates at night and in IFR conditions. Green and white alternating flashes means a civilian land-based airport. White-white-green signifies a military one, while white and yellow means a water airport for seaplanes, and white-yellow-green means a heliport. As we grew closer, I clicked the mic several times and the rest of the airport's lights sprang magically to life.

Landing at night should be done *exactly the same* as during the day—same speed, same glideslope, same round out and flare. This is easier said than done, however, due to the lack of visual references you normally rely so heavily on. Marana's runway was an island of light in a sea of inky blackness. The only other visible reference point at night was the line of interstate highway stretching towards Tucson through an otherwise light-less desert, along the outer edge of the traffic pattern. I had to trust to my altimeter—which I made sure to reset correctly from listening to the AWOS—that I was at a safe altitude over the unseen ground below.

Taxiways are fringed in blue lights, sometimes with green lights along their centerline. Runways have bright white lights defining their edges and centerline, but they can also get a lot more elaborate with green lights sometimes designating the near edge and red lights indicating that you're getting close to the far end. Often, as they were at Marana, runway lights can be one-directional, so that when I was on downwind they were dim and barely visible, and I had to infer the runway's location from the surrounding taxiway lights. Once I came abeam the numbers and began my descent, I couldn't see anything but pitch-black darkness ahead—though I knew a ridge of mountains waited there, just beyond the now-hidden White Stallion Ranch, if I didn't make my base turn on time.

The bright directional lights of Runway 30, as I swung from base onto final, were a welcome sight. But even here it can be tricky for pilots to interpret the visual clues and judge height and distance correctly. A runway that is sloping slightly downward (as it was here) or upward, or wider or narrower relative to its length, can throw perceptions off and make you think you are higher or lower on approach than you are. This is true in the day, but even more so at night. When the surrounding area is pitch dark—like it was here—and the runway's lights are the only reference point in sight, an illusion called the **black hole effect** can trick pilots into approaching too low and landing short of the runway. It has fooled even airline pilots and resulted in a number of deadly crashes before the adoption of visual approach aids like VASIs and PAPIs.[184] Fortunately, all of Marana's runways have a PAPI. As long as I had two white and two red lights all the way down, I knew I was on track.

Landing at night, it was even more important to keep my eyes raised to the distance, like I was driving down a dark highway, instead of looking down for a landing surface I could barely see. The cue to level off over the runway is the same sudden widening effect I observed during the daytime, except at night it was the edge lights I saw moving outwards in my peripheral vision. If anything, it's even more noticeable in the dark—as long as you're prepared and looking for it. That reassuring thump of the wheels touching down, after my flare, was even more welcome than usual. My landings had to be full-stop to qualify, but Runway 30 was long enough (almost 7,000 feet) to stop and then take off again, without exiting to taxi back. So we ran the same pattern over and over again, though the wind shifting to a brisk crosswind soon added another interesting challenge to the equation. Before I knew it, I had completed all 10 required landings. It was time to head back home.

The experience of flying at night was intimidating at first, but turned out to be another great adventure—my second that same day. Some time later, as we talked to Phoenix ATC and got clearance to cross the Bravo back to Scottsdale, we were greeted with a dazzling sight: below us, the lights of airliners taking off and landing on Sky Harbor's two main runways, and stretching towards the horizon, the blinking lights of the city spread out before us. I asked Brian to take the controls for a moment so I could snap a photo of this enchanting moment. I was almost sorry we had to land and call it a day.

Almost, but not quite. It was approaching midnight as I descended towards Scottsdale. The control tower was closed for the night, so I announced my own entry into the empty traffic pattern and came in to land. I had flown exactly 6.0 hours and over 350 nautical miles since lunchtime—basically, from Phoenix to Tucson and back, twice. I was exhilarated, but exhausted. I wouldn't be seeing Brian again—he had the next few days off—so I thanked him sincerely and wished him well on his own flying career. Then I trudged back to my hotel for an overdue good night's sleep.

FIGURE 1: SubLogic's *FS1 Flight Simulator* on the Apple II computer in 1979. Playing it as a kid, the primitive graphics and jerky motion convinced me that piloting an airplane must be insurmountably difficult. (Used with permission from Sublogic Corporation).

FIGURE 2: The set-up I assembled to play on my home PC, including yoke, throttle, rudder pedals, and radio stack. The photorealistic graphics of *Microsoft Flight Simulator 2020* are what sparked my interest in learning to fly, after being locked down during COVID-19. (Screen shows *Microsoft Flight Simulator 2020*, Microsoft Corp.)

FIGURE 3: A Cessna 172 lands at Lincoln Park Airport (N07) in northern New Jersey while I wait to begin my first lesson.

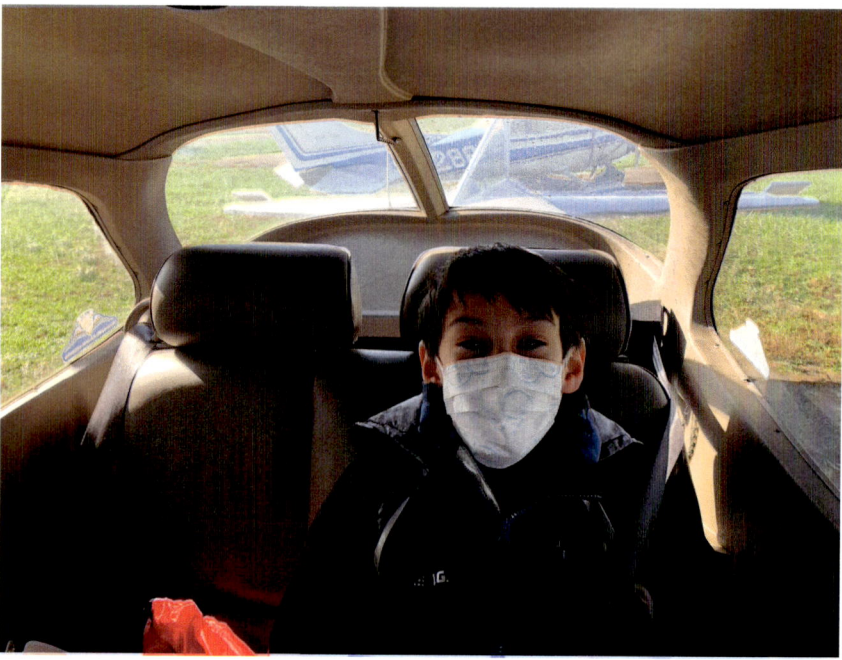

FIGURE 4: My 11-year-old son in the back seat of the Cessna 172, ready for our Discovery Flight.

FIGURE 5: A glimpse inside the cockpit of a Cessna 172. The pilot or student pilot sits in the left seat, while the co-pilot or instructor sits on the right.

FIGURE 6: Air density affects an aircraft's performance and handling. As fall turned to winter, the colder, denser air tended to give the wings more lift, requiring more forward pressure on the yoke.

FIGURE 7: A portion of a sectional chart showing the Class B (Bravo) airspace around New Orleans' Louis Armstrong International Airport (KMSY). The solid blue rings are actually upward steps in what looks, in three dimensions, like an upside-down wedding cake. The thin magenta circle on the very outside is the Mode C Veil. There are several other airports in the area: blue dots are towered airports, while magenta dots are non-towered.

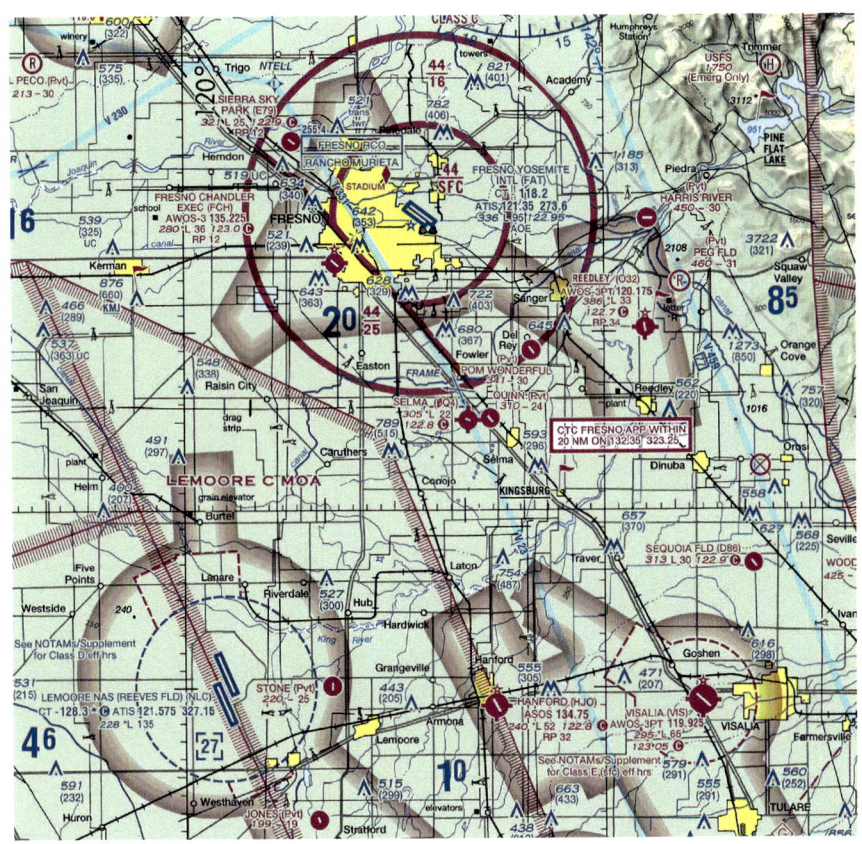

FIGURE 8: A portion of the sectional chart near Fresno, California, showing other types of airspace more clearly. The solid magenta circles around Fresno Yosemite (KFAT) show Class C (Charlie) airspace up to 4,400 feet MSL, in the shape of a small upside-down wedding cake. The dashed blue circle around Lemoore NAS (KNLC) signifies Class D (Delta) airspace up to 2,700 feet MSL. The dashed magenta circle and lines around Visalia (KVIS) show Class E (Echo) airspace down to ground level. Inside the irregularly shaped areas surrounded in shaded magenta lines, Class E airspace goes down to 700 feet AGL; outside of them, Class G (Golf) airspace goes up to 1,200 feet AGL. The chart also shows several MOAs (Military Operation Areas) bordered by magenta hatch-marked lines.

FIGURE 9: Flying on *MSFS 2020* gave me exposure to flying in weather conditions I might sensibly have avoided in real life, such as this rainstorm near Bear Lake in southern Idaho. It also gave me some familiarity with a digital "glass" cockpit. The PFD to the left integrates the main flight instruments, while the MFD to the right shows navigation and engine information. (Screenshot from *Microsoft Flight Simulator 2020*, Microsoft Corp.)

FIGURE 10: A brush with (virtual) disaster on this flight over the Alps in *MSFS 2020* taught me the dangers of ice forming on the airplane's surfaces. (Screenshot from *Microsoft Flight Simulator 2020*, Microsoft Corp.)

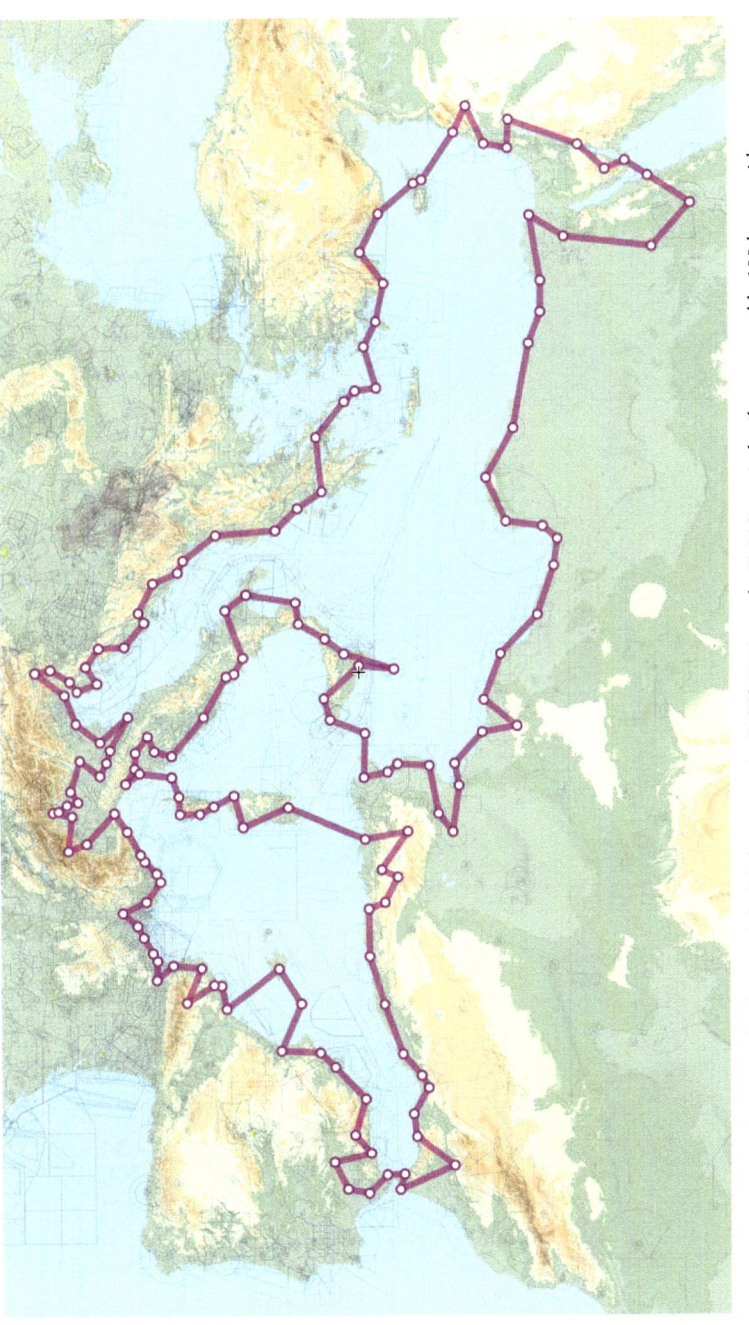

FIGURE 11: A map of my virtual trek around the Mediterranean in *MSFS 2020*: nearly 10,000 nautical miles over roughly 100 hours, with more than 100 takeoffs and landings. The trip helped me become familiar with the cockpit and the process of navigating a route. (Used with permission of SkyVector)

FIGURE 12: Studying hard for the written exam. Covering basic aerodynamics and mechanics, regulations, navigation, and weather, the test isn't difficult to pass—as long as you're well prepared.

FIGURE 13: A screenshot of the iPhone video I took, showing us on final approach to land on Runway 19, with my instructor Tess at the controls. One pilot blogger described arriving at Lincoln Park's short, narrow runway "like landing on a carrier without a tailhook," but reviewing this video second by second played a key role in helping me master the challenge. (Note Natalie's pink helicopter to the left).

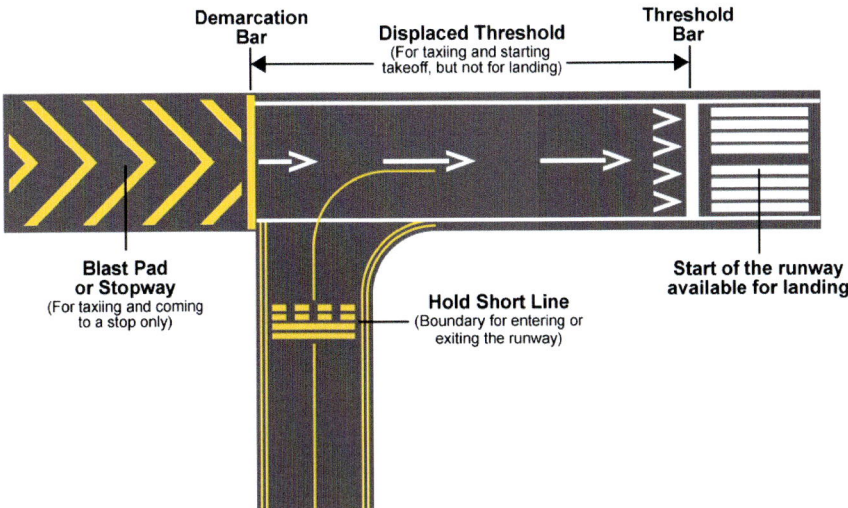

FIGURE 14: Because of surrounding terrain and obstacles, not all parts of a runway can be used to take off and land. Blastpads or stopways, with yellow arrows or chevrons, can only be used for taxiing and coming to a final stop on landing. The area of a displaced threshold, with white arrow or chevrons, can be used to begin a takeoff, but aircraft that are landing can only touch down beyond the white threshold bar.

FIGURE 15: Most airspeed indicators are now color coded. The white arc to the right shows the safe range of operation for the Cessna 172 when flaps are down (40-85 knots). The green arc shows the safe range of speeds when flaps are up (48-128 knots). The yellow shows speeds that are only safe in calm air, and the red line is the Never Exceed Speed (163 knots). The dial in the little window above can be adjusted, based on altitude and temperature, to translate the Indicated Airspeed (IAS) on the gauge into True Airspeed (TAS) on a sliding readout below.

FIGURE 16: A visit to the Glenn Curtiss Museum in Hammondsport, New York provided some inspiration when I was struggling with my landings. The early pioneers of aviation had to figure all this stuff out on their own, by trial and error, without anyone to teach them.

FIGURE 17: Finally, lined up on the runway at Lincoln Park to take off on my first solo flight.

FIGURE 18: A Stearman biplane at Scottsdale Airport in Arizona. Frustrated with the unpredictable weather back home, I came here for a week of intensive training, reminiscent of the "pilot mills" that taught thousands of enlistees to fly Stearmans like this one during World War II.

FIGURE 19: The view from the restaurant at Scottsdale Airport, after a long day of practice. The hot desert air and rugged terrain in Arizona created a very different environment for flying than back home in New Jersey, helping to round out my pilot's education.

FIGURE 20: The complicated airspace around Phoenix, Arizona. The solid blue lines show different shards of Class B airspace belonging to Phoenix Sky Harbor (KPHX), while the dashed blue circles show several Class D airports beneath it, including Scottsdale (KSDL).

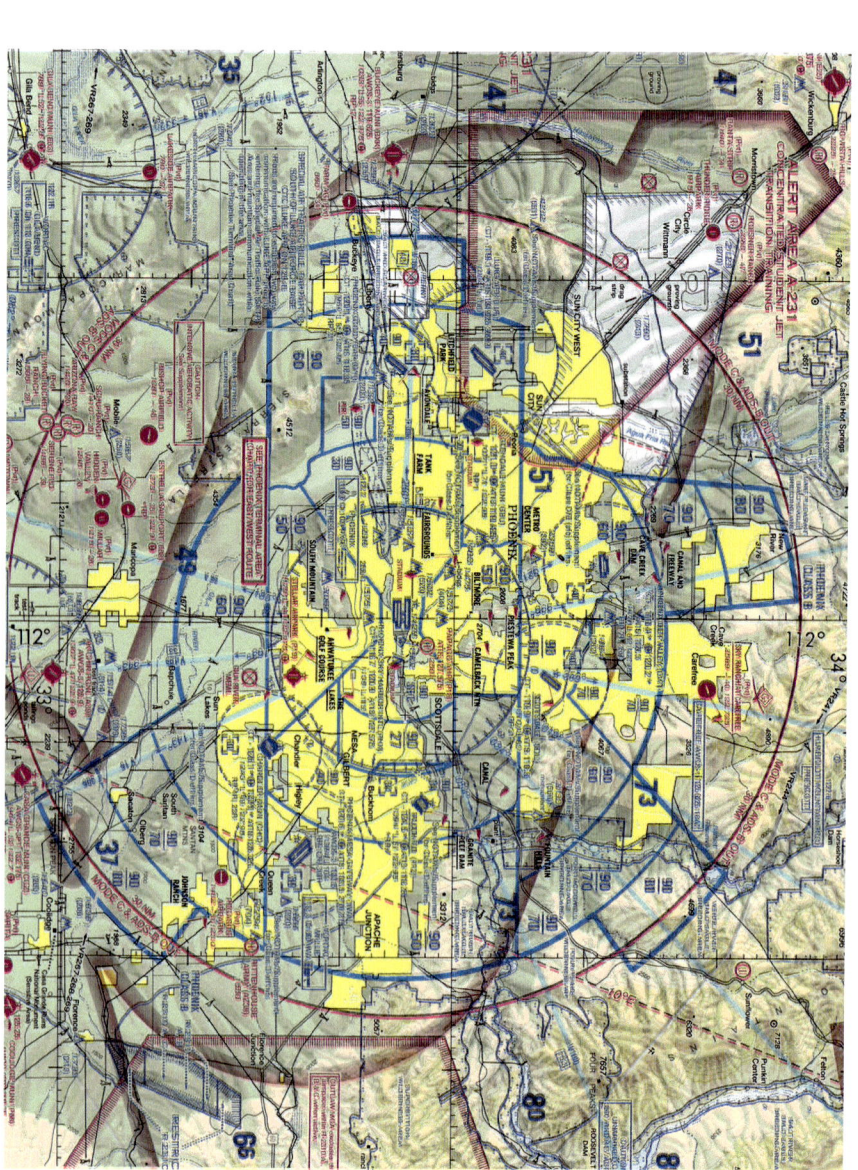

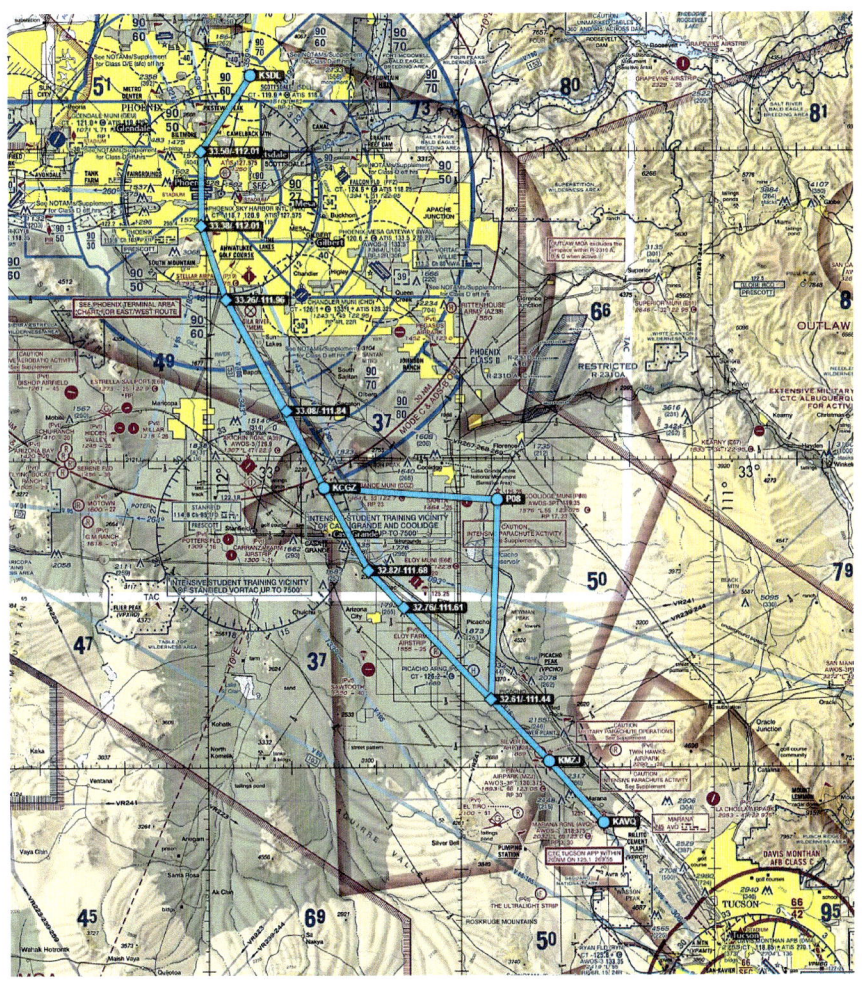

FIGURE 21: The flight plan (in *ForeFlight*) for my day-time cross-country in Arizona from Scottsdale (KDSL) south to Marana (KAVQ), with a stop at Coolidge (P08) on the way back. My night cross-country that same evening followed the same route, with the exception of the side trip to Coolidge. (Published with permission from ForeFlight LLC).

FIGURE 22: A year before, I took my family on a horseback riding vacation to White Stallion Ranch outside of Tucson. Seeing it from the air was a surprise treat during my cross-country flight to the nearby airfield at Marana.

FIGURE 23: Before taking off on my night cross-country, at Scottsdale Airport. Pilots use red light in the cockpit to help keep their eyes adjusted to the dark.

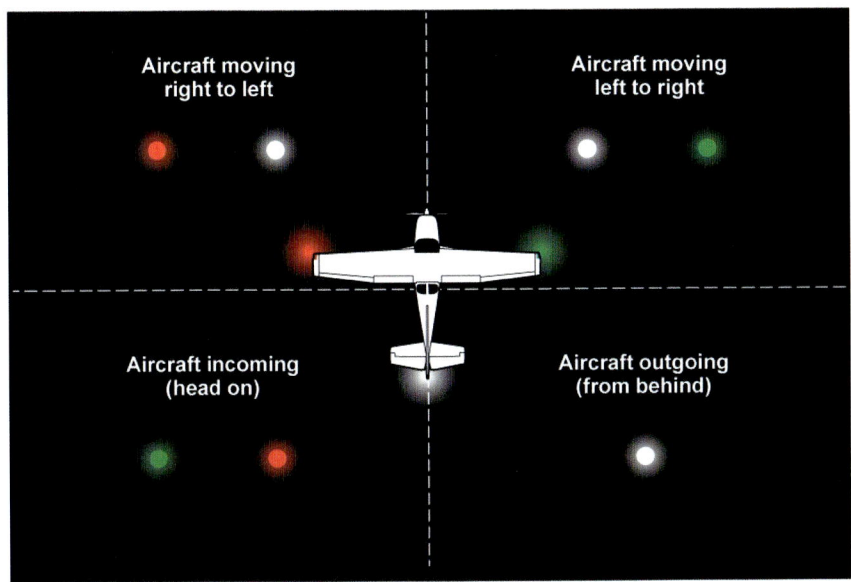

FIGURE 24: Different colored navigation lights on the airplane's wings and tail help other aircraft identify which direction it is going in the dark.

FIGURE 25: The bright lights of Phoenix from 4,500 feet MSL as I make the Bravo Transition over Sky Harbor Airport near the end of my night cross-country flight.

FIGURE 26: The view ahead over the wooded hills and lakes of northern New Jersey during my first solo cross-country up to Sullivan County Airport (KMSV).

FIGURE 27: Taking a quick selfie in the cockpit during my first solo cross-country.

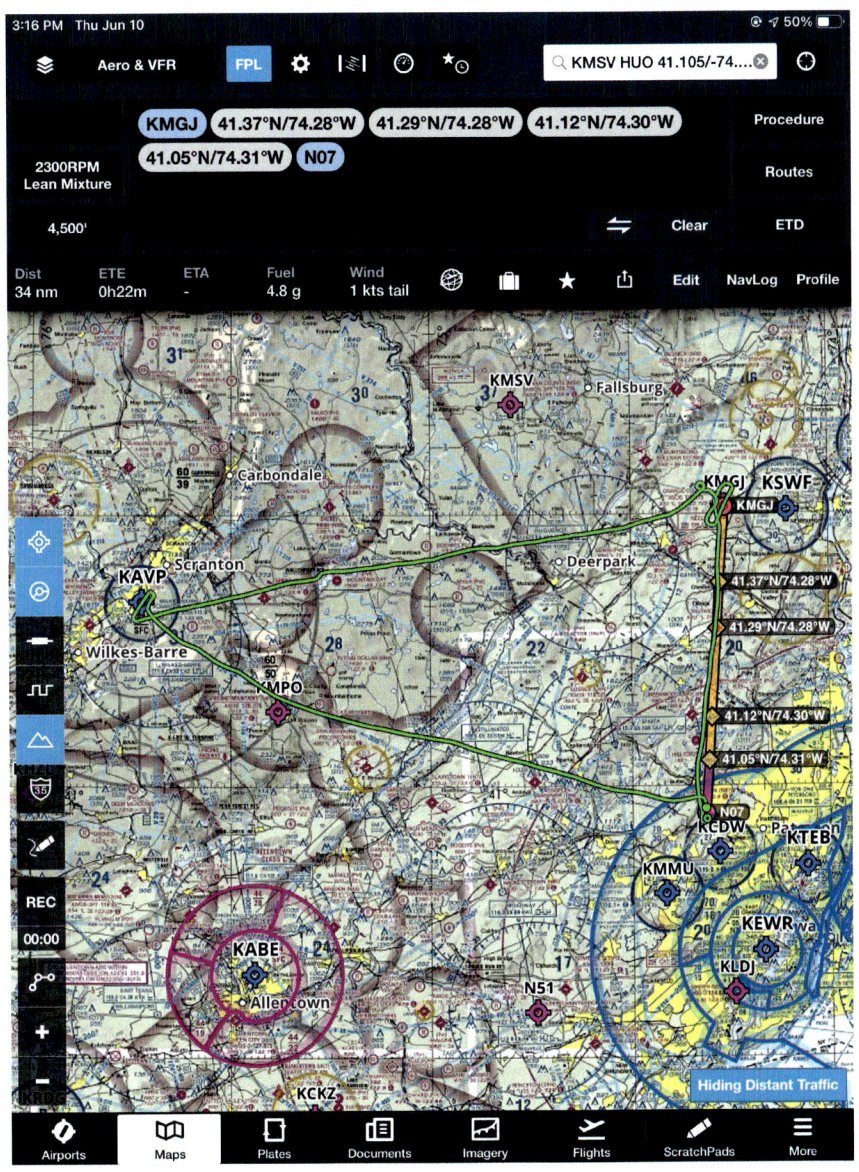

FIGURE 28: The green line on the screenshot from *ForeFlight* shows the ground track of my "long cross-country" to Wilkes-Barre (KAVP) and Orange County (KMGJ) shortly after my return to Lincoln Park. (Published with permission of ForeFlight LLC).

FIGURE 29: Looking down on the I-84 expressway towards Port Jarvis while pre-flying my first solo cross-country in *MSFS 2020*. (Screenshot from *Microsoft Flight Simulator 2020*, Microsoft Corp.)

FIGURE 30: The exact same scene in real life on my first solo cross-country, confirming that I was on course.

FIGURE 31: Flying over New York's Otisville prison complex in *MSFS 2020*, one of the easy-to-spot checkpoints I picked out while pre-flying my "long cross-country" solo in the sim. (Screenshot from *Microsoft Flight Simulator 2020*, Microsoft Corp.)

FIGURE 32: Identifying that same visual checkpoint out my window in real life on my "long cross-country" solo.

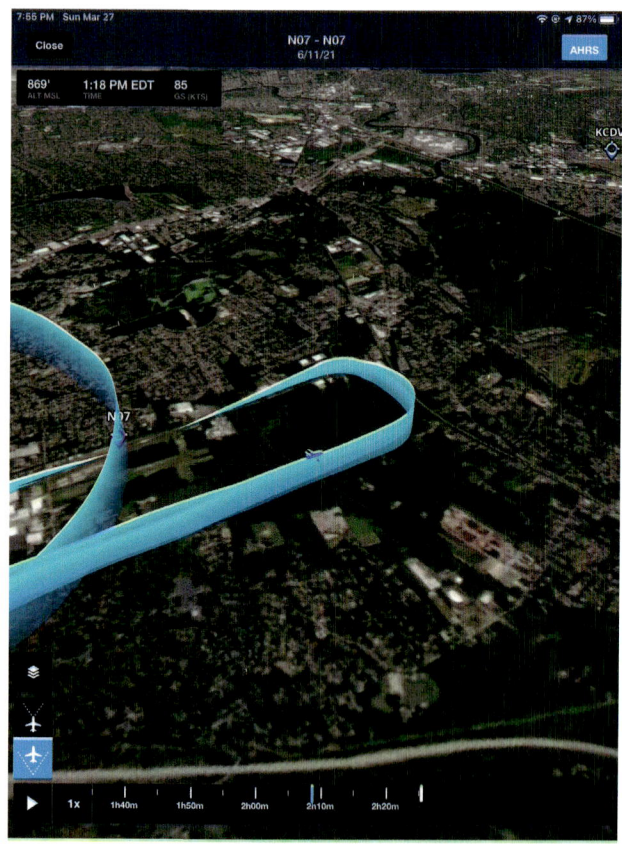

FIGURE 33: I recorded each of my solo cross-country flights in *ForeFlight* so I could review them later in 3-D. (Published with permission of ForeFlight LLC).

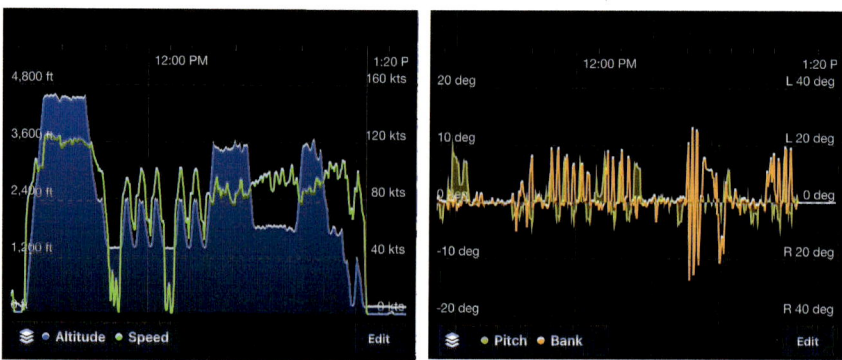

FIGURES 34 AND 35: *ForeFlight* also recorded my altitude and groundspeed at each moment of these flights, as well as my pitch and bank, for later analysis. (Published with permission of ForeFlight LLC.)

FIGURE 36: Ready for my introductory helicopter lesson in Natalie's pink R22 at Morristown.

FIGURE 37: In the cockpit of the R22 helicopter. I have control of the cyclic (the handlebar in front of me) but for the moment Natalie, to my left, still controls the collective and pedals.

FIGURE 38: The sectional chart of the area around Ocean County Airport (KMJX) where I would take my checkride.

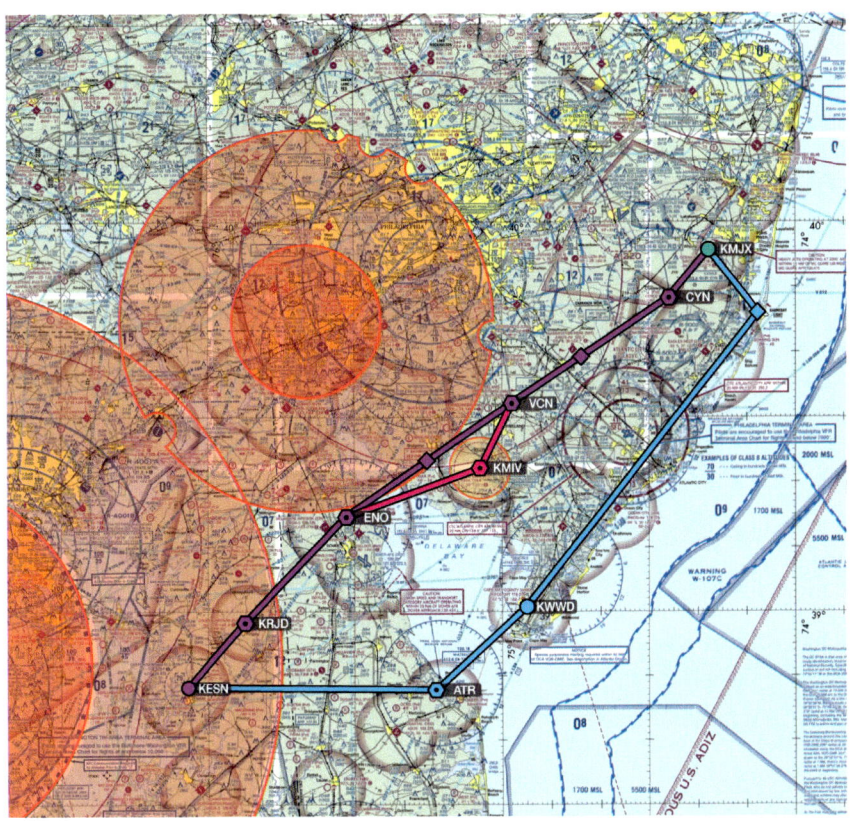

FIGURE 39: The two alternative routes from Ocean County (KMJX) to Easton (KESN), the planning scenario assigned by my checkride examiner. The coastal route (blue) follows the New Jersey shore, before crossing the mouth of Delaware Bay. The inland route (purple), which I decided to take instead, follows a series of VORs. However, Temporary Flight Restrictions (TFRs), shown by the red circles to the southwest, forced me to add an alteration to this route (pink) to avoid them.

FIGURE 40: Back from my checkride with my temporary license in hand. Not sure whether I'm more relieved that I passed, or that I'm safely back on the ground.

FIGURE 41: My private pilot certificate, received in the mail several weeks later.

CHAPTER 22

Radio

When I came into school the next morning on Friday, Celine the office manager took me aside to review the game plan. Brian was out for the next several days, and the chief instructor, who apparently needed to sign me off to solo, was also gone until Monday. I was leaving on Sunday, but Celine offered that if I was willing to stick around another week I could solo on Monday, knock out my required solo cross-country flights (the same trip down to Marana and back, twice, except now by myself), and—if all went well—pass my final checkride by next Friday.

Tempting as the idea was, it wasn't an option. Besides the fact that I needed to get home—it wouldn't be wise to impose too much on my wife's good humor—I didn't want to rush into the checkride just yet. I might have been able to squeak by, but I didn't feel comfortable with that. I sensed there were still things I needed to improve on. Had I been less tired, and less satisfied with what I had already accomplished, I might have been disappointed at not being able to solo in Arizona. As it was, I was happy to take the rest of the day off and come back the following morning for one last flight session with a new instructor—a chance to get yet another person's perspective on my flying.

Come Saturday morning I returned much refreshed, and Celine introduced me to Emily, another 20-something young woman dressed in a prim pilot's uniform. After reviewing Brian's notes, we both agreed that my biggest weakness, for the moment, was radio communication with ATC. I needed some practice, and we would spend the morning getting some. As usual, we would transition through the Bravo to the south. Then we would hop from Delta to Delta, hitting all the Class D airports in a broad semi-circle around Phoenix to the west and back to Scottsdale (an itinerary shown below). It was going to be a stressful, but hopefully productive, three hours.

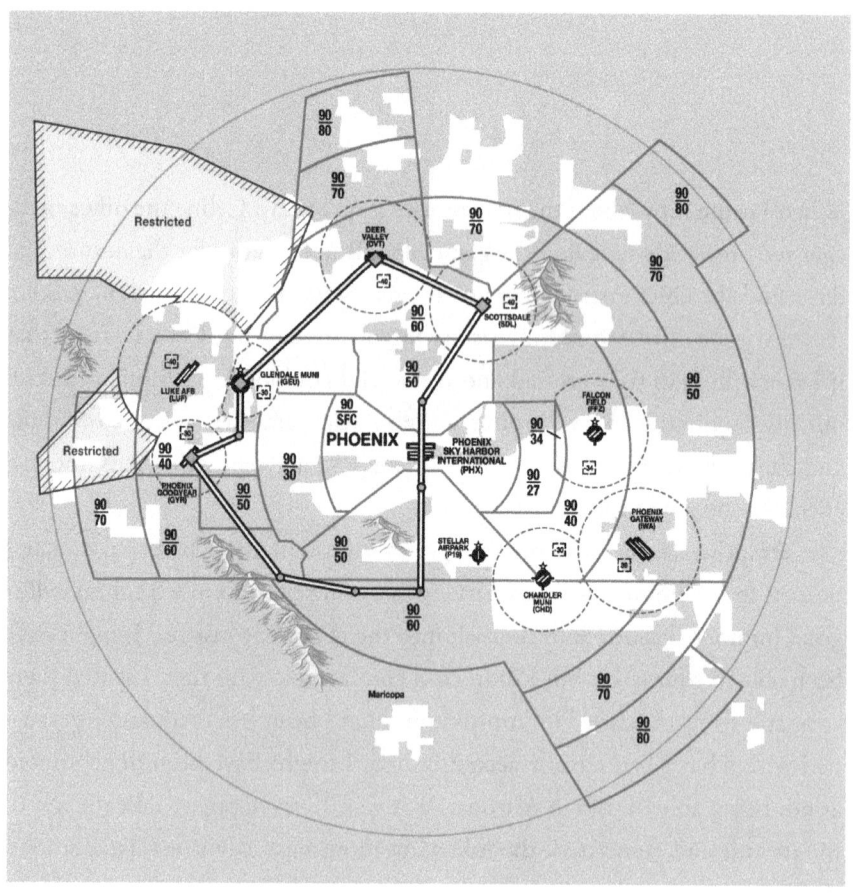

My short-hop itinerary around the Phoenix area to practice radio procedures.

A lot of pilots compare talking over the radio with ATC to learning a new language. To me, it felt like getting pulled over by a cop who spoke like an auctioneer. It combined the anxiety of trying to promptly comply with an authority figure with the difficulty of comprehending an unfamiliar patois going at a mile a minute. The fear of not hearing my call sign when the control tower gave me an instruction was stressful enough. Then there was understanding, repeating back, and *remembering* what that instruction was. There had been times over the past few days, I hate to admit, when I was so eager to spit an instruction back to the tower that I forgot what it was the moment it left my mouth, and I had to turn to my instructor and ask what I had just said. Yet I heard my instructors and other pilots sound reasonably at ease talking to ATC, so I figured there must be some way to get over this hurdle and become more like them.

By now, passing through the Bravo transition had become a bit easier, because I was starting to recognize—and anticipate—the pattern. I contacted ATC and made the request, they told me a code to squawk, which I did and then waited and circled if necessary. ATC eventually came back with a clearance and instructions, including an altitude to keep, and I repeated it back to them and crossed the Bravo. Halfway across, they often had me change frequencies and contact a new controller with my call sign and altitude. After a while, ATC told me I was clear of the Bravo, should squawk VFR (1200), and resume my own navigation. Sure, sometimes ATC might say something unexpected, but knowing what I *should* expect to hear cleared up 80% of the problem and made it easier to focus on the other 20%.

I've never been particularly good with foreign languages, but I have noticed that context helps immensely when trying to comprehend what's being said. If someone says something to you just out of the blue, your mind races because it could be anything. But if you're engaged in a somewhat predictable interaction—buying a ticket, getting a taxi, even engaging in "how's the weather" small talk—you can anticipate most of their questions and responses, and recognize them when you hear it. The same, I started to realize, is true of ATC. They're not just throwing random instructions at you. There's a pattern, which you can learn to anticipate.

Take approaching and landing at a Class D airport. After crossing south of the Bravo that day, we crept west, under and around its outer shelves, towards Phoenix Goodyear Airport (KGYR). The first step was to tune in and get the ATIS weather information. But as I listened, the runway numbers didn't seem to match up with those on the chart. It soon dawned on me that I must have read the wrong frequency off the chart and was listening to the ATIS from Glendale Municipal (KGEU) just next door. It was an easy mistake to make—the two airports are right next to each other, look almost the same, and have such similar ID codes—but it had the potential to cause a great deal of confusion, if I hadn't quickly recognized it.

A few moments later, I had the correct ATIS and could make my first call to Tower at Goodyear.

> *Goodyear Tower, Skyhawk Four-Eight-Two-Mike-Kilo, ten miles southeast with information Oscar, 3500, for full-stop landing.*

Now what was ATC going to say back to me? If I had a decent idea already, it would be easier to hear and understand. I knew from the (now correct) ATIS that the active runway was 21, facing into winds from the southwest. I was approaching from the southeast. The easiest thing for ATC to do, from their perspective, would be to have me enter on the left downwind, southeast of the runway. Of course, they might not, depending on traffic and other factors, but it was a reasonable guess.

> *Skyhawk Two-Mike-Kilo, enter left downwind Runway Two-One, report midfield.*

I repeated back:

> *Left downwind Runway Two-One, report midfield, Skyhawk Two-Mike-Kilo.*

My guess was correct. Two additional points to note, however: First, Tower had used an abbreviated call sign—just the last three numbers and letters of my plane's registration instead of the full five—which meant I could now use it myself in my radio calls to them. Second, Tower had not given me clearance to land yet. They said I should call and tell them when I was at midfield on my downwind leg, to get further instructions. When I arrived and entered the traffic pattern, that is just what I did:

> *Goodyear Tower, Skyhawk Two-Mike-Kilo, reporting midfield left downwind Runway Two-One.*

Now, I asked myself, what would ATC say next? If there were no other aircraft around, on the ground or in the air, they might immediately tell me I was cleared to land on Runway 21. Or they might tell me to look for other traffic and follow them in sequence. If it was really crowded, Tower might tell me to do a 360-degree circle, probably to the outside of the pattern, to buy time and space for other planes to take off or land.

> *Skyhawk Two-Mike-Kilo, you are number two behind Seneca one mile on final, Runway Two-One.*

I didn't immediately spot the small, twin-engine Piper PA-34 Seneca that Tower was talking about, so I replied, "*Looking for traffic.*" ATC is responsible for **sequencing**—telling you what order to land and who to follow—but pilots flying VFR are expected to share responsibility for **separation**—spotting and maintaining a safe distance from other aircraft. So I kept searching for the Seneca in front of me in line and when I saw it—ahead of me to the left, descending on final towards the runway—I broke in again to report "*Traffic in sight.*" Now that Tower knew I had the other plane in sight, I suspected they would probably go ahead and give me clearance to land after it. I was right:

📡 *Skyhawk Two-Mike-Kilo, cleared to land Runway Two-One, number two behind the Seneca.*

To confirm, I repeated back:

📡 *Cleared to land Runway Two-One behind the Seneca, Skyhawk Two-Mike-Kilo.*

It's crucial to hear the word "cleared" and repeat it back. Without it, I had no permission to land. If I had any doubt, I would ask. But there was no doubt, so from this point on, unless I heard otherwise from Tower, I could proceed through the rest of the pattern (to base and on to final) to land, following the Seneca in front of me at a safe distance.

Every other interaction—leaving the runway to taxi, holding short to take off, departing the area after takeoff, requesting to transition through the airspace—also follows a pattern. For the rest of the morning, we practiced each of them, hopping from Goodyear (KGYR) to Glendale (KGEU) to Deer Valley (KDVT) and back to Scottsdale. Normally, on approaching a new airport, you are supposed to make your first call to ATC from at least 10 miles out, to give them a chance to respond. But several of these airfields are less than 10 miles apart, which meant that after takeoff there was barely enough time to get the ATIS and contact the next tower before reaching their airspace. It was a wild, hectic ride, but a great learning experience.

One thing I took away from it was the importance of what pilots call "staying ahead of the plane"—being ready for what's coming next, instead of playing catch-up. Knowing how to make full use of the radio stack is a key part of this. The radio in a Cessna 172 has two communications channels, **COM1 and COM2**, either of which can be muted or unmuted as needed. Each has an active frequency—the one you can talk and listen to—and a stand-by frequency. To choose a new active frequency, you don't tune it directly like in an old car radio; you use the selector to change the stand-by

RADIO

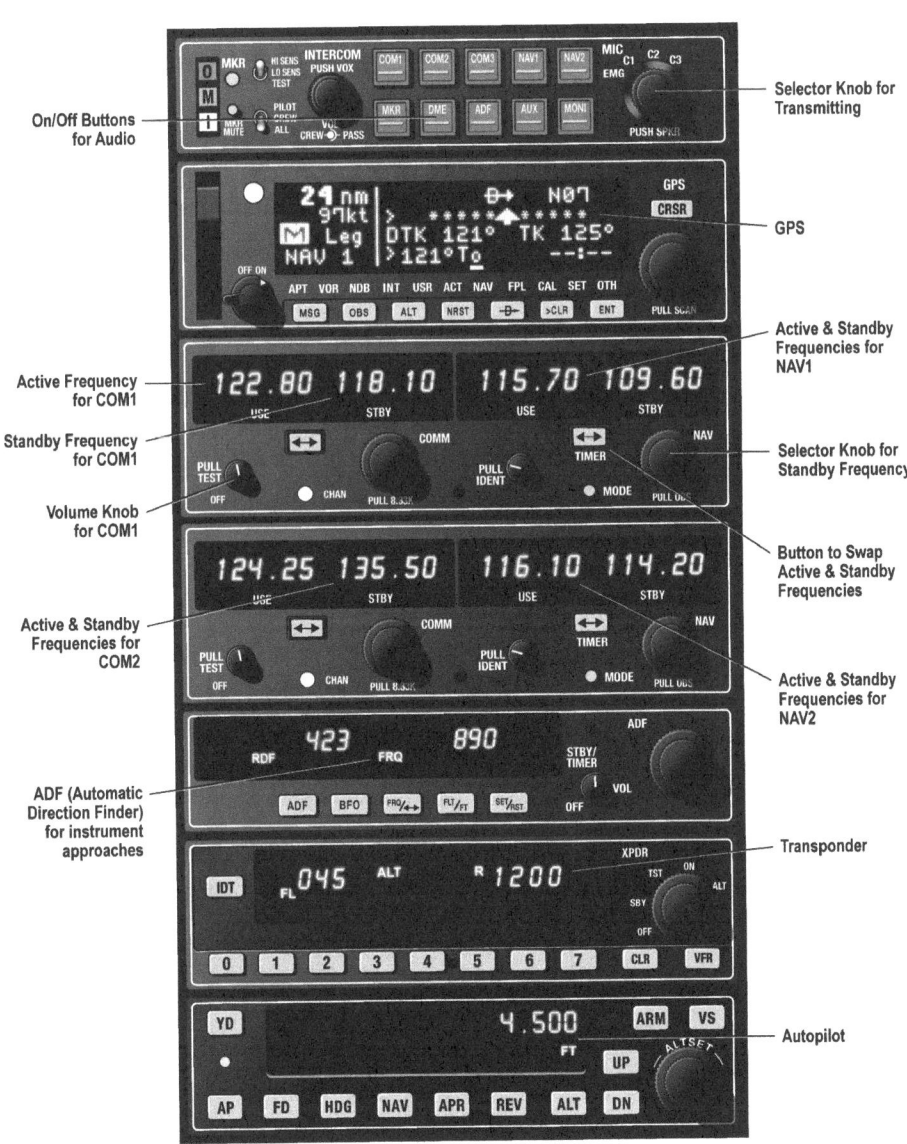

The radio stack in the center of the instrument panel of my Cessna 172.

frequency to what you want, then press a button to swap it to active. The important thing is, *a total of four frequencies can be entered at any time, potentially putting you three steps ahead of the game.* So while you're talking to one control tower on COM1, it's smart to enter the next ATC frequency you'll need on stand-by. While you're at it, have the next two ATIS frequencies entered as active and stand-by on COM2 so they're there when you need them. (Pilots typically use COM1 for ATC and COM2 for ATIS, but it depends on your needs.) But the main thing is, it takes thinking ahead. Taking a few moments prior to takeoff, or when things are less frantic in the air, can save a lot of fumbling around later when time is precious.

Another thing our outing taught me: circling is your friend. Sometimes the time and space available just isn't enough. In that case, there's nothing wrong with circling in place while you get things sorted out, especially if there's any risk you could violate airspace. If you find yourself at an inappropriate altitude—either too high or too low for whatever's coming next—you can fix it by circling. If you're already inside a tower's airspace, of course, you'll need to ask for permission to circle, but it's usually granted. Unless it's the result of bad planning, circling isn't wasting time; it is about controlling the pace of events and actively flying the plane, instead of letting it fly you.

Last but not least, I learned to stay flexible. Things are not always going to go according to plan—not even the ATC's plan. At Deer Valley, we were cleared and coming in on final when the airplane that landed in front of us didn't exit the runway in time. We advised Tower that we were going around—and then continued talking to them as they reinserted us back into the busy landing sequence. ATC can't always see what pilots are seeing, and many accidents take place when pilots assume that it can. Adapt and communicate. If you're unsure or concerned, it's okay to ask questions: "What do you want me to do? Can you say that again? Am I still cleared to land?" You don't want to chatter away, but I saw that it's important to be an active participant in the conversation, not just a passive recipient of instructions.

If I was a particularly attentive student that morning, the reason was simple: I knew that, soon after I returned home, I'd have to do all this again—by myself. One of the requirements for a Private Pilot License is to take off and land three times, to a full stop, at a towered airport solo. Students based at a towered airport, like Scottsdale, check this box as a matter of course when they do their first solos in the pattern. I had even listened over the radio to Tower gently coaxing a few of them through the process—usually in the early morning when there were few other aircraft around. If I had been able to solo in Arizona, that would have been me. Back in New Jersey, I faced a more difficult, and more realistic, scenario: I would have to fly from Lincoln Park to a towered airport (most likely Morristown), enter its airspace and join the traffic pattern as instructed, do my three landings and takeoffs there, then depart the area to fly back home—in a busy sky filled with who knows what other aircraft coming and going. In other words, exactly what I was practicing with Emily right now.

Of course, I knew Tess wasn't going to just send me off to Morristown on my own, not until we did a few practice runs there together to convince her I was ready. But as I boarded my airline flight back home, I also sensed that wouldn't be enough. Learning a new language—becoming comfortable and confident in it—isn't just a matter of attending classes and completing exercises. You have to put your heart into it and make it part of you. Just as I found out when learning to land the plane, a teacher can offer tips and guidance, but can only take you so far; you have to take it the rest of the way. And just like landing, I didn't know how I was going to make that happen. I only knew it was up to me to figure out how.

The traditional recommendation for someone in my shoes has always been to spend lots of spare time listening to the radio. By hearing other pilots interacting with ATC, especially at the same airport you'll be flying at, you gradually get a feel for the procedures and the language being used. It's true, so far as it goes, and the internet certainly makes it easier to do than ever. There's an Apple Store app called *LiveATC* that lets you listen in real time to the various frequencies at any airport in the country. At the same time, *ForeFlight* has a feature that pulls live air traffic data from the internet and displays it on the chart, much like ADS-B would in the cockpit. By opening both at the same time at home on my iPad, I could listen to aircraft taking off and landing at Morristown while seeing how that translated into what they were doing. Amusingly enough, I even recognized Tess's voice and our own plane's call sign once or twice as she did her lessons with other students.

Listening has its limitations, however, as it's a passive activity. Another iPhone app called *PlaneEnglish* (also known as *ARSim*) offers a more interactive approach. It presents you different scenarios, including charts and airport diagrams, then prompts you to record the appropriate radio calls or responses to ATC, and uses voice recognition to grade you on both accuracy and speed. The most basic sample lessons are free, but access to the full range of VFR dialogues cost $10 a month, and there's an additional subscription devoted to IFR for people working on their instrument training. The exercises are ploddingly predictable, but the whole value lies in the repetition, *saying* as well as hearing the same formulaic dialogues over and over again until they become instinctive habit.

Life, of course, is less predictable, and the real challenge of speaking a new language is how you respond when you get put on the spot. Before I left Arizona, my last instructor, Emily, mentioned vatsim.com as something to check out. *VATSIM* is flight-sim add-on that brings real people together as pilots and air traffic controllers and allows them to talk to each other in the course of virtual flights on *MSFS, X-Plane, Prepar3D*, or other PC-based sims. Of course, *Microsoft Flight Simulator* does have its own automated ATC as part of the sim, which works by clicking options from a menu bar. It's very cookie-cutter, however, and carries none of the urgency you feel in real life; in fact, you can ignore it entirely if you like with no consequences. With *VATSIM*, in contrast, you are talking via your headset and microphone with actual human beings reacting spontaneously to you in real time. The downside is that they, like you, are unpaid and possibly still learning the ropes, which means that the ATC coverage for any given location in the sim is often stretched thin and the quality can be uneven.

That's why I signed up instead with **pilotedge**.net, a paid service founded by Keith Smith, who served as a leading volunteer on *VATSIM* and decided to kick the concept up a notch. As one forum reviewer put it, "*VATSIM is a hobbyist enterprise with hobbyist trained controllers. PilotEdge is for 100% authentic flight operations, and is intended to be 100% in sync with real-world procedures. Their controllers are paid professionals.*"[185] To deliver a higher-quality experience, *PilotEdge* focuses on two coverage areas, Southern California and the rest of the Western U.S., with either one costing $20 per month to subscribe, or $35 for both.

When I first joined, I wasn't sure how or where to dive in, but soon I discovered their CAT (Communications and Airspace Training) program. This is a structured series of 11 virtual flights in and around the Los Angeles area which you can perform on a pass/fail basis, as a way of learning VFR radio procedures and improving your technique.[186] The scenarios start out simple, then step by step introduce more complex and challenging elements, so by the end you are navigating some of the most complicated, restrictive airspace out there:

CAT-01 – non-towered airport to non-towered airport
CAT-02 – non-towered airport to Class D airport
CAT-03 – traffic patterns at Class D airport
CAT-04 – Class D airport to Class D airport
CAT-05 – Class D airport to Class D airport with Flight Following
CAT-06 – Class D airport to Class D airport with Flight Following from the ground
CAT-07 – Class D airport to Class D airport via Class C Transition
CAT-08 – Class C airport to Class C airport
CAT-09 – Class C airport to Class D airport utilizing Flyways under Class B airspace
CAT-10 – Class D airport to Class C airport via Class B Transition
CAT-11 – Class B airport to Class B airport

There's also a whole other series for practicing IFR radio procedures, for pilots working towards—or keeping up to speed on—their instrument ratings.

Immediately on my return from Arizona, I set a goal of performing one CAT level on *PilotEdge* each day. This took a lot more than logging in and taking off. The key to success, as always, was preparation. Each scenario had a webpage that outlined the flight plan and the ATC procedures involved. Most importantly, it included a script of the main dialogues I could expect to have with ATC, as well as a video of those interactions being performed en route in *MSFS* from start to finish.[187] Once in the sim, my own flight might play out the same way, or the instructions I received might be a bit different. After all, I was dealing with human controllers in a dynamic world filled with all the other aircraft being "flown" in *PilotEdge* at the same time. But the script and the preview video gave me a game plan, which I could adapt as needed. I quickly found that preparing a script—writing down in advance what I expected to say to ATC, and what I was likely to hear back from them—could be an extremely helpful tool, even if I ended up deviating from it. It was one more way of "staying ahead of the plane."

Some of the procedures were new to me, at least in practice. **Flight Following** is a service that ATC facilities can often provide, so long as their other workload permits, to VFR aircraft. As the *PilotEdge* scenarios demonstrated, it can be initiated on the ground or in the air. Essentially, the closest ATC assigns you a distinct squawk code and keeps an eye on you en route, alerting you to other traffic and handing you off to the next ATC facility when the time comes. The later scenarios also introduce you to calling up **Clearance**, at larger airports, to get a squawk code and detailed departure instructions before contacting Ground to taxi. I had seen these procedures described in the Sporty's ground school videos, and even studied for them on the exam, but actually doing them on a virtual flight with live controllers brought it home for me in a whole new way.

At the start of each CAT flight, I informed the first Ground controller that I was going for a specific rating. Then after landing and taxiing to park, the last controller would inform me if I passed, allowing me to advance to the next scenario. There's something about talking to a real human being that instills that feeling of stage fright—the fear of making a mistake and looking stupid—which was the key thing I, like most student pilots, needed to overcome. But as I progressed through each stage, the process of talking to ATC became more familiar, and I became more confident. With confidence came the recognition that talking to ATC is not just a series of (their) directives and (my) responses, but a *conversation* in which I played an equally important role. Here's a simple example: After you land and exit the runway, Tower typically instructs you to change frequencies and contact Ground to taxi. But that doesn't always happen: If things are slow, Tower might have you stay on their frequency to taxi, and if they're extremely busy, they might be too preoccupied to realize that you're still waiting there. In Arizona, I often felt hesitant to ask what to do next. After a few flights on *PilotEdge*, I developed a sense of how long I should wait before giving them a helpful reminder I needed instructions.

To my surprise, two short weeks of intensive effort made a huge difference. By the time I had worked my way up to flying from one Bravo to another in *PilotEdge*, taking off and landing at a Class D airport was starting to feel like a piece of cake. I knew what to say, I knew what to expect, and I knew when to ask questions without sounding dazed or insecure. My first two lessons back with Tess, practicing at Morristown, confirmed to both of us that I had made huge strides, and was ready to handle whatever the tower threw at me. So the next time I came back, on May 18, she sent me up solo to complete my three takeoffs and landings at a towered airport.

Before takeoff, I got my radio stack ready. For the moment, my active frequency on COM1 was 122.8, the CTAF for Lincoln Park, but I dialed in 118.1 for Morristown Tower on the stand-by, ready to switch at the touch of a button. Meanwhile I had Morristown's ATIS, on 124.25, as the active for COM2, but on mute. Even though Morristown is just 10 miles to the southwest, I couldn't receive the ATIS on the ground, due to the hills in between. So instead of flying straight there, I took off to the north to give myself some time. After climbing above the traffic pattern at Lincoln Park, I could unmute COM2 and listen to the ATIS as I began my left turn to the south, writing down all the important information like the altimeter setting, wind speed and direction, active runway, and the letter identifying the current ATIS report.

Ten miles out, with the Boonton Reservoir serving as a landmark in front of me, I switched COM1 frequencies and made my first call to Morristown Tower. Along with the rest—my call sign, location, ATIS identifier, and intention to land—I added one more piece of information: "student pilot." It was a heads-up to the controller that he had a newbie on his hands, so he could factor that into his game plan for managing other traffic, and maybe treat me a little gently. I figured, hey, I won't have that card forever, so I better play it while I can.

My own game plan got thrown a curve ball right from the start. The ATIS indicated that Runway 23 was the active, so I figured that, since I was coming from the north, Tower would most likely instruct me to enter the pattern on right base, at a close right angle to land. That's what they usually did when I flew here with Tess. Instead, the controller told me to head way out for a four-mile straight-in approach, probably to keep me well away from other aircraft. Landing straight-in sounds like it should be easier, but not quite. Each turn in the normal pattern serves as helpful benchmarks for when you should be starting your descent, adding each stage of flaps, and reducing speed. Without them, you have to reconstruct each leg of the approach in your mind, minus the turns. Fortunately, I was prepared to adapt.

As I came in on final, I felt both grateful and chagrinned at the almost comical lengths the controller went to steer everyone well clear of me. The winds were somewhat variable, and aircraft were taking off from both of Morristown's runways, which cross each other like a T. I could tell that Tower would have liked to give me **LAHSO**—Land and Hold Short—instructions, to keep the other runway operating. It's a special kind of clearance that allows you to land *as long a*s you stop short of the intersecting runway. I knew, from flying into Morristown before, that there was still plenty of distance for me to come to a stop, well before I caused him any heartache. But student pilots aren't allowed to do LAHSO, so everyone had to cool their heels until I touched down and exited the runway.

Tower knew by now that I was planning to do two more laps to fulfill the

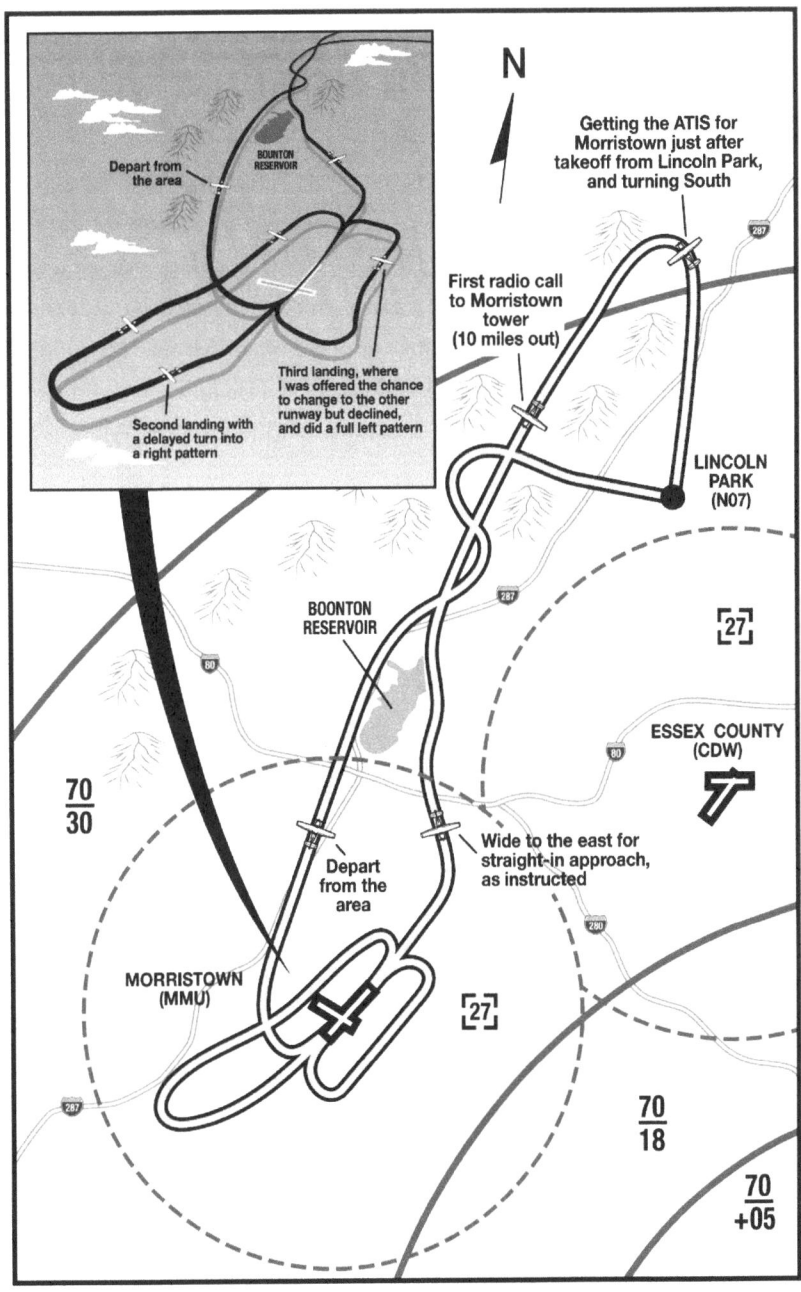

My required three solo takeoffs and landings at a towered airport, at Morristown (KMMU).

standard requirement, so instead of switching me over to Ground, he kept me on his frequency and I lined back up for takeoff. Morristown can be a surprisingly busy little airport, with plenty of small business jets coming in on long approach, due to their much faster speed. Instructions can change at a moment's notice, in response to traffic that isn't even in sight yet. On my first lap, Tower had me delay my first turn to crosswind, then follow a right-turning pattern instead of the standard left. On the second lap, due to another shift in the wind, he offered me the chance to turn my crosswind leg into a downwind and land on Runway 31 instead. I declined, because it would have put me behind on my descent and I was confident I could handle the crosswind on 23. A few weeks before, I probably would have felt paralyzed in the face of these rapid-fire conversations; now I just took them in stride.

Which brings us to the opening scene of this book, getting set for my third and last landing:

"*Morristown Tower, Skyhawk Niner-Juliet-Papa, midfield left downwind Runway Two-Three.*"

"*Skyhawk Niner-Juliet-Papa, cleared for the option Runway Two-Three.*"

"*Runway Two-Three, cleared for the option, Skyhawk Niner-Juliet-Papa.*"

"Cleared for the option" means you can do a touch-and-go or a full-stop landing, it's your call. It's your runway. I did a full stop, of course, to check one more box on the way to getting my license. But as I took off again and was flying home, the words stuck in my mind. A year ago, I would have never imagined myself doing this. Now I could see new options spreading before me, all the way to the distant horizon.

CHAPTER 23

Independence

Back in January, I had seen other students heading out on their own for their cross-country solos and wondered what that must be like. Now it was my turn.

After I got back from my flight to Morristown, I had a total of 58.6 flight hours, including 3.9 hours solo and 13.7 flying cross-country with an instructor. To earn my license, I would need 10 hours solo, including five flying cross-country by myself. For our purposes, **cross-country** (sometimes abbreviated XC) means any flight at least 50 nautical miles from point to point. The FAA also requires one of these solo flights, often called the "long cross-country," to meet certain criteria: It must be 150 miles total, make full stops at three different airports, and one of the legs must be at least 50 miles long. For each flight, the instructor assigns the destinations and, after reviewing your preparations, makes an endorsement in your logbook permitting you to fly it.

What makes the solo cross-country different isn't the distance, per se, though you do have to navigate without getting lost—a mishap which, of course, has been known to happen. What's different is the fact that you're on your own, with no one to tell you what to do. It's up to you to look and listen, decide what is safe or unsafe, or tackle any problem you might come across. If you don't remember something, no one is going to remind you. In other words, you're the pilot, and this is the real world. It's scary and liberating all at once.

The first flight Tess assigned me was to Sullivan County (KMSV) and back. It would be a pretty straight shot, and a familiar one, since Tess and I had flown there several times together for landing practice. Both airports are non-towered, and the route passes entirely through Echo airspace—so assuming everything went as planned, no need to interact with ATC. The hardest part was the unremarkable terrain I'd be navigating: miles and miles of rolling, forested hills with few discernable landmarks. There was a VOR about two-thirds of the way, though, which could keep me on the right path coming and going. But more importantly, there is no rule against using *ForeFlight* on solo cross-countries; unless it flaked out on me, I could track exactly where I was the whole time.

I'd still have to prepare a flight plan the old-fashioned way—a process that by now I was well acquainted with. But well before I got my weather briefing and ran my final calculations, I did something I hadn't been able to do in Arizona but proved immensely helpful now: I flew the entire trip in *Microsoft Flight Simulator 2020*. Previous generations of flight sims were useful for learning and practicing procedures, but for VFR navigation not so much. The grainy and generic landscapes simply weren't realistic enough to reliably or recognizably correspond to real life. But as I've already noted, my experiences flying in my home airport's pattern in *MSFS* fell nothing short of "virtual reality." One time, after getting back from the Onion Fields (our practice area) I went home and replicated the same flight in *MSFS*. I sent Tess a screenshot of an identical Cessna 172—displaying the same color scheme and registration number—flying over *the same tree*, in the middle of a field, that we had used for turns around a point. She emailed me back wondering how in the world I had taken a photograph of us during our lesson!

That's why a small but growing number of pilots are starting to pre-fly their flights on *MSFS*, and if they're lucky enough to live in an area of the country covered by *PilotEdge*, they can rehearse their radio interactions with live ATC to boot. New Jersey was outside their coverage zone, but I could still use my digital dry run to identify visual checkpoints along my planned route that were readily visible from the air. Of course, my heading and groundspeed would certainly vary from the real thing due to wind. But the ability to spot recognizable landmarks to confirm my location was a big reassurance. Much like my first solo, I could say to myself, "I've got this, because I've done this before."

During my actual cross-countries, I took a moment to snap some photos out my window, to compare with some of the screenshots from the sim I took while rehearsing. (As long as you're properly trimmed, it's not a critical stage of flight like landing or takeoff, and you're well clear of other traffic, taking a photo or two like this is perfectly alright.) When I got home, I posted them both, real and sim, on Twitter and asked if people could tell which was which. Usually they could—the airplane's surfaces in the sim looked a little too neat—but it was close enough to draw some astonished comments. You can compare them for yourself in Figures 29–32.

By the time I actually found myself in the air bound for Sullivan, tracking my progress on the iPad in my lap, I was feeling comfortable and well prepared. Still, every once in a while, I'd look up from the task at hand and marvel at where I was. I was alone in an airplane crossing mile after mile of countryside below—and I knew exactly what I was doing.

That's not to say everything went to plan. It was almost summer now, and about halfway back from Sullivan my iPad flashed a warning that it was overheating and would soon shut down. That wouldn't be a disaster: I knew pretty much where I was, and could find my way home without *ForeFlight*, if necessary. But it would be an inconvenience, especially as the Traffic overlay was an extra pair of eyes for other aircraft. I twisted the cabin's air vent open full and aimed it straight at my lap, hoping to cool the iPad down before it failed. That must have done the trick because the warning soon disappeared. It was a reminder, though, why the pen-and-paper notes and calculations I had done for my flight plan, and had stashed on the seat beside me, were more than a mere formality. The fact that I had a backup made the incident a hiccup, instead of a genuine worry.

It was a gusty day, a fact brought to my attention when a sudden wind pushed me well off centerline as I turned from base to final at Sullivan. I was far enough from the runway to correct, and landed without any problem. However, as I was coming in just over the trees to land on Runway 1 at Lincoln Park, the wind played the same prank on me again. What had been a steady, centered approached turned into a wild swing to the right. I responded quickly, pulling the plane back in line with the runway just before coming in over the threshold. But as I leveled off and flared, I touched down earlier than expected and bounced. Not high—probably just a few feet—but a definite bounce. Rather than overreact, I pulled gently back on the yoke to let more energy bleed off. The wheels touched down again … and bounced a second time, a shorter hop this time, before settling down. As the wheels finally gripped the runway, though, I felt a sudden sway to the left, which I countered with right rudder. This caused another sway to the right, before things finally settled down.

Though no one else had even seen it, the landing troubled me, and I thought a lot about it on the way home and into the evening. I would have liked to just dismiss it as a bit of bad luck, but if I was honest with myself—and it is important for a pilot to be honest with himself—it was my worst landing so far. There was no damage, and it wasn't an *unsafe* landing—but it could have been. My luck had been good luck, and you never want to take anything from the luck bag without putting something back into the experience bag. So what did the experience have to teach me?

The answer, I realized, was that when the gust blew me off course so close to the runway, *I should have gone around and tried again.* "A perfect landing begins with a perfect traffic pattern,"[188] and my pattern had been perfect—until it wasn't. It takes a certain *concentration* and *determination* to make a landing work. Precisely because of that, it's all too easy to get mentally locked onto completing the task, instead of recognizing that things have gone wrong. "I will make this work" must be willing to give way to "This isn't working." True, I recovered from the sudden gust, but at the cost of losing precise control over my speed and height in those critical last few seconds of flight. Rather than try to fix things at the last moment, I should have tried over again and gotten it right from the start.

My second flight, about a week later, was the "long cross-country." I was to fly nearly 70 nautical miles west to Wilkes-Barre Airport (KAVP) near Scranton, Pennsylvania, then east to Orange County (KMGJ) along the Hudson River valley in New York. Finally, I'd head back to Lincoln Park, for a total of 170 miles—a route shown in Figure 28. Including time on the ground, it would probably take about a little over two hours. This time, I would interact with ATC at a towered airport. Wilkes-Barre was technically a Class D airport, but it had a **TRSA** (Terminal Radar Services Area) marked in gray circles surrounding it out to 20 nautical miles. In effect, it's like Charlie airspace, but voluntary, at least for aircraft flying VFR.[189] I could ignore it and contact Tower directly, before entering the actual Delta, but that wouldn't be very polite. It would be smarter, and probably safer, to contact Approach at 20 miles out, inform them of my intent to land, get assigned a squawk code, and have them hand me off to Tower when I got closer. That was my plan.

Pre-flying my planned route in *MSFS* proved even more valuable this time, because it was unfamiliar ground. The most visible checkpoints from the air aren't always the most obvious ones, or even shown on the sectional chart. And as my screenshot/photo comparisons revealed, there's nothing like a sight picture you've seen before to verify where you are. More importantly though, the approach into Wilkes-Barre was tricky because the airport is located in a valley. Cruising at 4,500 feet MSL, I couldn't just suddenly drop down to a traffic pattern at 2,000; I had to manage my descent in stages, while staying safely above the surrounding terrain. Doing it two or three times in the sim helped me work out the best approach, and also recognize where that put me in relation to the airport's two intersecting runways when Tower gave me instructions to enter the pattern.

📡 *Wilkes-Barre Approach, Skyhawk Seven-Two-Niner-Juliet-Papa, ten miles southeast with information Yankee, 4500, for full-stop landing.*

📡 *Skyhawk Niner-Juliet-Papa, squawk 5521.*

📡 *Squawk 5521, Skyhawk Niner-Juliet-Papa.*

The routine of interacting with ATC was becoming, well, routine. I descended to 3,500 MSL, about 1,000 feet above the surrounding hills, and informed Approach when I had the airport in sight. They told me to switch frequencies and contact Tower. Because I was already in their system, I just had to tell Tower my call sign and altitude, and I was immediately cleared to land. I taxied back for takeoff and was on my way again.

The miles passed uneventfully as I flew east again, recrossing the Delaware River and beginning my descent into Orange County. KMGJ is a non-towered airport, and I already could see from the traffic on *ForeFlight* that it was buzzing with activity. As I tuned in the CTAF, I could hear five airplanes practicing in the pattern, with several others coming and going. It looked like one of those World War I dogfights in the movies. I recalled one of my takeaways from Arizona: If in doubt, circling is your friend. So I made a big arc west of the airport, about 500 feet above the pattern, until I could find a break in the traffic that would let me safely slip in.

Once I entered the downwind and was number two to land, I breathed a sigh of relief—but had to keep my eyes and ears sharp for what everyone else was doing. After I landed and taxied back to hold short for takeoff, another plane came in to land. He overshot his turn to final, and at one point was careening straight towards me on the taxiway, before he corrected and lined himself up with the runway. Needless to say, as I took off and climbed back above the frenzied traffic pattern, I was glad to put Orange County behind me.

My final landing back home at Lincoln Park was better this time, but I still bounced. I couldn't blame it on a last moment gust this time, so I searched my mind for an explanation. Bouncing means you're touching down with too much energy—the plane doesn't want to land yet, it has too much lift and still wants to fly. The remedy, once it happens, is to hold the yoke gently back and let it lose that excess energy before touching down again. That's what I was doing, alright, but what was causing the problem in the first place? One possibility was that I was coming in too fast, but I was pretty sure my airspeed was right on 65 knots. Finally, I figured it out: After two and a half hours in the air, I was just too eager to be on the ground again. The approach and round out were fine, but on flare, I wasn't holding the yoke back long enough to delay the touchdown. To land softly, I had to play "hard to get" with the runway. I made a note to exercise more patience in the future.

As always, it was two steps forward, one step back. But one positive step that I noticed: I was now landing with just my left hand on the yoke, without even being aware of it. That method, which felt so awkward at first, had become habit. That made me feel a little better.

On balance, my first two solo cross-countries had gone smoothly—too smoothly, in fact, because they hadn't eaten up all the time required. I now had 8.1 hours flying solo, of which 4.2 were cross-country. I'd need to do another flight. So the very next day after my "long cross-country," I came back to do one more flight to Sullivan County and back. The only planning required was to get the day's weather report and fill in the calculations with its new numbers.

This time, I kept a close eye on the watch. The last thing I wanted to do was land with 0.1 hours left to meet my requirements! I did a couple of patterns at Sullivan and practiced some ground reference maneuvers over the Onion Fields on the way back, until it was time to return.

On the last leg of my journey, it suddenly seemed as though every pilot in New Jersey decided it was a perfect day to go flying. The screen of my iPad was filled with aircraft popping up every which way. This was Echo airspace, so no control tower was going to tell us all where to go. It was, as I mentioned before, more like a rural intersection where everyone is expected to know and follow the rules of the road for themselves.

The first rule governing **right of way** is that more maneuverable categories of aircraft must give way to less maneuverable ones. So a more agile rotorcraft (such as a helicopter) must make way for an airplane, which makes way for an engine-propelled airship (like a blimp or dirigible), which makes way for a motorless glider. A drifting hot-air balloon takes precedence over all of them. But regardless of category, any aircraft in distress has right of way over all others.

So far, so good: All of the traffic around me also appeared to be airplanes and, I'm happy to report, none of them had declared an emergency. The next set of rules apply to aircraft within the same category. When two airplanes are converging on the same point, the one to the right has right of way, while the one on the left must give way, to avoid a collision. When overtaking another airplane, you must pass it to the right (that is why pilots normally begin their clearing turns to the left, in case there happens to be an unseen airplane passing from behind.) Two airplanes approaching each other head-on must both turn to their right. Determining the relative position of other aircraft, in this way, is a major reason why different-colored navigation lights on the wings and tail are so important at night.

Of course, flying VFR you can also change altitude to avoid other aircraft, but it's important to be aware of blind spots. A pilot flying a high-wing airplane like a Cessna 172 or Piper Cub may have difficulty seeing other aircraft above him; one in a low-wing airplane like a Piper Cherokee might not see traffic below him. The combination has sometimes been fatal. When approaching to land, the lowest aircraft has the right of way; however, you can't use this rule to cut someone off or overtake them. In theory, all small, unmanned aircraft (like drones) are supposed to make way for manned aircraft—but I wouldn't bet my life on it.

All the aircraft crossing my intended path, to and fro, forced me to alter course and altitude several times to avoid them, but I eventually inched closer to home. Ironically, for all the traffic around it, no one was taking off or landing at Lincoln Park, which could have helped clue me into the active runway. When I departed two hours earlier, the wind was from the north. I tuned in the ATIS at neighboring Caldwell Airport, and it said winds from the north.

There was a very good chance that was still true at Lincoln Park as well, but to make sure I overflew the field at 1,500 feet AGL, keeping a careful eye out for several planes *ForeFlight* was flagging in the immediate vicinity. I was distracted by this concern, but thought I saw the tiny windsock on top of the hangar below pointing in the expected direction. So I descended to join the pattern and come around again to approach Runway 1.

As I rounded off and started my flare, something didn't seem right. My airspeed over the threshold was fine, but I kept floating for an extended distance. I initially didn't give it much thought, but moments later I realized that I was halfway down the runway and my wheels had not touched down. In another second or two they probably would, but that wouldn't leave me much room to come to a stop. I must have been just a few feet off the runway, but I didn't hesitate: I pushed the throttle in full and called *"Going around!"* into the radio.

If I had the presence of mind, I would have looked at the windsock as I went by, but I was focused on gaining airspeed and—only then—altitude. As I've mentioned before, it's all too tempting to try to gain altitude first and pitch up, only to lose speed and stall. Worse yet, a pilot might "dump" the flaps, pulling them up all at once in the hope of gaining speed, only bringing the stall on sooner. It's the easiest way to get yourself killed on a go-around. Instead, I flew almost level over the remaining stretch of the runway, only raising the nose to a shallow climb, and lifted the flaps a stage at a time as my airspeed rose. It was some low flying at first, but trading speed for altitude would have been a foolish bargain and ended up costing me both.

When I came in over the trees on final the second time, I tried to keep my airspeed to a minimum, closer to 60 knots. I still floated a bit but touched down safely. Then I glanced up at the windsock on the hangar roof, towards the far end of the runway, and saw my problem. Despite the neighboring ATIS, despite what I *thought* I saw from 1,500 feet up, I had been landing in the wrong direction, with a stiff tailwind behind me. And on a short runway like this—less than 2,100 feet with the displaced threshold taken into account—that left no room for error. I should have spotted the windsock the first time, but I was preoccupied with my decision to go around. At least I did go around, though. It was the first time I had been forced to make that decision, and it was the right one. If I hadn't, I might have been able to stomp the brakes and stop in time. But I also might have gone right off the end of the runway.

Recounting some of these episodes may make it sound like my three solo cross-country flights were action-packed and full of drama. In fact, for large stretches they were rather tranquil. My chief memory of those 6.5 hours alone in the cockpit is listening to the steady hum of the engine over my earphones as the hills and trees and villages and rivers below glide noiselessly past, unveiling a constantly changing panorama. Cross-countries are a journey, and there's something about a journey that excites and rewards the imagination—albeit gradually, not all at once. The eye searches the horizon, as a long-awaited destination gradually takes shape, and a plan conceived in the mind transforms into reality—sometimes just as expected, sometimes taking an unexpected, even defiant twist. We rarely return from a journey unchanged. For me, they were my favorite part of flight training.

One reason I can recall so many events that happened on these flights, in such detail, is that I'm not relying solely on memory: I recorded every second of them in *ForeFlight*. Even now, as I write this, I can review them, forward and backward, in 3-D re-creation (Figure 33), along with charts showing my altitude, speed, pitch, and bank at any given moment (Figures 34-35). It's another example of the new tools technology has put within pilots' reach, and a great way to analyze—accurately and honestly—what I did right and what I did wrong.

I made a few mistakes on my cross-country adventures, and encountered some challenges, but I learned from them. I learned to never rely solely on electronics, however helpful they might be; to remain patient in holding off a landing, and bleed off that excess energy that might cause you to bounce; to never assume anything about the wind direction; and to never hesitate to go around again when a landing just doesn't look right. Far from discouraging or scaring me, confronting and dealing with these difficulties alone fostered a new sense of independence and self-reliance. In the end, my withdrawals from the luck bag had been modest and affordable; my deposits into the experience bag were substantial. And more than that, I was having a blast.

I was flying high. I had completed all the requirements for my Private Pilots' License, besides the final checkride. What I didn't know was, I still had a tough grind ahead of me.

CHAPTER 24

Performance

When I came home from Arizona, my thoughts began turning to the checkride. I knew all along, of course, that the checkride, consisting of both an oral interview and a practical demonstration of my flying skills, would be the final step to getting my license. But up to that point, it seemed such a distant prospect, with so many hurdles to overcome in the meantime, that—like a dental appointment scheduled many months in the future—it didn't seem worth worrying about. However, when the school in Scottsdale offered to schedule my checkride if I stayed around another week, it woke me up to the fact that my "date with destiny" was fast approaching, one way or another.

I began exploring a whole genre of videos that exists on YouTube devoted to "How to Pass Your Checkride." They fell into two main categories. The first were "mock checkrides." These focused mainly on the oral portion, which resembled something like a job interview. My main takeaway was that while there's a potentially huge amount of ground to cover, there are some standard questions that examiners tend to ask, which eat up a large chunk of the time available. If you're prepared to answer them, you'll probably survive the rest. One piece of advice I consistently heard: *Once you've answered a question, stop*. If the examiner needs to hear more, they'll ask. Rattling on because you're nervous will only expose the limits of your knowledge, which the examiner will home in on like a shark smelling blood in the water.

The second category of videos were usually titled "Why I Failed My Checkride" and were almost always about the practical portion, in the air. The typical narrative went as follows: *Everything was going fine, until the very end, when the examiner asked me to perform [an emergency procedure, a power-off approach, a short-field landing]. Then I [came in too fast, put my flaps in too soon, was about to overshoot or undershoot the runway] and the examiner just sadly shook his head.* In a word, they screwed up and had to come back and retake that part again. These videos had me a little worried, because while I was familiar with most of the procedures they described, I hadn't really practiced them much myself. I certainly wasn't very confident I could perform them to standard and avoid the same fate.

The good news was Tess was about to rectify that. Now that my solo cross-countries were completed, we were going to focus on the hard stuff that trips most people up on the checkride. And while the cross-country flights were thrilling and fun, this final phase of my training would take minute and sometimes tedious attention to detail.

To give you an idea what it involved, let me take you on another typical lesson. It's late June now, and Tess is back in the cockpit with me. There's no flight plan, because for the next two hours we'll be staying in the traffic pattern at Lincoln Park doing repeated takeoffs and landings. But not ordinary ones, no; these will be **performance takeoffs and landings**, designed to get the best possible performance out of the airplane in especially demanding situations.

Back when I was studying for my written exam, and later when I drew up weight and balance sheets as part of my flight planning, I calculated minimum takeoff and landing distances using the charts provided in the airplane's manual, its POH. It's actually an explicit regulatory requirement before every flight, and you're legally required to carry the calculations with you to prove that you did them. But if you look closely, next to those charts in the fine print it says that the results assume that short-field takeoff (or landing) techniques are being utilized—the precise methods and checklists for which are laid out, in detail, elsewhere in the POH.

There's no formal definition of "short-field"—it depends on the type of aircraft, as well as the pilot's experience and comfort level. Many pilots would say that Lincoln Park's 2,767-foot runway is already a "short-field," but in the past, the only concession we made to that was to add 10° of flaps on takeoff for a bit more lift. Many airplanes require flaps on every takeoff, but for a normal-size runway the Cessna 172 POH says that putting in the first 10° of flaps is optional. This initial degree of flaps produces more lift than drag, so it can be helpful in getting the airplane to lift off over a shorter distance. But it does slow the plane's acceleration on climb, so as soon as you're a safe distance above the runway (say 100 feet) and clear of any obstacles ahead, you need to remember to lift the flaps. Doing so will cause the nose to drop slightly, and require a bit more back pressure on the yoke. It may even cause the plane to sink slightly. But this is temporary, as the "clean" wing configuration reduces drag and allows the airplane to gain speed more quickly, for a sustained climb.

Today, however, we're going to do a short-field takeoff *by the book*, the way I'll be asked to do it on the checkride (regardless of the runway's actual length). First, I lower the flaps to 10°—a requirement now, not an option. Next, I taxi all the way back to the very end of the runway, using every foot available. By the time I turn around, the airplane's tail is dangling over the yellow line of the stopway. Then I press the brakes down hard with my feet and push the throttle in full. At full power, the airplane strains forward against the immobile brakes, like a horse against its harness. I make sure to check the engine gauges: all in the green.

Now before releasing the brakes and hurtling down the runway, I need to explain V_X and V_Y. These are specific airspeeds that I will aim for to get maximum performance out of the airplane on takeoff. Remember that for any given power setting—in this case, full throttle—airspeed is a function of pitch. The higher I raise the nose, the slower I fly. V_X is **best angle of climb**, the airspeed at which the airplane gains the most altitude over the shortest horizontal *distance* on the ground. V_Y is **best rate of climb**, the airspeed at which the airplane gains the most altitude over the shortest period of *time* rather than distance. These numbers vary by model of airplane, and were determined by the aircraft's designers and verified by test pilots when that model was first introduced. Neither are shown on the airspeed indicator—you just have to memorize them. For the school's Cessna 172S, V_X is 62 knots and V_Y is 74 knots. So if I want to fly at V_X, I need to pitch the nose higher than if I want to fly at V_Y.

V_X (Best Angle of Climb) and V_Y (Best Rate of Climb)

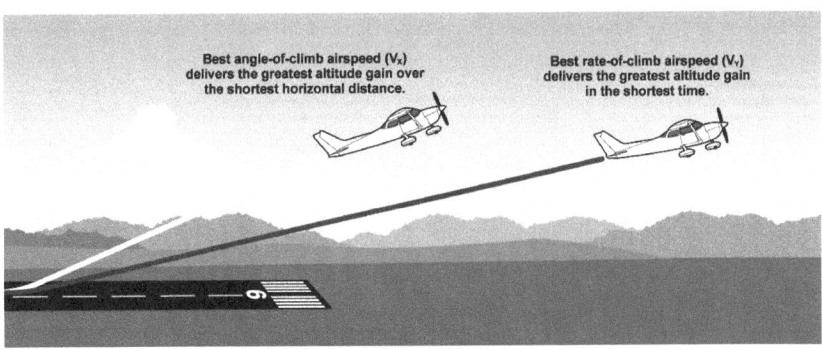

As I release the brakes and begin quickly gaining speed down the runway, my goal in a short-field takeoff is to get off the ground and climbing in as short a distance as possible. Depending on the airplane's weight, atmospheric air density, and headwind, in the Cessna 172 this could be as little as 600 feet. Today, on a warm day in June, I've calculated it's more likely to be around 860 feet. In any case, I'm going to rotate and lift off when the airspeed reaches 50 knots instead of the normal 55.

Once I'm off the ground, I'm still not done. Recall that the minimum takeoff distances include the possibility of having to clear a 50-foot obstacle (real or imagined) at the end of the runway. To do this, I need to gain that altitude over the shortest distance possible. So as soon as I rotate, I pull back farther on the yoke than normal, to keep my airspeed from rising above V_X, or 62 knots. Pitching the nose this far up, on takeoff, feels unusual and even dangerous. And it can be. Stall speed with no flaps is 48 knots, so there isn't much margin for error. If I pull back too steeply, the plane could easily slow and, instead of climbing, drop like a rock—exactly what we practiced power-on stalls to recognize and prevent. Normally on takeoff I'd just raise my nose to the horizon for a steady climb gradually accelerating to 80 knots, but here the nose needs to be above the horizon, leaving me few outside visual references. Instead, I need to keep at least one eye on the airspeed indicator and adjust my pressure on the yoke to keep it from rising or falling much beyond 62.

Short-Field Takeoff

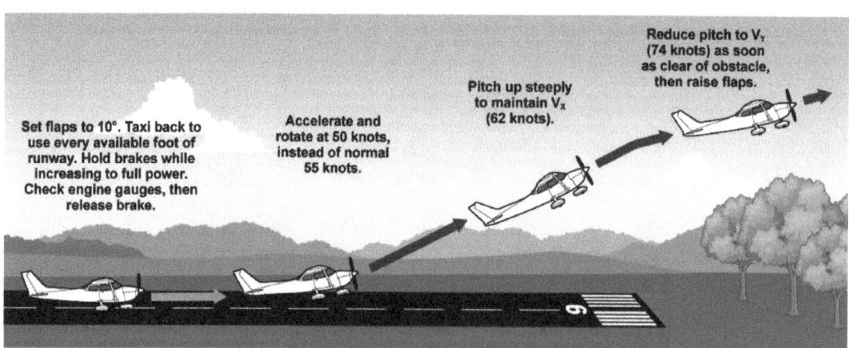

I only need to hold V_x for a few brief seconds to get above the 50-feet obstacle ahead. Then I can let the nose drop a bit and build up speed to V_y. Once I'm safely accelerating, I can raise the flaps. Holding 74 knots, instead of 80, still requires a slightly higher pitch than normal, but it gets me to my desired cruising altitude in the shortest period of time. By flying these speeds—rotating at 50 instead of 55, holding 62 to shoot up and over an obstacle, then climbing at 74 instead of accelerating straight to 80—I've reduced my margin of error over a stall, but I've also gotten a shorter takeoff distance and faster climb out of the airplane, if needed. The exact pressure on the yoke I need to exert to hit and maintain these speeds can vary depending on the day's weather, which makes the airplane feel more or less buoyant. So it takes a steady hand, a close eye on the instruments, and a good feel for the plane's responses.

"Good," says Tess, as we come around to downwind. "Now let's do a short-field landing." The goal here is to touch down, safely, a very short distance over the runway threshold, leaving as much room as I have left to brake (hard) to halt. For the checkride, I'll have to pick out a point—typically the runway numbers—and land right on it. I can get away with actually touching down about two runway stripes (200 feet) after it, but not before. Outside of those bounds, I'll fail. To do this, I fly the same approach as normal, with two differences. First, I keep my final approach speed at 60 knots, rather than 65, so there's less speed to bleed off once I flare. Second, I aim at the threshold of the runway, or even before it, so my round out happens directly over it. Again, it's all about reducing margin of error in exchange for shorter distances.

Short-Field Landing

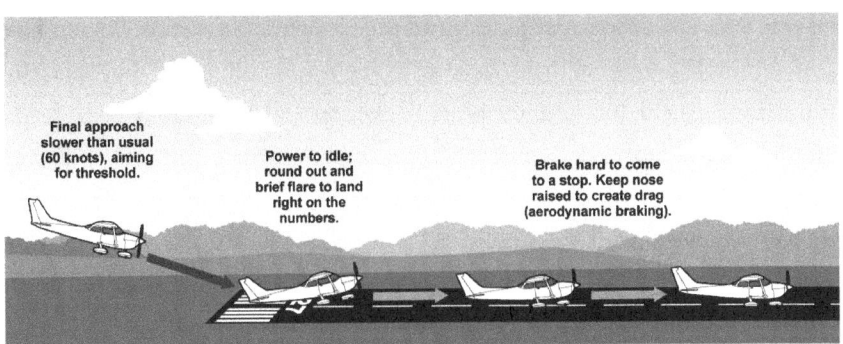

I'm not looking for the prettiest, softest landing here. I'm looking to plop the airplane down right where I want it. But I don't want to overdo it, either, because—as I had already learned—touching down too soon, with too much energy, only makes you bounce. Tess warned that some students get so eager (or desperate) to hit the target that they pitch down and land nose gear first. That might work on an aircraft carrier, in a jet fighter with specially reinforced landing gear, but in a Cessna 172 it will damage the plane and fail your checkride. I found that the best way was to flare normally but instead of holding the yoke back as much (playing "hard to get"), let the plane sink. If I did that, I usually hit the numbers or just after them. The main concern is overshooting, but one time—trying not to overshoot—I came in so low and slow I could see that I would touch down just short of the numbers (an automatic fail). If that happens, Tess advised, give it a tiny bit of throttle, just for a moment. The extra bit of thrust, she promised, would keep it in the air just long enough to reach my target.

Once I've touched down, I pull the yoke back more than normal to increase drag, a technique called **aerodynamic braking**. If this were an actual short-field landing, I'd stomp hard on the brakes. Both actions are intended to minimize my **roll**, the distance traveled between touching down and coming to a complete halt. When I'm just demonstrating the technique, though, I only *tell* my instructor (or checkride examiner) that I *would* be stomping on the brakes, as I come to a normal stop.

As we taxi back, Tess informs me that my next assignment is a soft-field takeoff. Not all runways are paved, and the Cessna 172 can take off and land perfectly well on a grass field, as long as it's reasonably level. But operating from a grass field (or a sandy beach) takes special techniques because the ground creates more friction than a nice, smooth tarmac and can easily snag your nose gear, causing the plane to get stuck or even flip over. The idea is to keep the weight off the nosewheel and get all the wheels off the ground as soon as possible—even sooner than in a short-field takeoff—to be able to build up the airspeed necessary to climb.

Most flight schools don't have you practice takeoffs and landings from an actual soft field because they don't want you accidentally getting stuck or damaging the landing gear. That might be educational for you, but not so much for the student scheduled for a lesson after you. So our practice—like the checkride—takes place on a normal paved runway, *as if* it were a grassy field.

Like the short-field takeoff, my first move is to lower the flaps 10° for added lift. But this time, as I enter the runway, I pull firmly back on the yoke to take as much weight off the nosewheel as possible. I line myself up and, *without stopping,* push the throttle in full. As the plane gains speed, I keep pulling the yoke all the way back with the nose pointing in the air, so that the nosewheel comes off the ground—kind of like doing a wheelie on a bicycle. Soon—a lot sooner than normal—the rear wheels start to lose their grip as well. The airplane is beginning to fly, but only because I'm in **ground effect**. The disruption in airflow caused by my close proximity to the ground is giving me extra lift. This effect extends about as high as half my wingspan, and if I continued to climb above that, at this low speed, I'd sink back down again and possibly even stall.

What I need to do, instead, is push forward on the yoke and level off, flying just a few feet above the ground. Free of the ground's friction, but still in ground effect, I can gain the airspeed I need more rapidly. If there's no obstacle in front of me, I'll let it rise to V_Y (74 knots) before pulling back on the yoke and starting to climb. If there is an obstacle, I'll pull back sooner and harder as soon as I reach V_X (62 knots), pitching the nose up into the air to pop up and over whatever's in my way. Once I'm clear, I can let the nose down to V_Y and, as I gain more speed, lift the flaps.

Soft-Field Takeoff

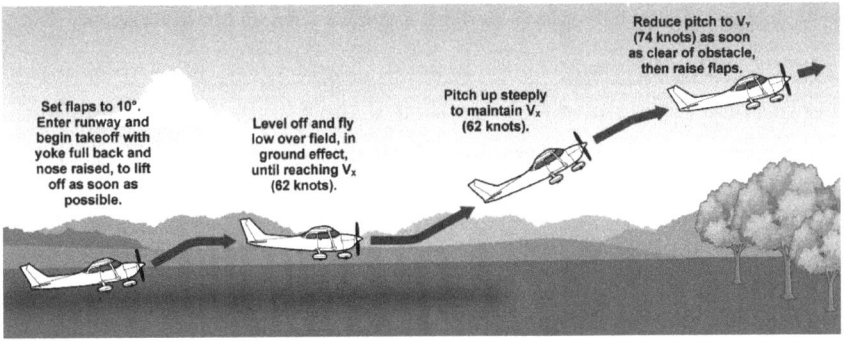

The best way I can describe a soft-field takeoff is like landing in reverse. When you level off and fly so low over the runway, it looks just like the round out on landing, except you're gaining speed instead of losing it. For me, the hardest part was knowing when I was actually aloft, because I was holding the nose up so high and the lift off was so gentle—though I imagine that in a real soft-field takeoff, an end to the rattling and bumping along the uneven ground would offer a better clue. In any event, I had to react rapidly to level off, because pitched up like that, I could gain unwanted height very quickly. At the time, it wasn't really possible to practice this maneuver on *Microsoft Flight Simulator* because with the yoke full back, the nose (incorrectly) angles up so high you get a **tailstrike** (the tail hits the ground). The only realistic way to practice was in real life. It could be pretty tricky, but I eventually got the hang of it and somewhat perversely found it to be a lot of fun. The low-level flying and abrupt changes in pitch make you feel like a real barnstormer.

"Alright," says Tess. "Now show me a soft-field landing." Unlike the short-field landing, I don't have to hit a target, I just have to land. But I also have to avoid getting stuck in the (for now, imaginary) grass. This time, I keep my final approach speed at the normal 65 knots and aim for the numbers as usual (not in front of them)—exactly the same as a standard approach. Then, just as I round out and flare, I must nudge the throttle slightly to give me about 100 RPM above idle. Not much, barely a purr, or I'll float down the field forever. Next, I pull back on the yoke like normal during my flare. Only once I touch down, I hold it back, keeping my nosewheel off the field as long as possible—another wheelie. Finally, no brakes. I let the friction from the ground, along with aerodynamic braking, slow me. Of course, when practicing this on a paved runway you do have to apply brakes, but you inform the instructor or examiner that you *wouldn't* if this were an actual soft-field.

Soft-Field Landing

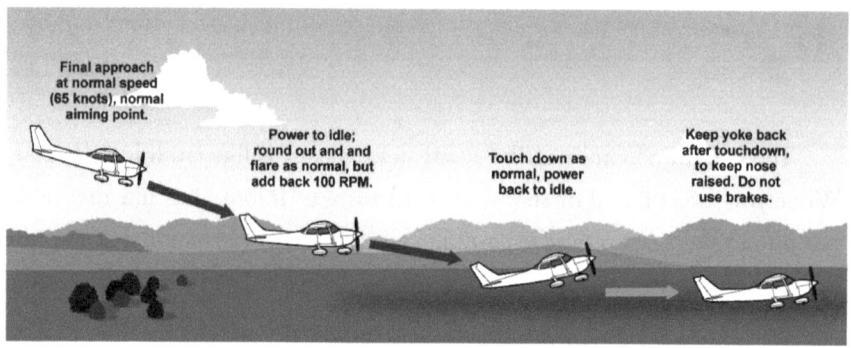

Though I never got the chance to takeoff or land from an actual grass field, Tess did take me around one afternoon, hopping from one short-field to another in the nearby area. After the repetitious practice at Lincoln Park, it was a welcome change of pace—and a fun challenge, because these were *really* short fields. Andover (12N) is a tiny airport nestled in the New Jersey hills with 1,981-foot runway right on the shore of a little lake. On final, I had to aim right at the shoreline where a group of kayakers were paddling about on the water. I cut the throttle to idle right over them, rounded out, and let the wheels come down right on the numbers 21. The kayakers seemed unfazed. While I was grateful for their vote of confidence, I wouldn't have liked to trade places with them.

Judging when to pull power to idle like this, on final approach, is all about having a feel for how the airplane will **glide**. A Cessna 172 can glide a fair distance without power, and understanding just how far it will go is the key to our last and final performance today: the **power-off landing**. In an emergency, if you lose your engine, this is the only way to land the plane, and you only get one shot. In real life there are no go-arounds without an engine.

Back at Lincoln Park, we're in the downwind leg of the traffic pattern, coming abeam of the numbers. But instead of pulling the throttle back to 1500 and beginning my powered descent, Tess leans over and pulls the power all the way out to idle. It will stay there until I land (unless it's going so badly that I need to throw in the towel and go around—this is practice, not a real emergency, after all.) Cutting the throttle like this makes a lot of students very nervous, because you can't control the rate of descent like you usually do by adding or taking out power. Instead, you have to *judge* where the plane is going to end up and make your turns to base and final accordingly. Putting it in other terms, there's a fixed amount of energy in the airplane, and you have to decide how and when to spend it so you run out just over the runway.

My first step may seem counterintuitive: I pull back on the yoke and pitch up, slowing the plane to its maximum glide speed of 68 knots. The only forward thrust I now have comes from gravity, and this is the speed where Cessna's test pilots have confirmed I'll get the most distance in exchange for altitude lost. In the meantime, I keep my flaps up. The added lift isn't worth the additional drag, which I have no power to counter.

My momentum isn't enough to carry me through the full remaining legs of the traffic pattern. But how much to cut them short? As I've come to learn, by about half. On my first try, I was afraid the plane wouldn't glide far enough, and shortened the turns so much that I actually ended up high on final approach. Eventually, I got a better feel for the rate of descent on glide and felt more confident that I could extend the legs out a bit and still make the runway. It's still probably better to err on the side of overshooting, rather than falling short. I can't regain lost energy if I'm too low and slow, but if I find myself too high, I can put in flaps to add drag so I lose that excess energy—and altitude—more quickly. For the commercial license checkride, pilots must hit a specific aiming point on the power-off landing, which means they have to judge the glide fairly well. For the private pilot checkride, all you have to do is land safely, anywhere on the runway. At Lincoln Park, that still doesn't give me much leeway. But on a more normal-size runway, I could come in high and fast and float for quite a while, and still be okay.

When I know I have the runway made, I finally put in my flaps, if I haven't already. From this point—and this is extremely useful to understand—it's just a normal landing. After all, with a Cessna 172, you always pull the power to idle as you come in over the threshold, and only keep your hand on the throttle in case something unexpected forces you to go around. So there's absolutely nothing unusual about a power-off round out and flare. It's judging the approach that's the entire game. And after becoming more comfortable, it did become a game to see how well I could do. After a few tries, I usually touched down exactly where I normally would.

Why do we learn performance takeoffs and landings, and why do they feature so prominently on the checkride? Many pilots go their entire careers without needing to operate from an extremely short field, much less a grass field. It's important to know how to glide, in the event of an emergency. The famous example of Captain "Sully" Sullenberger, who in 2009 glided US Airways Flight 1549 to a safe landing in the Hudson River after his plane hit a flock of geese and lost both engines, testifies to that.[190] But it's the kind of maneuver you hope you never *have* to do.

The real reason, in my opinion, is about learning to—and demonstrating that you've learned to—fly the plane with greater *precision*. The more precisely you can fly the airplane, at lower margins of error, the more effective those safety margins become when flying normally. Plus, you develop a better sense of how much further you *can* push the plane if you *need* to. Those skills, and that knowledge, are useful even when flying under much less demanding conditions.

Flying a short-field takeoff takes a close attention to airspeed, especially when attempting to climb quickly. A short-field landing takes concentration as well as nerve to aim and touch down on exactly the spot you want. A soft-field takeoff takes similar nerve to level off and fly just a few feet above the runway, as well as patience to gain the airspeed you need before pulling up and over a fast-approaching obstacle. A soft-field landing reminds you that the landing isn't over just because you've touched down. And a power-off landing teaches you to estimate, conserve, and expend the airplane's energy in a much more disciplined way.

The fact that it can save your bacon in a real emergency is just another added plus.

CHAPTER 25

Emergencies

One of the most hallowed rituals of flying as an airline passenger is the safety briefing. Some airlines go to great lengths to hold your wandering attention despite having heard it all hundreds of times before. (My personal favorite are the Air New Zealand videos, featuring the characters from *The Lord of the Rings*.)[191] If the content itself never seems to change, it's because FAA regulations define what the safety briefing must include. While not all of these requirements apply to smaller aircraft, private pilots are expected to brief passengers on safety—including on the checkride. Fortunately, there's a ridiculously convenient acronym to remember what topics to cover: SAFETY. It stands for:

Seat Belts
Airsickness/Air Vents
Fire Extinguisher
Exits/Evacuation Procedures
Talking/Traffic Spotting
Your Questions

A typical briefing might go like this:

Good morning. Your seat belt is located here, and this is how you buckle and release it. As a passenger, you need to have your seat upright and seat belt on, including shoulder harness if you have one, during taxi, takeoff, and landing. As crew, I have to wear my seat belt through our entire flight, but I can undo my shoulder harness en route. If you're feeling airsick, tell me. Turning on the air vents here and here can help. Looking outside at a fixed point on the horizon also helps.

The fire extinguisher is on the floor between our seats, and this is how you operate it. Your door opens and locks using this handle on the arm rest. Never open the door or exit the plane when the propeller is turning, except in an emergency. Regardless of whether the engine is on or off, always turn towards the rear when exiting, away from the propeller.

We have a **sterile cockpit** *rule, which means no unnecessary talking during critical phases of flight, like takeoff and landing, so I don't get distracted. But throughout our flight, I do need you to keep an eye out for other traffic and speak up if you see anything. Don't assume I've already seen it. Last but not least, do you have any questions for me?*

It's interesting: There are no door locks on the Cessna 172, just an armrest handle that serves as a latch. Every once in a while I noticed it get jostled and start creeping up, and had to push it back down again. Someone once told me a story, perhaps just an urban legend, about a checkride examiner who opened the door during flight to see how the pilot would react. According to the experts, a door opening in flight—at least for a non-pressurized airplane like the Cessna 172—poses only a minor safety risk, in itself.[192] The airflow will tend to keep it mostly shut, and you're supposed to be strapped to your seat in any event. The much greater risk is the pilot freaking out in response and forgetting to fly the plane. I told Tess this story and she laughed. "I hate heights," she said, and I agree. You might think that's strange for a pilot to say, but there's something psychologically reassuring about having even a fairly flimsy barrier between you and a several-thousand-foot drop.

My checkride examiner was unlikely to open a door on me mid-flight, but I knew he would present me with at least one emergency situation, which I'd be expected to respond to promptly and decisively. The checklists of procedures for each type of emergency are listed in the airplane's POH, but a real emergency is no time to be frantically searching through a manual. Some pilots carry a laminated sheet with all the checklists printed on them, but it can still take precious seconds to locate the right list and decipher the tiny print. At first, I tried to memorize the checklists, but I found my attempts to recall them made my reaction methodical and slow. Eventually, I came to realize that the best approach was to remember one or two critical go-to actions for each scenario which I could take immediately, along with an overall idea of what I was trying to accomplish. Then, time permitting, I could follow up by running through a laminated checklist to make sure I didn't forget anything important.

Flying back to Lincoln Park, at 3,500 feet, Tess suddenly reaches over and pulls the throttle back to idle. "Your engine is out," she explains, and sits back to watch my response. With an engine failure in flight, eventually I want to see if I can restart the engine. But my very first action is to establish my airspeed at 68 knots for maximum glide, just like I did for a power-off landing. Again it may seem counterintuitive, when I've just lost thrust from my propeller, to pitch up to intentionally *lose* speed. But the manufacturer has worked out that 68 knots gets me the most distance in exchange for altitude, absent power.

Next I need to look for some place to land and start heading towards it. As I've already discovered, it's surprising how far an airplane can glide. You might think you'd just drop out of the sky, but that's not the case. There's a chart in the POH, but the rule of thumb for the Cessna 172 is 1.5 miles for every 1,000 feet of altitude above ground. Keeping that in mind, as I slow, I next start looking around for an open space that's large enough to safely set down. In the Arizona desert that could be almost anywhere. Over the heavily wooded hills and suburban communities of northern New Jersey, my choices are a lot more limited.

Sometimes it's easy to overlook the obvious. Once, as I was scanning the unpromising terrain ahead, Tess nudged me and pointed to the small airport directly below her right-side window. A paved runway, familiar or not, is always the best option, and you never know where you might find one, so I made a mental note never to forget to look. Farm fields will do, as long as you make sure to land *with* the crop furrows, not against them. Golf courses can work. Busy highways are dangerous, for obvious reasons, but may be the best available option. In that case, you should always land *with* the direction of traffic. Smaller roads have less traffic, but even ones that are straight can be lined by trees or telephone wires. The most important thing, Tess advised, was to pick a decent option and commit to it, instead of wasting valuable time and glide energy wavering over which is best.

I pick out a farm field ahead and turn towards it. The priorities in an emergency are:

1. Fly the plane
2. Navigate
3. Communicate

Since I've done the first two, it's time for me to let someone else know what's going on. Any nearby aviation frequency will do—someone will probably hear it—but the emergency frequency anywhere in the U.S. is 121.5, which is monitored 24/7 by the Civil Air Patrol and other first responders. The FAA recommends that, if you don't have any other frequency you need to be using, you should tune in and monitor 121.5 while en route. If you wander into restricted airspace, they'll be trying to contact you there. You may also hear another aircraft in distress and be able to relay the message.

In an immediately life-threatening emergency (like losing an engine), yes, pilots really do call out **"MAYDAY! MAYDAY! MAYDAY!"** over the radio. The expression came about in the early 1920s and derives from the French *m'aidez*, which means "help me". It was widely adopted because it is easy to remember, recognizable, and gets everyone's attention.[193] Repeating it several times in a row makes it clear no one has misheard you saying something else. For less than life-threatening situations, like if a pilot is lost or having a mechanical problem, or if someone onboard is sick and needs medical attention, the expression to use instead is "**PAN-PAN,**" from the French word *panne*, which means "breakdown."[194] Saying one of these two things over the radio helps ATC, or whoever is listening, immediately gauge the level of urgency of your situation.

The transponder also has special emergency codes that alert ATC to your situation and help them track you on their radar as well. Squawking 7700 means a general emergency, like the situation I'm pretending to be in now, with an engine failure. I'll talk more in a moment about 7600, which means you have a communications failure. You never want to accidentally enter 7500, which is the code for a hijacking. Even if you recognize your mistake and change it later, ATC is going to assume you meant it, and you may get some F-16s showing up to check how your day is going.

Hopefully, after my initial surprise, it's only taken a few seconds to make all of these decisions. If I'm still fairly high up, I may have time to try to restart the engine. The basic rule of thumb, backed up by the checklist, is to scan "floor to door." I start at the center of the instrument panel and move down, looking for things that might have caused the engine to cut out. Is the fuel mixture knob full in? Has the fuel shutoff valve accidentally been pulled out? Is the fuel selector on the floor set to Both? As I witnessed in Arizona, running out of fuel is a surprisingly common cause of aircraft accidents. But sometimes the engine only runs out of fuel because the selector is set to the left or right tank only, and switching will restart the flow from the tank that's still full.

Next, I scan from the center to the left side: Switch the fuel pump on, in case the flow due to gravity has somehow been interrupted. Is the master switch on, for the starter to work? Is the ignition set to Both? Usually, as the plane glides, the airflow will cause the propeller to keep spinning. If all of these items have been checked, the windmilling propeller *should* restart the engine on its own. If the propeller is not turning, I can try to crank the starter. As I mimic running through these attempts, Tess informs me that none of them are working. With my engine still out, I will need to make a **forced landing**.

Landing in some random field is always going to be risky, but there are still steps I can take to improve my chances of walking away safely. First, I need to shut down and secure the engine, to minimize the chance of it catching fire on impact. Again, I go "floor to door," doing almost the exact opposite from when I was trying to restart the engine: pull the fuel mixture knob fully out; pull the fuel shut off valve out; turn the fuel selector to Off; make sure the fuel pump is off; turn the ignition to Off. I keep the electrical master switch on for the moment so I can continue to use the radio, as well as lower the flaps once I know I have the landing zone made. From here, it's a power-off landing like I've practiced back at Lincoln Park. If I'm too high when I arrive at my designated landing spot, I can descend in a circle until I'm low enough to land. As soon as I lower my flaps on final, I flip off the master switch and tell my passenger to open her door just a notch, and do the same on my side. That's to prevent us being trapped inside the aircraft if it gets damaged on landing.

If it's a hard landing, the **ELT** will go into action. The Emergency Locator Transmitter is a radio beacon that sends out a distress signal, which sounds kind of like a car alarm, over the standard 121.5 MHz emergency frequency, as well as 243 MHz (used by the military), so that ATC and other aircraft can hear and track it down. Newer ELTs also broadcast on 406 MHz, which is received by a satellite system and offers longer range and better accuracy for search and rescue efforts.[195] The ELT is designed to be automatically triggered when the aircraft experiences high g-forces, presumably due to a crash, though it can also be activated by hand. Sometimes if pilots have a particularly hard landing on the airport runway, the ELT can go off—but it has to be pretty hard. In any event, the ELT is supposed to transmit for at least 24 hours, which is the "golden period" in which most survivors are successfully found. All U.S.-registered civil aircraft are required to have an ELT, under a law Congress passed after a plane carrying Congressmen Hale Boggs and Nick Begich crashed somewhere in Alaska in 1972 and was never found.[196] The ELT antenna on the Cessna 172 sticks up just behind the rear cabin window, and the device must be regularly tested and inspected to make sure it is working.

Fortunately, we won't need the ELT today. In fact, as I glide down towards the field I've picked out, I'm not actually *doing* a lot of these actions, I'm just telling Tess what I *would* be doing in a real emergency. When we're still about 500 feet up and it looks like we'll make it, she calls a halt to our exercise and tells me to climb. I put the throttle back in and we fly away.

The worst time to have an engine failure isn't way up in the sky, it's immediately on takeoff. Altitude is your friend; it gives you time to think and distance to find a decent landing spot. On takeoff, you have neither. When time permits, many pilots also give a short briefing to passengers on what they will do if the engine fails while taking off. Ideally, if you catch the problem before rotating and lifting off, you abort the landing, cut the throttle, and brake to a stop on the remaining runway. If you've just lifted off and the runway is long enough, you might be able to continue straight and land on whatever portion is left. The most dangerous moment for the engine to fail is when there's no runway left but you're still below 1,000 feet. At this low altitude, climbing at relatively low airspeed, turning 180 degrees to get back to the departure runway is so treacherous it's called "the impossible turn."[197] You're almost certainly better off trying to land somewhere straight ahead on a road or a small field, though the options may be extremely limited.* Once you've reached the traffic pattern altitude, on the other hand, it should be possible to glide back to the airport and do a regular power-off landing onto the runway.

In theory, aircraft with more than a single engine should be safer because

---

* In 2015, the actor-pilot Harrison Ford, of Han Solo and Indiana Jones fame, landed his plane on a golf course in southern California after its engine failed on takeoff. The plane was badly damaged and Ford was injured, but he was credited with saving "several lives" by deciding to land where he did, rather than try to make it back to the airport.

they can continue to fly even if one of its engines fails. But staying in control of the airplane with one engine out takes training and practice (because the thrust from the remaining engine is off-center, causing the plane to yaw). Even pilots who have a multi-engine rating can easily fall out of practice and overestimate their abilities. As a result, the actual safety record of multi-engine planes is not noticeably better than single-engine.[198]

Sometimes engines catch fire. On the ground, an engine fire on start usually happens because the engine has been over-primed—too much fuel has been pumped into it in an effort to get it to start, often in cold weather. That excess fuel can pool just outside the cylinder, and when ignition finally takes place, it can catch fire all at once and burn its way back through the fuel system. Surprisingly, the best response is to keep cranking the propeller with the starter, because once started the engine will usually suck the fuel and flames into the combustion chamber, where it belongs. Then you run the engine at a high RPM (1800 or so) for a few minutes before shutting it down to go and inspect the damage. If the engine won't start, keep cranking, but pull the mixture knob and the fuel cut-off valve out to stop the flow of more fuel. At the same time—and again, somewhat counterintuitively—push the throttle in full, so that the flow of air from the open throttle can help evaporate or burn the fuel that's trapped in the engine. By this time, however, other components of the engine may have caught fire, and you may have to jump out with the fire extinguisher and try to put out the remaining flames, if possible. You're not going to be flying that day, but at least your disaster happened while you were still on the ground!

An engine fire in flight presents a greater threat to life and limb, instead of just property. It's another scenario that an instructor—or checkride examiner—can throw at you. We're back in the air and this time instead of saying "Your engine is out," Tess tells me, "Your engine is on fire." My response to this emergency is entirely different. Forget about gliding or finding a place to land; my first objective is to put out that fire. Immediately, I pull the fuel cut-off valve out and nose the airplane down into a steep dive. I could also scan floor to door, pull the mixture and throttle out, maybe turn off the master switch. But the vital thing is to stop fuel from flowing into the engine and feeding into flames, as quickly as possible. Meanwhile, I need to raise my airspeed, quickly, so that airflow over the engine can help blow the flames out. Closing the air vents in the cockpit can also help prevent noxious fumes from entering the cabin.

"Okay, the fire is out," Tess announced. I don't know how badly the engine is damaged or what caused the fire, so I'm not going to try to restart it. Without power, my only option is to proceed directly to a forced landing. Because of my dive to put out the fire, I've probably already lost a lot of altitude. Now I need to pull back on the yoke and slow all the way back to best glide speed, while scanning for a relatively safe place to land. From here, it's the same procedure as making a forced landing due to engine failure.

The engine isn't the only thing that can catch fire in an airplane. An electrical fire in flight can be caused by some sort of short circuit or dangerous overload on the instrument panel, with smoke rising and sparks flying. The immediate response: shut off the master switch and use the fire extinguisher in the cockpit, on the floor next to my seat, to put the fire out. The engine should keep running, because it's driven by the magnetos, not the battery or alternator. So once the fire is out, it's likely I can continue to fly and make a normal landing at the nearest airport.

The problem is, without electrical power from the battery or alternator, I can't operate the radio or flaps, and my transponder, turn coordinator, and fuel gauges won't work. If my airplane has a glass cockpit, the display screens will be down and I'll have only my backup steam gauge instruments to rely on. So if possible, I may try *very cautiously* to isolate the problem, and get at least some of my electrical power back. First I'm going to check the circuit breakers, which look like little black buttons arrayed across my instrument panel, and see if any of them popped out. If any did, that might have been the source of the problem, and I'll leave them out and inoperative. I'll also make sure the white avionics switch and any other electrical switches (such as lights) are all off, before turning the master switch back on. Finally, I'll turn each switch back on, one by one, watching carefully for any sign of smoke or sparks.

Losing radio communications, due to a fire or some other sort of malfunction, is a problem in itself. No longer having the ability to communicate your intentions or respond to instructions makes flying, even in less controlled airspace, an inherently more hazardous endeavor. If the transponder is still working you can squawk 7600, the code for radio failure, so at least ATC can see on their radar screens what the problem is. It's important to remember that unless the radio has been turned entirely off, the radio may be transmitting but not receiving, or vice versa. Even if you can't hear anything over the radio, you should still make radio calls over the normal frequency in case they can hear you. If you can hear everyone else talking but they don't respond to your calls, that's a different problem entirely (spoiler alert: this happens to me before the end of the book).

The best solution, if your radio isn't working, is probably to find the quietest non-towered airport nearby and, watching carefully for other traffic, enter the pattern and land. If that's not an option, it is *possible* to land at a towered airport using **light gun signals**. Approach the airport, observe traffic, and carefully enter the pattern. Once in the pattern, look to the control tower for a colored signal light. Flashing green means continue your approach; steady green means cleared to land. Steady red means give way to other aircraft and continue circling. Flashing red means the airport is unsafe, do not land. Alternating green and red mean use extreme caution, which you probably should be doing anyway. Once on the ground, similar light signals from the tower will instruct you whether to taxi or stop. The thing is, since light gun signals are so rarely used, few pilots can remember what they are, or have any practice responding to them.

A cabin fire—one that breaks out in the seating area of the cockpit itself, or spreads to it—is a pilot's worst nightmare. Until you're back on the ground, there's nowhere to escape, and in the meantime, it poses a direct threat to your ability to fly the plane. The POH says to turn off the master switch and use the fire extinguisher to hopefully put out the blaze. If that doesn't work, the only solution is to descend *very* rapidly and land as soon as possible, everything else be damned. Brian, my instructor in Arizona, sprang this on me one time, screaming all the way down that his legs were burning. Even knowing it was pretend, it was hard not to be rattled.

Every once in a while, I'd be flying along and suddenly a bird would pop up next to me. Soaring alongside a hawk could be a majestic sight, but it made me wonder just how much of a hazard accidentally colliding with a bird could be. It turns out there were 11,605 reported **birdstrikes** in the U.S. in 2020, down from a record 17,358 in 2019.[199] Over the past two decades, however, only 5% caused enough risk or damage to interfere with the flight.[200] The few that do can be serious, and have killed at least 293 people since 1988.[201] Birds tend to pose less of a danger to louder, slower-moving piston aircraft like the Cessna 172, which they can usually move quickly enough to avoid.[202] Flying at much faster speeds can turn even small birds into flying missiles capable of doing outsized damage.[203] Pilots have been killed outright by birds crashing through their windshield.[204] But the biggest problem is birds getting sucked into jet engines and destroying critical internal parts.[205] The FAA estimates that birdstrikes may cost as much as $500 million in repairs and lost flight time each year, in the U.S. alone.[206]

The risk of colliding with a bird, or the delightfully named Bird Aircraft Strike Hazard (BASH), decreases significantly with altitude: 71% of birdstrikes take place at or below 500 feet AGL, mainly on takeoff or landing.[207] However, collisions at higher altitudes are more likely to cause greater damage, due to the aircraft's higher speed.[208] While a close encounter with our fine feathered friends might not pose the danger I first imagined, it's still a good reason not to fly too low over designated wildlife refuges, and to steer well clear of the flocks of large geese flying in formation that I occasionally spotted from my cockpit.

The accident reporting system is a crucial part of aviation safety. The FAA defines an **accident** as any event during flight operations that causes serious injury or death, or substantial damage to the aircraft. Exactly what types of damage or injury meet these criteria are laid in in detail in its regulations. Events that didn't end up wreaking quite so much havoc but could still affect safety—like an engine or radio malfunction—are called an **incident**. When an accident happens, the National Transportation Safety Board (NTSB) must be notified immediately, and a report filed within 10 days. Certain types of incidents, including any in-flight fire, collision between aircraft, or flight control system malfunction, also require the NTSB to be notified, and a report to be filed if requested. The NTSB uses these reports, and the results of its own investigations, to identify the causes of specific accidents as well as shed light on larger safety trends. Sometimes possible defects or unknown safety issues are discovered in certain aircraft, which the FAA then requires to be fixed, during maintenance, per **Airworthiness Directives (ADs)**.

While we train to respond to all sorts of things that "just happen"—an engine cutting out, the instrument panel bursting into flames—the fact is that in 2019, mechanical malfunctions accounted for only 20% of **General Aviation** (non-airline) airplane accidents. A much larger portion, 62%, were due to pilot error.[209] Here, though, it's still possible to train pilots to become more aware of, and hopefully avoid, common mistakes. The Aircraft Owners and Pilots Association (AOPA)'s Air Safety Institute has an excellent (if sobering) series of free videos available on YouTube that analyze specific accidents, from innocuous start to often fatal finish, based on NTSB reports.[210] Because they are real-life stories, they tend to stick in your mind—hopefully at crucial moments when you might otherwise fall into the same trap. One such moment, for me, was on my last cross-country solo when I had that unexpected tailwind on landing and had to go around. A big reason I remembered not to raise my flaps all at once, despite wanting to quickly climb, was a similar case study I watched online which had a tragic outcome I didn't want to repeat.[211]

Mistakes and their consequences were far from my mind when I first started flying lessons—after all, I felt I was in the competent hands of my instructor. As time went on and I was making more of the actual decisions, I began to feel the weight of that responsibility. By the time I went to Arizona, I realized there was something I needed to do which hadn't even occurred to me before. I went online and bought insurance. Flight schools take out insurance, which often covers accidents involving students, but it's mainly designed to protect them, not you. The renter's insurance I bought online cost $105 to cover bodily injury and property damage, plus $120 for aircraft damage, for a total of $225 per year—about the same as a one-hour lesson. Hopefully I'd never need it. But far from encouraging morose thoughts, I felt like having insurance freed me to focus on what really mattered if I ever faced a real emergency.

For now, I had a different kind of anxiety to deal with. At long last, my lessons were drawing to an end. All the ground had been covered, all the boxes checked. With Tess's nod of approval, it was time to schedule my checkride.

CHAPTER 26

Stalling

It turns out there's a DPE shortage across the country. Designated Pilot Examiners (DPE) are experienced pilots authorized by the FAA to conduct checkrides and issue provisional licenses to those who pass. In recent years, the burgeoning number of new pilots has outstripped the limited number of DPEs, leading to backlogs. The examiner who usually worked with my flight school had just retired a few months before, and Fernando, the guy who had been filling in for him, was now busy starting a new business. It was early July, and he told Tess he could try to fit me in for August. However, I had a long-planned vacation scheduled then, driving the Oregon Trail with my son. It looked like I'd be cooling my heels until September.

I was curious about learning to fly a tailwheel airplane after getting my license, so I happened to be asking around. After explaining my situation to one local instructor named Andrew, he told me that he was a DPE and would be happy to schedule me for a checkride earlier. After linking him up with Tess, he told me the latest date he had available was Sunday, July 18, about two weeks away, since he would be out of town after that. That was sooner than I might like—I had hoped for a few more practice sessions with Tess—but I booked the appointment anyway.

With this date in my sights, I began reviewing for the oral portion of the checkride. I had flipped through ASA's *Private Pilot Oral Exam Guide* before, but now I started to systematically read each section, from start to finish. I soon realized that, while I may not have completely forgotten the material I learned for the written exam, I definitely needed a brush up. More importantly, there were some subjects in it, like risk management and decision-making, which the written exam hadn't focused on much. While they were not unfamiliar to me, I wasn't necessarily ready to face an interrogation about them either.

I also had a gnawing uncertainty about a few of the practical maneuvers I would be expected to perform. Each time I practiced, my second effort at a steep turn was always better than my first, which sometimes skirted the edge of losing or gaining too much altitude. I had never had much trouble with power-off stalls, but I just didn't feel right about my power-on stalls. Back on the ground, I had never gotten a chance to spend much time looking over and understanding the airplane's maintenance logs, which I knew I'd be quizzed on during the oral portion. There was a lot to do.

About a week in, I had made some progress in studying, but there were a few hiccups in the endorsements Tess had signed in my logbook for the checkride. Most DPEs don't require ground school time to be entered into the logbook, but Andrew pointed to a recent letter from the FAA that suggested it should be. Of course, I had plenty of unlogged ground school, including a certificate from Sporty's and the nine hours of formal instruction in Arizona. But my flight school didn't know Andrew and wasn't used to accommodating his request, so it caused some confusion and back and forth. On top of this, my wife informed me that the day before my scheduled checkride, we needed to drive to upstate New York to drop my two daughters off at summer camp. Distractions were starting to pile up.

When I checked in with Andrew that weekend, with a week left to go, he must have sensed my unease and asked me if I was sure I wanted to proceed. I told him I'd think about it and call him back promptly. On the one hand, I didn't want to chicken out. Even if you don't pass every aspect of the checkride, you get credit for the parts you do pass and only have to retake the parts you failed. So there was some rationale for just going ahead and passing as much as I could. On the other, I had to admit that I wanted more time to prepare, both with the study materials and in the plane. Was it so important to rush, possibly at the expense of my family? I decided it wasn't. A few minutes later, I called up Andrew and told him I'd like to postpone. He was very gracious and understood. There were others on the waiting list, he said, who could do it that day instead.

It turned out to be the right decision, in more ways than one. As I drove to drop off my daughters the next weekend, I felt immensely relieved I didn't have to worry about preparing for a checkride the very next day. Over the following weeks, I could study at a pace that didn't require me to ignore my family. Most importantly, I discovered that my power-on stalls really did need a lot of work.

Remember the power-on stall? Pull the throttle back to idle and let the airspeed slow while pulling back on the yoke to maintain altitude. Then when speed reaches 55 knots (the normal rotation speed at takeoff), push the throttle in full and pull the yoke back all the way. The airplane will pitch up steeply, so the only thing you see over the nose is sky, and it almost feels like you're going to topple over backward. As the stall horn warning blares, you keep pitching up and add right rudder to counter the airplane's multiple left-turning tendencies in this attitude. Finally, there will be a stall—the nose will dip—and you immediately let the nose drop to just below the horizon to pick up airspeed before resuming a more normal climb. The thing is, it's very easy to become uncoordinated and have the stall become a spin to one side or the other. If you fail to maintain a reasonably straight heading throughout, you fail the maneuver and you fail the checkride.

During the last days of July, before heading off on my father-and-son road trip, I had the chance to go up several times with Tess to practice maneuvers. Slow flight, turns around a point, and S-turns were all good. My steep turns got noticeably better. My response to emergencies got faster and more decisive. Performance takeoffs and landings, including power-off landings, were becoming almost fun. Power-off stalls took some effort and concentration, but posed no real problem. The power-on stalls, however, were another matter.

Entering the maneuver was not a problem. But whenever I was poised nose-up, approaching the stall, I always felt like the plane was a pencil balanced precariously on the tip of a person's nose. Unlike the power-off stall, which arrived with a noticeably lurch, I had a hard time telling when the power-on stall actually took place. By the time it became clear, I was usually toppling over, wing down, to one side or the other. I didn't go into a spin—I knew how to stop one from developing and recover—but I wasn't anywhere close to keeping the straight heading I needed, and lost way too much altitude in the process. Occasionally I'd get it right, but not often enough to feel confident I knew what I was doing, or could perform it the next time.

What was I doing wrong? This question plagued and frustrated me through two practice sessions, as July came to a close. Tess and I went up and did repeated power-on stalls over and over again, searching for the answers, or some kind of improvement. At one point I tipped over so many times in a row I realized that, for the first time, I was starting to feel airsick. I felt sweaty and a little dizzy from all the motion, and rather than play the tough guy, I asked Tess to take the controls for a while until I could take some slow breaths and recover. We practiced some performance landings and called it a day. At home, I took stock. Power-on stalls are apparently a challenge for many students. I found plenty of conversations and videos online about how to do them, and they all made it *look* easy—but it wasn't, at least not for me.

It was extremely frustrating. Here I was, "ready" to take my checkride, still struggling with a basic maneuver I had been introduced to in my very first lessons. But at the same time, I needed to be patient. I knew I had encountered hurdles, and even hit walls, before. Landing had seemed impossible, until I worked my way through it and it became possible. Same with talking on the radio to ATC. My power-on stalls would come around, if I just stuck with it.

At least one thing I recognized I was doing wrong was unconsciously trying to steer with the yoke. As you approach a stall, the ailerons lose their purchase on the airflow over the wing. To keep your heading, you have to use the rudder. I knew this, but still found my arms instinctively turning the yoke in the direction I wanted to go, or away from the spin as it began, which can actually make things worse. I had to consciously freeze my arms in place, willing them only to push in or out on the yoke, never sideways. That, at least, was a start.

The next part was controlling the rudder. At first, I looked to the turn coordinator on the instrument panel for guidance, without much success. Tess suggested I would do better to aim for a cloud above, using the rudder to prevent the nose from yawing away from it in one direction or the other. This, of course, depended on the weather; it wouldn't be much help under a clear blue sky. But that wasn't usually an issue, and once I got used to it, this method did help me keep the "pencil" balanced for at least a bit longer.

Still, I continued to have trouble, and I felt like it boiled down to three issues. First, like on takeoff, applying the correct amount of rudder is an art, not a science. I was afraid to not press the right rudder pedal enough and tip over to the left, and I was afraid to press it too hard and tip over to the right. But then I asked myself, which side am I usually tipping over toward? The answer, nine times out of ten, was to the left because of the airplane's left-turning tendencies. I had often heard the advice that, if you're consistently making the same mistake, try to overcompensate in the opposite direction. If you're always overshooting the turn to final, try to undershoot it; if you're always coming in too low on final approach, try to come in too high. My problem, 90% of the time, was too little right rudder, not too much. I needed to solve the problem I had, not the one I imagined I could have. I should press harder on the right rudder pedal, and if that became a problem, I'd worry about it then.

Second, Tess noticed that I was releasing the right rudder too quickly, immediately on breaking the stall. It was as though, when I let the nose drop, I was unconsciously declaring "all clear!" While lowering the nose did *reduce* the airplane's left-turning tendencies, it didn't *eliminate* them. I needed right rudder not just up to the stall, but *through* the recovery, to stay coordinated.

Third, I was holding the stall too long. In a power-on stall, the nose doesn't lunge, it falters. This slight dip can be easy to miss, and if you keep pulling back on the yoke, the stall will just continue. Keeping the "pencil" balanced is hard enough as the stall approaches, but during a stall it's all but impossible. One wing will soon become more stalled than the other and dip. The key was to recognize the stall early, and put the nose down, before it inevitably became uncoordinated. Yes, there was a risk of letting the nose down too early, before reaching a full stall. Again, however, it was better to overcompensate. The DPE wanted to see a quick reaction and recovery. On the checkride, if I didn't reach a full stall, he might have me do it over again. But if I held the stall too long and started to go into a spin, I'd fail.

Practicing at home on *MSFS* was helpful in trying these ideas out, but I also knew that in this situation, tiny handling differences between the sim and real life could make all the difference. As my short bout with airsickness demonstrated, this is a maneuver where physical sensations play a vital role, something that can't be fully replicated on a computer screen. The feeling of yaw, the exact amount of pressure on a foot pedal, the slight dip signaling the start of the stall—there was no real replacement for learning to recognize what they felt like in the air.

On August 2, a few days before I had to leave for vacation with my son, the weather was good and I got one last chance to see if all my analysis on the ground could translate into some improvement in the air. And like so many breakthrough moments before, after seemingly endless frustrations it finally worked. As I pulled the yoke back into a steep climb at 55 knots, I kept a firm foot on the right rudder. I kept my eyes on a cloud ahead and, if in doubt, erred on the side of more right rudder rather than less. At the very first sign the nose was faltering, I pushed the yoke forward to just below the horizon, letting up some *but not all* of the pressure of the right foot pedal, then quickly raised it back again into a normal climb as airspeed came back. Most importantly, the airplane flew straight ahead; neither of the wings dipped more than slightly. I tried it again, and again, to make sure it wasn't a fluke. It wasn't. Tess was relieved and happy for me.

While all this was going on, it turned out that Tess's original DPE contact, Fernando, had an opening available on Sunday, September 5. I decided to go with him. Andrew seemed like a great guy over the phone and had been both patient and helpful. But Fernando was a known quantity, both to Tess and my flight school. He had given previous students their checkride, so we had some sense of how he liked to run things. There might be fewer surprises, on both ends. The trick was, Fernando had moved to southern New Jersey and could only offer the checkride at Ocean County Airport (KMJX) near Atlantic City. So the next day, August 3, Tess and I flew the one-hour trip down to KMJX so it wouldn't be completely unfamiliar to me.

On the way back, Tess asked if I wanted to practice a few power-on stalls. No, I told her, I wanted to leave for my vacation on a positive note, which the previous day had given me. I could practice more once I got back. For now, I didn't want to think any more at all about stalling.

CHAPTER 27

Helicopter

Keeping my spirits up in that final stretch was harder than I expected. The past few weeks spent honing my maneuvers were necessary—and productive. But the unrelenting repetition and attention to detail were starting to wear me down. With the checkride approaching, I'd soon need all the energy and enthusiasm I could muster; instead, I could feel them fast draining away. I had heard many stories, directly and indirectly, of student pilots who had lost their momentum and let their lessons peter off—even in the later stages of training. I didn't want that to happen.

My batteries needed recharging, but how? A change of pace, perhaps—something to liven things up, engage my mind, and see flying from a fresh perspective. On the sim at home, I had begun to branch out and explore flying different kinds of aircraft. Acquainting myself with their history, their controls, their *feel* helped rekindle a curiosity that had gone numb from practicing day in, day out in the Cessna. It gave me the courage to pursue an idea that raised some eyebrows at the time, but ultimately proved exactly the pick-me-up I needed. Instead of just cooling my heels waiting for my checkride, I decided to take a flying lesson in a helicopter.

From my very first visit to the airfield at Lincoln Park, I noticed the helicopters. You could scarcely avoid noticing them. A small outfit operated tours of New York City, as well as lessons, out of the same building as my flight school. Their small, bug-like machines could often be seen parked besides our hangar or hovering over the runway. On calm days, a sudden blast of wind heralded their arrival or departure as I performed my own pre-flight inspection. When I approached the airport to land, their blips on the *ForeFlight* traffic overlay required extra attention. I could spot an airplane and, based on its trajectory, have a pretty good idea where it would be a few moments later; a helicopter, in contrast, could zig one way, then another, or rise or fall without even moving anywhere. They were ... unpredictable.

Airplane and helicopter pilots share the same space in the sky, and follow many of the same rules, but they belong to different tribes. The aerodynamics that allow both kinds of aircraft to fly are based on the same principles, but applied in entirely different ways. Both tribes firmly believe that their type of machine is more fun to fly, and safer. Both believe the other is crazy. There are some pilots who have both an airplane and rotorcraft rating, but they are few and far between.

When *MSFS 2020* first launched, it did not include any helicopters. After a while, however, a handful of hard-working developers figured out ways to adapt the flight model and get them to work. Out of sheer curiosity, I tried my hand at the Airbus H135, a popular modern helicopter, and the Bell 47, an early trailblazer that resembles a dragonfly and was most famously featured in the opening credits to the TV show *M*A*S*H*. Intrigued, I even ordered a copy of *The God Machine* by James Chiles, one of the few books I could find about the history of this odd and amazing machine.

People knew that rotary motion could produce lift ever since watching wing-shaped maple seeds spiral to the ground.[212] Leonardo da Vinci proposed some helicopter designs;[213] so did Thomas Edison[214] and our old friend George Cayley.[215] The problem wasn't lift, per se, but stability and control.[216] Through much trial and error, various pieces of the puzzle gradually came together, a few decades after the Wright brothers took flight. In the 1920s, a Spanish engineer named Juan de la Cierva introduced the autogyro, a kind of hybrid that uses a propeller to generate airflow over rotating blades, instead of a fixed wing, to produce lift.[217] The Germans designed some primitive but workable helicopters during World War II, but Allied bombing and competing priorities prevented all but a few prototypes from being built and flown.[218]

It was Igor Sikorsky, a Russian engineer who left his homeland after the 1917 Communist Revolution,[219] who brought all the elements together successfully.[220] On his arrival in America, Sikorsky gathered other displaced Russian émigrés, many of them languishing in odd jobs as janitors or language teachers, into a crack group of aircraft designers based out of New York's Long Island.[221] Initially he was famous for his gigantic flying boats,[222] but in the 1930s he increasingly turned his attention to the challenge of "vertical flight."[223] His first successful models were tested during World War II, but arrived a bit too late to see combat.[224] Their direct descendants, however, reshaped U.S. military operations in the Korean War, the Vietnam War, and beyond.[225] The ability of helicopters to hover in place, change directions on a dime, and take off and land from virtually anywhere have made them a ubiquitous part of modern life, not only on the battlefield but for search and rescue, medical evacuation, traffic reporting, sightseeing, and urban business travel.[226]

I rode as a passenger in helicopters plenty of times as an Army ROTC cadet. The pilots were mostly National Guard guys, making the most of their flight time by hugging the terrain at tree-top level, as we sat inches away from falling out the wide-open doors in back. One time we did this for what felt like hours on end, until one cadet finally threw up in his helmet. Flying at higher altitudes was disconcerting in a different way. In an airplane, there's a sensation of gliding; in the helicopter, I felt like we were being suspended from the sky like a tin can on a string. Still, there's an undeniable magic to it. Flying with my wife on a helicopter tour of the Grand Canyon, I'll never forget the moment we passed over the canyon's edge. One second we were low over the ground, perhaps 100 feet, the next the bottom dropped out and we were a mile high. So yeah, I've always been helicopter-curious, but to be honest I had no idea how they worked, or what you actually do to pilot them.

I wanted to find out, though. I looked up our neighbors, the helicopter folks, online, and it turned out they had just relocated a short distance from Lincoln Park to Morristown. No matter. When I called, I explained how I was familiar with them and that I was interested in a "discovery flight." Later that afternoon, an instructor named Natalie called me back and enthusiastically offered to take me up for a lesson. "So you want to see how the other half lives, huh?" she teased. It turned out Natalie was friends with my own instructor, Tess. "Natalie is *always* happy to take someone new up in her pink helicopter," Tess told me when I informed her of my plans. Pink? "Oh yeah, you'll see. She's a real character. You'll have fun." I asked Tess if she had ever gone up in Natalie's helicopter. She just nodded, laughed, and rolled her eyes as if to say *I'll stick to airplanes from now on, thank you very much.*

Before we scheduled a lesson, though, Natalie did strike one note of caution. In principle, once a pilot has a license to fly an airplane, expanding it to fly helicopters is only a new rating away. There's a checkride, but no need to take another written exam because you presumably already know about airspace, weather, navigation, and a host of other topics that all aircraft have in common. In practice, however, learning to physically handle a helicopter is an entirely new skill and takes as many hours to master, from scratch, as flying an airplane does. In fact, there's a great deal to un-learn, because the instincts and intuition that pilots develop in flying an airplane can lead them dangerously astray in a helicopter, and vice versa. For that reason, instructors usually discourage anyone from trying to learn both at the same time, since the training from one can easily contaminate and confuse the other. In my case, I was just going on one flight, to get some exposure and insight into just how different piloting a helicopter could be. So Natalie was happy to take me up and show me the ropes.

Flying helicopters depends even more on good weather than flying airplanes, so after a few canceled appointments, the day finally arrived. It's a strange thing about airports where you go to practice: I knew Morristown well from the air, but I'd never set foot in it from the ground. On meeting Natalie, I learned my very first lesson about helicopters: their headsets use a completely different type of plug than the airplane headset I brought with me. It's just a legacy issue and one more thing that separates the two tribes. Fortunately, Natalie had a set for me to borrow.

There it was on the tarmac, the pink helicopter, looking very pink. It was a Robinson R22, a small two-seat, single-engine, two-blade helicopter popular for initial pilot training, as well as for herding livestock. Unlike the slightly larger R44, there's no room for passengers, only an instructor and a student. Compared to an airplane, their positions are reversed with the instructor sitting on the left while the student (or solo pilot) sits on the right.

We began on the ground by walking through the pre-flight inspection. It seemed a lot more thorough, by comparison. For a Cessna, the pre-flight mainly consists of checking the outside surfaces and main control mechanisms for damage or malfunction; besides measuring the oil with a dip stick, you don't open up the metal engine cowling to look inside. In contrast, we popped open the engine compartment doors and jumped right into the guts of the helicopter, looking for leaks, cracks, or loosened parts. Then we went back to the tail rotor and searched for similar problems, running our hands over the blades themselves and turning them to make sure they were in working order. As I did this, our helicopter's sister-ship, a red R44 with room for two more passengers in back, floated loudly over us and settled down a few strides away.

The cockpit was like a glass bubble, with an unobstructed view in almost every direction. Natalie asked me if I wanted to fly with the doors on or off. Flashing back to my Army days, I went with "doors on"—I had enough to think about on my first helicopter flight, without that added thrill. Strapping ourselves into our seats, I saw a small instrument panel centered between us, with an altimeter, vertical speed indicator, and an airspeed indicator—which in this case simply indicated our forward speed of travel. Next to them was a manifold pressure gauge, showing the engine's power, and an RPM gauge with two needles. The left needle shows engine RPM, while the right one shows rotor RPM. The two have to be coordinated and kept near the top of the narrow green bands on the dial, ideally at 104%, which in the R22 equates to about 530 rotor RPM. Fortunately, the R22 has a computerized governor that, under normal circumstances, automatically keeps the main rotor turning at that speed without the pilot having to make constant changes to engine power by hand.[227]

The helicopter's blades—both the main ones on top and the tail rotor blades in back—are airfoils. They work just like the fixed wings or the blades of a propeller on an airplane. As air flows over them (in the case of a fixed wing, because of the airplane's forward motion; in the case of a propeller or rotor blade, because they are rotating), the pressure differential created generates lift. The higher the pitch—or more accurately, the greater the angle of attack—the more lift the airfoil produces, at the cost of greater drag. The way the pilot controls a helicopter is by altering the pitch of the main rotor blades using two inputs—the collective and the cyclic—and the pitch of the tail rotor blades using the foot pedals, to alter the amount and the direction of lift they each produce.

Let's take these controls one by one. Between the two seats, beside the pilot, is a lever called the **collective**, which looks sort of like the pull-up parking brake in some cars.[228] Pulling this lever up raises the pitch of the main rotor blades uniformly throughout their entire rotation. This increases the lift they generate as they spin through the air, causing the helicopter to rise. Push the lever down and it decreases the pitch uniformly, causing the aircraft to descend.

Increasing the pitch of the blades, however, also increases drag, causing the rotor to slow. This must be compensated by increasing engine power, to maintain RPM. When the R22's governor is on, this happens automatically, but there's also a twist-grip throttle on the collective that enables the pilot to do this manually if needed. If engine power isn't increased, RPM will slow, reducing the airflow over the airfoil. Just like in a fixed wing airplane, the pilot might try to compensate by increasing pitch until the angle of attack exceeds its critical point and the airfoil stalls. In a helicopter, the slowing blades may also tend to bend upwards or "cone," in an ever more desperate effort to support the aircraft's weight, until they finally fold up and collapse.[229] Either way, the helicopter will drop like a rock. Unlike in an airplane, this kind of blade stall is nearly impossible to recover from and, above a certain altitude, is almost always fatal.[230]

On the other hand, when blade pitch is reduced drag is reduced, and the throttle must be reduced as well to keep the rotor from overspeeding. If RPM goes too high, the blades will want to fling themselves off the rotor; they probably won't succeed, but a lot of important gear holding them together will get bent and damaged. The key thing to remember is that the helicopter's lift is controlled not by making the rotor spin faster or slower, but by changing the blades' pitch—an action called **feathering**—while keeping them spinning at the same speed.

A helicopter that just went straight up and down wouldn't be much fun. A vertical stick (or in the R22, a T-bar with grips for both pilots) called the **cyclic** makes the helicopter tilt in one direction or another, translating lift from the rotating blades into horizontal motion. The cyclic often looks much like the control stick that some airplanes have instead of a yoke, but it isn't connected to control surfaces like ailerons and elevators. Instead, what the cyclic does is feather the main rotor blades so they have a higher pitch as they come around one side of their rotation, and a lower pitch on the opposite side, creating a difference in lift.

Because of gyroscopic procession, the way this works is a little strange. Remember, a force applied to a rotating object will be felt 90 degrees forward in its rotation. In most American-made helicopters such as the R22, the main rotor turns counterclockwise when viewed from above (leftwards, when viewed from the cockpit). So if you want to create more lift on the rear side of the main rotor, to make the helicopter tilt and move forward you need to raise the blades' pitch on the left. If you raised it to the rear, the lift would be felt to the right and the helicopter would tilt and turn left. Fortunately, you don't have to think about this because the controls are already designed to compensate, so when you push the cyclic forward you tilt and move forward, push right to go right, and so on. But it's useful to understand what's really going on when you move the cyclic.

So what do the foot pedals do? As I mentioned, the R22's main rotor turns counterclockwise (many European helicopters do the opposite). Because of Newton's Third Law of equal and opposite reaction, the resulting torque makes the R22's fuselage want to turn clockwise, or nose right. Left to its own devices, the body of the helicopter would spin around uncontrollably. To counter this, the aircraft has a tail rotor. By spinning sideways like a propeller, these vertical blades produce enough horizontal force to counter the torque from the main rotor.

This torque changes throughout flight, however, depending on many factors, so the countering force constantly must be adjusted using the **anti-torque pedals** at the pilot's feet. These aren't rudder pedals, and they're not connected to one. Instead, like the collective, the pedals alter the pitch of the rotor blades—this time the tail rotor blades—so that they change the amount of thrust produced, to the right or the left. The effect feels very similar to using rudder pedals to yaw the airplane's nose right or left, but the mechanism is quite different. Unlike a rudder, which requires fast-moving airflow passing over it to work, the tail rotor can be used not only to counter torque, but to intentionally turn the helicopter around 360 degrees while standing otherwise still.

The ingenuity behind how helicopters work had piqued my interest. Now it was time to see it in action. I helped Natalie run through her start-up checklist, then placed my hands and feet on the controls as she lifted off. As we climbed and headed to the southwest, she introduced and handed over the three controls one by one, starting with the cyclic. With Natalie managing the collective and the pedals, I nudged the cyclic to keep us moving along the path of a highway about 500 feet below. Rather than trying to make large, dramatic corrections, gentle but firm pressure seemed to work best. In a few minutes, as soon as I got the hang of it, she gave me control of the collective as well.

When you tilt the rotor using the cyclic, you translate part of the rotor blades' lift from vertical to horizontal motion. That means you lose some vertical lift and have to compensate with more collective to maintain altitude. The steeper you tilt, the more collective is required. It's not unlike when you have to add power and back pressure on the yoke to compensate for the sideways lift when banking an airplane—and then take it out again once you level off. I had to keep an eye on the altimeter and vertical speed indicator and make constant small corrections to the collective to stay at a steady altitude.

Finally, Natalie gave me control of the anti-torque pedals. This wasn't too tricky while we were moving forward, because the helicopter tends to weathervane into the airflow. The R22 had no turn coordinator. Instead, Natalie had tied a piece of yarn to the front of the windshield as a makeshift yaw indicator, just like the Wright brothers used at Kitty Hawk. As long as the yarn blew straight up, we were pointed in the direction of travel. If it blew to the right, I needed to step on the left pedal to turn the nose left and bring it back head-on into the airflow. In this way, I guided the helicopter down the highway about 16 miles until we reached Somerset Airport (KSMQ). I wondered to myself what the motorists below me would think if they knew the helicopter above them was in the hands of a first-time pilot.

Glancing down at our airspeed indicator, I noticed that we were moving forward at a steady 70 knots. Forward motion has very different implications for a helicopter than for an airplane. In an airplane, airspeed is your friend, the thing that gives you lift and keeps you flying. An airplane typically stalls when airspeed gets too slow, requiring too high an angle of attack to produce the lift needed. You can usually avoid or recover from this by going faster, either by adding power or pushing the nose down. In a helicopter, it's just the opposite: The aircraft can hover motionless, lifted by its rotating blades, no problem. Once you start moving, things get more complicated.

Take a helicopter moving forward at 70 knots like I was. The main rotor is turning counterclockwise, with the outer blade tips moving at a speed of about 400 knots. When an airplane moves forward, both wings cut through the air at the same speed and produce roughly the same amount of lift on either side. In the helicopter, however, the main rotor blade swinging around on the right, from back to front, meets the airflow head-on, cutting through the air at 470 knots. The retreating blade on the left—even though it's rotating at the same speed—moves *with* the airflow and cuts through it at only

330 knots. A faster-moving airfoil should produce more lift, while a slower-moving one should produce less lift. Given this "dissymmetry of lift," why doesn't the helicopter tilt and roll to left?[231]

If the blades were completely inflexible and only able to rotate in a flat circle, that's pretty close to what would happen. Because of gyroscopic precession, the effect of greater lift wouldn't be felt on the right (advancing) side but 90 degrees further on in the rotation, causing the helicopter to pitch up. However, due to the way some blades are attached to the rotor, the angle of effect can be less than 90 degrees, causing the helicopter to pitch up *and* roll to the left.[232] Any way it works out, helicopters would be extremely hard, if not impossible, to fly.

To overcome this, a helicopter's blades are designed to respond to the oncoming airflow, along with the pilot's own feathering inputs, by **flapping** up and down, tracing an ever-shifting inclined path.[233] In rigid systems, where the blades are simply bolted to the rotor head, the blades themselves bend; in fully articulated systems, they each are allowed to rise and fall on a hinged joint. In the R22, which has a semi-rigid system, the two opposing blades teeter over a pivot, one up, the other down.[234] The pilot doesn't directly control blade flapping, it happens on its own—and can cause big problems if it exceeds certain limits. It sounds precarious, but within the proper parameters, the ability of the blades to flap on their own plays a crucial role in keeping the helicopter upright, especially once it gets moving.

Flying forward at 70 knots, it's happening too fast for me to see, but here's what happens. The advancing blade swinging around to my right encounters greater lift, causing it to flap (or in our case, teeter) upwards. The relative wind it meets from above reduces the blade's angle of attack, reducing the lift it produces. As it reaches the front and swings back around on the left, the reduced lift it encounters causes the blade to flap downwards, increasing its angle of attack and increasing the lift it produces. It's this rising and falling of the blades that negates the imbalance in lift that would be caused by them cutting through the oncoming air at different speeds.[235]

Just as an airplane can stall by flying too slow, a helicopter can stall by flying too fast. Keep in mind that the retreating blade's speed through the air is always reduced by the helicopter's own airspeed. The faster you go, the slower it cuts through the air and the greater angle of attack—produced by more flapping—is required to compensate. Beyond a certain airspeed, the angle of attack required will exceed the airfoil's critical point and the retreating blade will stall. At that point the helicopter will start to topple over and go into a spin, as at least the outer end of that blade stops producing lift. For this reason, helicopters also have a Never Exceed Speed (V_{NE}) on their airspeed indicators,[236] which for the R22 is 102 knots. Higher altitude, thinner air, greater weight, or turbulence can all reduce the speed at which a stall can happen.[237] The only way to stop an impending stall is to lower the collective, reducing the blade's angle of attack, and *slow* the aircraft's forward airspeed by pitching the nose gently upwards[238]—exactly the opposite what you would do in an airplane.

As we neared Somerset, I retained command of the controls as Natalie directed me how to land at the airport. Visually, it looked a lot like an approach in an airplane. I lined up with Runway 30 and reduced the collective so we maintained a steady glide path down toward the runway. In an airplane, once again, landing is all about managing airspeed: the goal is to come in at a precise margin above stalling so that you lose lift and stop flying just over the runway and not before. In a helicopter, airspeed was mainly a question of matching our forward motion with our rate of descent. Arriving over the spot where we wanted to set down, we lowered the collective to lose our remaining lift, touching down very gently right on the tarmac. Then Natalie had me raise the collective and go around the traffic pattern for the same approach again. The procedures and the sight pictures were virtually the same, but the control inputs, thought process, and reactions were completely different.

In addition to its paved airstrip, Somerset has two grass runways. After my second landing, we moved onto one of them to practice some low-level maneuvers: lifting off, setting down, hovering, and taxiing. All of these essentially boil down to the ability to hover, which most consider the most difficult part of flying a helicopter. The cool thing is, you can move a helicopter in any direction, regardless of where its nose is pointed. The aggravating thing is, it can wobble around in any direction it pleases, regardless of where its nose is pointed. I once heard a student joke that his first try at hovering in one spot was successful—as long as that "one spot" was a football field. I certainly found that it took a lot of work, suspended a few feet off the ground, to stop from drunkenly veering off in one direction, only to overcorrect and veer off in the other. At one point, a car full of people stopped by the side of the road to watch my efforts. I wanted to turn to them, spread my arms wide and ask, like Russell Crowe in *Gladiator*, "Are you not entertained?"[239]

Soon it was time to return back to Morristown, and I flew most of the way back on my own. By the time Natalie took the controls to land, my arm was aching. An airplane "wants to fly," and a stable airplane like the Cessna 172 wants to keep flying in straight line. A fighter plane trades some of that stability for agility. A helicopter goes all the way to other extreme: it's extremely agile, but extremely unstable. If a Cessna is properly trimmed, you can take your hands entirely off the controls, making only occasional corrections. The helicopter, in contrast, always wanted to go off in some random direction, requiring constant inputs from me to prevent it from doing so. It had been quite a tiring workout.

Airplane pilots will argue that lack of stability makes helicopters more dangerous to fly. And it's true that the accident rate for helicopters is slightly higher than airplanes, while the accident rate during training is actually twice as high.[240] Keep in mind, though, that helicopters are often asked to undertake tricky rescue missions that airplanes are not, due to their ability to perform the trickiest maneuver of all: hovering. Furthermore, the fatality rate is actually slightly lower for helicopters.[241] When an airplane loses an engine, it can glide, but must find a sizeable open area in which to land safely. When a helicopter loses an engine, it can autorotate—use its forward and downward momentum to spin its rotor, creating enough lift to descend safely—and has a much larger choice of potential landing places. When they do take place, many helicopter accidents occur at low speeds and low altitudes, reducing the chance of serious injury.[242]

Back on the ground, I thanked Natalie for the experience. There were still a thousand things I didn't know about helicopters, but they were no longer a complete mystery. Coming to grips with how a helicopter flies was a mental challenge, one that forced me to apply concepts I relied on to pilot an airplane, like angle of attack and airspeed, in wildly unfamiliar ways. By casting so many of my assumptions out the window, it clarified and sharpened my understanding of how an airplane behaves and why. I was coming to realize that for a pilot, any time spent wrapping your brain around the central, invisible problem of aerodynamics—how the air interacts with a surface to create lift, under a multitude of conditions—is time well spent. My session with Natalie gave my brain precisely the jump-start it needed.

It was also a whole lot of fun doing something I would have never dared to try just a short time ago. Flying a helicopter is cool, but I wouldn't have understood half of what Natalie told me, or felt half as confident following her instructions, had my training in an airplane not prepared me. This was the payoff which, marching single-mindedly toward the checkride, I had been unable to see and was glad to be reminded of. Especially near the end, it's tempting to see learning to fly as a race to the finish line—and get discouraged when that finish line seems in doubt or out of reach. But the checkride isn't a finish line. There's always more to explore, and earning my license was just one door that opened many other doors—a boundless range of new experiences to be tasted and new boundaries to be pushed.

In his book, James Chiles compares helicopters to the *deus ex machina*, "the god in the machine," a device in ancient Greek drama that shows up, out of nowhere, to rescue the play's ending from disaster. In my case, that's a bit *over*-dramatic: I wasn't ready to give up, I was just feeling down. But it's worth remembering that on any long journey, there are peaks and valleys, and you need to husband your strength to conquer both. When you hit a low, I learned, often the best medicine was a radical break from the routine. It doesn't have to be flying a helicopter—that just happened to work for me. Your *deus ex machina* can be anything, so long as it reawakens whatever spirit or drive pushed you to dare in the first place.

CHAPTER 28

Ready

Just one more hill to climb. That was the thought in my mind when I returned from my vacation in late August. My son and I drove over 4,000 miles exploring the historic migrant wagon trails from Missouri to Utah and Oregon, and it had been a welcome break. Now I was back, and as long as the weather cooperated, my checkride was still scheduled for Sunday, September 5. It was time to get down to business.

First and foremost, that meant getting back in the air with Tess a few times to shake the rust off. But an equally pressing concern, as the checkride date neared, was to finally get some time to sit down and become more familiar with the airplane's maintenance records, as well as get my pilot's logbook ready for inspection. I knew the DPE would ask me about both of them during the oral portion of the checkride. As I gathered from watching mock checkride videos on YouTube, most checkrides begin with two basic questions: First, how do you know that you are good to fly today? Second, how do you know that the airplane is good to fly today?

To answer the first, I'd need to name and show the three forms of identification I'm required to have with me as a pilot whenever I fly: a government-issued photo ID (driver's license or passport), my medical certificate, and my pilot certificate (the plastic license issued by the FAA). The DPE typically follows up by making sure you know when your medical certificate expires. For pilots under the age of 40, it's the end of the month five years after it was issued. I'm 40 or over, so for me it's two years. Since the date on my medical certificate said November 13, 2020, it would be good through November 30, 2022.

The pilot certificate never expires, but its privileges can only be exercised if you maintain **currency**. To begin with, that means either doing a flight review with an instructor or earning a new rating that required a checkride within the past two years. The FAA also has a safety program called Wings, where performing certain training activities and getting credit for them online can meet the qualifications for a flight review.

To carry passengers, a pilot also must have performed three takeoffs and three landings in the same class of aircraft (e.g., single-engine airplane) within the past 90 days. Of course, if you showed up at the airport with some friends and realized you were not current, you could solve this by flying three solo laps around the traffic pattern; then you could load them up and go. For tricycle-gear planes, these can be touch-and-goes to save time. If you're flying a tailwheel plane, on the other hand, it has to be three takeoffs and three full-stop landings *in a tailwheel*, because of the unique challenges of handling this type of plane. To fly passengers at night (from one hour after sunset to one hour before sunrise), you have to have done three takeoffs and three landings at night in the past 90 days to be current. For pilots who fly regularly, these currency requirements are rarely an issue. For those who fly only once in a while, it's a mandatory brush up before putting anyone's life on the line besides your own.

Sometimes the DPE asks the difference between currency and **proficiency**. Currency is a regulatory requirement. Proficiency is how good you actually are at something. I might be proficient at landing a tailwheel airplane, but if I haven't done it in three months, I'm no longer current. On the other hand, if I've done three recent takeoffs and landings, I'm current—but I still might not be proficient. The FAA requires you to be current, but as a pilot you have to use your own judgment whether you are genuinely up to the task or not. Besides proficiency in technical skills, you should also evaluate your own state of body and mind before flying. One common checklist is IMSAFE: Illness, Medicine, Stress, Alcohol, Fatigue, Emotion. Do any of these present risk factors that should make me think twice about flying today?

For a student pilot taking a checkride, currency is a quiz question: Do you understand the rules you must follow in the future, *after* you get your license? The more immediate requirement the DPE needs to see, for you to be able to fly that day, is that your logbook shows you have met all the FAA's requirements to take the checkride, including all the endorsements required from your instructor. Tess and I spent some time going through my logbook together, making sure everything was in order.

I heard from multiple instructors that DPEs hate hunting through a pilot's logbook to figure out whether they meet the checkride requirements or not. They want you to mark all the relevant entries, ideally with color-coded sticky labels, so they can understand them at a glance. Since I had some time to spare, I went all out, printing off a separate sheet listing each requirement, and flagging their color in the logbook. It sounds a bit ridiculous, but every instructor I ever met or listened to on YouTube said my DPE would love me for it, so that's what I did.

Now that we know the pilot is good to go, what about the airplane? There are three things that show the airplane is ready to fly: the list of documents required in the cockpit, the maintenance records, and the pre-flight inspection. The last of these is simply the physical inspection I learned to do on my very first lesson (and repeated every lesson since) based on the checklist in the POH. I'd be expected to do one, by the book, for the DPE at the start of the practical part of my checkride.

There are four, sometimes five, documents required to be in the cockpit that can be remembered with the acronym ARROW. The **Airworthiness Certificate** was issued when the plane was first manufactured, and is usually located in a clear plastic pouch by the pilot's left leg, but in any event must be displayed somewhere in the cockpit. It never expires, so long as the airplane is properly maintained. Next to it is typically the **Registration**, which indicates who owns the plane, and must be renewed every three years. The second R, a radio license, is only required if the airplane is going to be operated outside the U.S. (for instance, if we were flying across the border into Canada). The airplane's **Operating Limitations** can be found in the original POH, which must be carried and accessible inside the cockpit. The POH also describes what signs and placards must be placed in the cockpit, to warn pilots of certain operating limitations (e.g., "no intentional spins"). Finally, the **Weight and Balance** calculations for the current flight must be completed and available.

Although the airworthiness certificate never expires, it must be supported by the maintenance records. These are what I now sat down to try to make sense of, so I could explain what they contained during the oral part of the checkride. The records were in a hard-covered ring binder, which normally stays in the school's office but I would take with me on the day of the exam. At first glance, they seemed like a confused pile of lengthy entries in fine print, pasted or stapled into a number of separate booklets, along with a folded sheaf of printouts at the end. It was hard to make heads or tails of it all.

If I didn't know what I was looking *at*, at least I knew what I was looking *for*. To begin with, every airplane must have a comprehensive **annual inspection** once every 12 months as the name suggests. The airplane is opened up by trained mechanics and each important part gets thoroughly examined and, if necessary, replaced. Larger aircraft like airliners are allowed to go through what's called progressive inspection, so rather than being grounded for a lengthy period, the process gets completed bit by bit over time. But for a smaller airplane like the Cessna 172, it usually gets done all in one go and takes a couple of days.

In addition, airplanes that carry passengers for hire or are used for flight instruction must have a **100-hour inspection** after that many hours of flight time. There are actually two different types of time meters in the aircraft. The **Hobbs Meter** runs when the aircraft is in operation (depending on its design, either when the electrical master switch or when the engine is on) and is used to determine the pilot's logged flight hours, as well as to bill for aircraft rental or lessons. **Tach time**, shown on another meter, is based on RPM. It advances at normal rate when the engine is running at cruise speed, and slower when power is reduced or set to idle. Tach time is typically 10 to 20% less than Hobbs time, and Tach time is what gets entered in the maintenance logbook to determine when the next 100-hour inspection is required.[243]

The work done for a 100-hour inspection is virtually the same as for an annual inspection. The main difference is who must sign off on it. Any certified A&P (Airframe & Powerplant) mechanic can sign for a 100-hour, but only a mechanic further certified as IA (Inspection Authorized) can sign off on an annual. As a result, an annual resets the clock for the next 100-hour inspection, but a 100-hour inspection does not reset the clock for the next annual. In our case, though, the local mechanic was IA, so he signed off on a new annual every time our 100-hour came up.

Part of my initial confusion was that for many aircraft, including this one, maintenance work gets recorded in four separate log booklets for the airframe, engine, avionics, and propeller. So for each inspection there were four different entries, which I had to find by going to the end of each booklet and working back. It soon became clear, however, that all the dates matched up. I put more colored sticky tabs next to each so I could find them quickly and easily during the checkride, noted the information, and calculated the future expiration dates. It turned out the last annual inspection had been completed just a few days earlier on September 1. The Tach meter at the time had read 1419.6 hours. That meant the next annual would be due at the end of the month, a year later, on September 30, 2022, and the next 100-hour inspection (which would probably be signed off as an annual again) would be required when the Tach meter read 1519.6 hours.

What happens if you miss those deadlines, and the plane is overdue for an inspection? The short answer is, it can't fly. There is, of course, a somewhat longer answer. If we were flying and hit 1519.6 hours on the Tach meter, we wouldn't have to land immediately. We'd have a leeway of 10 hours to fly it back to somewhere the inspection could take place. However, that extra time would count against the plane's next 100 hours, which would still expire at 1619.6. There's no such extension for an annual inspection. If the plane must be moved to reach a mechanic, the owner must apply to the FAA for a **Special Flight Permit** to do so. The place to get one is usually the local **FSDO** (Flight Service District Office), which in our case was located at nearby Teterboro Airport (KTEB). Special Flight Permits are also frequently used to demonstrate or deliver new aircraft, as well as to evacuate ones that are parked at an airport and lack up-to-date maintenance records, in the case of an emergency like a hurricane.

When examining the maintenance records, I couldn't just stop at the latest inspection, however. There are a couple of specific requirements that are usually performed as part of a larger inspection, but maybe not the last one. For instance, the altimeter and pitot-static system must be inspected every 24 months. Looking back over the records, I saw that this was last performed on July 26, 2020, which meant it would be good until July 31, 2022. The transponder also has to be inspected every 24 months. The records showed that a new transponder was installed and tested on February 3, 2021, so we were good there until February 28, 2023. Finally, the ELT must be tested every 12 months, and the battery checked. This was performed during the latest annual inspection on September 1, so it had the same deadline as the next annual. The ELT battery was last replaced on August 17, 2020, and was still current. I sticky-tabbed each of these entries, so I wouldn't have to go hunting for them, and printed up all the dates and requirements on a separate sheet of paper for easy reference.

Last but not least, the airplane must conform to all relevant **Airworthiness Directives (AD)**. These are instructions issued by the FAA requiring potential defects in the airplane to be fixed, often in response to findings from an accident investigation. For instance, a specific part may need to be replaced, or regularly inspected. The mysterious sheaf of printouts in the back of the maintenance records was the result of the latest computer search performed by the mechanic on August 30, 2021, (a few days before) of all the relevant ADs, with the compliance status noted. There were perhaps over a hundred listed. Some were one-off requirements that had been completed in the past, while a handful were "recurring" and noted a future due date. While the specifics were often complicated and hard for a non-mechanic to understand, the list at least appeared to be in order.

I saw from the mock checkride videos that examiners often like to pose the following question, or one like it: You're doing your pre-flight inspection and realize that your navigation lights (or heading indicator, or flaps) don't work. Can you still fly today? Your first instinct is to say, "No, of course you can't fly if something is broken," but that's not always true. There's a process for determining whether you can or not.

Some aircraft, especially larger ones like airliners, have what's called a **Minimum Equipment List (MEL)**. Every single item, from the armrest on a passenger seat to the front windshield, is listed, along with the procedure for dealing with any deficiency. Some problems (like your broken armrest) can be "deferred," and the plane can still fly; others cannot be. Regardless, they need to be noted and the formal procedure followed. If you've ever sat in an airliner and heard the pilot announce that they're still working on some final "paperwork" before they can push back from the gate, this is most likely what's going on.

Smaller, privately owned aircraft like a Cessna 172 usually don't have an MEL. Instead, the pilot has two main places to look to determine if a certain piece of equipment is required to be in working order. First, the FAA regulations—found in a thick book published annually called the **FAR/AIM**—actually list the minimum equipment needed to fly VFR. It's a surprisingly short list, and some people try to memorize it using the acronyms ATOMATOFLAMES for day and FLAPS for the additional equipment required at night. To tell you the truth, I didn't bother with these acronyms since I knew I'd be able to bring and refer to a copy of the FAR/AIM during the checkride. In addition to checking the FAA regulations, the plane's POH also has an equipment list that indicates "required," "standard," or "optional," which can be important to check as well.

It turns out that you can take off without working navigation lights, as long as it's not night. You also don't legally need a heading indicator that works, only a magnetic compass. And the regulations say you don't need functioning flaps, as long as the POH agrees. Of course, it's always up to the pilot's own judgment to decide what they require to fly safely. If an optional piece of equipment doesn't work, however, it needs to be clearly labeled and rendered inoperable, before flying. For instance, the Cessna 172 that I trained in had a basic autopilot that, the entire time, wasn't working. Removing it would have required the airplane's empty weight and balance to be entirely remeasured. The much easier solution was to paste a label over it that said "INOPERATIVE" and pop the appropriate circuit breaker button out, to "unplug" it from the electrical system.

Pilots are allowed, by FAA regulations, to perform a certain number of limited tasks that fall under the heading of **preventative maintenance**. These include changing landing gear tires, hydraulic fluid, and light bulbs, as long as these actions are then entered into the maintenance records and signed by the pilot. Again, I wasn't going to try to memorize the entire list for the oral checkride, because it's listed in the FAR/AIM—which I probably would refer to anyway if I really had to repair something, rather than trust my memory.

Instead, to prepare for the checkride, I purchased the latest copy of the FAR/AIM from my flight school's small bookstore (more like a book*shelf*) and worked my way through it, marking each relevant section with yet more colored sticky tabs. What are the required VFR equipment items? What actions qualify as preventative maintenance? What qualifies as an aircraft accident versus an incident? What are the regulations for towing gliders, or for performing aerobatics? For non-everyday questions like these, most DPEs just want to know that you know how and where to look it up, without too much fumbling around. You're not expected to be a walking encyclopedia, just a knowledgeable pilot.

Pouring over maintenance records and bookmarking the FAR/AIM for hours on end wasn't my idea of fun. But these questions I've just gone over, while they might seem arcane, are a core part of the checkride. It's part of the transition from being a student to a licensed pilot. As a student, you ultimately look to others to ensure that you and the plane are safe to fly. Even on the solo cross-countries, the CFI must approve the flight plan and the flying conditions that day. A license, to a much larger degree, authorizes you to make the call on your own responsibility. And it allows you to take passengers up with you, trusting their lives to your decisions. If you cut corners, it's possible no one will know—until too late.

In addition to the thick 1,200-page FAR/AIM, I also collected a few more items for my packing list. The latest Airman Certification Standards (ACS), dated June 2018, listed all of the knowledge areas and maneuvers covered by the checkride, including the performance standards, in detail. Want to know the exact pass/fail cutoff for steep turns or power-on stalls, down to the bank angle or compass degree? It's in there, and was well worth looking at. I made sure I had the latest versions of the sectional charts for both Philadelphia (where Ocean County Airport is located) and New York (to get down there and back), along with the regional Chart Supplement (AFD) and Terminal Area Charts (TACs), all of which had been updated and reissued while I was on vacation. The last thing I wanted was to get tripped up by a foolish oversight like an out-of-date chart.

Tess informed me that, if I felt up to it, I could fly down to Ocean County on my own on the day of the checkride. She thought Fernando, my DPE, would take it as a vote of confidence, setting me off on the right foot. I agreed, but I also spent some time on *MSFS* at home, practicing the flight there and back. I took an additional few hours just flying over the vicinity of the airport, as well as studying the chart, to get familiar with the area (Figure 38).

Ocean County (KMJX) is located smack in the middle of the pine barrens of southern New Jersey. While the nearby coast offers a reference point, inland is mostly a monotonous expanse of sandy scrub forest—a wilderness haunted, at least according to legend, by the Jersey Devil, a beast with the face of a horse, the head of a dog, the wings of bat, a long tail, and cloven hooves.[244] This spooky folk tale is a reminder how lonely and trackless the surrounding landscape could be. When I was in Army ROTC in college, I spent a lot of time there on field exercises running all over the pine barrens and digging holes in the sandy soil, and I never had much of a clue where I was. From the air, there's not much to see, and not many places to do an emergency landing—even a pretend one.

Just to the north of KMJX is a Class D towered airport, Lakehurst (KNEL), where the German dirigible *Hindenburg* famously exploded in a huge ball of hydrogen flame in 1937.[245] Its immense airship hangers are the only notable landmarks for miles around. There are two blue hatchmarked Restricted Areas, next to McGuire Air Force Base (KWRI) to the north and over a smaller National Guard airfield (NJ24) to the south, which I flew over in the sim so I might recognize if I got too close to them in real life. Much of the rest of the area where my checkride would likely take place is covered by a magenta hatchmarked MOA, due to heavy military cargo jets flying in and out of McGuire. That meant keeping an eye out, not only for big planes but also their wake turbulence. Even more importantly, I took note of a VOR named Coyle just south of KMJX, located on the edge of a private dirt airstrip that formed a distinctive tan smudge amid the surrounding trees. I practiced tuning in this VOR and following it to its destination from several different directions, learning to recognize it visually from the air. I had a feeling that this virtual reconnaissance on *MSFS 2020* could end up proving valuable on my actual checkride.

In my spare time, I prepared a final packing list. Somehow, all of this fit into the same improvised flight bag, a blue student backpack, that I had taken to Arizona.

- Photo ID, student pilot certificate, medical certificate
- Pilot logbook, with colored tabs and annotated summary
- FAR/AIM book, with color-coded bookmarks
- Airman Certification Standards (ACS) book, latest edition
- Formal grade report for written exam, back in February
- Ground school endorsement from Sporty's, just in case

- E6B electronic aviation calculator, with extra batteries
- Radio headset, with extra batteries
- iPad with *ForeFlight*, fully charged
- Sentry receiver for ADS-B In, fully charged
- Portable electric recharger, just in case
- Latest sectional chart for New York, to fly down to Ocean County
- Latest sectional chart for Philadelphia, to mark with my scenario route
- Chart Supplement (AFD) for the Northeast U.S.
- Protractor, pencils, and pens
- Kneeboard and blank sheets of paper for taking notes in flight

I was ready. At least, as ready as I'd ever be.

CHAPTER 29

Checkride

The checkride is based around a scenario, a prospective flight to be planned beforehand and discussed during the oral portion. Then at the start of the practical portion, you typically fly the initial stage of that flight, to the first checkpoint, before breaking off to perform all the other maneuvers, takeoffs, and landings required to pass.

On Friday, two days before the checkride, my DPE texted me with instructions. I was to plan a flight from Ocean County (KMJX), where my checkride was taking place, to Easton (KESN), a Class D airport in Maryland. I should also be prepared to talk about runway incursions and Controlled Flight into Terrain (CFIT). Both of these topics suggested that safety would be a primary focus of the oral part of the checkride—a clue to the DPE's priorities. I looked up some articles on both subjects online, so I'd be armed with something useful to say.

Most of my time and effort, however, went into developing my flight plan. Now that I was actually faced with the task, I began to see how right I was to have postponed my checkride during that weekend I had to drop off my daughters at camp in July. I probably could have done it, somehow, but I would have been anxious and scrambling the whole time. Instead, with Saturday entirely to myself, I had the chance to think through my plan properly.

There were basically two options to fly from Ocean County to Easton: the coastal route and the inland route (both shown in Figure 39). The coastal route initially jogged east, to avoid the Restricted Area to the south. It then followed the New Jersey coast all the way south to Cape May and crossed over the mouth of Delaware Bay, before heading west across the Chesapeake Peninsula to my destination. The main advantage it offered was that, for much of the way, I could follow the shoreline by sight with little fear of getting lost. On the way, I'd have to either transition through or fly over the Class C airspace around Atlantic City (KACY) which topped out at 4,100 feet, but one or the other was certainly do-able.

The bigger challenge taking the coastal route would be crossing from Cape May over Delaware Bay, a 12nm stretch of open water, in a single-engine plane. At the midpoint, if anything happened, I'd be 6nm from a solid place to land in either direction—and that was assuming I navigated the narrowest point perfectly. Since the glide distance for the Cessna 172 is roughly 1.5 miles per 1,000 feet, I'd need an absolute minimum altitude of 4,000 feet MSL. Even then I'd be landing—at best—on the beach, with no margin for error. I'd need at least another 1,000 feet for safety, for an altitude of at least 5,000 MSL. Under normal circumstances, it could be done, but the latest weather reports suggested a possible cloud ceiling that day at around 4,000 feet. If I got to Cape May and found the clouds that low, and couldn't climb to a safe crossing altitude flying VFR, I'd have to take a long detour around the bay or turn around back home. Of course, this was all hypothetical: I wouldn't really be flying the full route at all, just presenting it. But I didn't want to propose an unrealistic flight plan that completely ignored the weather.

The alternative inland route looked like a nearly straight shot from Ocean County to Easton. In fact, it followed a series of VORs for navigation, since visible landmarks in southern New Jersey were few and far between. But it was shorter than the coastal route—107nm, compared to 129nm—and there were enough small airports along the way to serve as checkpoints I could spot from the air. More importantly, the inland route crossed the Delaware River at a point where it was less than half as wide (5nm), even if my navigation didn't turn out to be exact. Even if the clouds kept me to only 3,500 feet, I'd still be able to cross safely, with room to spare. Another advantage: the very first checkpoint—the one I would actually be flying to on the checkride—was the Coyle VOR, which I had practiced navigating to on the sim and knew how to recognize by sight from the air. For all these reasons, I chose the inland route.

With the major decision made, I sat down and worked out the details of my flight plan. By now, you know the drill: identifying checkpoints, plotting the course and distance for each leg, deciding my cruising altitude, noting down frequencies for airports and VORs, calculating weight and balance, and printing off taxi diagrams to take with me in the cockpit. As always, there was only so much I could accomplish before getting the full weather briefing the next morning, but I felt like things were well on track. Though I only drew up plans for one, I marked both routes I had considered on my sectional chart, in different color markers, to explain my decision-making process. It looked very pretty, if I might say so myself.

I wanted to get to bed early on Saturday night, because I knew I had a very early and very busy morning ahead of me. My checkride was scheduled to begin at Ocean County at 8:30 a.m. The oral part should take about two hours, so I set the scheduled departure on my flight plan at 10:30. That meant 4:30 a.m. (six hours before) was the earliest I could get a standard weather briefing and begin my final planning calculations. I needed to leave home by 5:30 to catch a car to Lincoln Park and take off by 7:00 to fly the hour-long journey all the way down to Ocean County. In the meantime, I could sure use some shut-eye.

At around 9:00 p.m. that night, I was just about to turn in when a thought occurred to me: Maybe I should get an outlook weather briefing, for my own peace of mind, just to avoid any big surprises. I went to www.1800wxbrief.com and entered the parameters for my flight. The moment I saw the report it generated, all my pretty flight plans crumbled to dust. Right in my proposed flight path, blocking my way, were two large yellow circles bordered in red and a smaller one bordered in blue. TFRs. Temporary Flight Restrictions.

I wondered if my examiner had thrown this curveball at me on purpose, to see whether I would catch it or not. Well, I had caught it, but what I would do with it was another matter. My first thought was to switch to the coastal route, but the cloud ceiling was still predicted to be too low for the long water crossing to be feasible. Fighting a rising sense of panic, I took a few deep breaths and started to read the fine print to see what options these TFRs left me and whether I could work out a way to deal with them.

The farthest TFR could not be avoided, because it included Easton, my assigned destination. However, it also turned out to present no real issue. Since 9/11, the FAA has imposed semi-permanent flight restrictions over the area around Washington, D.C. The inner ring requires certain procedures to enter, but Easton was only covered by the outer ring, and according to the weather briefing, the only restriction there was a speed limit of 230 knots. The Never Exceed Speed (V_{NE}) of the Cessna 172 is 163 knots, so if I ever went that fast, breaking some rule would be the least of my worries. This TFR, at least, wasn't going to spoil my day.

The second large TFR, centered on northern Delaware, posed a more substantial problem. It seemed that President Biden was spending the weekend at his home in Wilmington, and the entire area for many miles around was highly restricted. My current flight plan only brushed the edge of the outer ring, but to enter it at all I would need to request ATC clearance, much as if I were crossing a Bravo—and there was no guarantee they would grant it. Even to make the request, the notes said I would need to call ahead and get an assigned transponder code *before* takeoff, as well as file a formal VFR flight plan. Since I wasn't going to fly the full route, I didn't have to actually do these things; I could just explain to the DPE what I *would* do. But it sounded awfully complicated, and raised all sorts of questions I might not have a good answer for. Was it truly the best choice?

If I altered my flight plan somewhat, I could jog around the edge of the President's TFR, avoiding the need to jump through all these hoops. The potential problem was, this sent me right through the third, smaller TFR centered around Millville Municipal Airport (KMIV) in southern New Jersey. An airshow was taking place there on Sunday afternoon, and other aircraft were required to steer clear while it was going on. Fortunately, this TFR wouldn't go into effect until noon. I calculated that if I departed Ocean County on time, even if I was slowed by the 30-knot headwind that was predicted for tomorrow, I'd pass through the Millville area almost an hour before the TFR became active. I could just slip by, before the gates slammed shut. If I was running late, well, I'd have to take a short detour around it to the south, then jot back up to cross the Delaware at a narrower point. In any case, this was the most viable option I had given the unusual circumstances.

By the time I recalculated the two altered legs and marked the changes on my sectional chart, it was already 11:00 p.m. I clearly wasn't going to get the good night's sleep I had hoped for. Being all keyed up and anticipating a pre-dawn wake-up to complete my flight plan didn't make for a very restful slumber either. It could have been worse, though: I can only imagine my shock and last-minute anxiety if I had gone to bed earlier and only learned about those TFRs the next morning.

My alarm clock went off after what felt like a few short minutes of sleep. The sky outside was still dark as night. There was little change in the weather briefing from the evening before, and no notable weather hazards to speak of. Clouds were expected to be overcast at around 4,000 feet, which only confirmed my choice of flight plan. Winds aloft were supposed to be quite strong, 30 knots from the southwest, but closer to 7 knots near the ground, for takeoffs and landings. Maybe some light turbulence. Truth be told, a lot of students like a windy, bumpy day for their checkride because the examiner might be slightly more forgiving in tougher weather conditions. Well, I'd get to find out if that theory had any truth to it.

The next few hours passed on a flurry of activity: frantically completing my final calculations by flashlight while bouncing around in the back seat of the car to Lincoln Park; making sure not to forget the maintenance logbooks when Tess arrived to hand me the keys; taxiing for takeoff just as the sky began to grow light; making the radio call to transition through Morristown's Delta as I made my way south. After I was out from under the outer shelf of Newark's Bravo, I climbed to 3,500 feet to practice a few last-minute steep turns. Soon I spotted the huge airship hangars at Lakehurst and looped east around its airspace to descend and enter the traffic pattern at Ocean County. As soon as I landed and taxied off Runway 24, promptly at 8:30 a.m., a voice came over the radio: "Niner-Juliet-Papa, are you here for a checkride?" It was Fernando, and when I replied in the affirmative, he told me he would come outside and direct me where to park.

Fernando was one of the few people I met in aviation (besides Abbie, the owner of my flight school) who was actually older than me. A gruff but friendly man, sporting curly hair, arm tattoos, and a worn baseball cap, he greeted me and sat us down in a small conference room just off the lobby in the airport's main building. The oral portion of my checkride was about to begin.

All the work I put into color-coding my logbook felt pretty cheesy, at the time. But I have to say, it immediately paid off. Fernando broke into a wide grin when he saw it. "*This* is what I like to see!" he exclaimed. "You don't know how much time I waste searching through logbooks." He checked my IDs, then turned to my written exam results. "How did you manage to get 100?" he asked, and I muttered something suitably modest in reply. But I could tell that the score set me off on the right foot with Fernando. Between the logbook and the exam, he assumed I had my act together.

That was fortunate, because once we got into the oral interview, I was so nervous it felt like half my brains had fallen out of my head. Simple questions that I knew well and fully expected him to ask, like how long my medical certificate was good for, suddenly made my mind go blank. I felt like a babbling fool, to be frank, and it was purely a case of nerves. When he asked me how the fuel system worked—not exactly a difficult question—I was so busy trying to guess what he wanted to hear that I barely stumbled my way through a halting explanation. I must not have said anything too dumb, though, because he moved on.

Things settled down a lot when he asked me to pull out my flight plan to

Easton and explain it to him. I showed him the route I had chosen, the alternative I had considered, and finally, the TFRs that had almost ruined everything and forced me to make a slight adjustment to my route. It turned out he really hadn't known about all those TFRs in advance, but he was pleased that I had sorted through them and figured out a solution. He accepted my reasoning about the clouds posing a problem for crossing the mouth of Delaware Bay, and had me explain how I calculated the minimum safe altitude that could have allowed me to glide to land in an emergency. The curveball he had unintentionally thrown me, which kept me up so late the night before, turned out to be a blessing in disguise. By the time I was done presenting, I knew he felt good about my planning abilities and my understanding of relevant risk factors. (Another pilot wasn't so fortunate, to say the least. The day after my checkride, he flew his single-engine Diamond DA40 right into the same Presidential TFR, unawares, and got intercepted by an F-16. After some effort, ATC finally reached him by radio and he landed safely.)[246]

I could tell, as we became more comfortable, that because of my written exam score, Fernando was intentionally asking me harder questions to test the limits of my knowledge. I struggled through a few (like exactly how to call Flight Service through a VOR) but I also answered several he didn't expect me to know. It became a bit of a game: he was clearly trying to stump me. But it was good-natured, and he wasn't trying to flunk me, just probe my limits. I began to think that I might make it out of the oral portion alive.

Fernando wrapped up by asking me about runway incursions and CFIT, the two topics he told me to prepare for in his email. I suspected that one reason he brought up runway incursions was as a kind of helpful warning. Ocean County has crisscrossing runways, and to take off from certain ones, you have to taxi across others. If you don't stop, look, and announce that you're crossing, it's an automatic fail on the checkride. Tess and I had practiced this on our scouting visit here, to ingrain it into my mind, but it was nice to have the reminder.

With that, Fernando informed me that I had passed the oral portion of my checkride, and we could take a short lunch and bathroom break before beginning the practical portion. As soon as I was alone in the restroom, I stared dully at myself in the mirror and gave a huge sigh of relief. As I've mentioned, if you fail the checkride you only have to come back and retake the subjects or maneuvers that you failed, typically with the same examiner. Passing the oral portion meant I could put it out of my mind for good, no matter what happened next.

Over the quick meal of sandwich and chips I had brought with me, Fernando explained how he would conduct the practical part of the checkride. While I performed the pre-flight inspection, he'd ask me some spot-check questions, "But I won't ask you any knowledge questions in flight, I want you to focus on your maneuvers." If he used the word "blunder," that meant I had failed that element of the checkride. He might critique my performance or observe how I could have done it better, but unless I heard the word "blunder" I should assume I was still okay.

I found that very useful to know. I had heard many stories of students who thought they might have botched some maneuver, then spent the rest of their checkride preoccupied with wondering if they had just failed or not. It's all too easy to fall into the trap of replaying the *last* maneuver in your mind and get distracted from the *next* maneuver you're trying to perform. What's done is done; it's best to mentally block it out and move on. Even if I did fail a maneuver, I knew it was best to press on and knock out whatever else I could. I decided to treat anything I could pass as a kind of mini-victory, one less thing I'd have to practice and worry about for a re-test.

My first task, once I taxied and took off, was to fly the first leg of my planned route to Easton. I would have to do it, Fernando informed me, solely by dead reckoning and pilotage. I couldn't use *ForeFlight*—I already knew that—but nor could I use radio navigation, even though my first checkpoint was a VOR. Instead, we would put my flight planning calculations, including both heading and groundspeed, to the test and see if they panned out. Because the clouds were starting to move in quite low, Fernando told me, the initial climb would be to 2,500 feet instead of my planned cruising altitude of 4,500 and I should adjust my calculations accordingly.

After my pre-flight inspection, Fernando got in the right-hand seat. I gave him my safety briefing, started the engine, and began to taxi. As it happened, the direction of the wind, from the southwest, meant I didn't have to cross any runways after all. Still, my adrenaline was back, making me jumpy and nervous. "Relax," Fernando advised, "and stop riding the brakes." I forced myself to take a few deep breaths.

We started off with a soft-field takeoff. I pulled back on the yoke until I felt the wheels starting to lose contact with the ground, then pushed forward to level off just over the runway. At 62 knots, I pulled back again for best angle of climb. After we gained some altitude, I told Fernando that we had cleared the 50-foot obstacle, so I could reduce pitch to best rate of climb. "I didn't tell you there was any obstacle," he said. Damn. I had to listen more carefully. But other than that, I must have performed the takeoff to his satisfaction, because he didn't say "blunder" and let me proceed. I continued climbing and turned left, to the south, to follow my route to the first checkpoint.

Fernando asked what my heading should be on this initial leg, and I told him: 233°. "Well," he said, "let's see where that takes us." Almost as soon as the words left his mouth, my reconnaissance in *MSFS* paid off. Straight ahead of us I could see the distinctive tan smudge of Coyle airstrip and, right beside it, the tiny white cone of the VOR. "I already see it, right there," I declared, and could sense Fernando was a little vexed that I apparently solved the puzzle and located our destination so easily. "Stay on 233," he grunted, "and see if it really takes us there." It soon became evident that it would, but as I leveled off at 2,500 feet a different problem took shape. We were rapidly approaching the checkpoint and would be there shortly. "How much time did you estimate for this leg?" Fernando asked, with what I could swear was an impish grin. I groaned a little as I answered:

"Eight minutes."

I was going to get to the Coyle VOR too soon. The private pilot checkride standards allow only plus or minus five minutes leeway, versus my estimate, to pass. My initial estimate of nine minutes was based on the assumption that I'd spend the entire first leg, which was 9nm long, climbing to 4,500 feet at an airspeed of 80 knots. Against a strong headwind, that translated to a groundspeed of 60 knots or so, or one nautical mile per minute. Earlier when Fernando told me I'd only be climbing to 2,500 feet, I raised my projected speed and reduced my estimated time slightly—but not enough. Eager to get going, I factored in the reduced headwind at a lower altitude but forget to consider the effect of leveling off and accelerating to my 100-knot cruise speed much sooner, about halfway to my first checkpoint.

As we got closer and closer, I kept glancing anxiously at the instrument panel clock, willing it to advance faster. Fortunately, as I overflew the Coyle VOR it had reached the five-minute mark, within the acceptable margin of error. "My estimate would have been right if we climbed to 4,500 feet," I muttered to myself, rationalizing my mistake.

"I told you to adjust those numbers," Fernando replied. True, he did, and in my hurry to get airborne I had overlooked a key factor. Had this been a commercial pilot checkride, where the standard is plus or minus *three* minutes, I might have blown it. I was angry at myself—heck, I still am—but it wasn't time to focus on that. I needed to move on.

Next, as I somewhat expected, Fernando told me that the weather ahead had turned bad, and I needed to divert to another airport. Some DPEs tell you which airport you should divert to, and the correct response is to turn immediately in that direction, followed by some sort of rough, rule-of-thumb calculations of the time and fuel needed to get there. In my case, he didn't specify an airport, so I told him that given the Restricted Areas to either side, I thought the best solution would be simply to turn around and go back to Ocean County, where I took off. That was an acceptable answer for him, and he even elaborated: "If you ever find yourself flying into bad weather or poor visibility and don't know what else to do, turn around and fly back the way you came. If it was clear there a few moments ago, it probably still is." I had no idea at the time, but it was advice that would prove useful before the day was through.

What followed were a series of standard maneuvers: steep turns, then transition to slow flight for some careful, low-speed turns, climbs, and descents, finishing with a power-off stall. After recovering, we moved on to the dreaded power-on stall, where I made sure to keep pressure on the right rudder and let the nose drop the very first moment I sensed it faltering. Each went off without a hitch. With each maneuver completed (without a "blunder"), I quietly ticked off one more challenge that was permanently behind me.

At this point, Fernando asked me to put on the foggles, which I had brought with me. Unable to see anything besides the instruments in front me, I then followed his instructions through a series of turns, climbs, and descents. "Turn to a heading of 60°," for instance, "and descend to 2,000 feet, maintaining 100 knots." Banking carefully 20°, I reduced power and let the vertical speed indicator and altimeter gradually drop, while keeping a close eye on my airspeed.

"You ready for some **unusual attitudes**?" Fernando asked. Sure, I was game. Tess and I had practiced this curious drill a few times during my last couple of lessons with her, and I always found it an interesting challenge. With my foggles still on, I closed my eyes and put my head down while the DPE took control and took the airplane through an erratic series of twists and turns until I was thoroughly disoriented. Then he had me open my eyes and take immediate action to bring the aircraft back to straight and level flight. My first clue, even before looking at the artificial horizon, was the airspeed indicator. If it showed I was slowing, I knew I was nose up and had to add power and push the yoke forward to prevent a stall. If it showed I was fast, I was in a dive and had to reduce power and pull back on the yoke to pull out. Then I could turn my eyes to the attitude indicator, to bank or adjust my pitch to align myself back with the horizon. We did a couple of these, and I recovered quickly each time.

As soon as the foggles came off, I barely had a chance to look around when Fernando told me, "You have an engine fire." I immediately pulled the throttle back to idle, told him I'd pull the fuel cut-off valve out, and put the nose down into a banking dive to gain airspeed to put out the fire. "Faster! You need to dive faster to get it out!" Fernando urged, as I pushed the nose down harder than I ever had before and the airspeed indicator edged from green into yellow. "Alright it's out," he declared, and I leveled off about 1,000 feet above the ground.

I was about to pull back to glide speed and pick out a landing spot, but Fernando was apparently satisfied and instructed me to identify a landmark to do "turns around a point." The wind was blowing rather briskly from the southwest, and it took a lot of concentration and constant adjustments to avoid being blown with it. Still, I somehow managed to make a decent circle while keeping a steady altitude, and we moved on to S-turns along a nearby dirt road. "I like the way you look to both sides when you cross the road, to make sure you're really at a right angle," Fernando said when I finished. "Your ground references maneuvers were very good."

"Okay," he said, "take us back to Ocean County for some landings." After being under the hood and focused so intently on my maneuvers, I was suddenly aware I had no idea where we were. I was about to pull out the map and thinking about triangulating using VORs, when my virtual scouting of the area on *MSFS* saved the day again. As I looked around, some small open patches among the pine barrens reminded me of landscape I had seen in the sim, southwest of the airport. Since my heading indicator showed we were flying west, I turned my head to look past Fernando out the right-side window and, lo and behold, there was the airport, much closer than I had imagined. Instead of making an embarrassing to-do about being lost, I could confidently pretend I had known where I was all along.

Fernando had me do short-field landing first. Carefully managing my speed on final, I aimed at the very end of the runway instead of the numbers. Pulling up and leveling off just over the threshold, I plopped the plane down smack on the numbers themselves. "Come to a full stop," Fernando said, "and give me a short-field takeoff with a 50-foot obstacle." I raised the flaps, then lowered them back to 10°. My feet on the brakes, I pushed the throttle full in, and reported to Fernando that the engine gauges were all green. Then releasing the brakes, we accelerated until I rotated early at 50 knots, pulling steeply up to get best angle of climb at just over 60. Once we were over 100 feet, I resumed a normal climb back into the pattern and lifted the flaps.

"This time, when we come abeam the numbers, don't start your descent. Stay at traffic pattern altitude through base until you turn to final. Time to see your forward slip." When Fernando had mentioned wanting to see a forward slip, at the very end of my oral, my heart didn't exactly sink, but I took a deep breath. Remember, that's where you turn the ailerons one direction, the rudder the other, and nose down to drop quickly without gaining airspeed. I had only done one forward slip before, in Arizona. Tess and I had talked about practicing them, but somehow we never fit it in. I knew in theory what to do, but wished I had more experience.

As I turned from base to final, still a full 1,000 feet above ground, I saw the runway stretched out well below me. By this time, the wind had shifted so there was now a decent crosswind blowing from the left. So I banked left, into the wind, while pushing my rudder as far as it could go to the right. Then I put the nose down hard, and we rode the forward slip down like an elevator. "That's the stuff!" Fernando cried as the needle on my vertical speed indicator maxed out on its descent rate. Soon one light on the PAPI turned red, then the other, and I released the rudder and straightened out. From there it was a normal landing, except for a similar but less dramatic sideslip at the end to compensate for the crosswind.

As we came around for a third landing, Fernando told me he wanted a soft-field landing. At the last moment, however, he tested me on my go-around instead. As soon as he said the words "go around" I put in full throttle and stayed level to build up some speed, before climbing again into the traffic pattern, gradually lifting my flaps in stages.

For some reason, Fernando seemed convinced that I dreaded what was coming next: the power-off landing. Maybe other people felt that way, but unlike the forward slip, this was something I had practiced a lot with Tess. By now, I felt comfortable gliding the airplane, and estimating the distance it could go. Unlike the commercial pilot checkride, where you have to hit your aiming point, I just needed to land anywhere on the runway. At Lincoln Park, I still had to be pretty precise, but here, with a runway nearly 6,000 feet long, I could err on the side of cutting my base leg short and not worry about overshooting or descending too fast. So what if I floated, so long as I didn't fall short? In fact, I ended up judging it just right and touched down exactly on the normal aiming point.

"One more," Fernando said, as he had me take off again. "Normal landing this time, with the crosswind. But if you don't hit the centerline, you owe me a dollar. Use that rudder." I didn't touch down exactly on centerline, but I was pretty close. "See?" Fernando chuckled. "You can do it if you put your mind to it. This is your biggest issue to work on, like most new pilots. Get some training in a tailwheel and really learn to use the rudder. Now exit the runway and taxi over to parking."

I've heard warnings that some pilots fail their checkride on final taxi because they get too relieved or excited and forget something or go too fast. So I kept my mind on business until we pulled to a stop and cut the engine. Fernando nodded. "Congratulations, you passed the checkride. Grab your stuff and come inside."

In a daze, I followed Fernando into the airport lobby and down a corridor into an office. I was almost afraid to speak, or even breath, lest he change his mind. He logged into a PC and entered some information as I sat down and waited. The quiet clicking of the keyboard seemed to mock the wild adrenaline that had lost its focus, but still held me in its jittery grip. Then he printed out two copies of my temporary license, which I signed, one for him and one for me. I was stunned, elated, relieved, a bit dehydrated, and exhausted. I was, at long last, a pilot.

EPILOGUE

Killzone

While aircraft accidents are rare, statistics show that the greatest number of accidents take place when a pilot has between 50 and 350 hours of flight time. The author Paul A. Craig, who wrote a book on how and why fatal flying accidents happen, calls this the "Killing Zone."[247] Student pilots are inexperienced but aware of their limits, and fall under the guiding hand of an instructor, who decides when they can and cannot fly. More experienced pilots have made their mistakes and survived, and hopefully learned from them. It's the newly minted, full-fledged pilots just leaving the nest who are most likely to get in over their heads.

After receiving my temporary pilot's certificate from Fernando, I returned to the airport lobby and asked the people at the reception desk to arrange for my airplane to be refueled for the journey home. While they were taking care of that, I drank some water and tried to calm down. I was still a ways from home, and had at least another hour of flying ahead of me before I could relax in the backseat of a car ride from Lincoln Park back to New York City. I only slept about four hours the previous night and had gone through a stressful checkride, but I was still keyed up on adrenaline and eager to get back and tell the folks at my flight school, and later my family, that I had passed.

Several of the airport staff mentioned that the weather could close in as the afternoon progressed, so it might be best to get a move on now. I recall at least one of them saying that Morristown, along my route back, had turned IFR an hour or so earlier but was now VFR again. I checked the weather reports on *ForeFlight*, including the METARs (current conditions) and TAFs (forecasts), and they looked alright for the time being. But there was the prospect of rain showers moving in later, and if I waited too long, I risked being stuck in southern New Jersey for the night.

I said goodbye to Fernando and got in my Cessna 172, now fully loaded with fuel. It was overcast as I took off, but the cloud ceiling was at least 3,000 feet above ground. I could see clearly for many miles ahead as I climbed northeast to avoid Lakehurst's airspace, which lay directly to the north. *ForeFlight*, on my lap, showed there wasn't much air traffic. It wouldn't be a good flying day for very much longer, but I didn't intend to be in the air much longer either. All of a sudden, my cell phone buzzed with a text message. I glanced down and saw it was from Tess, asking me what I intended to do. I carefully typed a brief response so she wouldn't worry: "I'm halfway back now." From this point, I later learned, she logged into *FlightAware.com* and monitored the rest of my flight as it unfolded.

As I approached New Brunswick, along the New Jersey Turnpike, I came under the outer shelf of the Newark Bravo. Flying at 2,500 feet MSL, I planned to skirt around the western edge of the inner shelves (off to my right), transition through Morristown's Class D airspace, and continue a few more miles north to land at Lincoln Park, retracing the exact same route I had taken in the opposite direction that morning. But the clouds were looming thicker over the Newark area, and I had to descend to 2,000 feet to stay safely below them. There were pockets of clouds lower than this, but I could adjust my course to avoid them. Still, for a moment there was a light spray of rain on my windshield, and the visibility was becoming mixed.

I was okay for the time being, but I didn't want to fly inadvertently into IFR conditions, so I tuned in the Morristown ATIS a little early, on COM2, to get the current weather. The latest recording reported a broken cloud ceiling at 2,500 feet AGL and scattered clouds as low as 1,000, with visibility of five miles. That was VFR, but more marginal than I had flown before in real life, outside of the sim. It left room to fly over the field, but I'd have to be careful. And I didn't know what I'd find over Lincoln Park. If it didn't look good, I'd land at Morristown.

Ten miles south of Morristown, I entered its Tower frequency, 118.1, into COM1 and made my initial call:

📡 *Morristown Tower, Skyhawk Seven-Two-Niner-Juliet-Papa, 10 miles south, 2000, requesting transition to Lincoln Park.*

Seconds went by. No response. I called again. Dead silence.

I checked to make sure I had the correct frequency entered in. I did. I wasn't surprised that I couldn't hear any other chatter; *ForeFlight* indicated there wasn't any traffic in the area, so it made sense that, besides me, the frequency was silent. But for some reason Tower wasn't responding to my calls, and that was a problem.

At that moment, the visibility took a noticeable turn for the worse. I could still see the ground below me, out to a few miles in most directions. But straight ahead, blocking my way home, was a shadowy swirl of mist and rain. Even if I dared to enter it, I doubted it would be legal to try. That's it, I thought, recalling the DPE's advice just a few hours earlier. I'm turning around, back where I came from.

Turning south again, I was okay for the moment, but the weather was obviously very changeable. I wasn't afraid, but I knew I had to make sound decisions and have a plan in case things got worse. This wasn't an emergency—yet—but the priorities were the same: first, fly the plane; second, navigate; third, communicate. On the first two, at least, I had a couple of good things going for me. To begin with, I wasn't low on fuel. My tanks were virtually full, and I could stay in the air for several hours more if necessary, until I found a safe place to land.

Also, because of *ForeFlight* sitting on my lap, I knew exactly where I was. A quick glimpse at the digital chart showed the terrain below me at around 200 feet MSL, rising to a few hills as high as 600 feet. There were hardly any obstacles nearby, and none taller than 1,000 feet MSL. My altimeter showed 2,000 feet, and I had just gotten the pressure setting from the Morristown ATIS. Since it wasn't a particularly cold day, that was probably accurate. As long as I stayed at this altitude, I could be reasonably sure I wouldn't hit anything. One upside of the worsening weather: *ForeFlight* showed no other traffic nearby—one less thing to worry about.

The digital chart showed one ring of Newark's Bravo airspace about a mile to my east, and another 1,000 feet above me. Unless I declared an emergency, I needed to avoid both. If I needed to climb above 3,000 feet for any reason, I'd first have to head west or further south until I was clear of the outermost Bravo shelf. My default plan, at this juncture, was to keep flying back south at my present altitude until I could land at one of several airfields, towered or non-towered, I had passed on the way up.

In the meantime, I had to trust my instruments. I could see the ground below me, out to four or five miles, but beyond that was doubtful. It would be all too easy to mistake a shifting cloud or half-obscured ridgeline for the level horizon. I had to keep my eyes open, but I knew I couldn't trust them entirely. Only the instruments could provide a completely reliable picture.

Now that I was flying the airplane and navigating, my next critical task was to restore radio communications. The fact that Morristown apparently couldn't hear me was a problem. Even if I didn't plan to cross their airspace anymore, I might need to ask other ATC to guide me toward clearer weather, and I'd certainly need a working radio to land safely somewhere else. So I still tried to contact Morristown Tower. I quickly noticed that while I could turn the audio for COM1 on and off, COM2 stayed on, even when I hit the button. Well, I figured, if there's some sort of problem with one radio, that's why I have two. So I switched *both* radio frequencies to 118.1 and tried calling Tower again.

📡 *Morristown Tower, Skyhawk Seven-Two-Niner-Juliet-Papa, 10 miles south, 2000, please confirm you are hearing me.*

This time, I heard an immediate reply:

📡 *Niner-Juliet-Papa, I am hearing you loud and clear.*

Here's what I later found out had happened. During my checkride, I saw Fernando had tuned in McGuire Air Force Base on COM2, to listen for traffic in the MOA as a safety precaution. Maybe that's when it happened, I don't know, but somehow the transmitter got switched from COM1 to COM2. As I result, I was broadcasting not on COM1 as normal, but on whatever frequency I set for COM2, which most recently had been the ATIS. Of course I knew about the selector switch, but since I had never touched it that day the possibility just never crossed my mind. And because I hadn't expected a radio reply from anyone before calling Morristown, I did not notice a problem. Had I looked and seen it (duh!) I could have easily switched the transmitter back to COM1, in a heartbeat. But failing that, my impromptu, back-ended solution—using COM2 as my primary radio channel—got the job done: I now had communications.

With the situation somewhat stabilized, I decided to circle at least once, to assess the situation. As I came back around to the north, the previous wall of mist had dissipated, and I could now see Morristown Airport clearly ahead. The clouds above it were heavily overcast, but high enough—about 2,000 feet above the surface—to provide a decent margin of safety. This could obviously change, but at that moment, it looked like my best bet. Once I was over Morristown, I'd have a good view of what the weather looked like towards Lincoln Park, just a few miles further on. I could then make an informed decision whether to continue, or land at Morristown and call it a day. I asked and received permission from Morristown Tower to transition their airspace.

KILLZONE

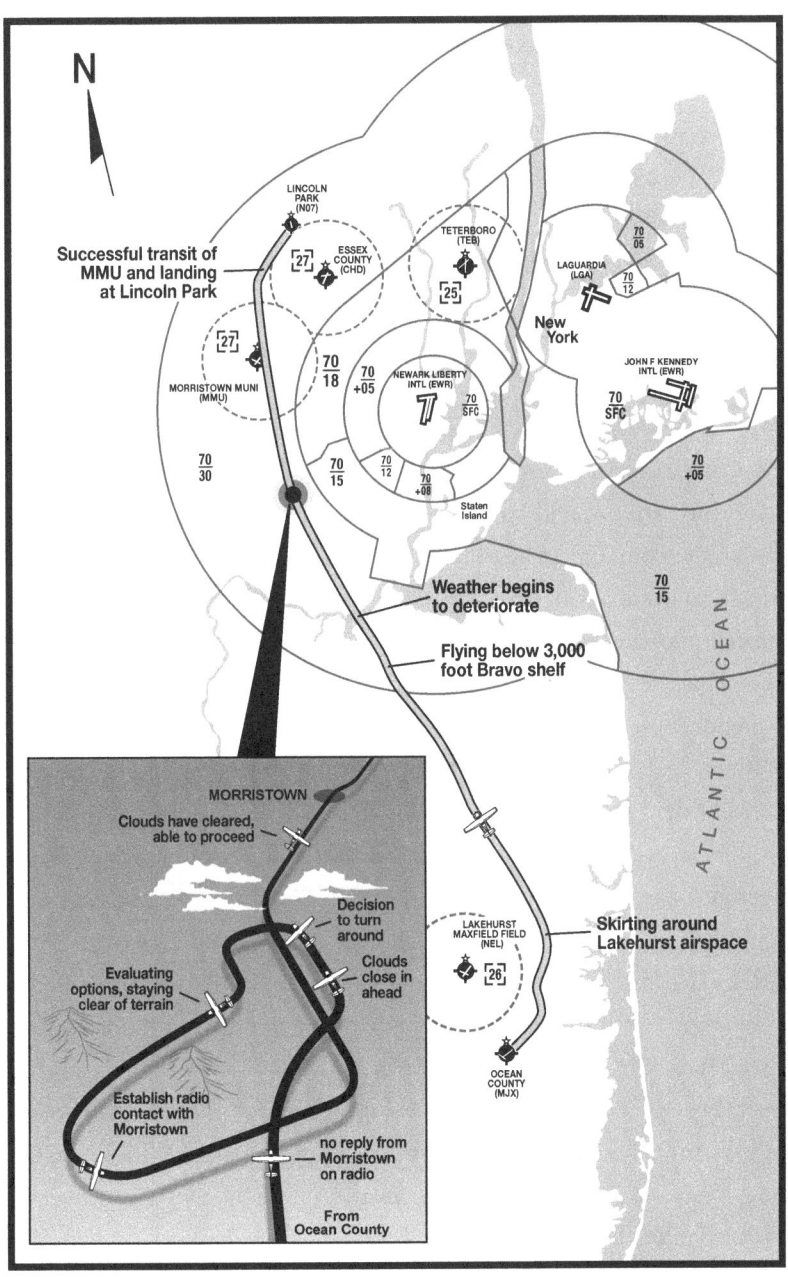

My eventful flight back from my checkride and into the "Killing Zone."

Once I reached Morristown, I was heartened by what I saw. I could definitely land on the field below me, if necessary. Ahead of me, aside from a few low-lying clouds clinging to the ridges, which I could easily skirt, the path home was still clear. With a mounting sense of relief, I followed the interstate highway past Boonton Reservoir and along the ridgeline toward Lincoln Park. Using both COM1 and COM2 on the same frequency, I announced my presence and overflew the field, to pirouette and enter the downwind leg for Runway 19. As I descended into the traffic pattern, safely below the looming layer of clouds, I knew I had reached my goal. The soft thump of the wheels touching down confirmed I was safely back on Mother Earth.

Tess and Abbie both came out to greet me as I taxied to park, to congratulate me on passing my checkride. They had been tracking my progress online, saw me turn around and circle before reaching Morristown, and assumed I must have encountered some kind of communications issue. We quickly figured out, to my chagrin, what had gone wrong with the radio. Then they took some cell phone photos of me holding my temporary pilot's certificate next to the plane. In the photo (Figure 40), I look relaxed and happy, but in fact I was drenched in sweat. It had been a long ordeal and I was ready to go home.

When I climbed in the cockpit at Ocean County, to head home from my checkride, I had 76.1 hours in my logbook, not including the checkride itself. I was keenly aware, even at that moment, that I was entering the most dangerous phase of my flying career. Yet I quickly found myself in a situation I would have avoided if I could, which could have ended up a lot worse than it did. I asked myself, when I got home: What could I have done differently?

To begin with, had I been in the habit of doing a radio check *on both channels* at each start-up, I would have caught and fixed my radio snafu before takeoff. Even if no one replied, simply going through the procedure of pressing the buttons would have ensured that I set the transmitter back to COM1. Instead, I assumed, and that assumption was wrong. By itself, my mis-set radio was only a hiccup, readily fixed. But most accidents are the result of a series of small errors that snowball and distract the pilot when dealing with bigger issues.

The bigger issue that afternoon—as it so often is—was the weather. One thing I could have done was call up Tess or the flight school before departing, to get their first-hand read on the weather. True, the METARs and TAFs looked okay; it even seemed like now was the best time to go. But I should have paid more attention to the fact that Morristown had flipped to IFR and back again, and realized that conditions might be more changeable than the weather reports implied. The folks back at Lincoln Park were on the scene. They could have looked out the window and told me what they saw, described how the weather had evolved throughout the day—and offered their advice, as more experienced pilots. I still might have ended up flying, but maybe not.

Student pilots are frequently warned of the dangers of "get-there-itis"— the pressure to reach your destination, which can override your better judgment. I didn't have a hardcore case of get-there-itis; I didn't *intentionally* risk poor weather conditions to get home. I was perfectly willing not to fly, even if it meant spending the night in southern New Jersey, if conditions warranted. But after a grueling but successful checkride, I did want to get home and probably was too willing to accept, at face value, the available weather information that appeared to confirm that desire. Unconsciously, my mindset was "I've been flying all day and the weather's been fine. What's one more hour?"

Reflecting more broadly, it's worth asking how I found myself making that choice, under those circumstances. When the idea was proposed to fly by myself down to Ocean County for my checkride, I thought mostly about the way there, not the way back. And my trip down that morning went fine—it was well within my abilities. I didn't consider, though, how I'd be feeling *after* the checkride, pass or fail, with just four hours of sleep the night before. Oh, I was keyed up and very alert—I wasn't falling asleep at the yoke. But stress and fatigue affect your decision-making in subtle ways. You might tend to rush to conclusions (the weather looks okay), overlook options (calling ahead to verify), or miss small details (the radio knob has been switched). Maybe having someone there to fly me home at day's end, or help make the go/no-go decision, would have been an asset. (That call was on me, by the way, not my instructor. To her credit, Tess phoned *me* to consult about the trip back, but

I was already on my way.)

In 2021, there were 1,157 general aviation accidents in the United States, of which 210 were fatal, resulting in 344 deaths.[248] (In contrast, as I'm writing, the U.S. has only had a handful of commercial airline fatalities since the Air Colgan crash in 2009, which led to the FAA's 1,500-hour rule for hiring airline pilots.)[249] The most deadly category of accidents involve "continued VFR into IFR conditions"—in other words, non-instrument-rated pilots flying into clouds and poor visibility.[250] According to Paul Craig, in *The Killing Zone*, through the first decade of the century, 62% of all weather-related accidents resulted in at least one fatality.[251] Typically, the pilot either became disoriented and lost control of the plane, or flew straight into either the ground or an obstacle because they could not see it. Sadly, between 70% and 75% of these fatal accidents happened after the pilot *chose* to keep flying into IFR conditions rather than turning around.[252]

The good news is that the statistics are improving. The number of general aviation accidents has fallen by 45% since 1992, while the number of people killed that year, 866, has dropped by 60%. The rate of fatal accidents per 100,000 hours flown, over those same years, fell from 1.82 to 0.95.[253] Weather-related accident deaths have shown a similar decline, after peaking in 2004.[254] Much of the improvement appears to have come from a safer flying record among less experienced, lower-hour pilots. The "Killing Zone" still exists, but the huge bulge that Craig identified in the first version of his book, published in 1999, diminished noticeably by the time he wrote an updated edition in 2013.[255]

It's probable that much of this progress stems from heightened awareness about the "Killing Zone" and steps taken to improve pilot training to address it.[256] The focus, during my checkride, on runway incursions, CFIT, and turning around when faced with IFR conditions was typical. And I think the results, at least in my case, paid off.

Because while I probably made a number of mistakes that day, I also did some important things right. I made an immediate, and correct, decision to turn back from harm's way. I remembered, first and foremost, to keep flying

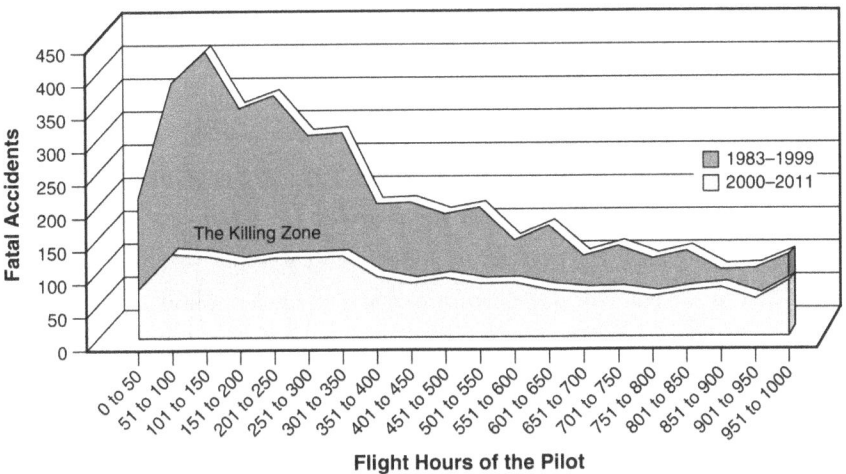

The Killing Zone comparison: 1983-2000 and 2000-2011. Reproduced with copyright permission from McGraw Hill, originally published in The Killing Zone by Paul Craig, 2nd Edition (2013).

the plane. I didn't panic, and quickly considered my options. I understood the limits of my abilities, and the dangers of ignoring them. I recognized the importance of reestablishing radio communications and improvised a way to do so. I remained flexible and altered my plan as the situation changed, while considering what my backup options were. Like the stranded astronaut in *The Martian*, I used the tools at my disposal to solve one problem, then the next one, and then the next, until I could come home. And while no one was with me in the cockpit to help me make those decisions, there were a whole bunch of people who helped *prepare* me to make them.

Technology helped too. Only a few years ago, I might have struggled with a paper chart and VORs to even figure out where I was, and where to go. Instead, with GPS and *ForeFlight* on an iPad, I had the equivalent of a modern, high-tech avionics suite right in my lap. By saving me time and energy, they allowed me to focus more of my attention on the rest of the problem. This is one of the keys to flying, I learned. There are always so many things to think about, but the better I became at processing information and reacting instinctively, the more I could focus on the decisions that really required careful thought. So much new technology in the cockpit can become distracting and overwhelming, if we let it. But used properly, it can radically reduce the pilot's workload in assessing and responding to a situation in the air.

In my opinion, *Microsoft Flight Simulator 2020* made a big difference as well. Initially, it was a toy that sparked my interest in flying. Later, however, it became a tool that let me practice my approaches and landings, over and over again every day, in a way that time, money, and weather would have never permitted in the real world. Add-ons to it helped me learn how to talk to Air Traffic Control, until it became second nature. And the ability to connect *ForeFlight* to *MSFS* gave me hours and hours of virtual flight time to become familiar and comfortable with using it to navigate in the cockpit.

Returning from my checkride was the first time I had encountered such marginal weather conditions in real life—but not in the sim. As I circled south of Morristown, surrounded by swirling mist and rain, I was reminded of a virtual flight I had made in southern France from Perpignan to Carcassonne, where I found myself dodging low-lying clouds and peering anxiously through opaque sheets of falling rain. I understood I wasn't qualified, by any means, to fly safely in such conditions, but being exposed to them on the sim gave me at least some basis for recognizing and coping with them. I had experienced, even sitting in front of my computer screen, how disorienting it was to suddenly lose all visual reference points, either in the dark or in a cloud, and how only the instruments could tell you up from down. Far from making me overconfident or blasé about flying in poor weather, these virtual experiences helped me recognize a dangerous situation when I saw one, and take steps to survive and land safely.

The convergence of new technology with the age-old principles of aeronautics makes this a fascinating moment in the story of human flight, oddly suspended between an enduring past and an onrushing future. The Cessna 172 in which I—like most people—learned to fly was designed in the 1950s, and many fundamentals of flight training have changed little since. I can flip through the pages of a World War II-era training manual and readily recognize its contents, or read about the Wright brothers tying a yaw string to their first Flyer, then spot the same simple device tied to the windshield of the helicopter I flew. It gives you a powerful sense of connection to all those who have flown before you, and a window into their world.

At the same time, I can glance down at the interactive charts on my GPS-enabled iPad, or sit at home and practice on a photorealistic simulator, and marvel at how much the experience of learning to fly has changed in just the past few years. A flood of digital technology has placed incredible tools in the hands of pilots and would-be pilots, transforming the way they work and learn. That's not to mention the development of remotely piloted or even fully autonomous flying drones, perhaps someday soon delivering online orders to our doorsteps.

Where is all this technology taking us? Some believe it will soon make pilots themselves obsolete, replaced by AI. Maybe sooner than we appreciate, a book like this one will be read as a nostalgic look back at a time when daredevils foolishly staked their lives on their own flawed perception, judgment, and reflexes, before pilotless airplanes and helicopters stepped in—alongside driverless cars—to get us from place to place with much greater convenience and safety. This final chapter, and my experience flying home from my checkride, might be cited as evidence of how crazy people once were to try to fly airplanes themselves.

For practical reasons, perhaps, it may eventually make sense to remove the unpredictable "human factor" from flying. But from the very beginning, people have always taken to the air for more than just practical reasons. I didn't have an immediate practical reason to learn how to fly. So why did I do it, instead of remaining a passenger for the rest of my life? Why am I *glad* I did it?

Once upon a time, pilots took to the air for the sheer wonder of seeing what the world looked like from up high. Antoine de Saint-Exupéry, a French airmail pilot best known for his small novel *The Little Prince*, wrote whole books filled with lyrical descriptions and philosophical reflections on the magic of touching the clouds or passing unseen over tiny villages below.[257] Lindbergh wrote that, "In flying, I tasted a wine of the gods of which they could know nothing."[258] You didn't find much poetry like that in this book, and maybe the absence of it surprised you. But the truth is, we've all looked out the window of an airplane by now. For better or worse, the novelty—the wonder—of a bird's eye view has worn off. You can enjoy it with a bag of pretzels, for less than $100, just by choosing window instead of aisle.

But I discovered that an even deeper, more enduring kind of wonder remains. It comes when you no longer shrug off the fact of flying as given, hold the controls in your own hands, feel the plane's responses, and realize that you are *in control* of a machine that is defying gravity. There isn't much time to feel as terrified by that realization as you rightfully should; the mind is primarily occupied following the procedures, recalling the facts, processing the information, and making the decisions drilled into it by hours of study and practice. Every once in a while, though, you look up and take in the wondrous fact that you are *floating on air*. What's more, you understand how and why it is happening.

It's a kind of wizardry, really, this command of the elements—including the invisible element which is often so imperceptible we dismiss it as "nothing" at all: the air. Mastering this ability to ride the air is a remarkable human achievement, and yet for each pilot it is a uniquely personal achievement as well, won by diligence, persistence, humility … and not a small dose of courage.

For this command, over the elements, is a fragile one. The slightest miscalculation, the slightest misstep—too steep a bank, too slow or fast an approach, misjudging the wind or weather, not realizing where the ground is—and the forces holding you up as solidly as concrete can dissolve back into nothingness. The price of the wonder I experienced, I came to understand, was the knowledge that every decision I made, on the ground or in the air, mattered and that nothing could be taken for granted.

But isn't that always true, whether we realize it or not? I mean, isn't that the way we should always live our lives? Flying only brought it to my attention—a good enough reason, by itself, to learn how to fly.

Almost 180 years ago, Henry David Thoreau went to live in a cabin by himself, in the woods near Walden Pond outside of Concord, Massachusetts. He later explained: *"I went to the woods because I wished to live deliberately, to front only the essential facts of life, and see if I could not learn what it had to teach, and not when I came to die, discover that I had not lived."*[259]

Pondering the result, Thoreau concluded: *"I learned this, at least, by my experiment; that if one advances confidently in the direction of his dreams, and endeavors to live the life which he has imagined, he will meet with a success unexpected in common hours ... If you have built castles in the air, your work need not be lost; that is where they should be. Now put the foundations under them."*[260]

Castles in the air. Thoreau lived in a world without airplanes, but his words resonate with me. Many of life's most meaningful adventures take unexpected form. But we are always cleared for the option.

My logbook entries for my flight training, from discovery flight to checkride.

2020 DATE	AIRCRAFT MAKE & MODEL	AIRCRAFT IDENT	ROUTE OF FLIGHT FROM	TO	DURATION OF FLIGHT	AIRCRAFT CATEGORY & CLASS AIRPLANE SEL		INSTRUMENT ACTUAL	SIMULATED	INSTRUMENT APPROACHES	HOLDS	NAV/ TRACK	SIMULATOR OR ATD
10/31	C172S		NO7	NO7	0:8	0:8							
11/10	C172S		NO7	NO7	1:2	1:2							
11/18	Redbird @AerosnByTraining												1:7
12/16	C172S		NO7	NO7	3:4	3:4			0:5				
12/19	C172S		NO7 KMSV NO7		2:2	2:2			0:3				
12/28	C172S		NO7	NO7	2:2	2:2							
12/30	C172S		NO7 KMPO NO7		2:8	2:8			0:9				
1/14	C172S		NO7	NO7	2:0	2:0							
2/04	C172S		NO7	NO7	1:6	1:6							
2/10	C172S		NO7	NO7	2:1	2:1			0:5				
THIS RECORD IS CERTIFIED TRUE AND CORRECT		PAGE TOTALS			18:3	18:3			2:2				1:7
		PREVIOUS TOTALS											
PILOT'S SIGNATURE		NEW TOTALS			18:3	18:3			2:2				1:7

2021 DATE	AIRCRAFT MAKE & MODEL	AIRCRAFT IDENT	ROUTE OF FLIGHT FROM	TO	DURATION OF FLIGHT	AIRCRAFT CATEGORY & CLASS AIRPLANE SEL		INSTRUMENT ACTUAL	SIMULATED	INSTRUMENT APPROACHES	HOLDS	NAV/ TRACK	SIMULATOR OR ATD
2/17	C172S		NO7	NO7	2:6	2:6			0:5				
3/3	C172		NO7	NO7	2:1	2:1							
3/10	C172		NO7 KMSV KMSV		2:7	2:7							
3/30	C172		NO7	UO7	2:1	2:1							
4/7	C172		NO7	NO7	2:0	2:0							
4/14	C172		NO7	NO7	2:8	2:8							
4/27	C172		NO7	NO7	2:4	2:4							
4/28	C172		NO7	UO7	3:0	3:0							
05/03	C172R		KSDL KDT KSDL		2:3	2:3							
05/04	C172S		KSDL 939 KSDL		2:5	2:5							
THIS RECORD IS CERTIFIED TRUE AND CORRECT		PAGE TOTALS			24:5	24:5			0:5				
		PREVIOUS TOTALS			18:3	18:3			2:2				1:7
PILOT'S SIGNATURE		NEW TOTALS			42:8	42:8			2:7				1:7

KILLZONE

LANDINGS		TYPE OF PILOT EXPERIENCE OR TRAINING					
DAY	NIGHT	GROUND TRNG REC'D	FLIGHT TRNG REC'D	CROSS COUNTRY	NIGHT	SOLO	PILOT IN COMMAND
1			0.8					Discovery Flight
1			1.2					Pre-flight, engine start, taxi, normal takeoffs, climbs, descents, turns, takeoffs and landings, slow flight, power off stall, steep turns, airspeed changes, traffic pattern
5			3.4					Taxi, takeoff, climb out, slow flight, steep turns, power off stall, power on stall, turns around a point, traffic pattern, atmosphere, VOR tracking, endurance
8			2.2	2.2				Cross country to KMSV, low band goes, traffic pattern, airspace work, nav back to NGY
7			2.2					Ruthand gas @ KMMU, slow flight, power off small traffic pattern turns around a point, 5 turns w/stall
2			2.8	2.8				XC to KMTO, slow flight, steep turns, power off & slow, power on stall, turns around a point, traffic pattern, VOR nav to and from KMTO, takeoff and landings
6			2.0					Slow flight, steep turns, power off stall, power on stall, power work, traffic patterns
2			1.6					Slow flight, power off stall, power on stall, steep turns, stalls, crosswind landing
5			2.1					Slow flight, power off stall, power on stall, steep turns, hard turns around a point, 5 turns, landing to full stop
37			18.3	5.0				
37			18.3	5.0				

LANDINGS		TYPE OF PILOT EXPERIENCE OR TRAINING					
DAY	NIGHT	GROUND TRNG REC'D	FLIGHT TRNG REC'D	CROSS COUNTRY	NIGHT	SOLO	PILOT IN COMMAND
8			2.6					Slow flight, steep turns, power off stall, power on stall, S-turns, turns around a point, xwind landings, @ KMMU, VOR
5			2.1					Slow flight, steep turns, power on stall, power off south, S turns, turns around a point, crosswind takeoff and landings @ KMMU, tower work
16			2.7	2.7				Landing @ KMSV, slow flight, steep turns, power off stall, steep turns, crosswind takeoffs, power on stall
10			2.1					Full stop, taxi back, slow flight, power off stall, power on stall, steep turns, crosswind takeoffs and landings
13			2.0					Full stop, taxi back, traffic pattern, radio calls
11			2.8					Full stop, taxi back, slow flight, power off & on, stall, power on stall, turns around a point, S-turns, crosswind takeoff on a land
10			2.0		0.4	0.4		First solo 1/3 takeoff & landing to a full stop, taxi back, soft field takeoff/landing, short field takeoff and landing
9			1.9 3.0		1.1	1.1		Solo full stop, taxi back to hot, dual takeoff land, slow flight, turns around a point, S-turns, power on stall, power off stall
3			2.3					2/23
5			2.5					3/23
90			23.0	2.7		1.5	1.5	
37			18.3	5.0				
127			41.3	7.7		1.5	1.5	

20 21 DATE	AIRCRAFT MAKE & MODEL	AIRCRAFT IDENT	ROUTE OF FLIGHT FROM	TO	DURATION OF FLIGHT	AIRCRAFT CATEGORY & CLASS AIRPLANE SEL		INSTRUMENT ACTUAL	SIMULATED	INSTRUMENT APPROACHES	HOLDS	NAV/ TRACK	SIMULATOR OR ATD
5/5	C172R		KSDL KF22	KSDL	2.2	2.2			0.3				
5/6	C172R		KSDL EAV PS8	KDL	1.9	1.9							
5/6	C172R		KSDL EAV	KSDL	3.1	3.1							
5/8	C172R		KSDL	KSDL	2.0	2.0							
5/12	C172S		N07	N07	2.0	2.0							
5/13	C172S		N07	N07	2.5	2.5							
5/18	C172S		N07 KMMU	N07	1.1	1.1							
5/20	C172S		N07 KASV	N07	1.8	1.8							
6/11	C172S		N07 KAVP KMG5	N07	2.4	2.4							
6/11	C172S		N07 KMSY	N07	2.3	2.3							
THIS RECORD IS CERTIFIED TRUE AND CORRECT			PAGE TOTALS		22.3	22.3			0.3				
			PREVIOUS TOTALS		42.8	42.8			2.7				1.7
PILOT'S SIGNATURE			NEW TOTALS		65.1	65.1			3.0				1.7

20 21 DATE	AIRCRAFT MAKE & MODEL	AIRCRAFT IDENT	ROUTE OF FLIGHT FROM	TO	DURATION OF FLIGHT	AIRCRAFT CATEGORY & CLASS AIRPLANE SEL		INSTRUMENT ACTUAL	SIMULATED	INSTRUMENT APPROACHES	HOLDS	NAV/ TRACK	SIMULATOR OR ATD
6/21	C172S		N07	N07	1.4	1.4							
6/25	C172S		N07	N07	2.1	2.1							
7/23	C172S		N07	N07	1.0	1.0							
7/27	C172S		N07	N07	1.8	1.8							
8/2	C172S		N07	N07	1.5	1.5			0.3				
8/3	C172S		N07 KMJX	N07	2.3	2.3							
9/3	C172S		N07	N07	0.9	0.9							
9/5	C172S		Private Pilot ASEL Flight Test Passed September 5, 2021										
9/5	C172S		N07	KMJX	1.0	1.0							
9/5	C172S		KMJX	N07	0.9	0.9							
THIS RECORD IS CERTIFIED TRUE AND CORRECT			PAGE TOTALS		12.9	12.9			0.3				
			PREVIOUS TOTALS		65.1	65.1			3.0				1.7
PILOT'S SIGNATURE			NEW TOTALS		78.0	78.0			3.3				1.7

LANDINGS		TYPE OF PILOT EXPERIENCE OR TRAINING					
DAY	NIGHT	GROUND TRNG REC'D	FLIGHT TRNG REC'D	CROSS COUNTRY	NIGHT	SOLO	PILOT IN COMMAND
7			2.2					
3			1.9	1.9				
	10		3.1	3.1	3.1			3/23 100nm xc w/ 10 TO/lnds
4			2.0					KSDL-KGXR-KGEU-KDVT-KSDL airspace controlled airport familiarization 10/27
8			2.0					
7			1.2			1.3	1.3	Solo slow flight, power off stall, steep turns & S-turns, turns around a point, tower work @ KMMU
4						1.1	1.1	Full stop taxi back @ KMMU solo
4				1.8		1.8	1.8	Solo cross country to KMSV
3				2.4		2.4	2.4	Long solo cross country
7				2.3		2.3	2.3	Solo cross country to KMSV
46	10		13.4	12.5	3.1	8.9	8.9	
127			41.3	7.7		1.5	1.5	
173	10		54.7	20.2	3.1	10.4	10.4	

LANDINGS		TYPE OF PILOT EXPERIENCE OR TRAINING					
DAY	NIGHT	GROUND TRNG REC'D	FLIGHT TRNG REC'D	CROSS COUNTRY	NIGHT	SOLO	PILOT IN COMMAND
8			1.4					Short field takeoff & landing, soft field takeoff & landing, power off approach
5			2.1					N07-4N1-12N-1N7-N51-N07
1			1.0					Slow flight, power off stall, power on stalls, steep turns
3			1.8					Slow flight, power off stall, power on stalls, steep turns, S-turns, soft field landing
2			1.5					Slow flight, power off stall, power on stall, steep turns, S-turns, turns around a point, high slow
5			2.3	2.3				XC Ocean to KMTN, short field takeoff, soft field landing
2			0.9					Slow flight, power off stall, power on stalls, steep turns
1				1.0		1.0	1.0	
1				0.9		0.9	0.9	
28			11.0	4.2		1.9	1.9	
173	10		54.7	20.2	3.1	10.4	10.4	
201	10		65.7	24.4	3.1	12.3	12.3	

Glossary

100-hour inspection: A thorough maintenance inspection required every 100 engine hours for any aircraft that carries passengers for hire or is used for flight instruction, in order to maintain airworthy status.

1500-hour rule: A new FAA rule, introduced in 2013, that requires pilots to have logged at least 1,500 flight hours to qualify for an ATP certificate in order to fly for the airlines, with a few exceptions.

abeam: At a right angle and parallel to. If an airplane is abeam the runway numbers, they are directly to its left or right, off the wingtip.

accelerated stall: A stall encountered at a higher-than-normal airspeed due to a higher load factor, typically brought on by a steep bank.

accident: An event that occurs during flight operations of an aircraft, either on the ground or in the air, that results in death or serious injury, or causes substantial damage to the aircraft.

active runway: The runway at an airport that points closest into a headwind, which other aircraft are using to take off and land.

ADS-B (Automatic Dependent Surveillance-Broadcast): A relatively new wireless surveillance technology that broadcasts an aircraft's position and other information not only to ATC but also to other receiving aircraft (ADS-B Out) and can also receive such data, as well as weather information, to aid in situational awareness (ADS-B In).

aerodynamic braking: The use of a higher pitch angle after landing, by pulling back on the stick or yoke, to increase drag and help slow the airplane.

AFD (Airport Facilities Directory): See *Chart Supplement*.

AGL (Above Ground Level): Altitude measured in feet above the surface of the terrain below (as opposed to MSL, above sea level).

aileron: A primary control surface, usually on the trailing edge of the wings, that alters the airplane's roll left or right around its longitudinal axis. Used to cause the airplane to bank and turn.

aiming point: The point just over a runway's threshold which a pilot aims for on final approach, and tries to keep centered on the same spot in the windshield, in order to maintain a steady glidepath.

airfoil: A structure designed so that air flowing around it produces lift. Examples include a wing, a helicopter rotor blade, or a propeller blade.

Airman Certificate: The formal FAA term for a pilot's license.

air mass: A large body of air in the earth's atmosphere with relatively uniform temperature, humidity, and pressure.

AIRMET: An advisory published by the U.S. government's Aviation Weather Center that warns of potential hazards to light aircraft and VFR pilots, including areas of obscured visibility, turbulence, and icing. They focus on less severe conditions than SIGMETs.

air pressure: The force exerted by the atmosphere on any surface in contact with it, which varies with weather, but steadily decreases with altitude.

airspeed: The speed of an aircraft through the surrounding air. Because of wind, this can differ from its speed over the ground below.

airspeed indicator: A primary flight instrument that compares the impact pressure of the oncoming airflow with ambient outside air pressure to estimate the aircraft's rate of movement through the air.

airworthiness certificate: An FAA-issued document that grants authorization for an aircraft to be operated in flight. It never expires, but must be supported by maintenance records.

Airworthiness Directive (AD): A regulation issued by the FAA instructing aircraft owners to fix a defect or safety hazard. Often issued after an accident investigation has revealed a problem previously unrecognized. The directive must normally be complied with for the aircraft to remain qualified as airworthy.

alternator: An electrical generator driven by the engine that provides power to the electrical equipment in the aircraft and also recharges the battery.

altimeter: A primary cockpit instrument that uses outside air pressure to estimate an aircraft's altitude above mean sea level (MSL).

altitude: An aircraft's vertical distance above either the ground below it (AGL) or mean sea level (MSL).

AME (Aviation Medical Examiner): A doctor authorized by the FAA to medically certify pilots.

ammeter: A gauge showing the flow of electricity to or from the aircraft's electrical system. A negative reading indicates a draw on the battery for power, while a positive reading indicates the battery is being recharged.

angle of attack: The angle at which the relative wind meets an airfoil, defined by its chord; instrumental in determining lift as well as induced drag.

angle of incidence: The angle at which an airplane's wings are attached to its fuselage. This is a design feature not to be confused with angle of attack.

annual inspection: A thorough maintenance inspection required every 12 months for every aircraft, in order to maintain airworthy status. Unlike a 100-hour inspection, it must be overseen and signed off by an Inspection Authorized (IA) mechanic.

anti-torque pedals: Foot pedals that control a helicopter's yaw, or rotation left or right around its vertical axis, by altering the pitch of its vertical tail rotor blades.

approach: 1) The process of an airplane flying towards or around an airport, often on a designated path, in order to land; 2) When capitalized, refers to the ATC frequency at a larger towered airport which serves as the initial point of contact for approaching aircraft that either wish to transit the airspace or land. In the latter case, Approach will eventually hand the aircraft off to Tower.

approach plate: Document that outlines the authorized instrument-based approaches to an airport, for pilots flying IFR.

arm: The distance from where a force, such as weight, is applied to a designated point which could serve as an axis, in order to determine the moment, or potential torque. In an airplane, the arm of different loads, measured from an arbitrary benchmark (such as the engine firewall), is used to calculate center of gravity (CG).

artificial horizon: See *attitude indicator*.

ASOS (Automated Surface Observing System): A recording over a designated radio frequency that is similar to an ATIS, but for non-towered airports. It typically does not identify the active runway, and is very similar to an AWOS.

ATC (Air Traffic Control): Ground-based personnel who direct air traffic in and out of airports, enforce FAA rules in controlled airspace, and provide advisory services to aircraft in flight.

ATIS (Automatic Terminal Information Service): A recorded radio transmission on a designated frequency that provides the basic weather information found in that airport's latest METAR as well as information on the active runway and instrument approaches. An approaching pilot is normally expected to tune in and listen to the ATIS before contacting Air Traffic Control. Also see *AWOS* and *ASOS*.

ATP (Airline Transport Pilot): The license that allows a pilot to fly for an airline.

attitude: The airplane's orientation relative to the horizon.

attitude indicator: A cockpit instrument that utilizes an artificial horizon, controlled by a gyroscope, to depict the airplane's pitch and bank relative to the earth's true horizon. It is of vital importance in maintaining controlled flight in the face of spatial disorientation.

autokinesis: A visual illusion that can occur when a person stares intently at a stationary light in the darkness, which causes it to appear to move.

autopilot: An automated system that flies the airplane based on certain instrument parameters set by the pilot.

avgas: High-octane gasoline used by most piston-driven airplane engines.

AWOS (Automated Weather Observing System): A recording over a designated radio frequency that is similar to an ATIS, but for non-towered airports. It typically does not identify the active runway, and is very similar to an ASOS.

balloon: When the aircraft unintentionally gains altitude due to a sudden increase in lift, often caused by lowered flaps or ground effect.

bank: The degree of an aircraft's rotation around its longitudinal axis, with one wing high and the other low. Also see *roll*.

base: The second to last leg of the traffic pattern, flying toward the intended runway at a right angle, that immediately precedes the last turn to final.

BasicMed: An alternate set of requirements for a pilot to retain certain flying privileges without renewing their FAA medical certificate, in consultation with a regular physician.

battery: The initial source of electricity when the aircraft's instrument panel is turned on but the engine and alternator are not yet engaged. It provides power to the starter and is recharged by the alternator when the engine is in operation.

beacon: 1) A red flashing light, typically at the top of an airplane's tail, that is always supposed to be on during aircraft operations as a warning to others; 2) A powerful rotating light, located at an airport, to aid pilots in identifying its position at night or in poor-visibility conditions.

Bernoulli's Principle: Principle of physics, stated in 1738, that the pressure of a moving fluid (including gas, such as air) decreases as its velocity increases.

best angle of climb (V_x): The airspeed that delivers the greatest gain in altitude over the shortest horizontal distance.

best rate of climb (V_y): The airspeed that delivers the greatest gain in altitude over the shortest period of time.

birdstrike: An in-flight collision between the aircraft and a bird.

black hole effect: A visual illusion that can occur on landing on dark nights when there are no ground lights between an aircraft and the runway, which can cause pilots to think they are higher than they actually are and fly dangerously low on approach.

blastpad: See *stopway*.

call sign: An aircraft's identifier in two-way communications by radio (typically based, in General Aviation, on its unique alphanumeric registration code).

carbon monoxide (CO): A colorless, odorless, toxic gas emitted in the engine's exhaust, which can have serious poisonous effects if breathed.

carburetor: A device in some airplanes that forces incoming air through a narrow throat, sucking in a metered amount of vaporized fuel on its way to be burned by the engine. In many aircraft, this mechanism is now replaced by a fuel injection system.

carburetor heat: Heat generated by the airplane's engine that can be redirected to warm the Venturi throat of the carburetor in order to melt and break up ice that has formed there. Warming the air flowing into the engine, however, makes that air less dense and reduces performance.

carburetor ice: Ice formed by moisture in the air condensing and freezing, even on a warm day, as it rushes through the throat of a carburetor, causing it to rapidly cool. This ice can block the passage of air and fuel into the engine, causing it to lose power or even fail.

CDI (Course Deviation Indicator): A cockpit instrument used to determine the heading to or from a VOR, or which indicates the change in course needed to follow a specific radial to or from a VOR.

center of gravity (CG): The point on which all the weight of an object balances, in all directions, though in an airplane the relevant balance is between fore and aft along the longitudinal axis. Calculated by dividing the aircraft's total moment by its total weight to get the weighted average arm.

centerline: The painted line midway between the two edges of a runway or taxiway, providing visual guidance for an aircraft to align itself for taxiing, takeoff, or landing.

CFI (Certified Flight Instructor): A pilot authorized by the FAA to give flying lessons, after taking a training program and passing a checkride.

CFIT (Controlled Flight Into Terrain): An unintentional collision with the ground (or an obstacle near the ground) despite the pilot being in full control of the aircraft.

chair flying: Visualizing and acting out each moment of a flight procedure, such as approach and landing, as practice outside the cockpit.

Chart Supplement: A book published and regularly updated by the FAA that provides detailed information on each airport in its region. There are seven multistate regions, each with its own book. Previously known and sometimes still referred to as an *AFD*.

checklist: A list of actions to be performed in the aircraft in a certain situation (such as start-up, takeoff, landing, engine failure, fire, etc.), followed to ensure nothing is forgotten.

checkride: The final test to obtain a pilot license or rating, conducted by an FAA-authorized examiner, and typically consisting of both an oral interview and a practical demonstration of skills.

chord: The imaginary straight line between the leading edge and trailing edge of an airfoil, which, compared to the relative wind, defines the angle of attack.

civil twilight: The period before sunrise or after sunset when the sun is no more than 6° below the horizon, when there is enough light for normal daytime activities. Night hours can be logged after the end of civil twilight until its beginning the next morning.

clean: Configured with flaps fully raised, landing gear raised (if possible), and no spoilers/air brakes deployed (if available), to reduce drag for normal flight.

clearance: 1) Explicit permission from Air Traffic Control to perform some action, usually to take off or land on a specific runway or enter restricted airspace; 2) When capitalized, refers to the ATC frequency at a larger towered airport that provides initial flight instructions to a departing aircraft, before contacting Ground to taxi.

clear ice: Structural icing caused by larger drops of moisture that spread before they freeze. It is more dangerous than rime ice because it causes greater disruptions to airflow and is harder to break apart.

cloud ceiling: The height in AGL of the lowest layer of clouds below 20,000 feet that covers more than half of the sky. If the ceiling gets too low, it becomes increasingly difficult, and potentially illegal, to fly VFR.

collective: The control on a helicopter, usually a horizontal lever, that raises or lowers the pitch of all the main rotors blades at once, increasing or decreasing overall lift. The collective often has a twist-grip throttle on it, as well.

COM1 and COM2: The two aircraft radios used for verbal communication. The frequencies for each can be selected independently, allowing the pilot to quickly switch from one to the other, or even listen to both at the same time. However, only one can be selected to transmit.

complex airplane: An airplane that has all three of the following elements: flaps, retractable landing gear, and a variable pitch propeller, requiring additional training and an instructor's endorsement to fly.

condensation: The transformation of water vapor in the air into liquid droplets, caused by the air's saturation at a certain temperature.

cones: The sensory receptors in the back of the human eye that are best at perceiving color and detail in well-lit conditions, and are largely ineffective at night.

constant speed propeller: A propeller whose blades are automatically adjusted in pitch by a governor to turn at an RPM set by the pilot, via the prop lever, apart from engine power.

coordinated turn: A turn in which the airplane's tail follows the path of its nose, causing the plane to neither "skid" nor "slip" sideways through the air.

Coriolis force: The deflection produced by the earth's rotation that causes air flowing from high to low pressure to move in a circular rather than straight line over the earth's surface.

Course: A pilot's intended direction of travel, not to be confused with heading (the direction the airplane is pointing).

CPL (Commercial Pilot License): A license that allows the holder to fly for hire.

crabbing: The practice of turning the aircraft's nose somewhat into the wind, left or right, in order to follow a desired course or ground track by flying along it diagonally, compensating for the speed and direction of the surrounding air.

critical angle of attack: The angle of attack beyond which an airfoil will stall, and cease producing lift. For most aircraft, this angle is somewhere between 15 and 20 degrees.

cross-country: For the purposes of earning an airplane Private Pilot License, any flight at least 50 nautical miles from point to point.

crosswind: 1) Any wind that blows across the intended path of an airplane, potentially causing it to drift sideways, especially on takeoff or landing; 2) The initial leg of the traffic pattern, at a right angle away from the runway, immediately after making the first turn following takeoff.

crosswind component: The force of the angled wind, measured in knots, that is pushing the aircraft in a lateral direction.

cruising altitude: The altitude, in MSL, that a pilot plans to climb to and maintain for most of the flight en route, and serves as a basis for flight planning calculations.

CTAF (Common Traffic Advisory Frequency): The designated radio frequency for aircraft to communicate with each other directly in the absence of Air Traffic Control.

cumulus: A fluffy, cotton-shaped cloud, signifying rising air and unstable conditions.

currency: Compliance with regulations that require a pilot to have performed certain actions within a recent period of time, in order to exercise certain flying privileges.

cyclic: The control stick in a helicopter that, by altering the pitch of the main rotor blades on one side and not the others, creates a differential in lift that causes the aircraft to tilt and move in the chosen horizontal direction (forward, back, left, or right).

cyclone: The counterclockwise motion of air around a low-pressure zone, caused by the effect of the Coriolis force on air moving from high pressure to low. A hurricane is an extreme example of a cyclone. The corresponding clockwise motion of air around a high-pressure zone is called an anti-cyclone.

cylinder: The metal casing in an engine that contains a piston and a chamber for igniting fuel and air in order to push that piston and produce mechanical power.

datum: An imaginary or arbitrary point used as a reference for calculation.

dead reckoning: The use of aircraft performance and weather data to estimate the required heading, groundspeed, time en route, and fuel consumption for an intended flight. The accuracy of these projections can be confirmed in flight by using pilotage.

density: The amount of air molecules in any given volume of space. Higher air pressure translates to higher density, while higher temperature and humidity translate to lower density.

density altitude: The altitude to which the prevailing air density would correspond given standard pressure and temperature conditions. It is the same as pressure altitude adjusted for temperature, and is primarily used to calculate and plan for aircraft performance, including true airspeed (TAS).

detonation: The sudden, explosive combustion of fuel and air in the engine's cylinder, which can cause damage to engine parts.

dew point: The temperature to which air must be cooled so that the water vapor in it condenses out in the form of water droplets. This varies depending on humidity, i.e., how much water vapor is present.

dihedral: A common design feature where an airplane's wings tilt upwards, from base to tip, in order to increase its stability.

dirty: Configured with flaps, landing gear, and/or air brakes/spoilers deployed, which increase drag, usually for takeoff or landing.

discovery flight: A first, introductory flying lesson.

displaced threshold: The part of a runway, marked with white arrows or chevrons, preceding the runway numbers that can be used for taxi and takeoff but not for landing, usually due to some obstacle on approach.

DME (Distance Measuring Equipment): A radio navigation aid, typically co-located with a VOR, that communicates the slant distance from the ground station to the receiving aircraft.

downwind: The leg of the traffic pattern where the airplane is flying parallel and in the opposite direction to the intended runway, with a tailwind behind it.

DPE (Designated Pilot Examiner): A person authorized by the FAA to conduct checkrides and issue provisional pilot certificates or ratings to those who pass.

drag: The force of resistance produced by an object's motion through the air around it, which counters the forward force created by thrust.

E6B: 1) A circular slide rule used to make numerous flight planning calculations, such as wind correction, density altitude, and time en route; 2) An electronic calculator especially designed to perform the same aviation-related calculations.

EFB (Electronic Flight Bag): A computer or smartphone app, such as *ForeFlight*, that provides pilots with accessible, and often integrated, digital versions of documents (sectional charts, chart supplements, POH, etc.) that are normally carried in the cockpit for reference.

EGT (Exhaust Gas Temperature): A gauge reading on some aircraft that the pilot can use to determine the most efficient fuel/air mixture.

elevator: A control surface, usually on the tailplane, that alters that airplane's pitch, up or down, around its lateral axis.

ELT (Emergency Locator Transmitter): A device that sends out a distress radio signal in the event of an accident to help rescuers locate the downed aircraft.

endorsement: A statement, entered into a pilot's logbook and signed by a CFI, that authorizes the student to perform solo training or take a test, or certifies that the pilot has received the required training to fly certain kinds of aircraft.

FAA (Federal Aviation Administration): The U.S. government agency that oversees all civil aviation, defines and enforces the rules for flying, and sets the standards and issues the licenses to become a pilot.

FADEC (Full Authority Digital Engine Control): A digital computer on some airplanes that automatically optimizes fuel/air mixture and propeller pitch based on input from a single power lever.

false horizon: A visual illusion, commonly encountered at night, in which a pilot mistakes a line of clouds or lights for the earth's horizon, causing potential disorientation.

FAR/AIM (Federal Aviation Regulations/Aeronautical Information Manual): A book published annually by the FAA containing the latest federal aviation regulations and advisory material.

feathering: 1) Turning the blades of an airplane's variable pitch propeller so their edges face into the airflow, no longer causing them to spin, to reduce drag following an engine failure; 2) Using the collective or cyclic to alter the pitch of the main rotor blades in a helicopter, for vertical and directional control.

final: The last leg of the traffic pattern, in which the airplane lines up with the runway and comes in to land.

flapping: The tendency of a helicopter's main rotor blades to rise and fall during rotation, in response to the forces experienced in flight.

flaps: Retractable extensions to the wings that alter its shape in order to provide greater lift as well as drag. Deploying flaps lowers the wing's stall speed and allows the pilot to make a steeper approach, at a slower speed, than otherwise possible.

flare: The final stage of landing, where the pilot gradually pulls back on the yoke to increase pitch, in order to delay touching down and bring the aircraft to, or close to, a stall.

Flight Following: An optional service offered, workload permitting, by Air Traffic Control facilities to VFR aircraft, monitoring their progress and providing traffic advisories en route.

flight plan: 1) Details of an intended flight filed with authorities (typically an FSS) to obtain required clearances and/or help in later search and rescue efforts; 2) Planning document carried by the pilot in the cockpit to aid in navigation and decision-making.

flight review: A refresher training session with a CFI to evaluate and update a pilot's skills, required every two years in order to retain flying privileges.

float: The tendency of an airplane to take more time and distance than desired to touch down on landing, due to some combination of excess speed, ground effect, or wind gusts.

fly-by-wire: A system in which the cockpit flight controls are linked to the airplane's control surfaces by electronic signals and computers, rather than mechanical means.

fog: Surface-based clouds, composed of either water droplets or ice crystals, which can restrict visibility. Can be caused either by a reduction in air temperature to its dew point, or the addition of moisture to the air, raising its dew point to the existing temperature.

Foggles: A popular brand name of restrictive viewing glasses used for instrument training, which has also become a generic term for such glasses. See *hood*.

forced landing: An emergency landing, typically due to an engine failure, often in whatever clearing, road, or field is available, in the absence of a paved runway.

ForeFlight: An integrated flight app on iPad, iPhone, or the web, available through a paid subscription, which provides electronic charts, location, weather, airport, and other information for use in flight planning and in-flight navigation. Also see *EFB*.

forward slip: A maneuver in which the pilot pushes the rudder full in one direction, turns the ailerons to bank in the opposite direction, and pitches the nose down, in order to create drag by presenting the side of the aircraft to the oncoming airflow. This allows the aircraft to lose altitude quickly without gaining unwanted speed, and can be performed when coming in much too high on final approach.

freezing rain: Supercooled liquid rain droplets that are kept from freezing by the surrounding warmer air temperature, but often freeze into ice on contact with surfaces.

front: The place, often drawn as a colored line on weather maps, where two different air masses meet. It can be called a cold front, warm front, stationary front, or occluded front depending on which air mass is advancing.

frost: Moisture that condensed onto the ground and other surfaces when the temperature is below freezing—essentially, frozen dew. It can disrupt air flow over an airplane's surfaces, significantly reducing lift and increasing drag, unless scraped off.

FSDO (Flight Standards District Office): A local field office of the FAA; pronounced "fizdo."

FSS (Flight Service Station): An FAA-contracted facility that provides information and services to pilots, including weather briefings and the filing of flight plans.

FTN (FAA Tracking Number): A long-term tracking number assigned by the FAA to a pilot, used in making applications within the IACRA system. Not to be confused with the pilot's certificate number.

fuel injection: System that injects a metered amount of fuel directly into the engine, as an alternative to a carburetor.

General Aviation (GA): All civil (non-military) aircraft operations besides commercial air transport (airliners), typically for private or recreational purposes.

glass cockpit: A cockpit where flight data is shown on digital display panels, often in an integrated form, instead of conventional instrument gauges.

glide: Flying without any artificial source of thrust, which can be simulated by pulling the throttle back to idle.

glideslope: The path of descent that will bring an airplane to its aiming point on the runway. The ideal glideslope is typically at a 3-degree angle to the surface.

go-around: The decision to abort a potentially unsafe approach or landing and proceed around the traffic pattern to try again.

GPS (Global Positioning System): A U.S. government-owned radio navigation utility that allows a receiving device to calculate its location anywhere on earth with reference to time and location signals from a network of orbiting satellites.

Ground: The ATC frequency at a towered airport that gives permission and instructions for aircraft to taxi on the ground, on either departure or arrival.

ground effect: An increase in lift and reduction in drag produced by the wings, caused by the distortions in airflow created when flying extremely close to the ground (typically about half the airplane's wingspan in height).

ground loop: When the tail of a tailwheel airplane abruptly swings out and whips the aircraft around, due to the center of gravity being located behind the main wheels; a particular hazard on landing, if the airplane is not properly aligned with the runway.

ground reference maneuvers: A series of training maneuvers designed to teach students how to adjust an aircraft's heading for wind direction in order to follow a desired ground track. They include turns around a point, S-turns, and rectangular course.

ground school: Courses which teach the requisite knowledge topics related to earning a pilot license; increasingly provided, today, in the form of online videos and materials.

groundspeed: The aircraft's rate of movement over the ground below it, which can differ from its airspeed due to the effect of wind.

ground track: The path of the airplane over the ground below it, ideally identical to the pilot's intended course.

gust: A brief increase in the speed of the wind, lasting a few seconds.

gyroscope: A spinning wheel or disk, mounted so that it can move independently in three dimensions and retain its orientation through the principle of rigidity in space.

gyroscopic precession: 1) The physical principle that a force applied to a spinning object acts at a 90-degree angle further along its rotation; 2) The left-turning tendency of a propeller-driven airplane caused by this principle when its pitch is reduced; 3) The tendency, caused by this principle, of an aircraft's heading indicator to drift out of alignment with the magnetic compass.

hail: Pellets of frozen rain which sometimes form in thunderstorms and can cause damage.

hand propping: Starting an airplane's engine by physically turning the propeller to engage the magnetos, without an electric starter.

heading: The direction the airplane's nose is pointing, not to be confused with course (the pilot's intended direction of travel).

heading indicator: A primary cockpit instrument that uses a gyroscope to indicate an aircraft's current directional heading around its yaw or vertical axis. It must be periodically aligned with the aircraft's magnetic compass.

headwind: Wind blowing from in front of the airplane, against its direction of travel. A headwind can slow an airplane's progress en route but improves its performance and safety during takeoff and landing.

high performance: An airplane that has an engine with over 200 horsepower, requiring additional training and an instructor's endorsement to fly.

Hobbs meter: A device in the cockpit that measures the time the aircraft is in operation (typically either when the engine or when the master switch is on) and is used as the basis for logging flight hours and charging for aircraft rental or lessons.

hold short: 1) The act of waiting behind a hold short line before entering a runway, to await clearance or safe conditions to proceed; 2) An ATC instruction to stop and wait at any designated point, while taxiing or landing.

hold short line: The boundary, designated by two solid yellow lines on the outer side and two dashed yellow lines on the inner side, defining the entrance/exit to a runway, which no part of an aircraft may pass to enter the runway without ATC clearance or (at a non-towered airport) announcing its intention over the CTAF.

hood: A device worn by a pilot to restrict their field of vision, in order to simulate IFR conditions and train to fly in reference solely to cockpit instruments.

horizontal stabilizer: The horizontal "wings" on the airplane's tail section, which normally generate negative lift to stabilize the plane, and which the elevators are attached to.

hyperventilation: Rapid breathing, often caused by excitement or panic, that can cause a depletion of CO_2 in the bloodstream, and a resulting constriction of oxygen flow to the brain. Symptoms include dizziness, shortness of breath, cold sweats, and confusion.

hypoxia: A serious medical condition caused by lack of oxygen supply to the brain. Causes can include low air density at high altitude, the effect of drugs or alcohol, CO poisoning, high g-forces, or other underlying medical conditions.

IACRA (Integrated Airman Certification and Rating Application): The website used by the FAA to process applications relating to pilot licenses, ratings, and checkrides.

ICAO airport code: A unique four-letter code assigned by the International Civil Aviation Organization to most airports around the world, distinct from the three-letter code assigned by the IATA (International Air Transport Association) for airline ticket and baggage handling; ICAO codes for airports in the Continental U.S. begin with K.

icing: The development of ice forming on an aircraft, from moisture in the atmosphere, in various ways that can impair its operation in flight.

idle: The lowest throttle setting, where the engine is still on but produces little or no forward thrust.

IFR (Instrument Flight Rules): The procedures, rules, and restrictions for flying solely with reference to cockpit instruments, regardless of outside visibility. A pilot must have an instrument rating to fly IFR, and must file a flight plan in advance.

ignition: The switch, operated by a key in the Cessna 172, that turns one or both magnetos, as well as the starter, on or off in order to operate the engine.

ILS (Instrument Landing System): A radio navigation system that provides both vertical and horizontal guidance to instrument-trained pilots for approach and landing under poor-visibility, IFR conditions.

IMC (Instrument Meteorological Conditions): Weather conditions where limited visibility and/or low clouds prevent pilots from flying safely or legally under VFR.

incident: An event associated with the operation of an aircraft that affects or could affect its safety of operation, but falls short of the definition of an accident.

inclinometer: A device that uses a ball in a sealed curved glass tube to display the inertial forces operating laterally on the aircraft. When the ball is centered, the aircraft is in coordinated flight; when it moves to the inside of a turn, the aircraft is slipping; and when it moves to the outside, the aircraft is skidding.[261]

Indicated Airspeed (IAS): The airspeed measured as a pressure differential by the pitot-static system and displayed on the airspeed indicator, not adjusted for altitude and temperature; used as the correct reference for flying the airplane, even though it does not reflect true airspeed (TAS).

induced drag: Drag that is caused by the wing's angle of attack in order to produce lift. This type of drag decreases as airspeed increases, because the required angle of attack decreases.

instrument rating: An additional qualification that authorizes a pilot to fly using IFR.

isobar: A line on a weather map showing where barometric air pressure is the same.

isogonic lines: Dashed lines on a sectional chart that indicate the difference (magnetic variance) at that location between true direction on the map and the magnetic readings from a compass, a number that changes across the United States from east to west. The number indicated on the line can be used to translate true course or heading into magnetic course or heading, or vice versa.

knots: Speed measured in nautical miles per hour.

LAHSO (Land and Hold Short Operations): An ATC procedure that clears an aircraft to land on one portion of a runway, so long as it halts before reaching a designated point, such as an intersecting runway or taxiway.

lateral axis: The line running from one wingtip of an airplane to the other. Rotation around this axis, up or down, is called pitch.

latitude: The angular distance north or south of the equator, expressed in degrees. Lines of latitude run east and west around the earth, parallel to the equator.

lean: 1) To reduce the amount of fuel in the fuel-air mixture, in order to improve engine performance; 2) A fuel-air mixture that is relatively low on fuel relative to air.

left-turning tendencies: Several physical properties that tend to cause the nose of a single-engine propeller airplane to yaw left, which at times must be offset by pushing the rudder to the right. These include gyroscopic precession, P-factor, spiraling slipstream, and torque.

lift: The upward force produced by an airfoil, which counters the downward force of gravity and causes an aircraft to fly.

light gun signals: Red, green, and white lights used by a control tower to send simple coded visual instructions to an aircraft that has lost radio communications.

load factor: The aerodynamic lifting force, and resulting stress, placed on an aircraft's structure during a turn or other maneuver, as a multiple of its weight.

logbook: 1) Booklet used to record a pilot's flying hours and training, along with any required endorsements; 2) Book used to record and certify any maintenance performed on an aircraft.

longitude: The angular distance east or west around the earth's circumference from the Prime Meridian running through Greenwich, England, expressed in degrees. Lines of longitude run north and south from one pole to the other, perpendicular to the equator.

longitudinal axis: The line running from the nose of the aircraft to its tail. Rotation around this axis, to the left or right, is called roll.

magnetic compass: A magnetized device that points towards the magnetic north pole, thus indicating the airplane's magnetic heading. It does not require any external source of power, but can be subject to certain errors caused by the aircraft's motion or electrical devices in the cockpit.

magnetic course: The magnetic compass direction a pilot intends to follow (as opposed to the direction defined by latitude and longitude on a map or chart).

magnetic deviation: The error introduced to a magnetic compass reading from the local magnetic fields created by electrical currents in the cockpit.

magnetic heading: The direction an aircraft's nose is pointing, according to the magnetic compass (as opposed to the directions on the map or chart, which are aligned with latitude and longitude).

magnetic variation: The difference in degrees between the true direction (based on a map oriented to the geographic north pole) and the reading from a magnetic compass (oriented to the magnetic north pole.) This difference varies by location, from east to west, across the U.S. and is indicated on the sectional chart along dashed isogonic lines. Used to translate true course or heading into magnetic course or heading, or vice versa.

magneto: A small electrical generator containing permanent magnets. In piston-driven airplanes, they are powered by the engine's rotation, and in turn deliver timed electrical charges to the spark plugs to keep the engine firing independent of the electrical system.

maneuvering speed (V_A): The airspeed beyond which moving the controls to their full extent could cause structural damage to the airplane before inducing a stall. Because it varies based on weight, it is not marked on the airspeed indicator.

manifold pressure: The pressure of the fuel/air mixture after passing through the throttle, on its way to the engine, as a result of the suction produced by the piston drawing air into the cylinder. In airplanes with constant speed propellers, it is used as an indicator of the power being generated by the engine, independent of RPM.

master switch: The two co-located switches, typically red, that turn the airplane's battery and alternator, and thus its electrical system, on and off.

Mayday: Internationally recognized code word used as a distress call over the radio to alert listeners to an emergency situation that poses an immediate danger to life or the aircraft. Derives from the French phrase *m'aidez*, meaning "help me."

MEL (Minimum Equipment List): A detailed list of all an aircraft's parts that lays out strict procedures for when they are inoperative, including whether the flight can proceed or not; used mainly in larger aircraft, rarely in smaller private ones.

METAR: A report usually issued every hour summarizing the current weather conditions at a given airport, often presented in an abbreviated coded format.

MFD (Multi-Function Display): A secondary digital display screen in a Glass Cockpit that shows engine gauges, navigation maps, and other flight information besides the primary instrument data displayed by the PFD.

microburst: A strong downdraft of air in a thunderstorm. Where it meets the ground, the air disperses in every direction, posing a risk of severe wind shear.

Microsoft Flight Simulator 2020 (MSFS 2020): The latest in a series of PC-based flight simulation games produced by Microsoft, released in August 2020.

mixture: The ratio of air and fuel, measured by density, being channeled to the engine's combustion chambers.

MOA (Military Operations Area): Special use airspace indicated on the chart by a hatched magenta boundary, where pilots should be aware that military aircraft may be performing abrupt, high-speed maneuvers. Aircraft do not require a clearance to enter an MOA but should exercise caution.

Mode C: The setting that instructs a transponder to transmit the aircraft's altitude to ATC.

Mode C veil: The circular boundary around a Class B airport, 30nm in radius, within which all aircraft must have an operating transponder set to Mode C, as well as ADS-B Out.

moment: The tendency of a force to move an object at a distance from an axis. Moment equals weight times arm, and can be used to calculate center of gravity. Also see *torque*.

MSL (Mean Sea Level): Altitude measured in feet above average sea level (as opposed to AGL, above the terrain below).

multi-engine rating: A rating that qualifies a pilot to fly an aircraft that has more than one engine; much of the training focuses on how to fly on the remaining engines if one is disabled.

nautical mile (nm): The measure of distance used on aviation charts, equivalent to 6,076 feet, or 1,852 meters, or approximately 1.15 statute miles. It is based on the earth's circumference, with one nautical mile equaling an average minute of latitude.

NAV1 and NAV2: The two aircraft radios used for radio navigation. The frequencies for each can be selected independently, allowing the pilot to quickly switch from one to the other, or navigate in reference to two different radio beacons at the same time.

navigation lights: An arrangement of colored lights (red on the left wing, green on the right wing, white on the tail) that help other observers identify an aircraft's relative position and direction of travel at night.

NDB (Non-Directional Beacon): A ground station in a known location that emits a radio signal, which aircraft can receive and follow to that location; an NDB's signal, however, lacks the inherent directional information which allows a pilot to fly a specific radial to or from a VOR.

Never Exceed Speed (V_{NE}): The designated airspeed beyond which it is not safe to fly the aircraft, due to structural limitations.

Newton's Third Law of Motion: "For every action there is an equal and opposite reaction," in other words, if Object A exerts a force on Object B, Object B exerts an equal and opposite force on Object A.

NOTAM (Notice to Air Missions, previously Notice to Airmen): A notice filed with an aviation authority to alert pilots to current conditions along the route or at locations (such as airports) that could affect the safety of the flight.

OBS (Omni Bearing Selector): The knob used to rotate the CDI's compass ring in order to identify the radial either to or from a VOR.

oil: Petroleum-based lubricating material that circulates throughout the engine to reduce friction between its moving parts, as well as carry away heat and contaminants.

oil pressure: Indication that signals whether oil is flowing adequately through the engine.

oil temperature: Indication that serves as the primary gauge of engine temperature in many airplanes, including the Cessna 172.

operating limitations: Instructions and guidelines that legally must be carried in the airplane either in the POH or on placards posted in the cockpit.

Pan-Pan: Internationally recognized code words used over the radio to alert listeners to an urgent situation that does not pose an immediate danger to life or the aircraft. Derives from the French word *panne*, meaning "breakdown".

PAPI (Precision Approach Path Indicator): A set of lights (typically four) arrayed horizontally next to a runway which change one by one from white to red to indicate whether the aircraft is above or below the recommended glideslope when approaching to land. If most of the lights are white, the aircraft is too high; if most are red, it is too low; if half are red and half are white, the aircraft is on the correct glideslope. Also see *VASI*.

parasitic drag: The resistance produced by an object's movement through the air around it, which increases with speed. Types of parasitic drag include form drag, interference drag, and skin friction.

Part 61: The FAA regulation governing flight schools or programs that customize training to each student's needs, based on a flexible curriculum and schedule.

Part 141: The FAA regulation governing flight schools or training programs that use a set, FAA-approved curriculum with fixed lesson plans, schedules, and benchmarks.

performance takeoffs and landings: Procedures used to get the optimal performance out of an airplane in order to operate safely on especially short or unpaved (soft) runways.

personal minimums: Explicit personal criteria set voluntarily by a pilot, based on their own experience and training, as a basis for deciding whether conditions are safe to fly; not a required practice, but advisable.

P-factor: One of several tendencies that can cause a single-engine aircraft's nose to yaw to one side (usually left), produced by the propeller blade taking a larger bite of the air and generating more thrust as it rotates downward than when it rotates upward, when flying at a high angle of attack.

PFD (Primary Flight Display): The digital screen in a glass cockpit that shows an integrated display of the primary flight instruments, usually superimposed on an artificial horizon.

PIC (Pilot in Command): The person who has final authority and responsibility for the operation and safety of the flight.

pilotage: The practice of navigating by visual references to known landmarks or checkpoints.

PilotEdge: A subscription-based network that allows pilots to practice talking to live air traffic controllers during virtual flights performed in *MSFS* or other PC-based flight simulators.

PIREP: A report submitted by a pilot, by radio, describing real-time weather conditions encountered in flight, including potential hazards, and distributed to other pilots via weather briefing and other information channels. Often presented in an abbreviated coded format.

piston: A moving disk inside a cylinder, which is pressed down by the explosive force of combustion, turning a crankshaft and transforming that energy into mechanical motion.

pitch: 1) The vertical position of the airplane's nose, up or down relative to its tail, around its lateral axis, usually controlled by the elevators by pushing the yoke or stick back (up) or forward (down); 2) The angle of an airplane's propeller blades as they cut into the air while spinning.

pitot-static system: The three cockpit instruments (altimeter, airspeed indicator, and vertical speed indicator) that rely on gauging outside air pressure to function, and the two devices (pitot tube and static port) that supply that pressure to them.

pitot tube: A device on their aircraft's outer surface that collects and channels the impact pressure from the oncoming airflow to the airspeed indicator, enabling it to function.

POH (Pilot Operating Handbook): The manufacturer's manual for operating a specific airplane, including technical specifications, procedural checklists, and performance information for planning purposes.

porpoising: A landing where, after initially bouncing or ballooning, the pilot overreacts and pitches down to hit nosewheel first, causing the airplane to bounce repeatedly forward and aft down the runway like a leaping porpoise, potentially damaging the plane.

power-off landing: Approach and landing performed with the throttle set to idle, in order to simulate gliding to a forced emergency landing with no engine power.

power-off stall: A training maneuver in which the student intentionally enters a stall by cutting power to idle in slow flight, with flaps down, in order to simulate a stall on flare and landing, and to learn how to recover safely from an unintended stall on approach to land.

power-on stall: A training maneuver in which the student intentionally enters a stall by pitching steeply up at full power, with flaps up, in order to simulate and learn how to recover safely from an unintended stall on takeoff.

PPL (Private Pilot License): A license which allows the holder to legally fly as Pilot in Command, either solo or carrying passengers, but not for compensation.

pre-flight inspection: A visual inspection of the aircraft performed by the pilot prior to any flight to ensure it is in safe working order, based on a checklist in the POH.

preignition: When the fuel/air mixture in an engine's combustion chamber ignites prematurely, out of sync with the piston stroke, typically due to a "hot spot" that has developed within the cylinder. It can reduce engine power and do damage to the engine parts.

pressure altitude: The altitude displayed on an altimeter when it is set to the standard 29.92 inches of mercury at sea level; in effect, a measure of the difference in air pressure, expressed in terms of height.

preventative maintenance: Minor maintenance tasks, such as changing oil or brake fluid, that FAA regulations allow pilots to perform themselves.

prime: Feed a small amount of fuel into the engine before starting it.

proficiency: The actual ability to do something well; not to be confused with currency.

prop lever: A control in some airplanes that adjusts the pitch of the propeller blades, either directly or (more often) indirectly via an RPM governor, to produce thrust more efficiently.

prop wash: The stream of air pushed back from the propeller and flowing over the control surfaces on the tail.

radial: The line along a specific magnetic compass bearing from a VOR, which the radio signal enables an airplane to follow either towards or away from the beacon, using the CDI.

radio stack: The radio selection panel in the cockpit, which typically includes two communications radios (COM 1 and COM2) and two navigation radios (NAV1 and NAV2).

rating: A qualification that authorizes a pilot to operate a particular category, class, or type of aircraft.

rectangular course: A standard training maneuver in which the student traces a box-like ground track around a rectangular set of features on the ground (such as a field or block of roads) while adjusting for wind direction and maintaining constant altitude and airspeed. It is meant to simulate following a traffic pattern.

registration: 1) Document indicating the aircraft's owner and its legal status with the FAA; 2) The unique alphanumeric code assigned to an aircraft, usually displayed on its tail and used as its call sign.

relative humidity: The ratio between the water vapor in the air and the maximum amount it could hold at that temperature, expressed as a percentage.

relative wind: The direction of the air moving past an aircraft or airfoil. It can be straight on (in level flight) or angled from below (in a descent) or above (in a climb).

Restricted Area: Special-use airspace that is restricted to aircraft with a clearance, due to special hazards or security concerns. Designated on the sectional chart by a blue hatched border.

reverse sensing: When the CDI needle indicates the opposite deviation it should because the pilot has mistakenly set the OBS to a TO instead of a FROM bearing, or vice versa.

rich: A fuel-air mixture that is relatively high on fuel relative to air.

right of way: Order of precedence among aircraft that encounter each other in the air, in lieu of ATC instructions, governing which may proceed and which must give way to avoid collision.

rigidity in space: The tendency of a spinning object to remain in a fixed position in the geometric plane in which it is spinning. See *gyroscope*.

rime ice: A crusty, opaque covering of ice that forms when tiny droplets of water freeze immediately and gradually accumulate on a surface.

rods: The sensory receptors in the back of the human eye that are best at perceiving peripheral motion and contrast, even in darkened conditions, and are vital to night vision.

roll: 1) The rotation of an aircraft around its longitudinal axis, with one wing moving upwards and the other downwards. Also see *bank*; 2) The distance required for an airplane to come to a complete halt, using brakes, after touching down on landing.

round out: When an airplane levels off its descent a short height above the runway, during landing.

RPM (Revolutions Per Minute): A measure of how fast a reciprocating piston engine, propeller, or rotor is turning.

rudder: A primary control surface, usually attached to the tail fin, that alters the airplane's yaw, left or right, around its vertical axis.

rudder pedals: Foot-operated pedals in the cockpit that operate the rudder and, in some airplanes, turn the nosewheel during taxiing on the ground.

running rough: When an engine sputters, coughs, or vibrates in an unusual manner instead of running steadily as normal.

run-up: A series of instrument, control, and engine checks performed prior to entering the runway for takeoff.

runway: A leveled strip of land designated for aircraft to take off and land. Runways, in either direction, are assigned numbers based on their magnetic compass direction (Runway 27 points towards 270° west, while at its opposite end, Runway 9 points towards 90° east).

runway incursion: The movement of an aircraft onto a designated airport runway without proper ATC clearance or in an unsafe manner.

sectional chart: The primary navigational maps used by VFR pilots, published and updated periodically by the FAA, which show key features including terrain, landmarks, airports and airport information, airspace, radio beacons, obstacles, etc. on a scale of 1:500,000. There are 37 sectional charts covering the Continental U.S.

separation: Maintaining a safe distance between aircraft in the airspace surrounding an airport, a responsibility that pilots flying VFR share with ATC.

sequencing: The order in which aircraft should take off and land, as instructed by ATC.

shock cooling: The possibility of damage occurring to an engine due to the rapid cooling of its parts, caused by an abrupt reduction in power setting.

sideslip: A maneuver in which the pilot turns the ailerons to bank into a crosswind, while pushing the rudder in the opposite direction, in order to counter the sideways drift caused by the wind while keeping the nose aligned with the runway. This can be performed all through final approach, or during round out and flare in the final moments before landing.

sight picture: The visual image a pilot becomes used to seeing out his or her windshield, which can be used to judge the airplane's position in performing maneuvers, takeoffs, or landings.

SIGMET: An advisory published by the U.S. government's Aviation Weather

Center that warns of potential hazards of concern to all aircraft, including major thunderstorms, hurricanes, dust or ash clouds, and hail. They focus on more severe conditions than AIRMETs.

sinking: The impression produced by the sight picture when the airplane descends at a faster rate than its current glideslope to the runway.

skid: An uncoordinated condition of flight in which the tail of airplane, during a turn, follows a path that is outside that followed by the nose, producing a lateral centrifugal force away from the direction of turn; typically countered using the rudder.

slip: An uncoordinated condition of flight in which the tail of airplane, during a turn, follows a path that is inside that followed by the nose, producing a lateral centripetal force into the direction of turn; typically countered by using the rudder.

slow flight: A training maneuver performed by student pilots, in which the airplane is slowed to just above stall speed, in order to gain experience handling the plane at low speeds during final approach and landing.

solo: When the pilot is the sole occupant of the aircraft.

spark plug: The device that delivers an electrical charge to ignite the fuel/air mixture in the combustion chamber of a piston-driven engine. In an airplane there are typically two per cylinder, actuated by separate magnetos, for redundancy.

spatial disorientation: The tendency of the pilot's physical sensations to create confusion over the airplane's movement and orientation, in the absence of sufficient visual clues. The main cure is to rely on the airplane's instruments for guidance.

Special Flight Permit: Permission issued by the FAA that allows an aircraft otherwise not qualified as airworthy to be flown to another location; also commonly called a Ferry Permit.

spin: A condition in which one wing is in a deeper stall than the other, causing the airplane to spiral uncontrollably and lose altitude. Because the wings are stalled, the ailerons are ineffective at correcting the turn. The pilot must rely on the rudder, and pitch the nose down to increase airspeed in order to break the stall.

spiraling slipstream: The airflow pushed back from the spinning propeller, which swirls around the fuselage in a corkscrew manner and, hitting the left side of the tail fin, pushes the tail right and the nose left. This is most pronounced when the propeller is fast and the airplane is slow, such as on takeoff.

squawk: To broadcast a designated transponder code.

stability: The tendency of an aircraft to resume its previous flight path when disrupted from it, either by some external force or a control input.

stall: When an airfoil, such as a wing, loses its ability to produce lift because the smooth airflow over it becomes disrupted, usually due to too high an angle of attack.

stall horn: An electronic or mechanical device that emits a loud noise to warn when the airplane's wings are at a high angle of attack and in danger of stalling.

stall speeds: The indicated airspeeds at which an airplane will stall with either flaps up (V_{S1}) or fully extended (V_{S0}), under the following conditions: level flight, maximum gross weight, and most forward center of gravity.[262] Often depicted on the airspeed indicator, though depending on the conditions, an airplane can stall at any airspeed and at any pitch attitude.

Standard Day: Temperature of 15°C (59°F) and air pressure of 29.92 in/Hg at sea level, used as a baseline for making adjustments to planning calculations and instruments based on deviations from these conditions.

Standard Rate Turn: A turn of 3° per second, which would take two minutes to complete a full 360-degree circle.

starter: The electric motor, powered by the battery, that when engaged causes the airplane's propeller to spin, engaging the magnetos to start the engine.

static port: An opening on the aircraft's surface that channels the ambient outside air pressure to the three cockpit instruments (altimeter, airspeed indicator, and vertical speed indicator) that rely on it as an input.

statute mile: The unit of distance equal to 5,280 feet which most people outside of aviation or sailing refer to simply as a "mile". It is roughly

0.87 nautical miles. Some aviation regulations, such as VFR minimum visibility requirements, are defined in statute rather than nautical miles.

steam gauge: Conventional, analog cockpit instruments, as opposed to digital display screens, dubbed this because of their resemblance to steam pressure gauges.

steep turn: A standard maneuver that involves turning the aircraft at a bank between 30° and 60° (typically 45°), to complete a full circle, while maintaining a constant altitude and airspeed.

sterile cockpit: The practice of avoiding unnecessary and distracting conversation in the cockpit, especially during critical phases of flight.

stick: See *yoke*.

stopway: The part of a runway, marked with yellow arrows or chevrons, that cannot be used either to begin takeoffs or to touch down on landings, but only to taxi or to roll to a final stop after landing if needed.

straight and level: Flying at a constant heading and altitude, with no bank.

stratus: A flat, uniform, featureless cloud that signifies relatively stable air conditions.

S-turns: A standard training maneuver consisting of alternating left and right half-turns along a linear feature on the ground, such as a straight road, while adjusting for wind direction and maintaining constant altitude and airspeed.

sumping: Draining samples of fuel from the airplane's tanks into a clear container, as part of the pre-flight inspection, in order to check for water or other contaminants.

TAC (Terminal Area Chart): An FAA-published map showing the area surrounding a major airport on a larger scale and in greater detail than the standard sectional chart.

tachometer: A cockpit instrument that shows the rate at which the engine is turning the propeller, in RPM, which with a fixed-pitch propeller is equivalent to the power put out by the engine. In a constant speed propeller, RPM is set independently and regulated by a governor.

Tach time: The number of hours the engine has been run at normal cruising speed, based on RPM, for the purpose of meeting maintenance requirements.

TAF (Terminal Aerodrome Forecast): A report issued four times per day (every six hours) summarizing the forecasted weather conditions at a given airport over the next 24 to 30 hours. Often presented in an abbreviated coded format.

tail fin: See *vertical stabilizer*.

tailplane: See *horizontal stabilizer*.

tailstrike: When the tail of an airplane hits the ground on takeoff or landing, due to the pilot pitching up too high.

tailwheel airplane: An airplane that, when on the ground, rests back on its tail instead of forward on a nosewheel; sometimes called "conventional gear" since they were once standard.

tailwind: Wind blowing from behind the airplane, in its direction of travel. A tailwind can hasten an airplane's progress en route, but seriously detracts from its performance and safety during takeoff and landing, which should always be made into a headwind.

taxi: Moving the aircraft on the ground, under its own power.

taxi diagram: Detailed map of an airport showing its runways, taxiways, parking areas, and major facilities.

taxiway: A designated path at an airport for aircraft to move on the ground, typically to or from runways. Taxiways are bordered by yellow lines, and often by blue lights at night.

temperature inversion: A situation where air temperature rises instead of falls with an increase in altitude, in which a layer of cooler air is trapped beneath of higher layer of warmer air, in many cases along with pollution and smog.

TFR (Temporary Flight Restriction): Airspace that is temporarily restricted to normal traffic due to special event or security risk.

throttle: 1) The control in the cockpit that regulates the amount of air and fuel allowed to enter the engine, to drive combustion, and thus the power it generates; 2) The valve that physically restricts the passage of air and fuel into the engine.

thrust: The forward-moving force pushing an aircraft forward, and generating airflow over its wings. It is usually produced by a propeller or jet exhaust, and is countered by drag.

torque: 1) Any twisting force, applied at a distance to the pivot point, that causes rotation; 2) the counter-rotation force created in reaction to any spinning object.

touch-and-go: Landing and taking off again on the same runway without coming to a complete stop.

traffic pattern: An established flying pattern in the air above an airport, at a certain altitude (usually 1000 feet above the surface, for smaller airplanes), that designates the path for aircraft to follow prior to landing and after takeoff.

transition: 1) To fly through an airport's restricted airspace, with ATC permission, without taking off or landing there; 2) Training in a new type of aircraft, usually to gain a new rating or endorsement.

transponder: An electronic device that provides information about an aircraft's identity and (in Mode C) altitude to ATC.

tricycle-gear airplane: An airplane, like the Cessna 172, that when on the ground rests forward on a nosewheel, instead of backward on its tail.

trim: The process of using the trim wheel to adjust the trim tab on the elevators, in order to relieve the active pressure on the yoke needed to maintain a certain pitch, often to maintain straight and level flight, or to climb or descend at a given speed. Some airplanes also give the pilot the ability to trim the rudder and ailerons.

trim tab: A hinged surface, set into the elevators, which when raised or lowered by using the trim wheel affects their default position up or down, in order to reduce the need to exert active pressure on the yoke. Some airplanes also have a trim tab for the rudder and/or ailerons.

trim wheel: The device in the cockpit that allows the pilot, by rolling it up or down, to adjust the trim tab and set the default position of the elevators.

TRSA (Terminal Radar Services Area): An area around a busy Class D airport where ATC provides optional guidance to aircraft approaching, departing, or transitioning, out to a radius that typically far exceeds the controlled airspace of that airport. Its boundaries are designated by gray circular lines on the sectional chart.

True Airspeed (TAS): The aircraft's true speed through the surrounding air, equivalent to its Indicated Airspeed (IAS) adjusted for air density.

true course: The direction a pilot intends to follow, relative to the directions defined by latitude and longitude on a map or chart (as opposed to the magnetic directions indicated by a compass).

true heading: The direction an aircraft's nose is pointing, relative to the directions defined by latitude and longitude on a map or chart (as opposed to the magnetic directions indicated by a compass).

turbocharger: A compressor that increases the density of the air flowing into the engine to drive combustion, compensating for lower air density at higher altitudes, which would otherwise reduce power. If it is powered by a turbine driven by the engine's exhaust gases, it is called a turbocharger; otherwise, it is called a supercharger.

turboprop: A hybrid type of jet engine where the gases expanded by combustion drive a turbine, which powers a propeller, instead of producing thrust directly by shooting out the back.

turbulence: Disturbances in the air surrounding an aircraft, which can cause abrupt variations in altitude, orientation, or airspeed.

turn coordinator: A primary cockpit instrument that uses a gyroscope to indicates the aircraft's yaw movement left or right around the vertical axis, in order to show rate of turn. It is typically paired with an inclinometer.

turns around a point: A standard training maneuver the involves flying in an even circle around some point on the ground, while adjusting for wind direction and maintaining constant altitude and airspeed.

type rating: A qualification needed to pilot a specific type of airplane, usually required for larger or jet-powered aircraft.

unusual attitudes: A drill where the instructor (or examiner) takes control of the airplane while the student closes their eyes. After a series of disorienting maneuvers, the student is asked to resume control and quickly take whatever actions are needed to return to straight and level flight. This can be performed either without foggles (relying on the outside sight picture) or with them (relying solely on instruments).

upwind: The leg of the traffic pattern that runs parallel to the runway, in the intended direction of landing.

UTC (Coordinated Universal Time): The time at the Prime Meridian, which serves as the standard reference in aviation, to avoid confusion over local time zones. Also called *Zulu Time*.

variable pitch propeller: A airplane propeller where the angle or pitch of the blades can be adjusted for different stages of flight, to produce thrust more efficiently. The most common kind now is a *constant speed propeller*.

VASI (Visual Approach Slope Indicator): Two (sometimes three) sets of lights arrayed vertically next to a runway, which change from white to red to indicate whether the aircraft is above or below the recommended glideslope when approaching to land. If both sets of light are white, the aircraft is too high; if both are red, it is too low; if the upper set are red and lower are white, the aircraft is on the correct glideslope. Also see *PAPI*.

vector: A magnetic heading given to an aircraft by ATC, to be flown for a certain time or distance, either to assist it in finding a desired course or to keep it clear of other air traffic.

vertical axis: The line running through the airplane from top to bottom. Rotation around this axis, left or right, is called yaw.

vertical speed indicator (VSI): A primary cockpit instrument that estimates an aircraft's rate of change in altitude by comparing two measures of air pressure, current and delayed.

vertical stabilizer: The vertical fin on the airplane's tail section, which helps stabilize it in flight and which the rudder is attached to.

VFR (Visual Flight Rules): The procedures, rules, and restrictions for flying in good visibility conditions. A pilot who lacks an instrument rating can only fly VFR, not IFR.

VFR over the top: Flying by VFR in good visibility above a cloud layer. It is legal, but requires a safe way to climb and descend without entering IFR conditions.

Victor airway: Designated pathway for aircraft to follow between two VORs, extending up to 18,000 feet MSL.

VOR (VHF Omnidirectional Range): A ground-based radio beacon that sends out a directional signal that allows an airplane to navigate to or from it along a chosen compass bearing, or radial.

VORTAC: A VOR that is co-located with a military TACAN beacon.

wake turbulence: Disturbed flow of air that descends behind and below a moving airplane, produced by the eddies of air around the tips of its wings (wingtip vortices) generated as a byproduct of the wing producing lift. The disruption is largest when an airplane is heavy, clean (flaps up), and slow, and can be a serious hazard to smaller aircraft.

weight: The effect of gravity on the airplane, pulling it down to earth; countered by lift.

weight and balance: The documentation required to be carried in the aircraft on every flight, showing the calculations performed to ensure the aircraft is operating within safe parameters, in terms of its loaded weight and center of gravity.

wind angle: The number of degrees that must be added to or subtracted from an airplane's intended course in order to find the heading it must fly in order to counter the force of the wind, which would otherwise blow it off course.

Winds Aloft: A type of weather report that forecasts wind speed and direction, as well as temperature, at different levels of altitude for use in flight planning.

wind shear: A rapid change in wind speed or direction, commonly encountered when crossing a weather front or from one stable layer of air to another.

wingtip vortices: Disruptions in airflow created by the wing generating lift, which can cause turbulence for other aircraft behind and below an airplane's path.

yaw: The horizontal position of the airplane's nose, left or right relative to its tail, around its vertical axis, usually controlled by the rudder via foot pedals.

yoke: A primary control in many airplanes that superficially resembles a steering wheel. Turning the yoke left or right operates the ailerons, while pushing it forward or back operates the elevators. In other airplanes, a vertical stick performs the same functions.

Zulu Time: See *UTC*.

Acknowledgements

There are several sets of people I must thank for making this book possible. The first are those who helped teach me to fly. Because they never expected to appear in a book—I didn't even plan to write one when I met them—part of my thanks must take the form of respecting their privacy. The fact that their real names are not used here, and their identities are often disguised, in no way diminishes my gratitude to them for benefiting from their knowledge, patience, and professionalism. In my "Note on Sources" I have already mentioned the various YouTube creators I never met whose advice and insights greatly assisted my flight training, for which I am grateful.

The second set of people I want to thank are those who helped me write and edit this book: James Fallows for his early encouragement after reading my rough draft, and his many generous introductions to others in the aviation community; David Thornton, for his conscientious proofread of an early draft; John Zimmerman of Sporty's, for deploying his expertise as both an airplane and helicopter pilot in reviewing my manuscript and offering suggestions; Mark Vanhoenacker, a 787 pilot and author, for catching a number of errors; Alex Fisher, for helping me correct and refine some of my explanations of aerodynamics; and Mike Forsythe, for guidance and advice as a fellow author on citations, as well as the publishing process. I'd like to thank Sam Taylor of ForeFlight, Kevin Meyers of PilotEdge, David Grave of SkyVector, and Stu Moment and Bruce Artwick of Sublogic for granting permission for me to use some of their company's images and materials, and for offering their helpful feedback on the manuscript. Similar thanks are due to Matthew Arpano, Sean Bradley, Jason Branski, Rachel Dodsworth, Melvin Edwards, Alex Gounares, Jorge Guajardo, Richard Hough, Dennis Kern, Frank Lavin, Phillip Romanelli, Tom Shugart, Robert Siegelbaum, Rob Teeter, Bruce Williams, and others who read all or part of my manuscript and offered their corrections, comments, and encouragement.

Special thanks must go to Carolyn Levin and her team for helping me navigate various legal issues, do all of the things I should do, and steer clear of the things I shouldn't; to Julie Broad and her team for helping me through the editing, printing, and marketing process, with special mention due to Jane Constantineau for her thoughtful developmental edits; to Jim Kopp for patiently working with me (and learning the intricacies of aviation charts) to develop the book's original illustrations; to Pete Garceau for designing the book cover; and to Rohesia Hamilton Metcalfe for designing my webpage.

Finally, I cannot conclude without thanking my wife and three children, to whom this book is dedicated. Learning to fly is time consuming and filled with frustrations. Writing a book is time consuming and filled with frustrations. They put up with all of it.

Note on Sources

I am not an expert in aviation; this entire book is the result of an experience learning from a wide range of teachers, directly and indirectly. Prior to being on the receiving end of their knowledge, I knew almost none of the information I've presented here.

Unless otherwise noted, the material presented in this book draws heavily from my direct interactions with my instructors and from FAA publications and instruction manuals, including the *FAR/AIM 2022, Airplane Flying Handbook, Pilot's Handbook of Aeronautical Knowledge, Pilot/Controller Glossary, Private Pilot—Airplane Airman Certification Standards,* sectional charts, and *Chart Supplements*. Other resources used during my training included Sporty's online *Learn to Fly Course*, American Flyers' student textbook *Private Pilot Flight*, ASA's *Private Pilot 2020 Test Prep*, and ASA's *Private Pilot Oral Exam Guide*. Since all of them cover the same ground in different ways—and repetition is the key to learning—I find it all but impossible to untangle their respective contributions. If I tried, the endnotes would be as long as the book itself.

Many specific facts and procedures come from the Pilot's Operating Handbook (POH) of the Cessna 172S, which is produced by its manufacturer, Textron Aviation Inc. Each individual aircraft's POH is unique, however, and the information it contains may vary, even within the same make and model, so you should always consult the POH of the aircraft you are flying.

There are several YouTube channels that post extremely helpful videos on aviation and flight instruction, free of charge. Ones I looked to the most during my training include MzeroA, Boldmethod, Fly8MA, Airplane Academy, The Finer Points, Rod Machado, Fly With The Guys, Cyndy Hollman, and King Schools. If I have overlooked the credit any of them (or others) are due for any particular aid or insight, it is because the abundance of useful perspectives they generously provided, over many months, outstrips my ability to keep track.

Although I found these sources to be useful in my own training, my mention of them does not imply any endorsement, not does it imply that any other authors, companies, organizations, or authorities have endorsed me or my book.

Selected Bibliography

3 Greens - Aviation Safety. "The Crash Which 'Changed' Aviation in America / Colgan 3407." April 15, 2021. Educational video, 16:31. https://www.youtube.com/watch?v=urF4GyF77_M.

Aircraft Owners and Pilots Association. "Emergency Locator Transmitter (ELT)." December 28, 2018. https://www.aopa.org/advocacy/aircraft/aircraft-operations/emergency-locator-transmitters.

Aircraft Owners and Pilots Association. "Vision: Monocular Vision." April 2016. https://www.aopa.org/go-fly/medical-resources/health-conditions/vision/monocular-vision.

Aircraft Owners and Pilots Association, Air Safety Institute. *31st Joseph T. Nall Report*. 2022. https://www.aopa.org/training-and-safety/air-safety-institute/accident-analysis/joseph-t-nall-report/.

Airlines for America. "Data & Statistics: Safety Record of U.S. Air Carriers." Airlines.org. November 11, 2021. https://www.airlines.org/dataset/safety-record-of-u-s-air-carriers/.

Airplane Academy. "How Many Flight Hours Before You Solo?" https://airplaneacademy.com/how-many-flight-hours-before-you-solo/.

Airplane Academy "This ONE Technique Instantly Improved My Landings."

September 21, 2020. Educational video, 6:12. https://www.youtube.com/watch?v=YMHw9QabSlg.

Air Safety Institute. "Accident Case Study: Traffic Pattern Tragedy." September 21, 2018. Educational video, 20:57. https://www.youtube.com/watch?v=mf3xhjXl454.

Air Safety Institute. "Reality Check: The Runway Behind You." June 4, 2021. Educational video, 9:37. https://www.youtube.com/watch?v=dFVFKq3QqXo.

Ambrose, Stephen E. *The Wild Blue: The Men and Boys Who Flew the B-24s Over Germany 1944-45*. New York: Simon & Schuster, 2001.

American Flyers. *Private Pilot Flight*, Version 19.1. Addison, TX, 2009.

ASA. *Private Pilot 2020 Test Prep*. Newcastle, WA: Aviation Supplies & Academics, 2019.

Asheville Regional Airport. "Breathe easy in the clouds: aircraft pressurization 101." Flyavl.com. February 16, 2017. https://flyavl.com/article/breathe-easy-clouds-aircraft-pressurization-101.

Aviator Inspirations. "How to Become a Flight Instructor" June 15, 2019. Educational video, 5:30. https://www.youtube.com/watch?v=Chd94s2xQSg.

AZ Stolman. "Choosing Lean of Peak or Rich of Peak." July 22, 2018. Educational video, 4:45. https://www.youtube.com/watch?v=C0-X_Flz4C8.

Beam, Christopher. "Hellish Copters: Why are choppers always crashing?" *Slate*, October 30, 2009. https://slate.com/news-and-politics/2009/10/why-are-helicopters-always-crashing.html.

Berge, Paul. "Rudders? We Don't Need No Stinkin' Rudders." AVweb.com. June 30, 2019. https://www.avweb.com/insider/rudders-we-dont-need-no-stinkin-rudders/.

Benson, Gene. "Deadly Turn – Base Leg to Final Approach." December 20, 2015. Educational video, 4:55. https://www.youtube.com/watch?v=3gKx2eh0urg.

Bill4LE Aviation. "Why Add Live ATC to Microsoft Flight Simulator 2020? (PilotEdge.net)." September 4, 2020. Educational video, 58:51. https://

www.youtube.com/watch?v=R6K6QAP9Ahs.

Borrows, David A. "Rotor RPM: Putting the Right Spin on It." AOPA.org. March 5, 1998. https://www.aopa.org/news-and-media/all-news/1998/march/flight-training-magazine/rotor-rpm.

Bousono, Carlos. "Pattern Primer: Essential Tools to Flying the Traffic Pattern." AOPA.org. January 1, 2017. https://www.aopa.org/news-and-media/all-news/2017/january/flight-training-magazine/pattern-primer.

Boyne, Walter J. *Dawn Over Kitty Hawk: The Novel of the Wright Brothers.* New York: Forge Books, 2005.

Boyne, Walter J. *The Leading Edge.* New York: Stewart, Tabori & Chang, 1986.

Boyne, Walter J., and Philip Handleman. *The 25 Most Influential Aircraft of All Time.* Guilford, CT: Lyons Press, 2018.

Briney, Amanda. "How Are Nautical Miles Measured?" ThoughtCo.com. April 10, 2019. https://www.thoughtco.com/what-are-nautical-miles-1435097.

Buck, Rinker. *Flight of Passage: A Memoir.* New York: Hyperion, 1998.

Cape Copters. "Retreating Blade Stall – Helicopter Ground School." February 15, 2021. Educational video, 4:23. https://www.youtube.com/watch?v=9ui6sVaKE_M.

Captain Joe. "AIRBUS HYDRAULIC SYSTEM how does it work?" July 6, 2017. Educational video, 7:29. https://www.youtube.com/watch?v=k5wNKAhCtyw.

Captain Joe. "How does FLY-BY-WIRE Work? The Future of Flight Controls!" January 14, 2021. Educational video, 13:40. https://www.youtube.com/watch?v=sqWCnsTieTU.

Captain Joe. "WING & ENGINE Anti-Ice Systems!" November 2, 2017. Educational video, 9:12. https://www.youtube.com/watch?v=K7R0wzM2y6M.

Center for Wilderness Safety. "Oxygen Levels at Altitude." https://wildsafe.org/resources/ask/altitude-safety/oxygen-levels/.

Chiles, James R. *The God Machine.* New York: Bantam Books, 2007.

Ciolac, Alin. "Why do aircraft use cabin pressurization." Honeywell

Aerospace. https://aerospace.honeywell.com/us/en/about-us/blogs/why-do-aircraft-use-cabin-pressurization.

Clark, James. "United CEO complains that the US military isn't training enough pilots for airlines to poach." Taskandpurpose.com. June 23, 2021. https://taskandpurpose.com/news/united-ceo-military-not-training-enough-pilots/.

CNBC International. "This invention changed flying forever / CNBC Reports." July 17, 2019. Broadcast video, 8:42. https://www.youtube.com/watch?v=5mYkS8A88Tk.

Collins, Mike. "How It Works: Marking Time." AOPA.org. September 1, 2018. https://www.aopa.org/news-and-media/all-news/2018/september/flight-training-magazine/how-it-works-hobbs-meter.

Craig, Paul. *The Killing Zone: How and Why Pilots Die*. Second Edition. New York: McGraw Hill, 2013.

Cummins, Nicholas. "How Dangerous Are Bird Strikes?" SimpleFlying.com. August 12, 2020. https://simpleflying.com/bird-strikes-danger/.

Cutler, Colin. "How A Constant Speed Propeller Works." Boldmethod.com. December 19, 2017. https://www.boldmethod.com/learn-to-fly/aircraft-systems/how-a-constant-speed-prop-works/.

Cutler, Colin. "How the Dihedral Keeps Your Wings Level." Boldmethod.com. May 5, 2015. https://www.boldmethod.com/learn-to-fly/aerodynamics/dihedral-keeping-your-wings-level/.

Culter, Colin. "The Four Steps of Spin Recovery, Explained." Boldmethod.com. December 14, 2021. https://www.boldmethod.com/learn-to-fly/maneuvers/the-four-steps-of-spin-recovery-explained-pare-fly-it-safely-to-recovery/.

Cutler, Colin. "Why Does Stall Speed Increase With Bank Angle?" Boldmethod.com. February 26, 2022. https://www.boldmethod.com/learn-to-fly/aerodynamics/why-does-aircraft-stall-speed-increase-with-bank-angle-aerodynamically-load/.

Deighton, Len. *Bomber*. London: Harper, 1970.

Deziel, Chris. "The Differences Between Kerosene & Jet Fuel." Itstillruns.

com. March 8, 2019. https://itstillruns.com/the-differences-between-kerosene-jet-fuel-12003828.html.

Encyclopedia Britannica. "Daniel Bernoulli." March 13, 2022. https://www.britannica.com/biography/Daniel-Bernoulli#ref200813.

Engstrom, Paul. "The Road Back After Heart Problems." Iflyamerica.org. https://iflyamerica.org/the_road_back.asp.

Epilepsy Foundation. "Pilot and Other Airline Positions." https://www.epilepsy.com/living-epilepsy/independent-living/employment/safety-sensitive-jobs/pilot-and-other-airline-positions.

Finer Points, The. "Operation 'Use More Rudder' – Learning to Fly With Rudder." April 12, 2019. Educational video, 14:42. https://www.youtube.com/watch?v=0L4oKP5xv-8.

Flight-club. "Adverse yaw explained in simple terms." February 16, 2021. Educational video, 4:03. https://www.youtube.com/watch?v=D9cIof2O6Mc.

Gibb, Randall W. "Visual Spatial Disorientation: Re-Visiting the Black Hole Illusion." *Aviation, Space, and Environmental Medicine* 78, no. 8 (August 2007). https://citeseerx.ist.psu.edu/viewdoc/download?doi=10.1.1.938.6343&rep=rep1&type=pdf.

Gleim Aviation. "The Blue Lever." https://www.gleimaviation.com/2020/04/27/the-blue-lever/.

Groom, Winston. *The Aviators: Eddie Rickenbacker, Jimmy Doolittle, Charles Lindbergh, and the Epic Age of Flight.* Washington, DC: National Geographic, 2015.

GVad The Pilot. "Landing on the Centerline – Flying Tips (MSFS)." July 20, 2010. Educational video, 5:36. https://www.youtube.com/watch?v=qX9ZI0xDFE4.

GVad The Pilot. "VOR Navigation Tutorial (Part I) – MSFS." December 3, 2009. Educational video, 8:34. https://www.youtube.com/watch?v=f67low6D-T0.

Hampton, Dan. *Chasing the Demon: A Secret History of the Quest for the Sound Barrier and the Band of American Aces Who Conquered It.* New York:

William Morrow, 2018.

Hampton, Dan. *The Flight: Charles Lindbergh's Daring and Immortal 1927 Transatlantic Crossing*. New York: William Morrow, 2017.

Hartzell Propeller. "Pilot Safety: Know What's in Your Tank." August 12, 2019. https://hartzellprop.com/know-whats-in-your-tank/.

Hayes, Michael D. *Private Pilot Oral Exam Guide*. 12th Edition. Newcastle, WA: Aviation Supplies & Academics, 2020.

Hayward, Justin. "The Miracle on the Hudson – The Full Story." SimpleFlying.com, April 15, 2021. https://simpleflying.com/the-miracle-on-the-hudson/.

Hayward, Justin. "What Is a Nautical Mile and Why Do We Use Them?" SimpleFlying.com. November 22, 2021. https://simpleflying.com/nautical-miles/.

Helicopter Lessons in 10 Minutes of Less. "Compensation for Dissymmetry of Lift in Helicopters." June 6, 2017. Educational video, 6:31. https://www.youtube.com/watch?v=culBbvszRpk.

Helicopter Lessons in 10 Minutes of Less. "Dissymmetry of Lift in Helicopters." June 3, 2017. Educational video, 5:21. https://www.youtube.com/watch?v=Cv74zHSLQ7A.

Helicopter Lessons in 10 Minutes of Less. "Retreating Blade Stall/VNE in Helicopters." July 14, 2018. Educational video, 9:41. https://www.youtube.com/watch?v=wZ0WIwrKSz8.

Helicopter Lessons in 10 Minutes of Less. "Types of Rotor Systems in Helicopters." January 19, 2018. Educational video, 8:41. https://www.youtube.com/watch?v=7gM3rMDpJt4.

Helicopter Online Ground School. "Low Rotor RPM and Blade Stall Helicopter Ground School Online." January 18, 2014. Educational video, 2:15. https://www.youtube.com/watch?v=ID8aeLqZS5A.

Helicopter Online Ground School. "Low Rotor RPM Blade Stall Accident Review." November 14, 2017. Educational video, 53:56. https://www.youtube.com/watch?v=ws_Vg02AwM4.

Hise, Phaedra. "How The Wright Brothers Blew It." *Forbes*, November

19, 2003. https://www.forbes.com/2003/11/19/1119aviation.html?sh=1ca007541bda.

History Channel. "Douglas Bader: The Double-Amputee Flying Ace of the Battle of Britain." https://www.history.co.uk/articles/douglas-bader-the-double-amputee-flying-ace-of-the-battle-of-britain.

Hoffman, Paul. *Wings of Madness: Alberto Santos-Dumont and the Invention of Flight*. New York: Theia, 2003.

Holliday, Shelby. "The 2013 FAA Rule That's Being Blamed for Today's Pilot Shortage." *Wall Street Journal*, December 21, 2021. Video, 7:07. https://www.youtube.com/watch?v=hmn7rquuzoI.

Hollman, Cyndy. "Leaning the Airplane (Private Pilot Lesson 2b)." April 29, 2018. Educational video, 8:11. https://www.youtube.com/watch?v=eR8Rig917z4.

Holthouse, Jerry. "Don McLean Reflects on the Tragic Inspiration Behind 'American Pie.'" Nashville.com. January 30, 2019. https://www.nashville.com/don-mclean-reflects-on-the-tragic-inspiration-behind-american-pie/.

Inside Edition. "Pilot Jessica Cox on Inside Edition." November 29, 2008. News video, 3:02. https://www.youtube.com/watch?v=b2IqpPSF9-U.

Interesting Engineering. "What happens when birds fly into airplane engines?" December 2, 2021. Educational video, 4:45. https://www.youtube.com/watch?v=619fct0KTPI.

JxJ Aviation. "Understanding Airplane's Longitudinal, Lateral & Directional Stability and the Need for Stabilizers." April 13, 2020. Educational video, 5:30. https://www.youtube.com/watch?v=uReN2Nd1yuo.

Johnson, Herbert A. "The Wright Patents and Early American Aviation." *Journal of Air Law and Commerce* 69, no. 1 (2004). https://scholar.smu.edu/cgi/viewcontent.cgi?article=1683&context=jalc.

Johnson, Tony. "Nautical Terminator – Nautical Mile." TradeWindsSailing.com. December 2, 2019. https://tradewindssailing.com/wordpress/?p=772.

Jones, Jamie. "Jessica Cox Flies in the Face of Challenges." *Smithsonian*

Magazine, March 4, 2021. https://www.smithsonianmag.com/blogs/smithsonian-affiliations/2021/03/04/jessica-cox-flies-face-challenges/.

Josephs, Leslie. "The last fatal US airline crash was a decade ago. Here's why our skies are safer." CNBC. February 13, 2019. https://www.cnbc.com/2019/02/13/colgan-air-crash-10-years-ago-reshaped-us-aviation-safety.html.

Korda, Michael. *With Wings Like Eagles: The Untold Story of the Battle of Britain*. New York: Harper Perennial, 2002.

KujoClips. "Leaning mixture with a constant speed prop." November 23, 2017. Educational video, 10:14. https://www.youtube.com/watch?v=N-OyeLKhq8k.

Landsberg, Bruce. "Safety Pilot Landmark Accident: The Day the Music Died." AOPA.org. February 1, 2009. https://www.aopa.org/news-and-media/all-news/2009/february/01/safety-pilot-landmark-accidents-the-day-the-music-died.

Langewiesche, Wolfgang. *Stick and Rudder: An Explanation of the Art of Flying*. New York: McGraw Hill, 1990.

Lawson, Ted W. *Thirty Seconds Over Tokyo*. New York: Pocket Star Books, 2002.

Learmount, David. "AOPA examines why 80% of student pilots drop out of training." FlightGlobal.com. February 25, 2011. https://www.flightglobal.com/aopa-examines-why-80-of-student-pilots-drop-out-of-training/98562.article.

Leishman, J. Gordon. "A History of Helicopter Flight." 2000. https://itlims-zsis.meil.pw.edu.pl//pomoce/WTLK/ENG/Sup/A_History_of_Helicopter_Flight.pdf.

Liebermann, Oren. "FAA to allow pilots with diabetes to fly commercial jets." CNN. October 31, 2019. https://www.cnn.com/2019/10/31/politics/faa-pilots-diabetes/index.html.

Ludovic, Andre. "'Black Hole' Approach." Smartcockpit.com. https://www.smartcockpit.com/docs/The_Black_Hole_Approach.pdf.

Lundgren, Miles. "TRSA Airspace: Everything You Need to Know." AirplaneAcademy.com, https://airplaneacademy.com/trsa-airspace-everything-you-need-to-know/.

Machado, Rod. "The Runway Expansion Effect." April 4, 2017. Educational video, 13:14. https://www.youtube.com/watch?v=9JfoZERqM7Q.

Mark, Rob. "How the Cirrus Combined Throttle/Prop Control Works." *Flying*, March 26, 2018. https://www.flyingmag.com/how-cirrus-combined-throttle-prop-control-works/.

McCauley, Kerry. *Ferry Pilot: Nine Lives Over the North Atlantic*. Middletown, DE, 2020.

McLanahan, David. "Open Door in Flight." AOPA.org. https://www.aopa.org/training-and-safety/students/solo/skills/open-door-in-flight.

National Business Aviation Association. "Business Aviation Insider: Mental Health Vital in Fitness for Duty." August 26, 2019. https://nbaa.org/aircraft-operations/safety/human-factors/mental-health-duty/.

National Postal Museum, Smithsonian. "The Suicide Club." https://postalmuseum.si.edu/the-suicide-club.

New York Times. "Col. Ocker is Dead; Aviation Inventor." September 18, 1942. https://timesmachine.nytimes.com/timesmachine/1942/09/18/85591260.html?pageNumber=22.

Noclip. "How Microsoft Flight Simulator Recreated Our Entire Planet." November 26, 2020. Educational video, 34:35. https://www.youtube.com/watch?v=0w7q1ZFfsxs.

Olson, Lynne. *Those Angry Days: Roosevelt, Lindbergh, and America's Fight Over World War II, 1939-1941*. New York: Random House, 2013.

Pallini, Thomas. "US airlines are combating the pilot shortage by raising pay, lowering requirements, and hiring from Australia," Business Insider. January 17, 2022. https://www.businessinsider.com/airlines-respond-to-pilot-shortage-higher-pay-lower-requirements-2022-1.

Peralta, Lina. "The importance of English language proficiency in aviation." Unitingaviation.com. November 12, 2021. https://unitingaviation.com/news/safety/the-importance-of-english-language-proficiency-in-aviation/.

Perdue, Scott. "Accident Review The Day the Music Died." FlyWire.

November 15, 2020. Educational video, 17:13. https://www.youtube.com/watch?v=hmn7rquuzoI.

Petzinger, Thomas Jr. *Hard Landing: The Epic Contest for Power and Profits That Plunged the Airlines into Chaos.* New York: Times Books, 1996.

Pilot Institute. "Women Pilot Statistics: Female Representation in Aviation." February 22, 2022. https://pilotinstitute.com/women-aviation-statistics/.

Pilot Nancy. "1500 Hour Rule Making It Harder To Become An Airline Pilot?" September 1, 2021. Educational video, 9:50. https://www.youtube.com/watch?v=A4FnTejkDtA.

Pilot Nancy. "Entry Level Pilot Jobs // Low Time Pilot Jobs." July 24, 2020. Educational video, 10:47. https://www.youtube.com/watch?v=Vmq5LJdu0N4.

Pilot Nancy. "United States Pilot Shortage Real in 2021?" October 3, 2021. Educational video, 6:01. https://www.youtube.com/watch?v=TZivnUNhksk.

Pilot Pro Academy. "60,000 Pilots Short | Post-COVID Pilot Shortage." July 3, 2021. Educational video, 5:48. https://www.youtube.com/watch?v=uZTkbeQMgBg.

Pisano, Dominick. "Wiley Post." Smithsonian Air and Space Museum. July 22, 2010. https://airandspace.si.edu/stories/editorial/wiley-post.

Powers, Rod. "Vision Requirements to Become a Military Pilot/Navigator." Thebalancecareers.com. January 8, 2019. https://www.thebalancecareers.com/vision-requirements-to-become-a-military-pilot-navigator-3332649.

Prichard, J. Laurence. *Sir George Cayley: The Inventor of the Aeroplane.* London: Max Parrish, 1961.

Purificato, Rudy. "Ocker, pioneer of 'blind flying.'" https://www.earlyaviators.com/eocker1.htm.

Pusey, Alexander. "Jan. 13, 1914: Wright brothers awarded patent on flying machine." ABAJournal.com. December 1, 2020. https://www.abajournal.com/magazine/article/wright-brothers-awarded-patent-on-flying-machine.

Pylypciw, Luke. "Should You Go To College For Aviation?" September 5, 2020. Educational video, 10:52. https://www.youtube.com/watch?v=tgnkroj_bxI.

RevelatorAlf. "What is rotor blade flapping?" December 21, 2017. Educational video, 2:54. https://www.youtube.com/watch?v=j_dfyBORSFo.

Reuters. "Chronology of the Crash of John F. Kennedy Jr.'s Plane." *New York Times*, July 19, 1999. https://archive.nytimes.com/www.nytimes.com/library/national/regional/071999kennedy-crash-timeline.html.

Ridley, Jonathan. "Leonardo da Vinci's helicopter: 15th-century flight of fancy led to modern aeronautics." The Conversation. May 3, 2019. https://theconversation.com/leonardo-da-vincis-helicopter-15th-century-flight-of-fancy-led-to-modern-aeronautics-116241.

Rigby, Sara. "How much horsepower does a horse have?" BBC Science Focus. December 5, 2020. https://www.sciencefocus.com/science/how-much-horsepower-does-a-horse-have/.

Rogoway, Tyler. "The Bird Strike Reminds Us It Doesn't Take a Missile to Down a Fighter." The War Zone. November 7, 2016. https://www.thedrive.com/the-war-zone/5892/this-bird-strike-reminds-us-it-doesnt-take-a-missile-to-down-a-fighter.

Sailing Saltwater Lanai. "Simple Way to Determine Aircraft Position Using a VOR, CDI, and OBS." December 20, 2018. Educational video, 8:27. https://www.youtube.com/watch?v=jrQ21zKjlVg.

Saint-Exupéry, Antoine de. *Wind, Sand and Stars*. Orlando: Harcourt Inc., 1939.

Schappert, Jason. "Don't Flare on Landings." MzeroA Flight Training. August 18, 2020. Educational video, 7:23. https://www.youtube.com/watch?v=0bOEiR6JuXY.

Schappert, Jason. "Help! I'm Landing Left of Center!?" MzeroA Flight Training. March 16, 2015. Educational video, 4:30. https://www.youtube.com/watch?v=iXubLPB9rEE.

Schappert, Jason. "Hypoxia – Aeromedical Factors – Day 14." MzeroA Flight Training. January 14, 2013. Educational video, 3:40. https://www.

youtube.com/watch?v=b_zSdpLCeAY.

Schappert, Jason. "JFK Jr Accident Analysis." MzeroA Flight Training. January 21, 2016. Educational video, 33:25. https://www.youtube.com/watch?v=PqnTA7KQFYE.

Schappert, Jason. "Master Landings With Jason Schappert." MzeroA Flight Training. April 6, 2021. Educational video, 22:46. https://www.youtube.com/watch?v=JSQxVe0H3JE.

Schappert, Jason. "Proper Spin Recovery." MzeroA Flight Training. September 22, 2015. Educational video, 6:21. https://www.youtube.com/watch?v=52tPNkBcfmg.

Schappert, Jason. "The Perfect Traffic Pattern." MzeroA Flight Training. August 11, 2020. Educational video, 4:45. https://www.youtube.com/watch?v=ac5c8nXSO0s.

Scott, Phil. "Crappy runways." Air Facts. April 18, 2012. https://airfactsjournal.com/2012/04/crappy-runways/.

Segarra, Marielle. "It's getting a lot more lucrative to become a pilot." Business Insider. December 28, 2017. https://www.businessinsider.com/its-getting-a-lot-more-lucrative-to-become-a-pilot-2017-12.

Shulman, Seth. *Unlocking the Sky: Glenn Hammond Curtiss and the Race to Invest the Airplane.* New York: Harper Perennial, 2002.

Silberman, Warren. "Disqualifying Psychological Conditions and Your Medical." January 12, 2015. https://pilot-protection-services.aopa.org/news/2015/january/12/the-medical-certification-of-the-five.

Silberman, Warren. "How Can Kidney Stones Impact Your Medical Certificate?" March 15, 2016. https://pilot-protection-services.aopa.org/news/2016/march/15/the-faa-and-kidney-stones.

Silk, Robert. "How the 1,500-hour rule created a pilot shortage." *Travel Weekly*, August 18, 2017. https://www.travelweekly.com/Robert-Silk/How-1500-hour-rule-created-pilot-shortage.

Skybrary. "Full Authority Digital Engine Control (FADEC)." https://skybrary.aero/articles/full-authority-digital-engine-control-fadec.

Smith, Oliver. "Introducing the most popular plane ever built." *The Telegraph*,

December 13, 2017. https://www.telegraph.co.uk/travel/comment/introducing-the-most-popular-plane-ever-built/.

Spoonts, Sean. "How High-Octane Gasoline Saved Untold Allied Pilots During WWII." Sofrep.com. November 5, 2021. https://sofrep.com/news/filler-up-how-high-octane-gasoline-saved-untold-allied-pilots-during-wwii/.

Squirrel. "Tutorial #9 – Autopilot Basics – Microsoft Flight Simulator." August 25, 2020. Educational video, 29:18. https://www.youtube.com/watch?v=7FizDT608bw.

Squirrel. "Tutorial #10 – How to set Mixture – Microsoft Flight Simulator." September 5, 2020. Educational video, 22:35. https://www.youtube.com/watch?v=8AGv8kSZTHQ.

Sterling, Bryan B., and Frances Sterling. *Forgotten Eagle: Wiley Post, America's Heroic Aviation Pioneer.* New York: Carroll & Graf, 2001.

Stone, Alex. *CFI! The Book: A Satirical Aviation Comedy.* Highland, IN: AWS Books, 2018.

Stromberg, Joseph. "Water really does swirl the other way in Australia." Vox, June 3, 2015. https://www.vox.com/2015/6/3/8723183/coriolis-effect-toilet-australia.

The Sim Pilot. "Microsoft Flight Simulator 2020 / G1000 Tutorial / Episode #1 / Basic Functions." August 27, 2020. Educational video, 30:55. https://www.youtube.com/watch?v=KJGrLb3EmvU.

The Trust. "Sea Breeze and land Breezes." March 27, 2020. Educational video, 1:42. https://www.youtube.com/watch?v=dN2SB2Jg77o.

Thomson, Greg. "8 Reasons Why Working As a Cargo Pilot Can Improve Your Career." Pilotjobcentral.com. June 1, 2018. https://pilotjobcentral.com/8-reasons-why-working-as-a-cargo-pilot-might-be-for-you/.

Thrust Flight Academy. "4 Year University Vs. Accelerated Flight School." July 30, 2020. Educational video, 4:00. https://www.youtube.com/watch?v=7T35-5oRKsM.

TotalEnergies. "The ultimate guide to jet and aviation fuel." November 18, 2019. https://services.totalenergies.uk/ultimate-guide-jet-aviation-fuel.

Trainor, Sean. "The Wright Brothers: Pioneers of Patent Trolling." *Time*, November 17, 2015. https://time.com/4143574/wright-brothers-patent-trolling/.

Truly. "Limb-itless: Pilot Born Without Arms Defies All Odds." June 29, 2015. Educational video, 5:41. https://www.youtube.com/watch?v=3g1ccsdMM0g.

Twombly, Ian J. "Aerodynamics: Nothing But a Number, A Closer Look at Stall Speed." AOPA.org. March 1, 2020. https://www.aopa.org/news-and-media/all-news/2020/march/flight-training-magazine/aerodynamics-stall-speed.

U.S. Department of Commerce, National Oceanic and Atmospheric Administration (NOAA). "History of the SARSAT program." https://www.sarsat.noaa.gov/history-of-the-sarsat-program/.

U.S. Department of Transportation, Bureau of Transportation Statistics. "U.S. General Aviation Safety Data." https://www.bts.gov/content/us-general-aviationa-safety-data.

U.S. Department of Transportation, Federal Aviation Administration. "Airmen Knowledge Test Statistics." https://www.faa.gov/data_research/aviation_data_statistics/test_statistics/.

U.S. Department of Transportation, Federal Aviation Administration. *Airplane Flying Handbook*, FAA-H-8083-3B. Washington, DC, 2016.

U.S. Department of Transportation, Federal Aviation Administration. *Commercial Pilot – Airplane Airman Certification Standards*, FAA-S-ACS-7A (with Change 1). Washington, DC, June 2018.

U.S. Department of Transportation, Federal Aviation Administration. "Controlled Flight into Terrain." https://www.faa.gov/news/safety_briefing/2018/media/SE_Topic_18-11.pdf.

U.S. Department of Transportation, Federal Aviation Administration. *FAR/AIM: Federal Aviation Regulations/Aeronautical Information Manual 2022*. Washington, DC, 2021.

U.S. Department of Transportation, Federal Aviation Administration. "ENR 1.15 Medical Facts for Pilots." https://www.faa.gov/air_traffic/

publications/atpubs/aip_html/part2_enr_section_1.15.html.

U.S. Department of Transportation, Federal Aviation Administration. "Pilot/Controller Glossary Basic with Change 1." December 2, 2021. https://www.faa.gov/air_traffic/publications/media/pcg_change_1_dtd_12-2-21.pdf.

U.S. Department of Transportation, Federal Aviation Administration. "Pilot Mental Fitness." June 9, 2016.

U.S. Department of Transportation, Federal Aviation Administration. *Pilot's Handbook of Aeronautical Knowledge*, FAA-H-8083-25B. Washington, DC, 2016.

U.S. Department of Transportation, Federal Aviation Administration. *Private Pilot – Airplane Airman Certification Standards*, FAA-S-ACS-6B (with Change 1). Washington, DC, June 2018.

U.S. Department of Transportation, Federal Aviation Administration. "U.S. Civil Airmen Statistics." https://www.faa.gov/data_research/aviation_data_statistics/civil_airmen_statistics/.

U.S. Department of Transportation, Federal Aviation Administration. "Wildlife Strike FAQs." https://www.faa.gov/airports/airport_safety/wildlife/faq/.

U.S. Department of Transportation, Federal Aviation Administration. "Wildlife Strikes to Civil Aircraft in the United States, 1990-2020." July 2021. https://www.faa.gov/airports/airport_safety/wildlife/media/Wildlife-Strike-Report-1990-2020.pdf.

U.S. National Transportation Safety Board. "Flying on Empty." Safety Alert, August 2017. https://www.ntsb.gov/Advocacy/safety-alerts/Documents/SA-067.pdf.

U.S. National Archives and Records Administration. "Ice Formation on Aircraft." ARC Identifier 75096, Local Identifier 428-MN-9487A. 1960. https://archive.org/details/gov.archives.arc.75096.

VASAviation. "Diamond DA-40 Busts into Presidential Restricted Area near Philadelphia, PA." September 7, 2021. https://www.youtube.com/watch?v=BZXKXWLWcec.

Verhovek, Sam Howe. *Jet Age: The Comet, the 707, and the Race to Shrink the World*. New York: Avery, 2010.

Vermuelen, Jan. "Computing power: Apple II vs iPhone5s, IBM PC vs Galaxy S5." Mybroadband.co.za. April 22, 2014. https://mybroadband.co.za/news/hardware/101004-computing-power-apple-ii-vs-iphone-5s-ibm-pc-vs-galaxy-s5.html.

vsTerminus. "DCS Mi-8: Retreating Blade Stall Tutorial." April 25, 2020. Educational video, 20:47. https://www.youtube.com/watch?v=PU3AIU8Sqxw.

Walsh, Amelia. "New Protocols for Pilots with Insulin-Treated Diabetes." AOPA.org. November 7, 2019. https://www.aopa.org/news-and-media/all-news/2019/november/07/new-protocols-for-pilots-with-insulin-treated-diabetes.

Warren, Chris. "Compression Ratio and Octane Ratings: What You Need to Know." How Stuff Works. February 10, 2021. https://auto.howstuffworks.com/compression-ratio-octane-ratings.htm.

Wendover Productions. "Why the World is Running Out of Pilots." October 2, 2018. Educational video, 11:35. https://www.youtube.com/watch?v=cognzTud3Wg.

We Are the Mighty. "Amputation couldn't keep these pilots out of the skies." March 31, 2018. https://www.wearethemighty.com/mighty-trending/amputation-couldnt-keep-these-pilots-out-of-the-skies/.

Williamson, Claire. "I'm surprised amputees are allowed to fly, pilot admits." *Belfast Telegraph*, August 15, 2014. https://www.belfasttelegraph.co.uk/news/northern-ireland/im-surprised-amputees-are-allowed-to-fly-admits-pilot-30510343.html.

ZeroByteInFlight. "Right Rudder! – A humorous analysis of my landing technique." April 12, 2014. Educational video, 3:39. https://www.youtube.com/watch?v=SEjNi1vPbuA.

Endnotes

1. Jamiel Lynch, Dakin Andone, and Pete Muntean, "A passenger with no flying experience landed a plane at a Florida airport after the pilot became incapacitated," CNN, May 11, 2022, https://www.cnn.com/travel/article/florida-passenger-lands-plane/index.html.

2. Jan Vermuelen, "Computing power: Apple II vs iPhone5s, IBM PC vs Galaxy S5," Mybroadband.co.za, April 22, 2014, https://mybroadband.co.za/news/hardware/101004-computing-power-apple-ii-vs-iphone-5s-ibm-pc-vs-galaxy-s5.html.

3. Jacob Ridley, "Microsoft Flight Simulator expected to generate $2.6B in PC hardware sales in 3 years," *PC Gamer*, August 21, 2020, https://www.pcgamer.com/microsoft-flight-simulator-expected-to-generate-dollar26b-in-pc-hardware-sales-in-3-years/.

4. Squirrel, "Tutorial #10 – How to set Mixture – Microsoft Flight Simulator," September 5, 2020, educational video, 22:35, https://www.youtube.com/watch?v=8AGv8kSZTHQ.

5. Oliver Smith, "Introducing the most popular plane ever built," *The Telegraph*, December 13, 2017, https://www.telegraph.co.uk/travel/comment/introducing-the-most-popular-plane-ever-built/.

6. Flying Magazine, "How Old Do You Have to Be to Fly a Plane?," May 25, 2022, https://www.flyingmag.com/guides/how-old-do-you-have-to-be-to-fly-a-plane/.

7. Lina Peralta, "The importance of English language proficiency in aviation," Unitingaviation.com, November 12, 2021, https://unitingaviation.com/news/safety/the-importance-of-english-language-proficiency-in-aviation/.

8. Earl Downs, "Sport Pilot and Man on the Moon: The Story of the Sport Pilot Rules," https://www.goldenageaviation.com/up-with-downs and Aero-news.net; and "Whenever Someone Talks About 'The Good Old Days' of Anything, It's Always

a Matter of Perspective and Personal Preference," http://www.aero-news.net/index.cfm?do=main.ajTextPost&id=5f37d641-f11c-4fae-a4ee-5e8d0d83507a.

9   U.S. Department of Transportation, Federal Aviation Administration, "U.S. Civil Airmen Statistics," https://www.faa.gov/data_research/aviation_data_statistics/civil_airmen_statistics/.

10 U.S. Department of Transportation, Federal Aviation Administration, "Airmen Knowledge Test Statistics," https://www.faa.gov/data_research/aviation_data_statistics/test_statistics/.

11 David Learmount, "AOPA examines why 80% of student pilots drop out of training," FlightGlobal.com, February 25, 2011, https://www.flightglobal.com/aopa-examines-why-80-of-student-pilots-drop-out-of-training/98562.article.

12 Warren Silberman, "How Can Kidney Stones Impact Your Medical Certificate?," March 15, 2016, https://pilot-protection-services.aopa.org/news/2016/march/15/the-faa-and-kidney-stones.

13 Rod Powers, "Vision Requirements to Become a Military Pilot/Navigator," The Balance Careers, January 8, 2019, https://www.thebalancecareers.com/vision-requirements-to-become-a-military-pilot-navigator-3332649; and U.S. Air Force, "How to Become a Pilot: Frequency Asked Questions," https://www.airforce.com/careers/detail/pilot.

14 Powers, "Vision Requirements."

15 Aircraft Owners and Pilots Association, "Vision: Monocular Vision," April 2016, https://www.aopa.org/go-fly/medical-resources/health-conditions/vision/monocular-vision.

16 Bryan B. Sterling, and Frances Sterling, *Forgotten Eagle: Wiley Post, America's Heroic Aviation Pioneer* (New York: Carroll & Graf, 2001), pp. 53–54, 64–65.

17 Sterling, *Forgotten Eagle*, p. 73.

18 Dominick Pisano, "Wiley Post," Smithsonian Air and Space Museum, July 22, 2010, https://airandspace.si.edu/stories/editorial/wiley-post.

19 U.S. Department of Transportation, Federal Aviation Administration, "ENR 1.15 Medical Facts for Pilots," https://www.faa.gov/air_traffic/publications/atpubs/aip_html/part2_enr_section_1.15.html.

20 Epilepsy Foundation, "Pilot and Other Airline Positions," https://www.epilepsy.com/living-epilepsy/independent-living/employment/safety-sensitive-jobs/pilot-and-other-airline-positions.

21 Paul Engstrom, "The Road Back After Heart Problems," I Fly America, https://iflyamerica.org/the_road_back.asp.

22 National Business Aviation Association, "Business Aviation Insider: Mental Health Vital in Fitness for Duty," August 26, 2019, https://nbaa.org/aircraft-operations/safety/human-factors/mental-health-duty/.

23 Warren Silberman, "Disqualifying Psychological Conditions and Your Medical," January 12, 2015, https://pilot-protection-services.aopa.org/news/2015/january/12/the-medical-certification-of-the-five.

24 Amelia Walsh, "New Protocols for Pilots with Insulin-Treated Diabetes," AOPA.org, November 7, 2019, https://www.aopa.org/news-and-media/all-news/2019/november/07/new-protocols-for-pilots-with-insulin-treated-diabetes; and Oren Liebermann, "FAA to allow pilots with diabetes to fly commercial jets," CNN, October 31, 2019, https://www.cnn.com/2019/10/31/politics/faa-pilots-diabetes/index.html.

25 Claire Williamson, "I'm surprised amputees are allowed to fly, pilot admits," *Belfast Telegraph*, August 15, 2014, https://www.belfasttelegraph.co.uk/news/northern-ireland/im-surprised-amputees-are-allowed-to-fly-admits-pilot-30510343.html; and We Are the Mighty, "Amputation couldn't keep these pilots out of the skies," March 31, 2018, https://www.wearethemighty.com/mighty-trending/amputation-couldnt-keep-these-pilots-out-of-the-skies/.

26 Michael Korda, *With Wings Like Eagles: The Untold Story of the Battle of Britain* (New York: Harper Perennial, 2002), pp. 180–181.

27 History Channel, "Douglas Bader: The Double-Amputee Flying Ace of the Battle of Britain," https://www.history.co.uk/articles/douglas-bader-the-double-amputee-flying-ace-of-the-battle-of-britain.

28 Inside Edition, "Pilot Jessica Cox on Inside Edition," November 29, 2008, https://www.youtube.com/watch?v=b2IqpPSF9-U; Truly, "Limb-itless: Pilot Born Without Arms Defies All Odds," June 29, 2015, educational video, 5:41, https://www.youtube.com/watch?v=3g1ccsdMM0g; and Jamie Jones, "Jessica Cox Flies in the Face of Challenges," *Smithsonian Magazine*, March 4, 2021, https://www.smithsonianmag.com/blogs/smithsonian-affiliations/2021/03/04/jessica-cox-flies-face-challenges/.

29 Paul Berge, "Rudders? We Don't Need No Stinkin' Rudders," AVWeb.com, June 30, 2019, https://www.avweb.com/insider/rudders-we-dont-need-no-stinkin-rudders/.

30 Center for Wilderness Safety, "Oxygen Levels at Altitude," https://wildsafe.org/resources/ask/altitude-safety/oxygen-levels/.

31 Asheville Regional Airport, "Breathe easy in the clouds: aircraft pressurization 101," flyavi.com, February 16, 2017, https://flyavl.com/article/breathe-easy-clouds-aircraft-pressurization-101; and Alin Ciolac, "Why do aircraft use cabin pressurization," Honeywell Aerospace, https://aerospace.honeywell.com/us/en/about-us/blogs/why-do-aircraft-use-cabin-pressurization.

32 Jason Schappert, "Hypoxia – Aeromedical Factors – Day 14," MzeroA Flight Training, January 14, 2013, educational video, 3:40, https://www.youtube.com/watch?v=b_zSdpLCeAY.

33 Len Deighton, *Bomber* (London: Harper, 1970), pp. 378-381.

34 Famous Scientists, "Niels Bohr," Famous Scientists, December 19, 2015, www.famousscientists.org/niels-bohr/; and New World Encyclopedia, "Niels Bohr," https://www.newworldencyclopedia.org/entry/Niels_Bohr.

35 Stephen E Ambrose, *The Wild Blue: The Men and Boys Who Flew the B-24s Over Germany 1944-45* (New York: Simon & Schuster, 2001), p. 96.
36 James R. Chiles, *The God Machine* (New York: Bantam Books, 2007), p. 30.
37 Encyclopedia Britannica, "Daniel Bernoulli," March 13, 2022, https://www.britannica.com/biography/Daniel-Bernoulli#ref200813.
38 Wolfgang Langewiesche, *Stick and Rudder: An Explanation of the Art of Flying* (New York: McGraw Hill, 1990), pp. 7–8.
39 Langewiesche, *Stick and Rudder*, p. 9.
40 Langewiesche, *Stick and Rudder*, pp. 6, 9–11.
41 Langewiesche, *Stick and Rudder*, p. 15.
42 Walter J. Boyne, *The Leading Edge* (New York: Stewart, Tabori & Chang, 1986), p. 126.
43 Colin Cutler, "How A Constant Speed Propeller Works," Boldmethod.com, December 19, 2017, https://www.boldmethod.com/learn-to-fly/aircraft-systems/how-a-constant-speed-prop-works/.
44 Cutler, "Why Does Stall Speed Increase With Bank Angle?" BoldMethod.com, February 26, 2022, https://www.boldmethod.com/learn-to-fly/aerodynamics/why-does-aircraft-stall-speed-increase-with-bank-angle-aerodynamically-load/.
45 Gene Benson, "Deadly Turn – Base Leg to Final Approach," December 20, 2015, educational video, 4:55, https://www.youtube.com/watch?v=3gKx2eh0urg.
46 CNN, "Sudden shift in heavy cargo apparent cause of deadly 747 crash," June 3, 2013, news broadcast video, 2:22, https://www.youtube.com/watch?v=KCCy-ojQMcE.
47 Flight-club, "Adverse yaw explained in simple terms," February 16, 2021, educational video, 4:03, https://www.youtube.com/watch?v=D9cIof2O6Mc; and JxJ Aviation, "Understanding Airplane's Longitudinal, Lateral & Directional Stability and the Need for Stabilizers," April 13, 2020, educational video, 5:30, https://www.youtube.com/watch?v=uReN2Nd1yuo.
48 Langewiesche, *Stick and Rudder*, pp. 125–127.
49 Colin Cutler, "How the Dihedral Keeps Your Wings Level," Boldmethod.com, May 5, 2015; and Langewiesche, *Stick and Rudder*, pp. 125–127.
50 Langewiesche, *Stick and Rudder*, pp. 125–127.
51 Walter J Boyne, *Dawn Over Kitty Hawk: The Novel of the Wright Brothers* (New York: Forge Books, 2005), p. 42–44, 109–110, 140; and Boyne, *The Leading Edge*, pp. 18–19.
52 Boyne, *Dawn Over Kitty Hawk*, pp. 42, 128–130, 164–166.
53 Boyne, *Dawn Over Kitty Hawk*, pp. 42–44, 71, 108, 141, 146; and Boyne, Walter J., and Philip Handleman, *The 25 Most Influential Aircraft of All Time*, (Guilford, CT: Lyons Press, 2018), pp. 4–5.
54 Boyne, *Dawn Over Kitty Hawk*, pp. 42–43.

55 Shulman, Seth, *Unlocking the Sky: Glenn Hammond Curtiss and the Race to Invest the Airplane* (New York: Harper Perennial, 2002), p. 123.

56 Shulman, *Unlocking the Sky*, pp. 133, 160.

57 Boyne, *Dawn Over Kitty Hawk*, p. 323.

58 Shulman, *Unlocking the Sky*, pp. 159–160; and Dan Hampton, *Chasing the Demon: A Secret History of the Quest for the Sound Barrier and the Band of American Aces Who Conquered It* (New York: William Morrow, 2018), p. 47.

59 Shulman, *Unlocking the Sky*, pp. 177–178; and Hampton, *Chasing the Demon*, p. 48.

60 Shulman, *Unlocking the Sky*, pp. 205–206, 210–212, 223–224; Phaedra Hise, "How The Wright Brothers Blew It," *Forbes*, November 19, 2003, https://www.forbes.com/2003/11/19/1119aviation.html?sh=1ca007541bda; Sean Trainor, "The Wright Brothers: Pioneers of Patent Trolling," *Time*, November 17, 2015, https://time.com/4143574/wright-brothers-patent-trolling/; and Hampton, *Chasing the Demon*, p. 51.

61 Herbert A Johnson, "The Wright Patents and Early American Aviation," *Journal of Air Law and Commerce* 69, no. 1 (2004), https://scholar.smu.edu/cgi/viewcontent.cgi?article=1683&context=jalc; Alexander Pusey, "Jan. 13, 1914: Wright brothers awarded patent on flying machine," ABA Journal, December 1, 2020, https://www.abajournal.com/magazine/article/wright-brothers-awarded-patent-on-flying-machine; and Boyne, *The Leading Edge*, p. 38.

62 Boyne, *The Leading Edge*, p. 19.

63 Boyne, *Dawn Over Kitty Hawk*, pp. 295–296.

64 Langewiesche, *Stick and Rudder*, pp. 66, 68.

65 Langewiesche, *Stick and Rudder*, pp. 152–155.

66 Benson, "Deadly Turn."

67 Deighton, *Bomber*, p. 241; and Ambrose, *The Wild Blue*, pp. 21, 77.

68 Captain Joe, "AIRBUS HYDRAULIC SYSTEM how does it work?," July 6, 2017, educational video, 7:29, https://www.youtube.com/watch?v=k5wNKAhCtyw.

69 Captain Joe, "How does FLY-BY-WIRE Work? The Future of Flight Controls!," January 14, 2021, educational video, 13:40, https://www.youtube.com/watch?v=sqWCnsTieTU; and David Bellm, "Electric Jet – How the F-16 Became the World's First Fly-By-Wire Combat Aircraft," F-16.net, https://www.f-16.net/articles_article13.html.

70 The Air Combat Tutorial Library, "DCS F/A-18C #3 - Understanding 'On Speed' AoA," October 5, 2021, educational video, 14:02, https://www.youtube.com/watch?v=1XnLON9RkKk; Ravagetalon, "DCS World Tutorial – F/A-18C Hornet – On-Speed AoA and Landing," October 16, 2019, educational video, 15:12, https://www.youtube.com/watch?v=5JYf-AEOl_A; and Flight-Sim-Fan, "How To Maintain On Speed AOA In the DCS F-18 [Making The F/A-18C Easy]," August 13, 2018, educational video, 6:41, https://www.youtube.com/watch?v=hhXgnxNjzvc.

71 Langewiesche, *Stick and Rudder*, pp. 50–51.
72 Colin Culter, "The Four Steps of Spin Recovery, Explained," BoldMethod.com, December 14, 2021, https://www.boldmethod.com/learn-to-fly/maneuvers/the-four-steps-of-spin-recovery-explained-pare-fly-it-safely-to-recovery/; and Jason Schappert, "Proper Spin Recovery," MzeroA Flight Training, September 22, 2015, educational video, 6:21, https://www.youtube.com/watch?v=52tPNkBcfmg.
73 Schappert, "Proper Spin Recovery."
74 Boyne, *Dawn Over Kitty Hawk*, pp. 295–296.
75 Dan Hampton, *The Flight: Charles Lindbergh's Daring and Immortal 1927 Transatlantic Crossing* (New York: William Morrow, 2017), p. 138.
76 Gleim Aviation, "The Blue Lever," https://www.gleimaviation.com/2020/04/27/the-blue-lever/.
77 Rob Mark, "How the Cirrus Combined Throttle/Prop Control Works," *Flying*, March 26, 2018, https://www.flyingmag.com/how-cirrus-combined-throttle-prop-control-works/.
78 Skybrary, "Full Authority Digital Engine Control (FADEC)," https://skybrary.aero/articles/full-authority-digital-engine-control-fadec; and Gleim, "The Blue Lever."
79 Paul Hoffman, *Wings of Madness: Alberto Santos-Dumont and the Invention of Flight* (New York: Theia, 2003), pp. 3, 218.
80 Jonathan Parker, "Take To The Skies With These Luxury Pilot Watches," *Luxe Digital*, April 22, 2022, https://luxe.digital/lifestyle/style/best-pilot-watches/.
81 National Postal Museum, Smithsonian, "The Suicide Club," https://postalmuseum.si.edu/the-suicide-club.
82 Ted W Lawson, *Thirty Seconds Over Tokyo* (New York: Pocket Star Books, 2002).
83 CNBC International, "This invention changed flying forever / CNBC Reports," July 17, 2019, broadcast video, 8:42. https://www.youtube.com/watch?v=5mYkS8A88Tk.
84 Winston Groom, *The Aviators: Eddie Rickenbacker, Jimmy Doolittle, Charles Lindbergh, and the Epic Age of Flight* (Washington, DC: National Geographic, 2015), pp. 163–170.
85 Rudy Purificato, "Ocker, pioneer of 'blind flying,'" https://www.earlyaviators.com/eocker1.htm; and "Col. Ocker is Dead; Aviation Inventor," *New York Times*, September 18, 1942, https://timesmachine.nytimes.com/timesmachine/1942/09/18/85591260.html?pageNumber=22.
86 Thomas Petzinger Jr, *Hard Landing: The Epic Contest for Power and Profits That Plunged the Airlines into Chaos* (New York: Times Books, 1996), pp. 9–11.
87 Lynne Olson, *Those Angry Days: Roosevelt, Lindbergh, and America's Fight Over World War II, 1939-1941* (New York: Random House, 2013), p. xiv; and Groom, *The Aviators*, p. 177.
88 Groom, *The Aviators*, pp. 177–178.

89 Groom, *The Aviators*, pp. 178–179; and Petzinger, *Hard Landing*, p. 11.
90 Olson, *Those Angry Days*, p. xiv.
91 Bruce Landsberg, "Safety Pilot Landmark Accident: The Day the Music Died," AOPA.org, February 1, 2009, https://www.aopa.org/news-and-media/all-news/2009/february/01/safety-pilot-landmark-accidents-the-day-the-music-died; and Scott Perdue, "Accident Review The Day the Music Died," FlyWire, November 15, 2020, educational video, 17:13, https://www.youtube.com/watch?v=hmn7rquuzoI.
92 Perdue, "Accident Review The Day the Music Died."
93 Landsberg, "The Day the Music Died."
94 Landsberg, "The Day the Music Died."
95 Jerry Holthouse, "Don McLean Reflects on the Tragic Inspiration Behind 'American Pie,'" Nashville.com, January 30, 2019, https://www.nashville.com/don-mclean-reflects-on-the-tragic-inspiration-behind-american-pie/.
96 Landsberg, "The Day the Music Died."
97 Reuters, "Chronology of the Crash of John F. Kennedy Jr.'s Plane," *New York Times*, July 19, 1999, https://archive.nytimes.com/www.nytimes.com/library/national/regional/071999kennedy-crash-timeline.html.
98 Jason Schappert, "JFK Jr Accident Analysis," MzeroA Flight Training, January 21, 2016, educational video, 33:25, https://www.youtube.com/watch?v=PqnTA7KQFYE.
99 CNBC, "This invention changed flying forever."
100 Squirrel, "Tutorial #9 – Autopilot Basics – Microsoft Flight Simulator," August 25, 2020, educational video, 29:18, https://www.youtube.com/watch?v=7FizDT608bw.
101 Cecil Adams, "Is 'dead reckoning' short for 'deduced reckoning'?," Straightdope.com, November 21, 2002, https://www.straightdope.com/21343189/is-dead-reckoning-short-for-deduced-reckoning.
102 Hampton, *The Flight*, pp. 25–27.
103 Hampton, *The Flight*, p. 66.
104 Hampton, *The Flight*, p. 172; and Groom, *The Aviators*, p. 138.
105 Hampton, *The Flight*, pp. 188–190.
106 Tony Johnson, "Nautical Terminator – Nautical Mile," TradeWindsSailing.com, December 2, 2019, https://tradewindssailing.com/wordpress/?p=772.
107 Amanda Briney, "How Are Nautical Miles Measured?," ThoughtCo.com, April 10, 2019, https://www.thoughtco.com/what-are-nautical-miles-1435097.
108 Justin Hayward, "What Is a Nautical Mile and Why Do We Use Them?," SimpleFlying.com, November 22, 2021. https://simpleflying.com/nautical-miles/.
109 U.S. Department of Transportation, Federal Aviation Administration, "Controlled Flight into Terrain," https://www.faa.gov/news/safety_briefing/2018/media/SE_Topic_18-11.pdf.

110 Hampton, *The Flight*, p. 67.

111 The Trust, "Sea Breeze and land Breezes," March 27, 2020, educational video, 1:42, https://www.youtube.com/watch?v=dN2SB2Jg77o.

112 Joseph Stromberg, "Water really does swirl the other way in Australia," Vox, June 3, 2015, https://www.vox.com/2015/6/3/8723183/coriolis-effect-toilet-australia.

113 Storm Shield App, "Why are they called fronts?," December 7, 2015, educational video, 1:13, https://www.youtube.com/watch?v=BLIZT2MuV_c.

114 Kerry McCauley, *Ferry Pilot: Nine Lives Over the North Atlantic* (Middletown, DE, 2020), pp. 17–18.

115 U.S. National Archives and Records Administration, "Ice Formation on Aircraft," ARC Identifier 75096, Local Identifier 428-MN-9487A, 1960, https://archive.org/details/gov.archives.arc.75096.

116 Captain Joe, "WING & ENGINE Anti-Ice Systems!," November 2, 2017, educational video, 9:12, https://www.youtube.com/watch?v=K7R0wzM2y6M.

117 Sam Howe Verhovek, *Jet Age: The Comet, the 707, and the Race to Shrink the World* (New York: Avery, 2010), pp. 127, 135.

118 Ambrose, *The Wild Blue*, p. 177.

119 *The Martian*, directed by Ridley Scott (20th Century Fox, 2015).

120 Rigby, Sara. "How much horsepower does a horse have?" BBC Science Focus, December 5, 2020. https://www.sciencefocus.com/science/how-much-horsepower-does-a-horse-have/.

121 McCauley, *Ferry Pilot*, pp. 113–123.

122 Chris Warren, "Compression Ratio and Octane Ratings: What You Need to Know," How Stuff Works, February 10, 2021, https://auto.howstuffworks.com/compression-ratio-octane-ratings.htm.

123 Sean Spoonts, "How High-Octane Gasoline Saved Untold Allied Pilots During WWII," Sofrep.com, November 5, 2021, https://sofrep.com/news/filler-up-how-high-octane-gasoline-saved-untold-allied-pilots-during-wwii/; and Boyne, *The Leading Edge*, p. 126.

124 Chris Deziel, "The Differences Between Kerosene & Jet Fuel," Itstillruns.com, March 8, 2019, https://itstillruns.com/the-differences-between-kerosene-jet-fuel-12003828.html.

125 TotalEnergies, "The ultimate guide to jet and aviation fuel," November 18, 2019, https://services.totalenergies.uk/ultimate-guide-jet-aviation-fuel.

126 Hartzell Propeller, "Pilot Safety: Know What's in Your Tank," August 12, 2019, https://hartzellprop.com/know-whats-in-your-tank/.

127 Cyndy Hollman, "Leaning the Airplane (Private Pilot Lesson 2b)," April 29, 2018, educational video, 8:11, https://www.youtube.com/watch?v=eR8Rig917z4; and

KujoClips, "Leaning mixture with a constant speed prop," November 23, 2017, educational video, 10:14, https://www.youtube.com/watch?v=N-OyeLKhq8k.

128 Taking Off, "LOP vs ROP Smackdown – InTheHangar Ep 112," November 6, 2020, educational video, 28:02, https://www.youtube.com/watch?v=ovciZR86YKA; and AZStolman, "Choosing Lean of Peak or Rich of Peak," July 22, 2018, educational video, 4:45, https://www.youtube.com/watch?v=C0-X_Flz4C8.

129 Sailing Saltwater Lanai, "Simple Way to Determine Aircraft Position Using a VOR, CDI, and OBS," December 20, 2018, educational video, 8:27, https://www.youtube.com/watch?v=jrQ21zKjlVg.

130 U.S. Department of Transportation, Federal Aviation Administration, "Airmen Knowledge Test Statistics," https://www.faa.gov/data_research/aviation_data_statistics/test_statistics/.

131 *Top Gun*, directed by Tony Scott (Paramount Pictures, 1986).

132 Wendover Productions, "Why the World is Running Out of Pilots," October 2, 2018, educational video, 11:35, https://www.youtube.com/watch?v=cognzTud3Wg.

133 Wendover Productions, "Why the World is Running Out of Pilots."

134 Ch-Aviation, "US lawmakers support FAA flight-hour rule," December 10, 2021, https://www.ch-aviation.com/portal/news/108560-us-lawmakers-support-faa-flight-hour-rule.

135 Robert Silk, "How the 1,500-hour rule created a pilot shortage," *Travel Weekly*, August 18, 2017, https://www.travelweekly.com/Robert-Silk/How-1500-hour-rule-created-pilot-shortage.

136 Shelby Holliday, "The 2013 FAA Rule That's Being Blamed for Today's Pilot Shortage," *Wall Street Journal*, December 21, 2021, video, 7:07, https://www.youtube.com/watch?v=hmn7rquuzoI.

137 Paul Craig, *The Killing Zone: How and Why Pilots Die*, Second Edition (New York: McGraw Hill, 2013), pp. 28-29; and Pilot Nancy, "1500 Hour Rule Making It Harder To Become An Airline Pilot?," September 1, 2021, educational video, 9:50, https://www.youtube.com/watch?v=A4FnTejkDtA.

138 Airlines for America, "Data & Statistics: Safety Record of U.S. Air Carriers," Airlines.org, November 11, 2021, https://www.airlines.org/dataset/safety-record-of-u-s-air-carriers/; and Leslie Josephs, "The last fatal US airline crash was a decade ago. Here's why our skies are safer," CNBC, February 13, 2019, https://www.cnbc.com/2019/02/13/colgan-air-crash-10-years-ago-reshaped-us-aviation-safety.html.

139 Holliday, "2013 FAA Ruling."

140 Pilot Nancy, "United States Pilot Shortage Real in 2021?," October 3, 2021, educational video, 6:01, https://www.youtube.com/watch?v=TZivnUNhksk; and Pilot Pro Academy, "60,000 Pilots Short | Post-COVID Pilot Shortage," July 3, 2021, educational video, 5:48, https://www.youtube.com/watch?v=uZTkbeQMgBg.

141 Wendover Productions, "Why the World Is Running Out of Pilots"; and Pilot Nancy, "1500 Hour Rule Making It Harder To Become An Airline Pilot?"

142 James Clark, "United CEO complains that the US military isn't training enough pilots for airlines to poach," Task and Purpose, June 23, 2021, https://taskandpurpose.com/news/united-ceo-military-not-training-enough-pilots/.

143 Luke Pylypciw, "Should You Go To College For Aviation?," September 5, 2020, educational video, 10:52, https://www.youtube.com/watch?v=tgnkroj_bxI.

144 Thrust Flight Academy, "4 Year University Vs. Accelerated Flight School," July 30, 2020, educational/promotional video, 4:00, https://www.youtube.com/watch?v=7T35-5oRKsM; and Pylypciw, "Should You Go To College For Aviation?"

145 Thrust Flight Academy, "4 Year University Vs. Accelerated Flight School."

146 Thrust Flight Academy, "4 Year University Vs. Accelerated Flight School."

147 Fly8MA.com, Flight Training, "5 Pilot Jobs for 500hr Pilots," January 14, 2019, educational video, 8:19, https://www.youtube.com/watch?v=RpZ4p2m0GsY; and Pilot Nancy, "Entry Level Pilot Jobs // Low Time Pilot Jobs," July 24, 2020, educational video, 10:47, https://www.youtube.com/watch?v=Vmq5LJdu0N4.

148 Greg Thomson, "8 Reasons Why Working As a Cargo Pilot Can Improve Your Career," Pilotjobcentral.com, June 1, 2018, https://pilotjobcentral.com/8-reasons-why-working-as-a-cargo-pilot-might-be-for-you/.

149 Fly8MA.com, "5 Pilot Jobs for 500hr Pilots"; and Pilot Nancy, "Entry Level Pilot Jobs"

150 Aviator Inspirations, "How to Become a Flight Instructor," June 15, 2019, educational video, 5:30, https://www.youtube.com/watch?v=Chd94s2xQSg.

151 Pilot Institute, "Women Pilot Statistics: Female Representation in Aviation," February 22, 2022, https://pilotinstitute.com/women-aviation-statistics/.

152 Thomas Pallini, "US airlines are combating the pilot shortage by raising pay, lowering requirements, and hiring from Australia," Business Insider, January 17, 2022, https://www.businessinsider.com/airlines-respond-to-pilot-shortage-higher-pay-lower-requirements-2022-1.

153 Wendover Productions, "Why the World Is Running Out of Pilots"; and 74 Gear, "Worldwide Pilot Shortage [2019] Is the pilot shortage real?," October 28, 2018, educational video, 8:40, https://www.youtube.com/watch?v=i5aE97LGgOw.

154 Marielle Segarra, "It's getting a lot more lucrative to become a pilot," Business Insider, December 28, 2017, https://www.businessinsider.com/its-getting-a-lot-more-lucrative-to-become-a-pilot-2017-12.

155 74 Gear, "Worldwide Pilot Shortage."

156 Wendover Productions, "Why the World Is Running Out of Pilots."

157 Alex Stone, *CFI! The Book: A Satirical Aviation Comedy* (Highland, IN: AWS Books, 2018), p. 12.

158 Stone, *CFI! The Book*, p. 17.

159   Carlos Bousono, "Pattern Primer: Essential Tools to Flying the Traffic Pattern," AOPA. org, January 1, 2017, https://www.aopa.org/news-and-media/all-news/2017/january/flight-training-magazine/pattern-primer.

160   Jason Schappert, "Don't Flare on Landings," MzeroA Flight Training, August 18, 2020, educational video, 7:23, https://www.youtube.com/watch?v=0bOEiR6JuXY.

161   Phil Scott, "Crappy runways," Air Facts, April 18, 2012, https://airfactsjournal.com/2012/04/crappy-runways/.

162   Scott, "Crappy runways."

163   Aero Safety Training, "It's time to live your dream. Learn to fly with us," http://lpawings.com/learn-to-fly.

164   Jason Schappert, "The Perfect Traffic Pattern," MzeroA Flight Training, August 11, 2020, educational video, 4:45, https://www.youtube.com/watch?v=ac5c8nXSO0s.

165   *Dodgeball: A True Underdog Story*, directed by Rawson Marshall Thurber (20th Century Fox, 2004).

166   Langewiesche, *Stick and Rudder,* p. 155.

167   Aeroflight Services, "Pitch and Airspeed Techniques for a Good Landing," December 19, 2014, educational Video, 1:59, https://www.youtube.com/watch?v=TjwxwPfvSms.

168   GoFly Online, "Debunking the Myth Power vs Ptich – GoFly Fix," December 27, 2019, educational video, 16:47, https://www.youtube.com/watch?v=LoSF-YtEeug.

169   William Shakespeare, *Hamlet, Prince of Denmark* (Act I, Scene V, 166-167), *The Complete Signet Classic Shakespeare*, edited by Sylvan Barnet (San Diego: Harcourt Brace Jovanovich, 1963), p. 927.

170   Jason Schappert. "Help! I'm Landing Left of Center!?," MzeroA Flight Training, March 16, 2015, educational video, 4:30, https://www.youtube.com/watch?v=iXubLPB9rEE.

171   ZeroByteInFlight, "Right Rudder! – A humorous analysis of my landing technique," April 12, 2014, educational video, 3:39, https://www.youtube.com/watch?v=SEjNi1vPbuA; and Schappert, "Help! I'm Landing Left of Center!?"

172   GVad The Pilot, "Landing on the Centerline – Flying Tips (MSFS)," July 20, 2010, educational video, 5:36, https://www.youtube.com/watch?v=qX9ZI0xDFE4; and Schappert, "Help! I'm Landing Left of Center!?"

173   Rod Machado, "The Runway Expansion Effect," April 4, 2017, educational video, 13:14, https://www.youtube.com/watch?v=9JfoZERqM7Q.

174   Airplane Academy, "This ONE Technique Instantly Improved My Landings," September 21, 2020, educational video, 6:12, https://www.youtube.com/watch?v=YMHw9QabSlg.

175   The Supremes, "You Can't Hurry Love," *The Supremes A' Go-Go*, Motown, 1966; and Phil Collins, "You Can't Hurry Love," *Hello, I Must Be Going!*, Atlantic Records, 1982.

176   "How Many Flight Hours Before You Solo?," Airplane Academy, https://airplaneacademy.com/how-many-flight-hours-before-you-solo/.

177 Arizona Flight Training Workgroup, "Arizona Practice Areas and Reporting Points," AFTW.org. https://aftw.org/arizona-practice-areas/.

178 Rinker Buck, *Flight of Passage: A Memoir* (New York: Hyperion, 1998), pp. 289-291.

179 Buck, *Flight of Passage*, p. 8.

180 12 News, "Plane lands on Pinnacle Peak Road in north Phoenix," May 4, 2021, https://www.12news.com/article/news/local/valley/plane-lands-on-pinnacle-peak-road-in-north-phoenix/75-53d54536-87bb-49eb-9883-1e8535878d99.

181 U.S. National Transportation Safety Board, "Flying on Empty," Safety Alert, August 2017, https://www.ntsb.gov/Advocacy/safety-alerts/Documents/SA-067.pdf.

182 12 News, "Plane land on Pinnacle Peak Road."

183 Robert Frost, "Stopping by Woods on a Snowy Evening," in *The Poetry of Robert Frost*, edited by Edward Connery Latham (New York: Henry Holt, 1969).

184 Randall W Gibb, "Visual Spatial Disorientation: Re-Visiting the Black Hole Illusion," *Aviation, Space, and Environmental Medicine* 78, no. 8 (August 2007), https://citeseerx.ist.psu.edu/viewdoc/download?doi=10.1.1.938.6343&rep=rep1&type=pdf; and Andre Ludovic, "'Black Hole' Approach," Smartcockpit.com, https://www.smartcockpit.com/docs/The_Black_Hole_Approach.pdf.

185 XPlane.org, "Vatsim vs PilotEdge," December 21, 2015, https://forums.x-plane.org/index.php?/forums/topic/91884-vatsim-vs-pilotedge/.

186 PilotEdge, "VFR Communications and Airspace Training (CAT) Program," https://www.pilotedge.net/pages/cat-ratings.

187 For example, see: PilotEdge, "CAT-07 Flight: Class D to Class D with Class C Transition," https://www.pilotedge.net/pages/cat-07-rating.

188 Schappert, "The Perfect Traffic Pattern."

189 Miles Lundgren, "TRSA Airspace: Everything You Need to Know," AirplaneAcademy.com, https://airplaneacademy.com/trsa-airspace-everything-you-need-to-know/.

190 Justin Hayward, "The Miracle on the Hudson – The Full Story," SimpleFlying.com, April 15, 2021, https://simpleflying.com/the-miracle-on-the-hudson/.

191 Air New Zealand, "An Unexpected Briefing," October 31, 2012, Safety video, 4:27, https://www.youtube.com/watch?v=cBlRbrB_Gnc.

192 David McLanahan, "Open Door in Flight," AOPA.org, https://www.aopa.org/training-and-safety/students/solo/skills/open-door-in-flight.

193 Captain Joe, "'MAYDAY vs PAN PAN' Why do pilots use these CALLS? Explained by CAPTAIN JOE," December 27, 2018, educational video, 13:22, https://www.youtube.com/watch?v=UWpwl-NPnrM.

194 Captain Joe, "'MAYDAY vs PAN PAN.'"

195 Aircraft Owners and Pilots Association, "Emergency Locator Transmitter (ELT)," AOPA.org, December 28, 2018, https://www.aopa.org/advocacy/aircraft/aircraft-operations/emergency-locator-transmitters.

196 U.S. Department of Commerce, National Oceanic and Atmospheric Administration (NOAA), "History of the SARSAT program," https://www.sarsat.noaa.gov/history-of-the-sarsat-program/.

197 Air Safety Institute, "Reality Check: The Runway Behind You," June 4, 2021, educational video, 9:37, https://www.youtube.com/watch?v=dFVFKq3QqXo.

198 Sporty's, "Introduction," *Multiengine Training Course*, educational video, 3:59-4:15; and J. Mac McClellan, "Wrong Worry in Twins vs. Singles," *Flying*, February 1, 2003, https://www.flyingmag.com/wrong-worry-twins-versus-singles/.

199 U.S. Department of Transportation, Federal Aviation Administration, "Wildlife Strikes to Civil Aircraft in the United States, 1990-2020," July 2021, https://www.faa.gov/airports/airport_safety/wildlife/media/Wildlife-Strike-Report-1990-2020.pdf, p. v.

200 FAA, "Wildlife Strikes," p. vi.

201 FAA, "Wildlife Strikes," p. v.

202 Nicholas Cummins, "How Dangerous Are Bird Strikes?," SimpleFlying.com, August 12, 2020, https://simpleflying.com/bird-strikes-danger/.

203 Tyler Rogoway, "The Bird Strike Reminds Us It Doesn't Take a Missile to Down a Fighter," The War Zone, November 7, 2016, https://www.thedrive.com/the-war-zone/5892/this-bird-strike-reminds-us-it-doesnt-take-a-missile-to-down-a-fighter.

204 Cox News Service, "Vulture Caused F-16 Crash in Florida, Air Force Says," *Orlando Sentinel*, January 19, 2000, https://www.orlandosentinel.com/news/os-xpm-2000-01-19-0001190179-story.html.

205 Interesting Engineering, "What happens when birds fly into airplane engines?," December 2, 2021, educational video, 4:45, https://www.youtube.com/watch?v=619fct0KTPI.

206 U.S. Department of Transportation, Federal Aviation Administration, "Wildlife Strike FAQs," https://www.faa.gov/airports/airport_safety/wildlife/faq/.

207 FAA, "Wildlife Strikes," p. vi.

208 FAA, "Wildlife Strikes," p. vi.

209 Aircraft Owners and Pilots Association, Air Safety Institute, *31st Joseph T. Nall Report*, 2022, https://www.aopa.org/training-and-safety/air-safety-institute/accident-analysis/joseph-t-nall-report/.

210 Air Safety Institute, https://www.youtube.com/user/AirSafetyInstitute/featured.

211 Air Safety Institute, "Accident Case Study: Traffic Pattern Tragedy," September 21, 2018, educational video, 20:57, https://www.youtube.com/watch?v=mf3xhjXl454.

212 Chiles, *The God Machine*, pp. 7, 28.

213 Jonathan Ridley, "Leonardo da Vinci's helicopter: 15th-century flight of fancy led to modern aeronautics," The Conversation, May 3, 2019, https://theconversation.com/leonardo-da-vincis-helicopter-15th-century-flight-of-fancy-led-to-modern-aeronautics-116241; and J. Gordon Leishman, "A History of Helicopter Flight,"

2000, https://itlims-zsis.meil.pw.edu.pl//pomoce/WTLK/ENG/Sup/A_History_of_Helicopter_Flight.pdf.

214   Leishman, "A History of Helicopter Flight."
215   Chiles, *The God Machine*, pp. 30–34.
216   Chiles, *The God Machine*, p. 8.
217   Chiles, *The God Machine*, pp. 73–78.
218   Chiles, *The God Machine*, pp. 89–92.
219   Chiles, *The God Machine*, pp. 93–97.
220   Chiles (Sikorsky brought all the elements together).
221   Chiles, *The God Machine*, pp. 98–99.
222   Chiles, *The God Machine*, p. 100.
223   Chiles, *The God Machine*, p. 101.
224   Chiles, *The God Machine*, p. 115.
225   Chiles, *The God Machine*, p. 9.
226   Chiles (hover, ubiquity).
227   Corsaire Helicopter Flight Training, "R22 Governor (Engine RPM)," July 12, 2020, educational video, 5:10, https://www.youtube.com/watch?v=UGpTN-adq3c.
228   Chiles, *The God Machine*, p. 21.
229   Helicopter Online Ground School, "Low Rotor RPM and Blade Stall Helicopter Ground School Online," January 18, 2014, educational video, 2:15, https://www.youtube.com/watch?v=ID8aeLqZS5A; Helicopter Online Ground School, "Low Rotor RPM Blade Stall Accident Review," November 14, 2017, educational video, 53:56, https://www.youtube.com/watch?v=ws_Vg02AwM4; and David A Borrows, "Rotor RPM: Putting the Right Spin on It," AOPA.org, March 5, 1998, https://www.aopa.org/news-and-media/all-news/1998/march/flight-training-magazine/rotor-rpm.
230   Helicopter Online Ground School, "Low Rotor RPM Blade Stall Accident Review"; and Robinson Helicopter Company, Safety Notice SN-24, June 1994.
231   Helicopter Lessons in 10 Minutes of Less, "Dissymmetry of Lift in Helicopters," June 3, 2017, educational video, 5:21, https://www.youtube.com/watch?v=Cv74zHSLQ7A.
232   vsTerminus, "DCS Mi-8: Retreating Blade Stall Tutorial," April 25, 2020, educational video, 20:47, https://www.youtube.com/watch?v=PU3AIU8Sqxw.
233   RevelatorAlf, "What is rotor blade flapping?," December 21, 2017, educational video, 2:54, https://www.youtube.com/watch?v=j_dfyBORSFo; and iKalams, "Cyclic Inputs Control Blade Flapping," August 6, 2014, Educational video, 2:13, https://www.youtube.com/watch?v=Mx7vLB3KP1w.
234   Helicopter Lessons in 10 Minutes of Less, "Types of Rotor Systems in Helicopters," January 19, 2018, Educational video, 8:41, https://www.youtube.com/watch?v=7gM3rMDpJt4.

235 Helicopter Lessons in 10 Minutes of Less, "Compensation for Dissymmetry of Lift in Helicopters," June 6, 2017, educational video, 6:31, https://www.youtube.com/watch?v=culBbvszRpk.

236 Helicopter Lessons in 10 Minutes of Less, "Retreating Blade Stall/VNE in Helicopters," July 14, 2018, educational video, 9:41, https://www.youtube.com/watch?v=wZ0WIwrKSz8.

237 Cape Copters, "Retreating Blade Stall – Helicopter Ground School," February 15, 2021, educational video, 4:23, https://www.youtube.com/watch?v=9ui6sVaKE_M.

238 Cape Copters, "Retreating Blade Stall."

239 *Gladiator*, directed by Ridley Scott (DreamWorks Pictures and Universal Pictures, 2000).

240 Christopher Beam, "Hellish Copters: Why are choppers always crashing?," Slate, October 30, 2009, https://slate.com/news-and-politics/2009/10/why-are-helicopters-always-crashing.html.

241 Beam, "Hellish Copters."

242 Sporty's, "Introduction," *So You Want To Fly Helicopters*, educational video, 4:10-4:25.

243 Mike Collins, "How It Works: Marking Time," AOPA.org, September 1, 2018, https://www.aopa.org/news-and-media/all-news/2018/september/flight-training-magazine/how-it-works-hobbs-meter.

244 Pinelands Preservation Alliance, "The Jersey Devil and Folklore," https://pinelandsalliance.org/learn-about-the-pinelands/pinelands-history-and-culture/the-jersey-devil-and-folklore/; and Jean Shepherd, "The Jersey Devil," WOR Radio, March 22, 1977, https://www.youtube.com/watch?v=71dWQ9dN_cM.

245 Atlas Obscura, "Hindenburg Crash Site, Lakehurst, New Jersey," https://www.atlasobscura.com/places/hindenburg-crash-site.

246 VASAviation, "Diamond DA-40 Busts into Presidential Restricted Area near Philadelphia, PA," September 7, 2021, https://www.youtube.com/watch?v=BZXKXWLWcec.

247 Craig, *The Killing Zone*, p. 2.

248 U.S. Department of Transportation, Bureau of Transportation Statistics, "U.S. General Aviation Safety Data," https://www.bts.gov/content/us-general-aviationa-safety-data.

249 Airlines for America, "Data & Statistics: Safety Record of U.S. Air Carriers," Airlines.org, November 11, 2021, https://www.airlines.org/dataset/safety-record-of-u-s-air-carriers/; and Leslie Josephs, "The last fatal US airline crash was a decade ago. Here's why our skies are safer," CNBC, February 13, 2019.

250 Craig, *The Killing Zone,* p. 35.

251 Craig, *The Killing Zone,* p. 35.

252 Craig, *The Killing Zone,* p. 36.

253 BTS, "U.S. General Aviation Safety Data."

254 Craig, *The Killing Zone*, p. 35.
255 Craig, *The Killing Zone*, pp. 5, 12.
256 Craig (better training, fewer accidents).
257 Antoine de Saint-Exupéry, *Wind, Sand and Stars* (Orlando: Harcourt Inc., 1939).
258 *Time*, "Heroes: The Lone Eagle's Final Flight," September 9, 1974, https://content.time.com/time/subscriber/article/0,33009,904095,00.html.
259 Henry David Thoreau, *Walden and Other Writings*, edited by Joseph Wood Krutch (New York: Bantam Books, 1962), p. 172.
260 Thoreau, *Walden*, p. 343.
261 Pilot Ahmad, "Turn and Slip Indicator", https://pilotahmad.wordpress.com/turn-and-slip-indicator/
262 Ian J Twombly, "Aerodynamics: Nothing But a Number, A Closer Look at Stall Speed," AOPA.org, March 1, 2020, https://www.aopa.org/news-and-media/all-news/2020/march/flight-training-magazine/aerodynamics-stall-speed.

Index

100-hour inspection 300, 301, 340, 342
121.5 emergency frequency 267
1500-hour rule 158, 340

A

abeam 164, 167, 169, 191, 192, 223, 261, 320, 340
accelerated stall, *see stall*
accident (aviation) 79, 302, 304, 328, 340, 342, 350, 357
    case studies 80-81, 275
    causes 80, 208, 232, 274-275, 328, 330
    CFIT 105
    Colgan Air 158
    helicopter 295
    insurance 275
    reporting 274-275
    statistics 274, 295, 322, 330
ADS-B 96-98, 107, 108, 109, 123, 194, 233, 307, 340-341, 360
Aegean Sea 82
aerodynamic braking 258, 260, 341
Aeroflex-Andover Airport (12N) 261
AFD (Airport Facilities Directory), *see Chart Supplement*
Africa 140

AGL (altitude Above Ground Level) 67, 341, 342, 361
    airspace 107, 108, 109, 146
    birdstrikes 274
    clouds 126, 324, 347
    obstacles 105
    overflying filed 249
    safe altitude 105
ailerons 44, 51, 165, 290, 341, 372, 376
    crosswind taxi and takeoff 186-187
    forward slip 206, 320, 352
    inspection 15-16
    mechanism 52
    origin 45-46
    sideslip 367
    stall and recovery 60-61, 281, 368
    trim 53, 372
aiming point 2, 10, 170, 172, 177, 181, 341, 353
    power-off landing 262, 320, 321
    runway numbers 20, 165, 181
    short-field landing 257, 261, 263, 319
    soft-fielding landing 260
Airbus A320 (airliner) 52
Airbus H135 (helicopter) 285

airfoil 34-36, 38, 341, 342, 346, 348, 353, 358, 366, 369
    helicopter blades as 289, 293, 294
    propeller as 36-37, 49
    Wright brothers 43
airmail 79, 80, 333
Airman Certificate (pilot's license) 23, 24, 26, 298, 306, 328, 341, 350, 353
Airman Certification Standards 305, 306
air mass 115, 116, 341, 353
AIRMET 121, 341, 368
Air New Zealand 264
air pressure 29, 31, 34, 67, 68, 69, 70, 71, 115, 117, 122, 132, 135, 146, 341, 342, 349, 357, 363, 365, 369, 374
Air Safety Institute (AOPA) 275
airspace 21, 87, 100, 215, 230, 233, 267, 326, 342, 343, 347, 372. *Also see Class A-G airspace, MOA, Restricted Area, and TFR.*
    ADS-B requirement 97
    and radio failure 273, 325
    and VFR rules 78, 147
    around New York 12, 56, 194
    around Phoenix 194-195
    at Lakehurst 313, 323
    circling 232
    PilotEdge 235
    sequencing and separation 367
    shared knowledge with helicopters 287
    shown in *ForeFlight* 97
    shown on charts 87, 106, 367
    Sport and Recreational Pilot's License 24
    types of 106-100, 194, 360, 366, 371, 373
airspeed 65, 80, 83, 84, 118, 208, 318, 341, 365, 373. *Also see airspeed indicator.*
    and angle of attack 38
    and control surfaces 48, 51, 55
    and drag 357
    and engine fire 272, 318
    and flaps 53, 249
    and pitch 176, 254
    and spiraling slipstream 49
    and wind 20, 61, 118, 186, 354
    approach and landing 164, 176, 181, 206, 247, 249
    autopilot 84
    climb 199, 258
    engine cooling 143, 199
    flight planning 87, 89, 99, 147, 317, 349
    ForeFlight 96
    gliding 266
    helicopter 292-294, 296
    in bank/turn 39, 63, 340, 370, 373
    indicated vs true 69-70, 87, 357, 373
    in skid or slip 51, 207, 320
    maneuvering speed 359
    never exceed speed 361
    on go-around 249
    on PFD 76, 130
    slow flight 58
    stall and recovery 59-60, 61, 279, 282, 292, 369
    takeoff and climb 18, 82, 199, 245-255, 258, 259, 263, 270, 344
airspeed indicator 18, 66, 67, 69, 87, 164, 181, 206, 256, 318, 341, 363, 369
    depicted speeds 39, 70, 255, 357, 359, 369
    in helicopter 288, 292
    in unusual attitudes 318
    malfunction 71, 130, 133
airworthiness certificate 41, 299, 300, 341
Airworthiness Directive (AD) 275, 302-303, 342
alcohol 30, 299, 356
alternator 139-140, 272, 342, 344, 359
altimeter 21, 66, 67-69, 85, 108, 197, 222, 288, 292, 318, 325, 342, 363, 365, 369
    barometer setting 68, 69, 85, 88, 108, 122, 196, 202, 222, 237, 325, 365
    inspection 302
    malfunction 71
    on written exam 150

INDEX 415

altitude 10, 27, 56, 65, 67, 82, 83, 129, 130, 131, 164, 194, 220, 232, 248, 316, 341, 342, 344, 361, 368. *Also see AGL and MSL*.
    air density 9, 28, 135, 373
    air pressure 67, 70, 341
    air temperature 88, 116, 119, 371
    and airspeed 69-70, 71, 357
    and altimeter 67-69
    and true airspeed (TAS) 69
    approach and landing 165, 173, 176
    ATC 198, 201, 202-203, 227, 246
    autopilot 84, 85
    best angle of climb 254, 255, 344
    best rate of climb 254, 256, 344
    birdstrikes 274
    cruising 88, 108, 120, 210-211, 310, 315, 348
    density altitude 88, 199, 212, 349, 350
    during maneuvers 39, 45, 57, 58, 59, 61, 62, 63, 64, 202, 278, 279, 280, 319, 365, 370, 373
    emergency 270, 272
    ForeFlight 96, 97, 250
    forward slip 207, 320, 352
    fuel mixture 9, 44, 128
    gliding 262, 266
    go-around 249
    helicopter 286, 290, 291, 292, 294, 295
    lift and weight 38-39
    medical issues 29-31, 356
    on PFD 76
    performance 37, 199, 212
    pitch and power 47, 51, 176
    pressure altitude 70, 149, 349, 365
    safety 39, 40, 58, 61, 105, 222, 309, 314, 325
    traffic pattern 164, 191, 211, 320, 372
    transponder 97, 107, 201, 360, 372
    turbulence 118, 123, 205, 373

    vertical speed indicator (VS) 71, 374
    Winds Aloft 87-88, 121, 317, 375
AME (Aviation Medical Examiner) 25, 26, 27, 31, 342
American Pie (song) 81
angle of attack (AoA) 35-36, 52, 176, 296, 342, 346
    and airspeed 38
    and banking 39-40, 57
    and center of gravity 40-41
    and dihedral 42
    critical angle of attack 36, 127, 348
    elevators as AoA lever 47
    flare and landing 181
    helicopter blades 289, 293-294
    induced drag 38, 357
    left-turning tendencies (p-factor) 57, 363
    propeller 37, 49
    stall and recovery 36, 38-39, 60, 292, 369
angle of incidence 35, 342
annual inspection 300, 301, 302, 342
anti-torque pedals 290, 291, 292, 342
AOPA (Aircraft Owners and Pilots Association) 275
Apple II computer 5, 6
Approach (ATC frequency), *see ATC*
approach (to landing) v, 7, 20, 69, 105, 163, 173-174, 181, 184, 190, 205, 238, 240, 247, 334, 342, 353, 367
    aiming point 181, 341
    airspace 107, 200
    airspeed 51, 53, 165
    at Lincoln Park 167-170, 172, 175, 249
    crabbing 187
    flaps 53, 351
    forward slip 206-207, 352
    hazards 51, 59, 61, 118, 345, 350, 364
    in helicopter 294
    instrument 109, 111, 343, 357
    left-turning tendencies 49
    night 223, 345
    other traffic 192, 248

pitch and power 176-177
planning 211, 245
power-off approach 253, 261-262, 364
practicing 170, 171, 176, 177, 189, 281, 332, 346, 368
radio failure and light gun signals 273
short-field landing 257, 261
soft-field landing 260
sight picture 22, 170, 172, 176
visual guidance 174-175, 223, 362, 374
approach plate 111, 343
arm (measurement) 147, 343, 345, 361
ARROW 299-300
ARSim, see PlaneEnglish
artificial horizon 66, 72, 75, 79, 81, 82, 83, 131, 221, 318, 343, 363. *Also see attitude indicator*
ASOS 123, 343, 344. *Also see ATIS and AWOS.*
ATC (Air Traffic Control) v, 7, 20, 102, 146, 194, 199, 202, 224, 242, 243, 325, 343, 355, 357, 366, 367, 372, 373, 374
    and ADS-B 97, 201, 340
    and transponder 201, 360, 372
    Approach (frequency) 200-201, 245, 246, 342-343, 373
    ATIS 123
    Clearance (frequency) 236, 346
    communication with 226-229, 230, 232, 233-237, 245-246, 280
    control tower 1, 20, 21, 87, 101, 102, 108, 164, 174, 194, 198, 211, 224, 227, 232, 247, 273, 358
    deviation from instructions 112, 198, 367
    emergencies 208, 268, 269, 273
    Flight Following 236
    Ground (frequency) 196, 200, 209, 236, 237, 240, 347, 354
    IFR 111, 210, 212
    lost procedures 91
    non-towered airport 109, 112, 123, 194, 206, 211, 235, 242, 246, 273, 325, 343, 344, 355
    regional center 211
    TFR 311, 314
    Tower (frequency) 1, 197-199, 200, 205, 208, 228-230, 232, 233, 237, 238-240, 245-246, 324, 325-326, 343
    towered airport 106, 109, 110, 194, 196, 233, 237, 239, 245, 273, 306, 325, 342, 347, 345
    VFR waypoints 201
ATIS 123, 343, 344. *Also see ASOS and AWOS.*
    at Caldwell 124, 248, 249
    contacting ATC 196, 205, 228, 230
    flight planning 211
    on return from checkride 323, 325, 326
    staying ahead of the plane 232, 237-238
Atlantic City, New Jersey 283
Atlantic City International Airport (KACY) 309
ATP (Airline Transport Pilot license) 158, 159, 160, 161, 340, 343
attitude 35, 166, 279, 343, 369. *Also see attitude indicator and unusual attitudes.*
attitude indicator 66, 67, 72, 74, 83, 85, 221, 318, 343. *Also see artificial horizon.*
autogyro 285
autokinesis 221, 343
autopilot 83-84, 98, 304, 343
avgas, *see fuel*
AWOS 123, 211, 222, 343, 344. *Also see ASOS and ATIS.*

B

Bader, Douglas 28
balloon (aircraft) 33, 36, 166, 248
balloon (motion) 164, 166, 191, 344

bank 6, 19, 44, 44, 81, 94, 172, 250, 318, 334, 340, 341, 344, 366, 367, 370
    attitude indicator 72, 343
    forward slip 207, 320, 352
    load factor and stall speed 39-40
    parachute 146
    PFD 76
    sideslip 188, 367
    slow flight 58
    spatial disorientation 81
    stability 41, 42
    steep turns 56-57, 305, 370
    S-turns 64
    turbulence 56
    turn coordinator 74
    turns around a point 62-63
base (leg) 21, 198, 230, 238, 261, 320, 344
    airspeed 165
    at Lincoln Park 167, 169
    turn from base to final 40, 51, 187, 206, 223, 244, 320
    turn from downwind to base 164, 167, 169, 223
BasicMed 25, 344
battery 17, 75, 113, 139-140, 272, 302, 342, 344, 359, 369
beacon (airport) 101, 222, 344
beacon (light) 17, 219, 344
beacon (radio) 91-92, 95, 99
Bell 47 (helicopter) 285
Bernoulli, Daniel 34
Bernoulli's Principle 34, 35, 136, 344
best angle of climb (V_X) 254, 255, 256, 259, 316, 319, 344
best rate of climb (V_Y) 255, 256, 259, 316, 344
Biden, President Joseph 311
birdstrike 274, 344
black hole effect 223, 344
blastpad 169, 345
Bohr, Niels 29
Boldmethod 7, 380
Boonton Reservoir 238, 328
bounce (landing) 166, 177, 244, 246, 250, 257, 364
Boyne, Walter 37
brakes 9, 17, 18, 209, 250, 316, 366

    on soft-field landing 260
    on short-field landing 258
    on short-field takeoff 254-255, 319
Bravo transition, *see Class B (Bravo) airspace*
Buck, Rinker 207
Buffalo, New York 158
bush trip 10, 82

C

cabin fire 273-274
Caldwell Airport, *see Essex County Airport (KCDW)*
call sign vi, 20, 198, 201, 202, 227, 234, 238, 246, 345, 365
    abbreviated 229
carbon monoxide (CO) 30, 345
carburetor 136, 137, 345, 353
carburetor heat 136, 345
carburetor ice 136, 345
Carcassonne, France 332
Cartier, Louis 77
Casa Grande Municipal Airport (KCGZ) 211
Cayley, George 33, 285
CDI (Course Deviation Indicator) 91-95, 148-149, 150, 345, 361, 365, 366
centerline 9, 18, 50, 165, 166, 171, 174, 177, 180, 199, 222, 244, 321, 345
center of gravity (CG) 40, 41, 49, 127, 148, 343, 345, 354, 361, 369, 375
Cessna 152 (airplane) 8-9
Cessna 172 Skyhawk 5, 8, 14, 104, 110, 158, 195, 200, 208, 274, 284, 323, 332
    172R (compared to 172S) 199
    autopilot 83, 84, 304
    cabin 16, 29, 30, 43, 135, 265
    center of gravity 40, 147
    checklists 208
    controls 51, 52, 53, 76, 254
    crosswinds 186, 189
    design and stability 42, 47, 48, 50, 295
    ELT 270
    engine 30, 50, 134, 135, 136, 137, 139, 140-143, 362

fuel capacity 136
gliding 261, 266, 309
high wing 164, 248
history 14-15
icing 130
in *Microsoft Flight Simulator* 82,
84, 98, 125, 131, 189, 242
inspection 288
instruments 65, 69, 70, 71, 75, 76,
91, 98
landing 19, 164, 165, 257, 262
landing gear 49, 257, 372
lights 220
maintenance 300, 303, 304
operating altitude 30, 128, 134
payload 41
performance 55, 59, 61, 132, 189,
199, 255, 258
power settings 18, 56, 76, 164,
166, 262
propeller 37, 76
radio 230-231
speeds 18, 40, 70, 146, 165, 191,
255, 261, 311
starting 16-17, 356
structural limits 31, 39, 311
Cessna 182 Skylane 76
Cessna 210 Centurion 140
Cessna 402 (airplane) 122
CFI (Certified Flight Instructor) vi, 17,
155, 160, 162, 194, 218, 305, 346
as PIC 13, 160
CFI! The Book (novel) 162
flight review 157, 352
logbook endorsements 156, 350
seating position 16, 160, 288
training and checkride 160, 161,
195
CFIT (Controlled Flight Into Terrain) 106,
308, 314, 330, 346
chair flying 170, 346
Chandler Municipal Airport (KCHD) 211
Chart Supplement 111, 112, 124, 193,
305, 307, 341, 346, 350, 379
checklists 15, 16, 17, 18, 208, 209, 220,
254, 266, 268, 291, 299, 346, 364

checkride 1, 121, 124, 145, 208, 225, 252,
258, 277, 280, 284, 296, 298, 312,
314, 326, 330, 336, 346
examiner, *see DPE*
flying to and from 305, 312-313,
322-329, 332, 333
for other ratings 157, 160, 262,
287, 317, 320
IACRA and FTN 23
oral portion 204, 278, 300, 304,
310, 313-315
partial pass 279
practical portion 315-321
preparation 297-312
requirements 24, 156, 251, 278,
299
scenario 308
scheduling 276, 277, 278-279,
283, 308
standards 64, 254, 257, 262, 264,
279, 282, 299, 305, 314,
316-317, 320
written exam report 153
YouTube videos 252-253
Chiles, James 285, 296
China 3, 6, 151, 161
chord 35, 39, 342, 346
Cierva, Juan de la 285
Cirrus SR22 76
Civil Air Patrol 267
civil twilight 217, 218, 346
Class A (Alpha) airspace 68, 106
Class B (Bravo) airspace 106, 109, 194,
235, 237
around Newark 194, 313, 323, 325
around Phoenix 194-195, 197-198,
199, 211, 215, 220, 226,
228
clearance 200, 202, 224, 311
dimensions 107-108, 199-200
frequencies 200
Mode C veil 201, 360
speed limits 146
student pilots 2000
transition 197, 200, 201-203, 205,
210, 214, 224, 226, 227,
235, 372

transponder 109
Class C (Charlie) airspace 106, 194, 212, 235, 245
    dimensions 108-109
    requirements 109, 200
    speed limits 146
    transition 235, 309, 372
Class D (Delta) airspace 106, 169, 194, 198, 199, 200, 201, 212, 228, 235, 237, 245, 306, 308, 372
    around Phoenix 194-195, 197, 226
    dimensions 108-109
    requirements 109, 200
    transition 230, 313, 323, 324, 326
Class E (Echo) airspace 106, 109, 110, 182, 194, 197, 200, 211, 242, 247
Class G (Golf) airspace 106, 109, 110, 197
clean configuration 53, 254, 346, 375
Clearance (ATC frequency), *see ATC*
clearance (permission) 346, 351, 355
cleared for the option v, 1, 240
    for landing 229-230, 238
    for takeoff 199
    to cross or enter runway 112, 367
    to enter airspace 110, 198, 200, 202, 224, 227, 311, 360, 366
    IFR 106, 212
clear ice 129, 347
clouds 114, 147, 314, 333, 352, 357
    AIRMETs 121
    cloud base (calculation) 146
    cloud ceiling 78, 122, 128, 309, 310, 312, 323, 324, 326, 347
    cumulus 119, 348
    formation 116, 117, 118, 120
    icing 126-127, 128, 132
    IFR 79, 91, 357
    METARs 122
    on checkride and return 315, 323, 324, 326, 328
    on *Microsoft Flight Simulator* 126-132, 332
    SIGMETs 368
    spatial disorientation 79, 81, 85, 218, 330, 351

stratus 119, 370
    VFR rules 78, 81, 82, 147, 357
Colgan Air Flight 3407 158, 330
collective 289, 291-292, 294, 347, 351
COM1 and COM2 91, 123, 230, 232, 237, 238, 323, 324, 325, 326, 328, 347
complex airplane 156-157, 347
condensation 116, 117, 118, 119, 120, 127, 136, 137, 347, 349, 353
cones (vision) 218-219, 347
constant speed propeller, see propeller
control tower, see ATC
Coolidge Municipal Airport (P08) 210, 211, 212, 215
coordinated turn 50, 75, 347, 357
Coriolis force 116, 347, 349
course (direction) 49, 59, 61, 62, 84, 89, 90, 91, 94, 95, 100, 128, 129, 187, 199, 210, 212, 213, 244, 248, 345, 347, 348, 354, 365, 374, 375
    magnetic course 88, 94, 95, 357, 359
    true course 87, 88, 89, 147, 357, 359, 373
COVID-19 1, 3, 4, 6, 8, 11, 25, 144, 158, 161, 190, 215
Cox, Jessica 28
Coyle VOR 306, 310, 316, 317
CPL (Commercial Pilot License) 13, 157, 158, 159, 161, 348
crabbing 62, 187, 188, 348
Craig, Paul A. 322, 330, 331
critical angle of attack, *see angle of attack*
Croatia 10, 82, 125
cross-country 10, 79, 156, 160, 185, 253, 348
    in Arizona 210-214, 225
    night 216, 217-224
    requirements 156, 157, 217, 348
    solo 156, 225, 241-251, 275
crosswind (leg) 21, 240
crosswind (weather) 51, 61, 106, 186, 348
    component (calculation) 186, 189, 348
    forward slip 207, 320

landing and sideslip 186, 187-189, 206, 223, 240, 320, 321, 367
taxi 186-187
takeoff 187
cruising 37, 212, 245
    altitude 88, 105, 108, 210-211, 256, 310, 315, 348
    throttle setting 56
CTAF (Common Traffic Advisory Frequency) 102, 112, 211, 221, 237, 246, 348, 355
cumulus, *see clouds*
currency 298, 299, 348, 365
Curtiss, Glenn 43, 45, 183
cyclic 289, 290, 291, 348, 351
cyclone 116, 349
cylinder (engine) 9, 134, 135, 137, 138, 141, 142, 143, 271, 349, 359, 363, 364, 368

D

datum 147-148, 349
Da Vinci, Leonardo 285
Davis Monthan Air Force Base (KDMA) 212
dead reckoning 86, 90, 97, 210, 315, 349
Deer Valley, *see Phoenix Deer Valley Airport (KDVT)*
Deighton, Len 29
Delaware Bay 309, 314
Delaware River 246, 310, 312
Dell Alienware 11 PC 6
density (air) 28, 69, 87, 135, 136, 146, 191, 255, 349, 350, 356, 360, 373
density altitude, *see altitude*
detonation 141, 349
deus ex machina 296
dew point 116, 119, 120, 122, 146, 349, 352
Diamond DA40 314
Diamond DA42 NG 76
dihedral 42, 349
discovery flight 13, 14, 56, 161, 287, 336, 349
displaced threshold 169, 249, 349

DME (Distance Measuring Equipment) 92, 350
Dodgeball (film) 173
Doolittle, Jimmy 79, 91, 141
downwind (leg) 1, 21, 163, 187, 198, 205, 223, 228, 229, 240, 246, 257, 261, 328, 350
    45-degree entry 22
    airspeed 165
    at Lincoln Park 164, 167, 169, 181, 191, 328
    extending 192
DPE (Designated Pilot Examiner) 2, 278, 282, 305, 318, 324, 346, 350
    logbook 299, 313
    oral portion 124, 153, 252-253, 297, 298, 299, 303, 304
    practical portion 253, 258, 260, 265-266, 271, 312, 317, 373
    retesting 315
    scenario 308, 311
    scheduling checkride 277, 283
    shortage 277
drag 33, 37, 350, 351, 372
    aerodynamic braking 258, 341
    and adverse yaw 41
    and altitude 28
    flaps 53, 58, 206, 254, 262, 346, 349, 351
    frost 353
    ground effect 354
    helicopter blades 289, 290
    induced drag 38, 342, 357
    in steep turn 57
    parasitic drag 37, 362
    skidding and slipping 50, 51, 207, 352
    spoilers 53

E

E6B calculator 88, 89, 147, 307, 350
Easton Airport (KESN) 308, 309, 311, 314, 315
Edison, Thomas 285
EFB (Electronic Flight Bag) 112, 350
EGT (Exhaust Gas Temperature) 142, 350

electrical fire 272
elevators (control) 16, 44, 46-47, 51, 52, 60, 186, 207, 290, 350, 356, 364, 372, 376
    and center of gravity 40-41
Eloy Municipal Airport (E60) 211, 221
ELT (Emergency Locator Transmitter) 269-270, 302, 350
endorsement (logbook) 157, 350, 358, 372
    complex 156, 347
    deficiencies on written exam 153
    high performance 156, 355
    tailwheel 50, 156
    to enter Bravo 200
    to fly solo 190, 241
    to retake written exam 153
    to take checkride 278, 299
    to take written exam 145, 152, 306
engine failure in flight 208, 266-268
engine failure on takeoff 270
English (language) 24
ERCO 415-C Ercoupe 28
Essex County Airport (KCDW) 81, 109, 124, 169, 248
eyesight requirements 26-27

F

F-16 (fighter plane) 52, 212, 314
F-35 (fighter plane) 212
F/A-18 (fighter plane) 42
FAA (Federal Aviation Administration) 23, 102, 105, 220, 267, 311, 350
    aircraft certification vi, 189, 275, 302, 341, 342, 365
    and flight simulators 85, 170
    facilities 120, 302, 353
    medical certification 25-28, 32, 342, 344
    pilot instruction and certification 24, 156, 158, 241, 277, 278, 298, 299, 330, 340, 341, 346, 350, 362
    publications v, 35, 86-87, 89, 111, 150, 303, 346, 351, 367, 370, 379
    regulations vi, 29-30, 41, 97, 264, 274, 298, 303, 304, 343, 365, 368
    websites 23, 31, 25, 111, 152, 353, 356
    written pilot exam 7, 12, 28, 35, 153
FADEC (Full Authority Digital Engine Control) 76, 351
false horizon 221, 325, 351
FAR/AIM (Federal Aviation Regulations/ Aeronautical Information Manual) 303, 304, 305, 306, 351, 379
feathering 290, 293, 351
final (leg) 21, 174, 184, 192, 205, 229, 230, 232, 238, 351, 367, 368
    aiming point 181, 257, 260, 261, 319, 341
    airspeed 51, 165, 176, 249, 257, 260, 319
    at Lincoln Park 167, 169, 172, 175
    crabbing 187
    flaps 165, 269
    forced landing 269
    forward slip 206, 320, 352
    left-turning tendencies 49
    power-off landing 261-262
    risk of stalling 59, 61, 118
    sight picture 22, 281
    turn from base to final 2, 40, 165, 187, 223, 244, 246, 281, 344
    visual guidance 174
Flagstaff, Arizona 10
flapping (rotor blades) 293, 294, 351
flaps 1, 7, 44, 52, 53, 172, 208, 220, 253, 346, 349, 351, 375
    and required equipment 303
    and stall speed 39, 40, 70, 165, 256, 369
    approach and landing 10, 164-165, 206, 238
    ballooning 154, 344
    complex airplane 156, 347
    electrical power 140, 272
    forced landing 269
    go-around 166, 249, 275, 320

inspection 15-16
power-off landing 262
slow flight 58
stall recovery 59-60, 364
takeoff 18, 254, 256, 258, 259, 319
touch-and-go 175
FLAPS (acronym) 304
flare (landing) 5, 163, 205, 223, 249, 351
   at night 222
   bouncing 244, 247
   during sideslip 188, 367
   first solo 191
   power-off landing 262
   power-off stall 59, 364
   short-field landing 257
   soft-field landing 260
   struggling to master 166, 171, 177, 181, 182, 184
Flight Following 235, 236, 351
flight level (FL) 68-69, 106
flight plan 209, 222, 236, 253, 305, 348, 350, 351
   autopilot 84, 98
   checkride scenario 308-312, 313, 315
   filing 212-213, 353, 356
   ForeFlight 97, 121, 213, 214, 352
   IFR 95, 110, 210, 356
   MFD 77
   pen and paper 112, 213, 216, 242, 243
   weather briefing 121, 123, 353, 375
   written exam 100, 147
flight review 157, 298, 352
flight school 7, 8, 14, 24, 145, 162, 170, 258, 300
   airline-run 161
   and DPEs 277, 278, 283
   at Lincoln Park 13, 14-15, 18, 55, 152, 153, 162, 167, 189, 190, 285, 304, 313, 322, 329
   finding 12-13
   in Scottsdale 190, 192, 193, 195, 196, 204, 210, 213, 214, 216, 219, 225, 252
   insurance 275
   Part 61 156, 157, 161, 362
   Part 141 156, 157, 159, 161, 190, 362
   universities 159
Flight Service, *see FSS*
float (motion) 165, 175, 180, 186, 249, 260, 262, 321, 352
floor to door scan 268, 269, 271
Fly8MA 7, 380
fly-by-wire 52, 352
fog 81, 82, 116, 119-120, 122, 126, 127, 147, 352
Foggles 78, 80, 83, 85, 86, 90, 92, 318, 352. *Also see hood.*
forced landing 269, 272, 352
Ford, Harrison 270
ForeFlight 112, 121, 124, 126, 131, 193, 196, 307, 315, 332, 350, 352, 378
   and ADS-B 97
   and *Microsoft Flight Simulator* 98
   displays 96, 114
   flight planning 97, 213, 214
   flight recording 97, 250
   in-flight weather 123, 129
   on return flight from checkride 323-325, 331
   on solo cross-countries 242, 243, 246, 249, 250
   relative cost 98
   traffic 233, 246, 249, 285, 324
   weather briefing 121
forward slip 51, 206-208, 320, 352
freezing rain 127, 129, 352
front (weather) 116-118, 120, 126, 353, 375
frost 127, 353
Frost, Robert 216
FSDO (Flight Standards District Office) 302, 353
FSS (Flight Service Station) 120, 121, 124, 211, 212, 314, 351, 353
FTN (FAA Tracking Number) 23, 353
fuel 156, 313, 317, 323, 324, 371-372

INDEX

avgas 136, 137, 141, 344
   Cessna 172 system and capacity 136-137, 313
   cooling function 141-142
   efficiency/rate of burn 28, 37, 89, 91, 97, 132, 142, 213, 349
   emergency procedures 268-269, 271, 318
   fuel injection 137, 345, 353
   gauges 272
   in carburetor 136, 345
   in jet engine 36, 141
   in piston engine 134, 138, 139, 141, 349, 359, 364, 368
   Jet A 141
   leaded 141, 144
   mixture 9, 44, 76, 128, 135, 138, 142, 350, 351, 358, 360, 366
   octane 141, 344
   priming 17, 137, 271, 365
   refueling 101, 322
   reserves 214
   running out 90, 208, 268
   sumping 15, 16, 137, 370
   weight and balance 39, 40, 41, 146, 147-148

G

Garmin G1000 98, 129
Gasmire, Charlie 182-183
General Aviation (GA) 345, 353
   accident statistics 275, 330
glass cockpit 66, 77, 98, 131, 132, 272, 353, 360, 363
Glendale Municipal Airport (KGEU) 228, 230
glide (power-off) 105, 163, 165, 177, 206, 261-262, 266, 267, 268, 270, 294, 295, 314, 353
   best glide speed 261, 266, 272, 319
   maximum distance 96, 266, 309
glider 43, 75, 98, 248
glideslope 95, 165, 173, 175, 177, 207, 222, 353, 362, 368, 374

go-around 21, 58, 131, 166, 206, 249-250, 261, 262, 275, 320, 353
GPS (Global Positioning System) 17, 96, 98, 140, 146, 331, 333, 353
Greece 10, 82
Grintovec, Slovenia (mountain) 131
Ground (ATC frequency), see ATC
ground effect 166, 259, 344, 352, 354
ground loop 49, 354
ground reference maneuvers 61, 64, 187, 247, 319, 354
ground school 7, 9, 10, 145, 195, 204, 236, 278, 306, 354
groundspeed 20, 89, 96, 213, 243, 315, 317, 349, 352, 354
ground track 62, 348, 354, 365
gust (wind) 2, 41, 56, 165, 186, 188, 189, 244, 246, 354
gyroscope 67, 72, 74, 75, 79, 83, 343, 354, 355, 366, 373
gyroscopic precession 49, 73, 74, 293, 354, 358

H

hail 119, 355, 368
Hammondsport, New York 183
hand propping 139, 355
heading (direction) 57, 58, 61, 62, 64, 65, 72, 80, 83, 84, 87, 90, 91, 96, 97, 99, 201, 213, 243, 315, 316, 318, 347, 349, 354, 355, 370, 375
   and magnetic compass 73-74
   during stalls 279, 280, 281
   magnetic heading 88, 89, 97, 123, 147, 214, 357, 358, 359, 374
   runway heading 199
   true heading 88, 89, 357, 359, 373
   VOR TO/FROM 94, 95, 345
heading indicator 66, 67, 72, 75, 79, 89, 91, 319, 355
   and magnetic compass 73-74
   gyroscopic precession 73
   in glass cockpit 76
   required equipment 303, 304
headset 17, 193, 234, 287, 307

headwind 20, 21, 61, 62, 118, 150, 186, 187, 255, 312, 317, 340, 355, 371
helicopter 284-296, 333, 351, 377
    and airplanes (comparison) 285, 286, 287, 292, 294, 295
    Army 26, 286, 288
    at Lincoln Park 284-285, 287
    at Morristown 287
    blades as airfoils 289, 341
    blade flapping 293
    controls 289-291, 342, 347, 348
    dissymmetry of lift 292-293
    German 286
    Grand Canyon 286
    hovering 292, 294-295
    in *Microsoft Flight Simulator* 285
    inspection 288
    rating 287
    retreating blade stall 293-294
    right of way 248
high performance 157, 355
Hindenburg (airship) 306
Hobbs meter 300, 355
Hochosterwitz, Austria 128
hold short (action) 112, 196, 238, 246, 355
hold short line 18, 184, 191, 197, 355
Holly, Buddy 81
hood 78, 80, 86, 156, 185, 205, 319, 352, 355. *Also see Foggles.*
Hoover, President Herbert 80
horizontal stabilizer 40, 41, 356, 371. *Also see tailplane.*
horsepower 60, 135, 157, 199, 355
Huguenot VOR 92-95
hyperventilation 31, 356
hypoxia 29, 30, 31, 356

I

IACRA (Integrated Airman Certification and Rating Application) 23, 356
IATA airport code 102, 356
ICAO airport code 102, 356
icing 71, 120, 121, 127, 129-132, 341, 347, 356
idle (setting) 135, 318, 353, 356
    descent 206

emergency drills 266, 318
landing 10, 131, 166, 167, 181, 184, 205, 260, 261, 262
power-off landing 261, 262, 364
power-off stall 59, 364
power-on stall 59, 279
run-up 18
stall recovery 61
tach time 301
IFR (Instrument Flight Rules) 90, 94, 356, 374
    charts and approach plates 110, 111, 343
    clearance 106, 212
    conditions 121,126, 222, 323, 329, 330, 355, 357, 375
    flight plan 84, 95, 210, 212
    instrument rating 80, 157, 357
    radio procedures 234, 235
ignition 128, 140, 142, 271
    switch 17, 18, 139, 144, 268, 269, 356
ILS (Instrument Landing System) 95, 356
IMC (Instrument Meteorological Conditions) 80, 357
IMSAFE 299
incident (safety) 16, 275, 304, 357
inclinometer 74, 75, 357, 373
Indicated Airspeed (IAS) 69, 70, 87, 357, 373
induced drag, *see drag*
Inspection Authorized (IA) mechanic 301, 342
instrument rating 80, 81, 85, 91, 95, 106, 157, 161, 218, 235, 356, 357, 374
insurance 275-276
isobar 115, 117, 357
isogonic lines 89, 147, 357, 359

J

Jersey Devil 305
John F. Kennedy International Airport (KJFK) 107, 194
Julian Alps 126, 128

INDEX

K

Kennedy, John F., Jr. 81-82
kidney stones 26, 27, 32
Killing Zone 322, 327, 330, 331
Klagenfurt, Austria 126-128
knots 18, 80, 103, 318, 357
    airspeed indicator 70
    approach speeds 164-165, 247, 249, 257, 260
    autopilot 84
    best angle of climb 255, 256, 259, 316
    best rate of climb 255, 256, 259
    climb speed 19, 82, 256, 317
    groundspeed 89, 317
    helicopter 292, 293, 294
    maneuvering speed 57
    maneuver standards 57
    maximum glide speed 261, 266
    never exceed speed 311
    power-on stall 59, 279, 282
    slow flight 58
    speed limits 146, 311
    stall speeds 40, 56, 165, 256
    takeoff speed 9, 18, 199, 255, 319
    true airspeed (TAS) 69, 89
    wind speed 88, 122, 186, 189, 312, 348
Kos, Greece 82

L

LaGuardia Airport (KLGA) 194
LAHSO (Land and Hold Short Operations) 238, 357
Lakehurst Maxfield Field (KNEL) 306, 313, 323
Langewiesche, Wolfgang 35, 47, 176, 177
lateral axis 47, 51, 350, 358, 364
latitude 102-104, 105, 358, 359, 361, 373
lean (fuel mixture) 9, 128, 142, 144, 358. *Also see fuel.*
left-turning tendencies 48-50, 53, 57, 60, 73, 279, 281, 354, 358
lift 10, 33, 34-36, 37, 43, 55, 130, 132, 135, 177, 292, 296, 341, 358
    ailerons 44-45
    and angle of attack 36, 38, 42, 342, 348, 357
    and crosswind 186, 187, 188
    and flaps 53, 58, 164, 254, 258, 262, 344, 351
    and gusts 186
    and ice/frost 127, 353
    and speed 36, 38, 47, 70
    and weight 39
    autorotation 295
    banking 39-40, 57
    blade flapping 294
    center of lift 40
    dissymmetry of lift 293
    floating 247
    ground effect 166, 259, 344, 354
    helicopter 285-286, 289, 290, 291, 292, 294, 347, 348
    negative lift (tailplanes) 40, 46-47, 130, 356
    stall 36, 59, 60, 294, 369
    vortices 202, 375
light gun signals 273, 358
Lincoln Park Airport (N07) 64, 81, 171, 190, 209, 233, 244, 245, 246, 253, 261, 266, 269
    CTAF 102, 237
    depiction on chart 101-102
    elevation 21, 102
    flight school 13, 152
    flight to and from checkride 310, 312
    helicopters at 284-285, 287
    lack of weather information 124, 248-249
    non-towered procedures 20, 164
    runway 18, 19, 102, 169-170, 173-175, 254, 262, 320, 322-329
    taxiway 112
    traffic pattern and landing approaches 21, 166-168, 180
    vicinity 105, 108, 109
Lindbergh, Charles 75, 80, 81, 90, 91, 112, 333
LiveATC 233

Ljubljana, Slovenia 126, 129, 131
load factor 39, 40, 57, 58, 340, 358
logbook (pilot) 156, 162, 185, 195, 328, 358
    endorsements 156, 191, 241, 278, 350
    logging ground school 278
    preparing for checkride 297, 299, 306, 313
    record of training entries 336-339
logbook (maintenance), *see maintenance records*
longitude 87, 102, 103, 104, 105, 358, 359, 373
longitudinal axis 44, 51, 341, 344, 345, 358, 366
Los Angeles International Airport (KLAX) 107
Louis Armstrong New Orleans International Airport (KMSY) 107
Luke Air Force Base (KLUF) 212

M

Machado, Rod 180, 380
Magdalensberg, Austria 128
magnetic compass 20, 73-74, 75, 87, 89, 90, 147, 304, 355, 357, 358, 359, 365, 367, 373
magnetic course, see course.
magnetic deviation 73, 90, 359
magnetic heading, *see heading*
magnetic variation 88, 89, 214, 359
magneto 18, 138-139, 140, 144, 272, 355, 356, 359, 368, 369
maintenance records 297, 299, 300, 301, 302, 304, 312, 341, 358
maneuvering speed (VA) 56, 359
manifold pressure 76, 288, 359
Marana Regional Airport (KAVQ) 210, 211, 212, 213, 214, 215, 218, 221, 222-223
Maria Saal, Austria 128
Martian, The (film) 133, 331
M*A*S*H (TV show) 285
master switch 16, 52, 139, 140, 219, 359
    and Hobbs meter 300, 355

emergency procedures 268-269, 272, 273
Mayday 208, 267, 360
McCauley, Kerry 125, 140
McGovern, George 132
McGuire Air Force Base (KWRI) 306, 326
medical certificate 23, 25, 32, 297-298, 306, 313, 344
medications 27, 31
Mediterranean Sea 10, 82, 84, 125
MEL (Minimum Equipment List) 303, 360
METAR 121, 122, 123, 126, 150, 212, 323, 329, 343, 360
MFD (Multi-Function Display) 77, 360
microburst 118, 360
Microsoft Flight Simulator 2020 (MSFS 2020) 360
    automated ATC 234
    exposure to autopilot 83-85
    exposure to challenging conditions 82-83, 84-85, 120, 125-133, 332
    flying other aircraft 50, 285
    initial experiences 8-10
    Mediterranean journey 82, 84-85, 125-126
    photorealism 4, 6, 171, 242, 243
    relevance to real-world training 170-172, 176, 178, 189, 191, 194, 220, 236-237, 242-243, 245, 260, 282, 305-306, 316, 319, 332
    triggering interest in flying 4, 6, 7, 13
    using glass cockpit 75, 98
    with *ForeFlight* 98, 332
    with *PilotEdge* 234, 236-237, 242-243
    with VR helmet 171-172, 189, 191
Millville Municipal Airport (KMIV) 312
mixture, *see fuel*
MOA (Military Operations Area) 110, 212, 306, 326, 360
Mode C 107, 201, 360, 372
Mode C veil 107, 201, 360
moment (measurement) 147-148, 343, 345, 360-361

Morristown Airport (KMMU) 1, 109, 174, 194, 234, 241
    airspace 109, 194
    helicopter lesson 287, 295
    solo takeoffs and landings 233, 237-240
    to and from checkride 313, 323-328, 329, 332
MSL (Mean Sea Level) 67, 126, 128, 131, 164, 246, 309, 323, 342, 361
    airspace 106, 108, 109, 197, 200
    and density altitude 88
    cruising altitude 210, 211, 245, 348
    inaccuracies 67-68
    obstacles 103, 105, 325
    speed limits 146
    versus AGL 67, 341
multi-engine airplanes 50, 270-271
multi-engine rating 158, 159, 271, 361
MzeroA 7, 380. Also see Schappert, Jason.

N

nautical mile (nm) 18, 103-104, 114, 165, 197, 201, 217, 224, 241, 317, 348, 357, 361
NAV1 and NAV2 91, 92, 94, 361, 365
navigation lights 217, 219, 248, 303, 361
NDB (Non-Directional Beacon) 91, 92, 361
Never Exceed Speed (V_{NE}) 70, 294, 311, 361
Newark Liberty International Airport (KEWR) 56, 108, 109, 194, 200, 313, 323
Newton's Third Law of Motion 35, 48, 291, 361
New York City 3, 4, 12, 13, 89, 194, 285, 322
night 1, 84, 106, 112, 140
    aircraft lights 16, 219-220, 248, 303-304, 344, 361
    airport lights 102, 222-223, 344, 371
    cross-country 210, 216-224
    currency 218, 298
    definitions 217-218, 346
    fog 120
    gear 193
    hazards 82, 211, 218, 223, 344, 351
    landing 222, 223
    night solo for CPL 157
    night vision 218-219, 347, 366
    pilotage 221
    required equipment 303-304
    requirements for PPL 156, 217
    VFR 81, 218
north pole 89, 358, 359,
nosewheel 9, 44, 48, 49, 55, 156, 186, 258, 259, 260, 364, 367, 371, 372
NOTAM (Notice to Air Missions) 121, 361
NTSB (National Transportation Safety Board) 275

O

OBS (Omni Bearing Selector) 91-94, 361
Ocean County Airport (KMJX) 283, 305, 306, 305, 307, 308, 309, 310, 312, 313, 314, 317, 319, 328, 329
Ocker, William C. 79
octane, *see fuel*
oil 362
    function in engine 142-143
    inspection 16, 288
    oil pressure 37, 142, 143, 362
    oil temperature 142, 143, 199, 362
    preventative maintenance 365
operating limitations 300, 362
Orange County Airport (KMGJ) 245, 246

P

Page, Arizona 5
Pan-Pan 268, 362
PAPI (Precision Approach Path Indicator), 174, 175, 223, 320, 362
parasitic drag, *see drag*
PARE (stall recovery) 60-61
Part 61, *see flight school*
Part 141, *see flight school*

performance takeoffs and landings 253, 262, 279, 362
Perpignan, France 332
personal minimums 189, 363
P-factor 49, 358, 363
PFD (Primary Flight Display) 75, 77, 360, 363
Phoenix, Arizona 194, 197, 205, 208, 210, 211, 224, 226
Phoenix Deer Valley Airport (KDVT) 197, 205, 230, 232
Phoenix Goodyear Airport (KGYR) 228-230
Phoenix Sky Harbor International Airport (KPHX) 194-195, 197, 199-203, 224
PIC (Pilot in Command) 13, 160, 363
pilotage 86, 90-91, 210, 221, 315, 349, 363
PilotEdge 235-237, 242, 363, 378
Pinal Airpark (KMZJ) 211, 214
Piper Cub 207, 248
Piper Cherokee 248
PIREP 121, 122, 150, 363
piston 9, 134-135, 138, 141, 143, 274, 344, 349, 359, 363, 364, 366, 368
pitch (aircraft) 47, 250, 358, 363, 368, 371
    aerodynamic braking 341
    and angle of attack 35, 47
    and speed 47, 51, 176, 254
    approach and landing 164-165, 176-177, 257, 351
    attitude indicator 72, 343
    autopilot 84
    controls 46-47, 51, 350
    forward slip 352
    gliding 261, 266
    helicopter 293, 294
    icing 130
    in turns 57, 63, 64
    left-turning tendencies 49, 354
    on go-around 249
    on PFD 76
    parachute 146
    slow flight 58
    stall and spin recovery 59-60, 84, 256, 279, 318, 364, 368, 369
    takeoff and climb 49, 52, 56, 82, 199, 220, 255, 256, 259-260, 316
    trim 52, 372
pitch (rotor blade) 289-290, 291, 342, 347, 348, 351, 370, 374
pitch (propeller) 37, 76, 347, 351, 365
pitot heat 72, 130, 133, 140
pitot-static system 72, 302, 357, 363-364
pitot tube 16, 69, 71-72, 130, 364
PlaneEnglish 234
POH (Pilot Operating Handbook) vi, 204, 350, 364, 379-380
    checklists 208, 254, 266, 273, 299, 364
    equipment list 303, 304
    operating limitations 300, 362
    performance calculations 89, 253, 266
    weight and balance 148
porpoising 166, 364
Po Valley, Italy 126
power-off landing 261-262, 263, 266, 269, 270, 320-321, 364
power-off stall, *see stall*
power-on stall, *see stall*
PPL (Private Pilot License) 24, 61, 80, 156-157, 159, 161, 217, 218, 233, 251, 316, 348, 364
pre-flight inspection 15-16, 52, 55, 137, 142, 208, 209, 285, 303, 364, 370
    at night 219
    on checkride 315, 316
    on helicopter 288
    requirement 299
preignition 141, 364
pressure altitude, *see altitude*
preventative maintenance 304, 365
prime (engine), *see fuel*
Prime Meridian 104, 358
proficiency 24, 298, 299, 365
propeller 14, 40, 44, 47, 143, 291, 364, 365
    and left-turning tendencies 48-50, 60, 73, 354, 358, 363, 369
    and piston engine 135, 138, 139, 140

INDEX 429

and turboprop engine 135, 373
as an airfoil 36-37, 49, 289, 341
autogyro 285
constant speed propeller 37, 76, 142, 157, 347, 359, 370, 374
feathering 351
fixed pitch propeller 37, 76
icing 127
idle setting 10
inspection 16
maintenance records 301
RPM 8, 76, 366, 370
safety 139, 209, 265
starting 17, 139, 269, 271, 355, 369
thrust 10, 17, 36, 37, 266, 372
variable pitch propeller 37, 347, 351, 374
windmilling 268-269, 351
prop lever 76, 347, 365
prop wash 47, 365

R

radial 92, 93, 94, 95, 345, 361, 362, 365, 375
radio stack 91, 92, 230, 231, 237, 365
rating 23, 157, 285, 287, 298, 346, 350, 356, 365, 372. *For more on specific ratings, see instrument rating, multi-engine rating, type rating.*
Recreational Pilot License 24
rectangular course 62, 354, 365
registration vi, 20, 41, 189, 229, 242, 300, 345, 365
relative humidity 116, 365
relative wind 35, 47, 59, 60, 293, 342, 346, 366
Restricted Area 110, 212, 306, 309, 317, 366
retreating blade stall, *see stall*
reverse sensing (VOR) 95, 366
rich (fuel mixture) 142, 143, 144, 366. Also see fuel.
Richardson, J.P. "The Big Bopper" 81
Rickenbacker, Eddie 80

right of way 247-248, 366
rigidity in space 72, 354, 366
rime ice 129, 346, 366
Robinson R22 288
Robinson R44 288
rods (vision) 218-219, 366
roll (landing/takeoff) 258, 366, 370
roll (bank) 42, 44, 51, 57, 60, 293, 341, 344, 358, 366
Roosevelt, President Franklin D. (FDR) 80-81
round out 163, 166, 170, 171, 177, 181, 182, 205, 222, 247, 366, 367
    power-off landing 262
    short-field landing 257
    soft-field landing 260
    soft-field takeoff 259
RPM (Revolutions Per Minute) 8, 135, 144, 366
    and carburetor ice 136
    approach and landing 76, 164, 260
    constant speed propeller 37, 347, 359, 365
    cruise 76
    descent 76
    engine fire 271
    in helicopter 288, 289, 290
    leaning fuel mixture 9, 142
    performance 89
    recognizing sound 170
    run-up 18, 139
    slow flight 58, 59
    start-up 17
    tachometer 76, 370
    tach time 301, 371
    takeoff and climb 56, 76
    taxiing 17
rudder 5, 28, 44, 48, 51, 366, 368, 374, 376
    and center of gravity 40-41
    and left-turning tendencies 48-49, 50, 56, 358
    and tailwheel airplanes 49-50
    and turn coordinator 75
    approach and landing 165, 178, 180, 244, 321
    coordinated turn 50, 57

effect of airspeed 55
forward slip 51, 206, 320, 352
inspection 16
mechanism 47-48, 52
sideslip 51, 188, 367
stall and spin recovery 60, 61, 279, 281-282, 318, 368
trim 53, 372
rudder pedals 19, 44, 51, 112, 291, 366-367, 376
    brakes 17
    Ercoupe 28
    for sim 6, 9
    landing 182
    mechanism 47-48
    step on the ball 75
    takeoff 9, 18, 182, 191
    taxiing 9, 17
    tendency to ignore 48
running rough 143-144, 367
run-up 18, 139, 191, 196, 208, 367
runway 200, 202, 224, 249, 250, 253, 285, 354, 367, 371
    active 20, 112, 123, 196, 228, 238, 248, 340, 343, 344
    and traffic pattern 21-22, 62, 163-164, 187, 191, 192, 211, 228, 344, 348, 350, 351, 374
    clearance 1, 229-230, 240, 346
    closures 121, 123
    emergency 267, 270, 352
    exiting 230, 232, 237, 238, 313, 321
    holding short 197-198, 230, 238, 355, 357-358, 367
    incursion 112, 308, 314, 330, 367
    instrument approach 91, 95
    landing 2, 5, 6, 10, 20, 38, 51, 131, 163, 165-166, 170, 172, 174, 177, 180-184, 186-188, 191, 205, 223, 244, 247, 257, 260, 261, 262, 269, 319, 320, 364, 366, 372
    length 18, 53, 87, 102, 150, 174-176, 185, 205, 207, 223, 249, 254, 261, 262, 320, 363-364
    lights 82, 83, 102, 111, 131, 220, 221, 222-223
    markings 7, 18, 164-165, 169-170, 197, 257, 345, 349-350, 355, 370
    numbers 20, 123, 169-170, 182, 228, 340, 367
    on chart 101, 102
    orientation 19-20, 21, 101, 111, 166, 186, 245, 316, 367
    other traffic 246
    sight picture 165, 176, 180, 368
    soft field 258-261, 294, 352, 363-364
    takeoff 9-10, 18, 20, 48, 50, 55, 82, 191, 199, 220, 254-255, 258-260, 263, 316, 372
    visual approach 40, 49, 53, 131, 132, 163-165, 167-169, 172, 174-177, 206-207, 223, 294, 320, 341, 345, 353, 368
    visual guidance 174-175, 223, 362, 374
Runway 1 (Lincoln Park) 20, 166, 167, 169, 244, 249
Runway 19 (Lincoln Park) 20, 164, 167, 169, 184, 190, 328
Ryan Airfield (KRYN) 212

S

safety briefing 264-265, 270, 316
Saguaro National Park 212
Saint-Exupéry, Antoine de 333
Santorini, Greece 82
Santos-Dumont, Alberto 77
Sardinia, Italy 84
Schappert, Jason 166, 170. *Also see MzeroA.*
Scottsdale, Arizona 190, 193, 218, 252
Scottsdale Airport (KSDL) 194, 196-199, 205, 208, 210, 213, 216, 224, 226, 230, 233
seat belts 33, 264-265

sectional chart 86-87, 88, 89, 100, 104-105, 111, 112, 113, 193, 210, 211, 214, 245, 367, 370, 379
    airport information 101-102, 123, 222
    airspace 106-110. 197, 366, 373
    for checkride 305, 307, 310, 312
    ForeFlight/EFB 96-97, 357
    isogonic lines 89, 359, 366
    longitude and latitude 102-104
    VFR waypoints 201
    Victor airways 95, 110
    VOR 92-94, 110, 124, 149
Sedona, Arizona 8
Sentry (ADS-B device) 96, 97, 193, 196, 307
separation 229, 367
sequencing 229, 367
shock cooling 143, 367
short-field landing 253, 257-258, 260, 261, 263, 319
short-field takeoff 253, 254-256, 258, 263, 319
sideslip 51, 187, 188, 206, 320, 367
sight picture 58, 165, 170, 171, 176, 180, 182, 189, 245, 294, 367, 368, 374
SIGMET 121, 341, 367
Sikorsky, Igor 286
sinking 176, 177, 368
skid 41, 50, 75, 347, 357, 368
SkyVector 100, 126, 378
slip 50, 51, 57, 75, 188, 347, 357, 368. *Also see forward slip and sideslip.*
slow flight 58-59, 64, 166, 182, 205, 279, 364, 368
    transition to 57-58, 317
Smith, Keith 234
soft-field landing 260, 263, 320
soft-field takeoff 258-260, 263, 316
solo 55, 155, 162, 288, 298, 364, 368
    first solo 8, 23, 163, 185, 186, 189, 191-192, 193, 215, 243
    historic solo flights 27, 75
    night solo (for CPL) 157, 217
    pre-solo exam 191, 210
    requirements for PPL 233, 241

    requirements to fly 23, 24, 191, 200, 225, 350
    solo cross-countries 153, 156, 225, 241-251, 253, 275, 305
    solo takeoffs and landings at towered airport 233, 237-240
Somerset Airport (KSMQ) 292, 294
spark plug 134, 138-139, 140, 141, 142, 359, 368
Sparta VOR 92, 94
spatial disorientation 78, 81, 82, 343, 368
Special Flight Permit 302, 368
Sperry, Elmer 79, 83
Sperry, Lawrence 83
spins 1, 51, 60, 146, 294, 300, 368
    fatal accidents 61, 81, 105
    power-on stall 61, 279, 280, 281, 282
    recovery (PARE) 60-61, 281
spiraling slipstream 49, 358, 369
spoilers 53, 346, 349
Sport Pilot License 24, 28
Sporty's 7, 8, 145, 151, 152, 221, 236, 278, 306, 377, 379
squawk 201, 203, 227, 236, 245, 246, 273, 369. *Also see transponder.*
    emergency codes 268, 273
stability 40-42, 48, 50, 285, 295, 349, 369
stall 36, 38, 131, 132, 146, 165, 205, 256, 292, 348, 359, 369
    accelerated stall 40, 340
    accidents 105, 158
    and center of gravity 40-41
    and flaps 53, 249, 351
    and icing/frost 127
    and load factor 40, 50, 57, 58
    and weight 39
    autopilot 84
    flare and landing 5, 58, 166, 181, 294, 351
    go-around 249
    low RPM blade stall 289-290
    microbursts 118
    power-off stall 59, 60, 64, 166, 278, 280, 318, 364

power-on stall 59-60, 61, 64, 256, 278-283, 305, 318, 364
retreating blade stall 293-294
safe practice altitude 58
slow flight 58, 368
spins 50, 60-61, 279, 368-369
stall speeds 39, 40, 50, 70, 165, 256
unusual attitudes 318
stall horn 59, 60, 130, 279, 369
stall speeds 39, 40, 41, 50, 53, 57, 58, 127, 165, 256, 351, 368, 369
Standard Day 69, 369
Standard Rate Turn 74, 369
starter 17, 139, 268, 269, 271, 344, 355, 356, 369
static port 67, 69, 71, 364, 369
statute mile 18, 78, 104, 361, 369
steam gauge 66, 98, 272, 370
Stearman (airplane) 195, 207, 209
steep turns 56-57, 61, 64, 205, 278, 279, 313, 317, 370
    checkride standard 305
    load factor and stall speed 40, 50
sterile cockpit 265, 370
stick (control) 5, 44, 51, 341, 364, 370, 376
Stick and Rudder (book) 35, 47, 176
Stone, Alex 162
stopway 169, 254, 370
Storžic, Slovenia (mountain) 131
straight and level flight 8, 52, 57, 75, 83, 85, 318, 370, 372, 374
stratus, *see clouds*
S-turns 64, 205, 279, 319, 354, 370
Su-27 (fighter plane) 42
Sullenberger, "Sully" 262
Sullivan County Airport (KMSV) 174, 242, 247
sumping, *see fuel*

T

TAC (Terminal Area Chart) 193, 305, 370
TACAN 92, 375
tachometer 76, 135, 370
Tach time 301, 370

TAF (Terminal Aerodrome Forecast) 121, 122, 150, 212, 323, 329, 371
tail fin 41, 50, 371. *Also see vertical stabilizer.*
    icing 129, 131
    lights 219
    rudder 48, 366
    spiraling slipstream 48, 369
tailplane 40-41 42, 46, 129, 131, 350, 371. *Also see horizontal stabilizer.*
tailstrike 260, 371
tailwheel airplane 49, 50, 156, 166, 186, 277, 298, 321, 354, 371
tailwind 20, 61, 62, 89, 106, 118, 187, 249, 275, 350, 371
taxi diagram 96, 111-113, 196, 214, 310, 371
taxiing 15, 22, 55, 74, 82, 143, 169, 205, 214, 230, 236, 254, 310, 312, 313, 315, 316, 321, 328, 349, 355, 371
    across runway 314
    airplane lights 2200
    crosswinds 186-187
    Ground ATC 196, 200, 209, 220, 236, 237, 347, 354
    light gun signals 273
    rudder pedals 9, 17, 44, 48, 367
    seatbelts 265
    sight picture 180
    speed 9
    tailwheel airplane 49
    taxi back 175, 191, 215, 223, 246, 258
taxiway 111, 112, 191, 196, 198, 214, 246, 345, 358, 371
    closures 121
    lights 221, 222
temperature inversion 119, 371
Teterboro Airport (KTEB) 302
TFR (Temporary Flight Restriction) 131, 371
    on checkride 311-312, 314
Thirty Seconds Over Tokyo (book, film) 79
Thoreau, Henry David 334, 335
throttle 1, 8, 9, 28, 44, 353, 371
    and altitude 10, 47, 52
    and manifold pressure 76, 359

INDEX 433

and RPM 76
and thrust 44, 356
autopilot 84
cut to idle on landing 10, 166,
   167, 177, 181, 182, 184,
   205, 261
emergency procedures 266, 270,
   271, 318
for sim 6, 172
go-around 166, 205-206, 249,
   262, 320
helicopter 289, 290, 347
in turns 57
mechanism 135-137, 371
on approach 2, 10, 164, 176, 206
power-off landing 261, 364
run-up 18
short-field landing 258
short-field takeoff 254, 319
slow flight 58
soft-field landing 260
stall and spin recovery 59-60, 279
start-up 17
takeoff and climb 9, 18, 56, 191,
   199, 208, 220, 259
touch-and-go 175
thrust 10, 33, 36, 43, 258, 261, 266, 353,
   356, 372
   and drag 37, 350
   and icing 127, 132
   and throttle 44
   helicopter tail rotor 291
   jet engine 36
   multi-engine 271
   propeller 37, 49, 363, 365, 374
   turboprop 135, 373
thunderstorm 84, 117-119, 121, 355, 360,
   368
Top Gun (film) 3, 155
torque 48, 291, 343, 372
   helicopter 291, 342
   left-turning 48, 358, 372
touch-and-go v, 175, 240, 298, 372
Tower (ATC frequency), *see ATC*
traffic pattern 10, 21, 170, 187, 222, 223,
   224, 237, 238, 242, 244, 247, 249,
253, 294, 313, 319, 320, 328, 344,
348, 350, 351, 353, 372, 374
   ATC 22, 198, 229, 230, 233, 235,
      238, 240, 245
   at Lincoln Park 164, 167-169
   entering 22, 67, 164, 198
   extending 192
   first solo 163, 190-191, 233
   information 67, 96, 191, 124, 191,
      211
   other traffic 192, 246
   overflying 192, 124
   power-off landing 260-261, 270
   practicing 163, 171, 174, 180,
      184, 189, 298
   radio failure and light gun signals
      273
   rectangular course 62, 365
transponder 97, 194, 302, 311, 360, 369,
   372. *Also see squawk.*
   airspace requirements 107, 108,
      109, 201
   electrical power 140, 272
   emergency codes 268, 273
   ident button 201-202
   inspection 302
   VFR code 201, 203
tricycle-gear airplane 186, 298, 372
trim 52-53, 57, 58, 243, 295, 372
   tab 52, 372
   wheel 42, 52, 58, 372
TRSA (Terminal Radar Services Area) 245,
   372
True Airspeed (TAS) 69-70, 87, 89, 147,
   349, 357, 373
true course, *see course*
true heading, *see heading*
Tucson, Arizona 210, 215, 222, 224
Tucson International Airport (KTUS) 212
Tunisia 84, 85
turbocharger 135, 373
turboprop 135, 158, 373
turbulence 42, 56, 85, 132, 212, 294, 312,
   373
   AIRMETs 121, 341
   mountain 129, 211
   PIREP 123

thunderstorm 118
    wake turbulence 202, 306, 375
turn coordinator 66, 67, 74-75, 79, 272, 281, 292, 373
turns around a point 62-63, 205, 242, 279, 319, 354, 373
type rating 157, 161, 373

U

United States Air Force 26, 159
United States Army 26, 79, 80, 195, 222, 286, 288, 305-306
United States Navy 26, 52
unusual attitudes 318, 373
upwind (leg) 21, 374
UTC (Coordinated Universal Time) 122, 374

V

Valens, Ritchie 81
variable pitch propeller, *see propeller*
VASI (Visual Approach Slope Indicator) 174, 175, 223, 374
VATSIM 234, 235
vector 91, 374
Venice, Italy 126
vertical axis 44, 48, 51, 342, 355, 366, 373, 374, 376
vertical speed indicator (VSI) 66, 67, 70-71, 164, 288, 292, 318, 320, 363, 369, 374
vertical stabilizer 41, 371, 374. *Also see tail fin.*
VFR (Visual Flight Rules) 78, 157, 245, 248, 309, 323, 330, 341, 374
    airspace corridors 200
    ATC services 236, 351
    charts 87, 110, 367
    cruising altitudes 210
    eyes outside 83, 95, 229, 367
    flight plan 212, 311
    flight simulators 242
    minimum conditions 109, 110, 126, 147, 324, 347, 357, 370

minimum equipment 303, 304
    night flying 81, 82-83, 218
    pilotage 90
    radio procedures 234, 235
    squawk VFR 201, 203, 227
    VFR over the top 126, 374
    VFR waypoints 201
    weather briefing 121-122
Victor airway 95, 110, 375
Volkermarkt Reservoir, Austria 128
VOR (VHF Omnidirectional Range) 96, 97, 185, 331, 345, 350, 361, 362, 365, 375
    contacting FSS via 124, 314
    depiction on chart 92-93, 110
    flight planning 210, 242, 309-310
    flying to or from 94-95
    locating position using 93-94, 148-149
    on checkride 306, 309 -310, 315-317, 319
    physical appearance 92
    tuning 92
VORTAC 92, 375

W

wake turbulence, *see turbulence.*
water crossing 309-311
weather briefing 120-121, 123, 124, 132, 212, 213, 242, 353, 363
    for checkride 310-312
weight 33, 39, 147-148, 150, 289, 343, 361, 375
    allowance 41
    and center of gravity 40, 41, 132, 345
    and load factor 39, 358
    and maneuvering speed 359
    and nosewheel 258
    and stall speed 39, 294, 369
    of fuel 146
    passenger 15
    performance 255
    torque 48

weight and balance (calculation) 41, 146, 147-148, 204-205, 214, 253, 300, 304, 310, 375
White Stallion Ranch 215, 223
Wilkes-Barre Scranton International Airport (KAVP) 245, 246
wind angle 62, 89, 147, 375
Winds Aloft 87-88, 121, 123, 212, 312, 375
wind shear 118, 119, 360, 375
wingtip vortices 202, 375
women in aviation (statistics) 160
Wright brothers 33, 43, 45, 285, 292, 332
wristwatch 77
written exam 1, 7, 12, 23, 28, 35, 37, 73, 100, 114, 121, 144, 145, 155, 156, 163, 205, 214, 236, 253, 278, 306
    and checkride 153, 313, 314
    CFI 160
    commercial pilot 157
    experience taking 152-153
    helicopter 287
    pre-solo 191, 210
    preparing for 145-152
    retaking 153
    scheduling 152
    statistics 24, 153
    when to take 153-154

Y

yaw 48, 178, 182, 355, 358, 363, 366, 374, 376
    helicopter 291, 342
    in coordinated turn 50
    in forward slip 206
    in sideslip 188
    multi-engine 271
    power-on stall 281, 282
    turn coordinator 74-75, 373
    yaw string 75, 292, 332
yoke 19, 43-44, 46, 64, 130, 140, 172, 290, 329, 364, 370, 376
    aerodynamic braking 258, 341
    and navigation 92, 221
    autopilot disengage 84
    crosswind taxi and takeoff 186-187

descent 164
Ercoupe 28
forward slip 206-207
gliding 261, 272
Honeycomb 6, 7
landing 28, 166, 177, 181, 184, 191, 205, 244, 247, 258, 260, 351
mechanism 51-52
one hand 205-206, 221, 247
pitch and speed 47, 56, 58
power-off stall 59
power-on stall 59-60, 279, 281, 282
sideslip 188
slow flight 58, 58
spins 60-61
steep turns 57, 292
takeoff 10, 18, 55, 199, 254, 255, 256, 258-259, 260, 316
transmit button 196
trim 52, 372
unusual attitudes 318
YouTube 4, 7, 12, 41, 49, 149, 166, 170, 180, 182, 188, 299, 377, 380
    accident case studies 275
    failed checkrides 253
    mock checkrides 252, 297

Z

Zulu time, *see UCT (Coordinated Universal Time)*